XML Schema Essentials

R. Allen Wyke

Andrew Watt

Wiley Computer Publishing

John Wiley & Sons, Inc.

Publisher: Robert Ipsen
Editor: Cary Sullivan
Developmental Editor: Scott Amerman
Associate Managing Editor: Penny Linskey
Associate New Media Editor: Brian Snapp
Text Design & Composition: D&G Limited, LLC

This book is printed on acid-free paper. ♾

Published by John Wiley & Sons, Inc.

Published simultaneously in Canada.

Library of Congress Cataloging-in-Publication Data:

ISBN: 0-471-412597

Printed in the United States of America.

10 9 8 7 6 5 4 3 2 1

Contents

Introduction

Back in February 1998, XML 1.0 was released among the most hype and media coverage that the Internet community had seen since the first version of Java. XML was supposed to solve many of the problems that existed in heterogeneous environments, where applications were forced to communicate and exchange data in proprietary formats. The explosion of the Web had introduced the common HTML format for marking up and exchanging documents, but the structure and potential of HTML to be more than that simply did not exist.

XML, whose foundation was based on SGML, provided a means for people, companies, or entire industries to define languages that could be used to mark up data in a method that others could support and understand. Simply conforming to the well-formed and valid (which is technically optional) requirements of XML was a huge step, and if you coupled that with inherit structure of *document type definitions* (DTD), users were able to provide a wealth of knowledge to partners with whom they exchanged data. XML offered some datatyping, however, and did not really support a more flexible means of defining schemas.

To help accommodate these deficiencies, other standards such as *Datatypes for DTDs* (DT4DTD), *Schema for Object-Oriented XML* (SOX), XML Data, and

Document Definition Markup Language (DDML) were developed and combined with XML data for exchanges. But while these provided many of the features that users needed, integrating multiple standards were cumbersome and less desired than a single, standard approach. Enter *XML Schema* (XSD).

XSD, which was inspired by all the previously mentioned standards, does not necessarily replace XML—but in many senses of the word, it can be thought of as XML on steroids. It can be the perfect solution for large solutions that include many various types of data integration. When you have applications or entire systems that need to communicate yet have very diverse methods of storing data, XSD can act as the bridge between these systems. These complex solutions need more, and XSD offers that.

What to Expect

In *XML Schema Essentials,* our job as authors is to expose you to the various publications that are part of the XSD Recommendations. For those of you who have attempted to read and study the recommendations, you know that it can be complex and hard to follow. But just knowing and understanding the standard is only half the battle. We will also expose you to using it to solve real-world problems as well as have discussions about best practices and how you can get the most out of your implementation.

Our goal is simple: for you to finish this book and not only understand XSD but also understand what you can do with it.

Book Organization

In our attempt to teach you XSD, we have taken the approach of stepping through the recommendations from a functional standpoint rather than from top to bottom. The book itself is divided into four parts. The first part, "Getting Started," introduces you to XSD. You will learn the basic concepts, how to define elements, and how to add attributes to those elements.

Part Two, "Going beyond DTDs," will focus on functionality that is open and beyond that found in XML DTDs. You will learn about datatypes and how to derive your own datatypes. There are also a couple of chapters that focus on data facets, which are ways you can constrain things such as datatypes. There is also a chapter on grouping elements and attributes. One of the things you will quickly learn about XSD is that you can define more than one root element.

The third part of the book, "Next Steps," is just that: next steps. In the final two chapters of the book, which are contained in this section, you will learn about some advanced topics that revolve around the use of XSD schemas and essentially expose yourself to a deeper level of topics than covered in previous chapters. You will also work through an example that ties together everything you have learned up until this point to result in a full understanding of XSD.

Finally, in Part Four, which contains Appendixes A and B, we have included a reference for both the datatypes (primitive and derived) and the facets available in the XSD Recommendations. We hope that you will use the material contained here even after you have finished reading the book, because it can serve as a valuable reference.

A Final Thought

This brief introduction should basically prepare you for what to expect from the pages that follow. We did not want to waste your time here rambling on about random thoughts of how XSD will solve the world's problems. Simply put, we want you to come to your own conclusions. So, we have saved our discussion of why and how XSD could possibly do so, at least in the computing world, for the chapters and pages within the book itself.

R. Allen Wyke
Andrew Watt

Acknowledgments

R. Allen Wyke

On the publishing side, I would like to thank Bob Kern of TIPS Publishing and my co-author, Andrew, for their professionalism, hard work, and overall support in the proposing and writing of this book. I would also like to thank all the people at Wiley who worked on the book and helped make sure it was the best it could be.

Andrew Watt

I would like to thank my co-author, Allen, for his contribution to the development and writing of this book. Thanks, too, to Scott Amerman, Penny Linskey, and the team at Wiley for doing all that was necessary to bring this book to fruition.

I would like to dedicate this book to the citizens of New York City, the United States of America, and the world for their perseverance and strength following the tragic events that occurred September 11, 2001.

R. Allen Wyke

I would like to dedicate this book to the memory of my late father, George Alec Watt, a very special human being.

Andrew Watt

About the Authors

R. Allen Wyke

R. Allen Wyke of Durham, North Carolina is the Vice-President of Technology at Blue292, a pioneering company on the forefront of environment, health, safety, and emergency management software and services. At Blue292, he works with management and engineering to help ensure and create products that have the proper vision and direction while fulfilling customers' expectations. He is constantly working with Java, XML, JavaScript, and other related Internet technologies—all of which are part of the framework used for the Blue292 systems.

Allen, who wrote his first computer program at the age of eight, has also developed intranet Web pages for a leading telecommunications and networking company in addition to working on several Internet sites. He has programmed in everything from C++, Java, Perl, Visual Basic, and JavaScript to Lingo as well as having experience with both HTML/XHTML and DHTML. He has also published roughly a dozen books on various Internet technologies that include topics such as Perl, JavaScript, PHP, and XML. In the past, he has also written the monthly "Webmaster" column for *SunWorld* and a weekly article, "Integrating Windows and Unix," for ITworld.com.

Andrew Watt

Andrew Watt is an independent consultant and author based in the United Kingdom with an interest and expertise in the growing family of XML technologies. He wrote his first programs in 6502 Assembly Language and BBC Basic around 1985 and has programmed in Pascal, Prolog, Lotus Domino, and a variety of Web and other technologies including HTML/XHTML and JavaScript. He works with XML, XSLT, SVG, and various other XML technologies on a regular basis and is excited by the progressive transition of the XML technologies from potential to reality as the pieces of the XML jigsaw puzzle appear one by one from the *World Wide Web Consortium* (W3C).

Andrew is the author of *Designing SVG Web Graphics* (published by New Riders) and *XPath Essentials* (published by Wiley) as well as being co-author or contributing author to *XHTML, XML & Java 2 Platinum Edition* (published by Que), *Professional XSL, Professional XML 2nd Edition* and *Professional XML Meta Data* (published by Wrox), and *Sams Teach Yourself JavaScript in 21 Days* (in press at Sams).

Getting Started

CHAPTER

1

Elementary XML Schema

The World Wide Web Consortium's XML Schema is arguably one of the most important and far-reaching recommendations related to XML to come from the W3C.

Since its introduction as a W3C recommendation in 1998, *Extensible Markup Language* (XML) has had a rapidly growing impact on the World Wide Web and as a basis for electronic business. As the impact of XML has grown, the need to integrate XML with existing technologies, such as programming languages and relational database management systems, and the need to exchange information expressed in XML has led to demands for a schema language written in XML that will constrain the allowed structure of a class of XML documents with precision and that can also constrain the datatypes that are permitted at individual locations within such a structure. The need for a new schema language arose, in part, from the limitations of the *Document Type Definition* (DTD), which was the form of XML schema defined within the XML 1.0 Recommendation of February 1998.

As well as being one of the most important recommendations, the W3C XML Schema Recommendation is one of the most complex, and at times abstract, XML technology specifications. In this book, we will be emphasizing aspects of W3C XML Schema that are practical, using many examples of W3C

XML schemas and introducing the theory that sheds light on the practical use of schemas.

Let's take a quick look at a simple XML schema so that you can see what one looks like. An XML document that is described by an XML schema is called an *instance document*. Listing 1.1 shows a very simple XML instance document.

A schema expressed in W3C XML Schema syntax that describes the permitted content of Listing 1.1 is shown in Listing 1.2. The details of the syntax are not essential for you to understand at this stage.

As you can see, the schema of XML Schema is substantially longer than the document it describes or defines. For the moment, do not worry about the detail of the schema. The <xsd:annotation> and <xsd:documentation> elements enable us to document the purpose of a schema for a human reader. The <xsd:element> and <xsd:attribute> elements enable us to declare elements and attributes that are permitted in instance documents. The <xsd:complexType> element enables us to define the permitted complex type content of certain elements. How to use XSD Schema elements such as <xsd:element>, <xsd:complexType>, <xsd:attribute>, and so on will be introduced a little later in this chapter.

NOTE The World Wide Web Consortium, or W3C, has termed its version of a schema language as simply XML Schema. In reality, a number of other XML schema languages existed for some time before W3C completed the development of XML Schema. So, to avoid ambiguity, when we refer to the specification for the W3C flavor of XML Schema, we will use the terms W3C XML Schema or XSD Schema to refer to W3C's type of XML Schema, because an earlier name for the W3C XML Schema was XML Schema Definition Language, abbreviated to XSD. When we refer to a specific example of a schema written in the XSD Schema language (with the upper-case initial letter of Schema), we will use the term XSD schema (with the lower-case initial letter of schema).

Throughout this book, we will be using the indicative namespace prefix *xsd* to refer to elements such as <xsd:complexType> (which are part of XSD Schema).

```
<?xml version="1.0"?>
<Book>
  <Title>XML Schema Essentials</Title>
  <Authors>
   <Author>R. Allen Wyke</Author>
   <Author>Andrew Watt</Author>
  </Authors>
  <Publisher>John Wiley</Publisher>
</Book>
```

Listing 1.1 Simple XML instance document (Book.xml).

```
<?xml version="1.0" encoding="UTF-8"?>
<xsd:schema xmlns:xsd="http://www.w3.org/2001/XMLSchema" >

<xsd:annotation>
   <xsd:documentation>
    This is a sample XML Schema for Chapter 1 of XML Schema
Essentials.
   </xsd:documentation>
</xsd:annotation>

<xsd:element name="Book">
   <xsd:complexType>
    <xsd:sequence>
     <xsd:element name="Title" ref="Title"/>
     <xsd:element name="Authors" ref="Authors"/>
     <xsd:element name="Publisher" ref="Publisher"/>
    </xsd:sequence>
    <xsd:attribute name="pubCountry" type="xsd:string"/>
   </xsd:complexType>
</xsd:element>

<xsd:element name="Title" type="xsd:string"/>

<xsd:element name="Authors">
 <xsd:complexType>
    <xsd:sequence>
      <xsd:element name="Author" ref="Author" minOccurs="1"
maxOccurs="unbounded"/>
    </xsd:sequence>
 </xsd:complexType>
</xsd:element>

<xsd:element name="Author" type="xsd:string"/>

<xsd:element name="Publisher" type="xsd:string"/>
</xsd:schema>
```

Listing 1.2 W3C XML Schema syntax describing content of Listing 1.1 (Book.xsd).

What Is XML Schema?

XML Schema is the W3C-recommended schema definition language, expressed in XML 1.0 syntax, which is intended to describe the structure and constrain the content of documents written in XML. It is explicitly intended to improve on the schema functionality that was provided by the DTD, which was the original form of schema for XML documents that the W3C recommended in 1998 when XML was first released.

The W3C XML Schema became a full W3C recommendation in May 2001. Unusually, the final recommendation was released in three parts. The first part, Part 0, is a primer that is intended to introduce XML Schema in a non-formal way (from W3C's point of view) and is located at www.w3.org/TR/2001/REC-xmlschema-0-20010502/. Part 1 is a normative W3C document, defines structures that XML Schema supports, and is located at www.w3.org/TR/2001/REC-xmlschema-1-20010502/. Part 2 is also a normative W3C document, defines the datatypes that W3C XML Schema supports, describes mechanisms for creating new datatypes, and is located at www.w3.org/TR/2001/REC-xmlschema-2-20010502/.

An XSD Schema schema is intended to define the structure and constrain the content of a *class* of XML documents. Given the terminology "class," such documents are often termed *instance documents*.

NOTE Instance "documents" need not exist as document files but can exist as a stream of bytes or as a collection of XML Information Set items.

How Does an XML Schema Processor Work?

In much of this book, we will refer to the relationship between an XSD schema and instance documents as if an XSD schema-aware validating processor actually directly processed the instance document. In fact, an XSD schema-aware processor operates on a set (called the *information set*) of *information items* rather than on the instance document itself. This method is similar to the way that an XSLT/XPath processor operates, in reality, on a source tree of nodes rather than directly on the elements in a source XML document. Later in this chapter, we will take a look at the XML Information Set specification and examine how the XML Information Set is relevant to XSD Schema.

It isn't surprising that an XSD Schema processor does not operate directly on an XML instance document; after all, an instance document is simply a series of characters. An XML parser extracts a series of logical tokens by parsing the characters in the serialized document. In the case of a parser that is XML Information Set-aware, the logical tokens are termed information items. There is, for example, a document information item (broadly corresponding to the document entity) that has several *properties*. Among the properties of the document information item is the [children] property. Note that the name of a property of an information item, such as the [children] property, is written enclosed in square brackets. One of the information items in the [children] property of the document information item is the element information item, which represents the document element of the instance document.

What Is XML Schema for?

The purpose of XML Schema is to define the structure of XML instance documents. By defining and constraining the content of XML instance documents, it becomes possible to exchange information between applications with greater confidence and with less custom programming to test and confirm the structure of an instance document, or to confirm that the data in a particular part of the document is of a particular datatype.

XSD Schema adds the capability to combine schemas from more than one source. For example, we could generate an invoice perhaps by combining a schema from a customer's purchase order (which includes information such as shipping address, billing address, and so on) and billing information from our own accounts department (describing information such as price, discount allowed, and so on). This technique would enable schemas to be reused in a variety of combinations, thus improving efficiency.

XSD Schema Schema Components

The W3C XML Schema Recommendation indicates that an XSD schema comprises 13 types of *schema components* that fall broadly into three groups: primary, secondary, and helper components.

The XSD Schema Recommendation refers to the following *primary components*:

- Simple type definitions
- Complex type definitions
- Attribute declarations
- Element declarations

Primary components that are type definitions can have names. Attribute declarations and element declarations must have names.

The following are the *secondary components:*

- Attribute group definitions
- Identity-constraint definitions
- Model group definitions
- Notation declarations

The final five XSD Schema components are referred to as *helper components* and provide parts of other components:

- Annotations
- Model groups

- Particles
- Wildcards
- Attribute uses

This chapter introduces the syntax to enable you to use many of the components just mentioned. Later chapters will detail how they are to be used.

Other Schema Languages for XML

Other schema languages are written in XML and are designed for use in defining and describing XML instance documents. This book does not describe them in detail because that is not its intended purpose. You should be aware of the existence of these other schema languages, however, and where you can obtain information about them.

XML-Data Reduced, often known simply as XDR, is a schema language that antedated the XSD Schema language. XDR is routinely used within the BizTalk Framework (www.biztalk.org) sponsored by Microsoft and is supported by Microsoft's MSXML parser.

Another important alternative schema language for XML is now termed RELAX NG. RELAX NG, standing for RELAX New Generation, is an amalgam of two embryonic schema languages, RELAX and TREX. RELAX NG is being developed by the *Organization for Advancement of Structured Information Standards* (OASIS), found at www.oasis-open.org.

These XML schemas are written for XML as well as being written in XML. The original schema for XML 1.0 was the DTD that was, however, not written in XML.

The DTD Descended from SGML

The first form of schema for XML documents was the Document Type Definition. Definitive information about the XML Document Type Definition is contained in the XML 1.0 Recommendation. At the time that XML became a recommendation, few people envisaged how it would evolve from being a document description language into one that would be used for many data-centric, rather than document-centric, applications. Not surprisingly, then, the DTD created largely with document-centric use in mind was found to have inadequacies when routinely applied in a data-centric context.

Among the limitations of the DTD are the following:

- Datatyping is very weak.
- DTDs have a limited range of content models.

- The content cannot be validated precisely where it is of mixed content type.
- Cardinality is limited to being defined to zero, one, or many occurrences.
- DTDs lack named element or attribute groups that would enable us to reuse them.
- XSD Schema was designed, among other things, to provide superior datatyping to the DTD, to provide greater flexibility but yet with control of content models, and to provide definitions of cardinality not possible using a DTD.

Later in the chapter, we will look in a little more detail at comparisons between DTDs and XSD schemas once you have been introduced to some commonly used XSD Schema constructs.

XSD Schema Tools

You might well already have your own favorite tools with which to create XML documents and XSD schemas. If so, then feel free to use these as you work through the examples in this book. The tools mentioned here include tools that the authors use on an ongoing basis. We are making no specific claims for their superiority for a particular purpose, but they do enable us to work with XSD Schema to explore its capabilities and complexities.

NOTE Each of the XSD Schema tools is an early implementation; therefore, you can expect to find some situations where inappropriate error messages are issued or where an error in a schema is overlooked.

Schema Checkers

At this writing, an online XSD Schema checking service is available using XML Schema Validator provided at the W3C Web site. The schema validation service for the May 2001 Recommendation is located at www.w3.org/2001/03/webdata/xsv. Figure 1.1 shows part of the form that you must use in order to get a schema validated. Essentially, your schema needs to be accessible via a URL in order to be validated.

The online checking service can check an XSD schema for validity (that is, conformity to the W3C Recommendation), or it can validate an instance document against a schema.

The online schema checking service can be used to process files that are accessible at a URL, or you can upload files for checking.

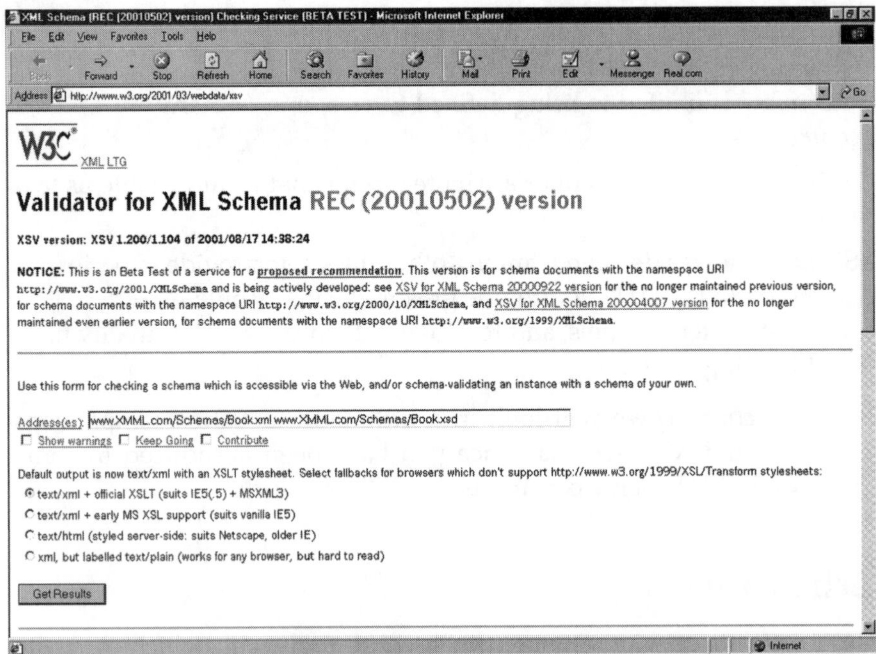

Figure 1.1 Online XSD schema validation service from the W3C.

Figure 1.2 shows the form filled in just prior to asking the processor to validate an instance document (Book.xml, Listing 1.1) against its XSD schema (Book.xsd, Listing 1.2).

Be careful to include the http:// part of the URL; otherwise, the schema checker interprets the URL as being a relative one, as shown in Figure 1.3. Relative URLs are not permitted in XSD Schema.

The output from validating Book.xml, using Book.xsd, is shown in Figure 1.4.

NOTE XSV is undergoing continuing development. At this writing, not all parts of the W3C Recommendation are supported. The download page mentioned earlier provides details of areas not yet fully implemented.

The W3C schema checker requires that you either make the file(s) available at a URL or upload them by using the online form. If you are unable or unwilling to do that, an alternate approach is to download the schema checker that lies behind the W3C schema checking service.

Two schema checkers are available for download. One from Henry Thomson at the University of Edinburgh (also of the W3C XML Schema Working Group) is the basis of the W3C schema checking service. The other download is available from IBM.

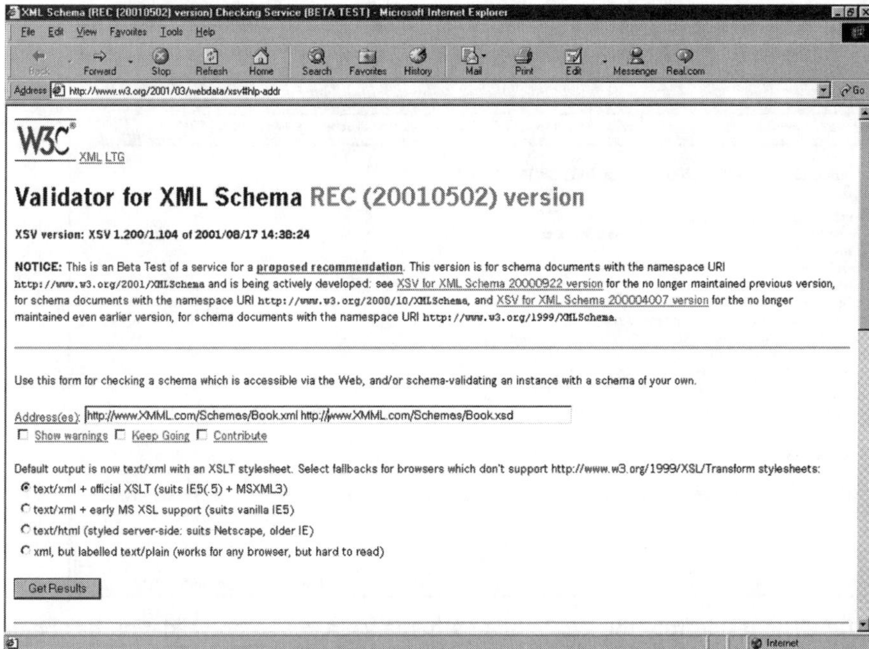

Figure 1.2 Using the online schema checker.

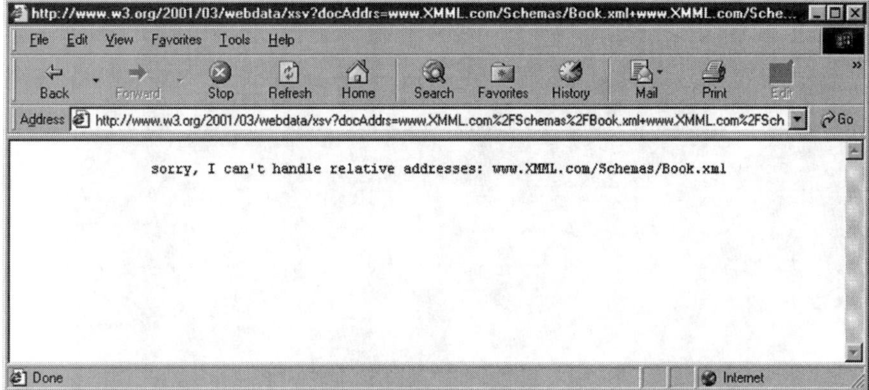

Figure 1.3 Error message if http:// is omitted.

The download version of XML Schema Validator, XSV, corresponds to the online schema checking service at W3C. Further information about downloading XML Schema Validator can be found at www.ltg.ed.ac.uk/~ht/xsv-status.html.

To check the validity of the Book.xsd schema, copy it to the XSV directory (or place the directory containing Book.xsd in the PATH) and issue the following command:

```
xsv -i Book.xsd
```

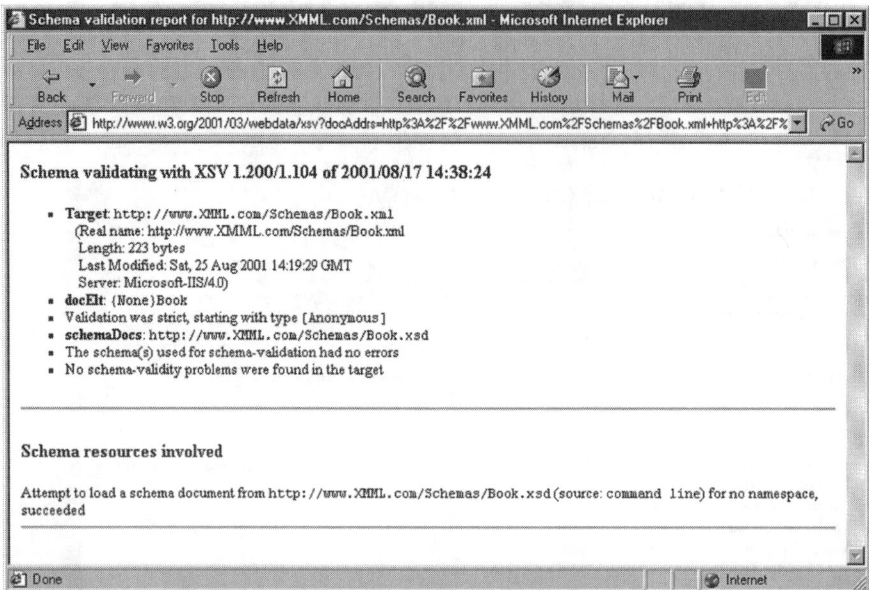

Figure 1.4 The result from the W3C online schema validator when validation has been successful.

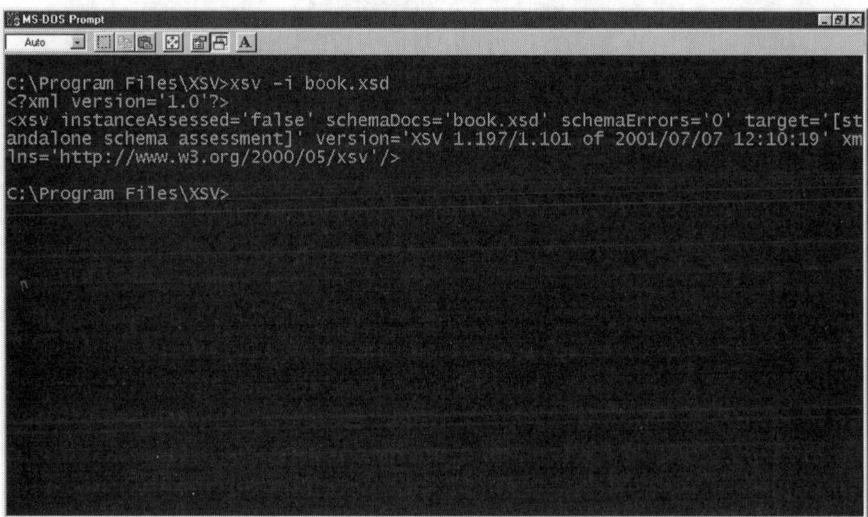

Figure 1.5 Output of validating Book.xsd by using the XSV schema validator.

and you will see output like that in Figure 1.5. Note that there are zero schema errors.

Alternatively, you can issue the command

```
xsv  -o output.xml -s xsv.xsl -i Book.xsd
```

And, if you have MSXML3 installed, you will see output similar to the display of the output file output.xml, as shown in Figure 1.6.

The IBM XML Schema Quality Checker can be downloaded from www.alphaworks.ibm.com/tech/xmlsqc. The IBM XML Schema Quality Checker checks whether or not an XSD schema corresponds to the W3C Recommendation. It does not, at least at this writing, validate instance documents against the XSD schema.

As well as standalone schema validation tools such as those just described schemas can be validated by using schema authoring tools.

Schema Authoring Tools

XSD Schemas can be created by using any XML editor, but editors that are not XSD Schema-aware are limited as learning and production tools. They can spot basic XML syntax errors and can indicate that the syntax is well-formed, but are incapable of providing information about the correctness or incorrectness of a schema you have created. Therefore, you would be well-advised to consider, if you have not already done so, acquiring a schema editor such as Turbo XML (from TIBCO Extensibility) or XML Spy (from Altova). Both have free evaluation downloads available from their respective Web sites. Turbo XML

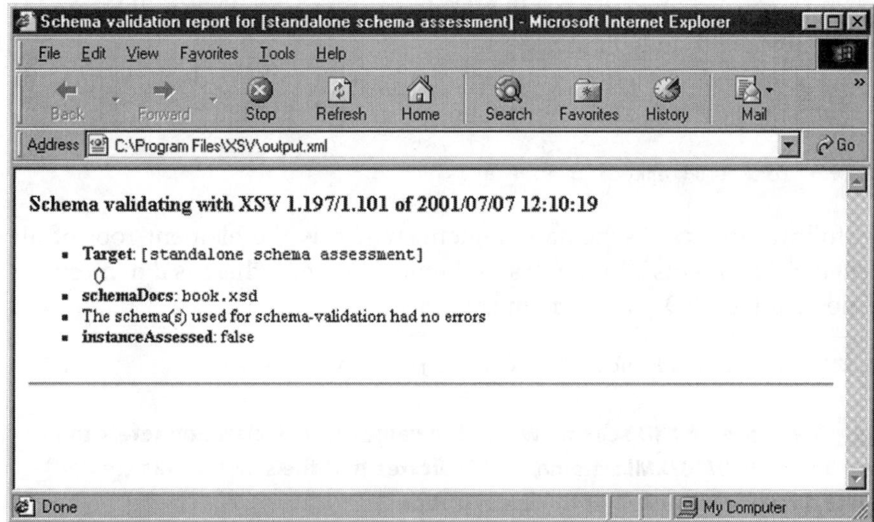

Figure 1.6 Using XSV schema validator and an XSLT stylesheet to generate an output file, output.xml.

can be downloaded from www.extensibility.com/downloads/trial_downloads.htm, and XML Spy can be downloaded from www.xmlspy.com/.

Turbo XML is available for various flavors of 32-bit Windows operating systems, multiple flavors of Unix and for Mac OS X. Occasionally version 2.2.1 overlooks schema errors correctly identified by XML Spy.

NOTE If you have Turbo XML version 2.2.1 running, you might find that you cannot start the Netscape 6 browser. If you use Netscape 6, start the browser before starting Turbo XML.

The generally available version of XML Spy at this writing is version 4.0. Version 3.5 does not use the final XSD Schema namespace. XML Spy Version 4 supports the full XSD (W3C XML) Schema Recommendation.

XML Spy is generally easy to use. One irritation with XML Spy 4.0 is that it reformats code, however. For example, it introduces tabs instead of spaces. In addition, occasional spurious error messages are produced.

Despite the minor problems just mentioned, both Turbo XML and XML Spy are powerful and useful tools for XSD Schema development. Each is capable of validating an instance document against a schema as well as validating an XSD schema for conformity to the W3C XML Schema Recommendation.

XML Schema Document

In this section, we will look briefly at the general structure of an XML Schema schema such as the one that you saw earlier in Listing 1.2. The description of each part of a schema document will be brief, and many points will be developed in greater depth in later chapters.

An XSD Schema document begins, optionally, with an XML declaration with required version attribute and optional encoding and standalone attributes:

```
<?xml version="1.0" encoding="UTF-8"?>
```

Then follows the <xsd:schema> element, which is the element root of all XSD Schema documents. On the <xsd:schema> element, there is a namespace declaration for the XSD Schema namespace:

```
<xsd:schema xmlns:xsd="http://www.w3.org/2001/XMLSchema" >
```

NOTE If you see an XSD schema where the namespace declaration refers to www.w3.org/2000/10/XMLSchema, that indicates that the schema was created by using a non-final version of the specification.

```
<xsd:annotation>
   <xsd:documentation>
```

```
    This is a sample XML Schema for Chapter 1 of XML Schema Essentials.
   </xsd:documentation>
</xsd:annotation>
```

Optionally, you can include an <xsd:annotation> element nested as above—within which you can include descriptive information indicating the purpose of the schema or otherwise documenting it. The content of <xsd:documentation> elements are intended for use by human readers.

```
<xsd:element name="Book">
   <xsd:complexType>
    <xsd:sequence>
     <xsd:element name="Title" ref="Title"/>
     <xsd:element name="Authors" ref="Authors"/>
     <xsd:element name="Publisher" ref="Publisher"/>
    </xsd:sequence>
<xsd:attribute name="pubCountry" type="xsd:string"/>
   </xsd:complexType>
</xsd:element>
```

An XSD schema will typically include a number of element declarations, such as the element declaration for the <Book> element shown earlier. In this example, the <Book> element is to have complex content; that is, either child elements, an attribute, or both are permitted or required for the <Book> element in an instance document. The presence of complex content is indicated by the <complexType> element. We will return to examine how to define complex types a little later.

```
<xsd:element name="Title" type="xsd:string"/>
```

An element declaration can simply associate an element name—in this case, "Title" with a built-in datatype, in the earlier code, xsd:string.

```
<xsd:element name="Authors">
 <xsd:complexType>
    <xsd:sequence>
      <xsd:element name="Author" ref="Author" minOccurs="1"
maxOccurs="unbounded"/>
    </xsd:sequence>
 </xsd:complexType>
</xsd:element>

<xsd:element name="Author" type="xsd:string"/>

<xsd:element name="Publisher" type="xsd:string"/>
</xsd:schema>
```

The final section of the XSD schema contains other element declarations and is completed by the end tag, </xsd:schema>.

As we move through the chapter, we will examine other foundational structures in XSD schemas.

Root of an XML Schema Document

The root of all W3C XML Schema documents is the <xsd:schema> element. A namespace declaration within the <xsd:schema> element associates it with the W3C XML Schema namespace:

```
<xsd:schema
     xmlns:xsd="http://www.w3.org/2001/XMLSchema">
```

Of course, if you are using the xsd prefix, then a namespace declaration is essential if the namespace prefix is to conform to the requirements of the Namespaces in XML Recommendation and to be processed by applications that implement that recommendation.

You might also see the namespace prefix xs associated with the W3C XML Schema namespace.

Declaring the Location of Your XML Schema Document

The instance document that you saw in Listing 1.1 made no reference to being associated with any particular schema. There is no direct equivalent to the DTD of XML 1.0. XSD Schema uses a more indirect approach.

For the moment, we will look at how we associate an instance document that does not use namespaces with an applicable schema document. Listing 1.3 shows how this job can be done.

```
<?xml version="1.0"?>
<Book pubCountry="USA"
  xmlns:xsi="http://www.w3.org/2001/XMLSchema-instance"
  xsi:noNamespaceSchemaLocation="C:\My Writing\XML Schema
Essentials\Ch01\Book.xsd">
 <Title>XML Schema Essentials</Title>
 <Authors>
  <Author>R. Allen Wyke</Author>
  <Author>Andrew Watt</Author>
 </Authors>
<Publisher>John Wiley</Publisher>
</Book>
```

Listing 1.3 Instance document that does not use namespaces (Book02.xml).

The association of an instance document is a two-stage process. The namespace declaration

```
xmlns:xsi="http://www.w3.org/2001/XMLSchema-instance"
```

associates the namespace prefix xsi with the URI shown. The xsi:noNamespaceSchemaLocation attribute, which belongs to the namespace

```
http://www.w3.org/2001/XMLSchema-instance
```

indicates the location of the schema. The xsi:noNamespaceSchemaLocation attribute can only be used when the xsi namespace prefix has been declared. The value of the noNamespaceSchemaLocation attribute indicates the location of the schema. In the case of this example, the schema is located on drive C: at the location indicated:

```
C:\My Writing\XML Schema Essentials\Ch01\Book.xsd
```

XSD Schema processors are free to ignore or to override the schema suggested by using the mechanism just described.

Declaring Elements and Defining Types

Because XML instance documents contain one (and typically many more) element(s), one of the foundational techniques of W3C XML Schema is the declaration of elements.

In XML Schema, there is a substantive difference between *declaring* an element that has content that is either a simple type or complex type and is permitted to occur in an instance document and *defining* a new type, which can be either *simple type* or *complex type*.

NOTE The terms definition and declaration in XML Schema have no close relation to the terms Document Type Definition and Document Type Declaration of XML 1.0.

First, let's look at how we declare an element the content of which is of simple type in an instance document.

Defining Simple Types

Elements that contain other elements or that possess attributes are termed *complex types*, and we will discuss them in the next section. Elements that have neither child elements nor possess attributes are termed *simple types*, and we will discuss these in this section. All attributes have simple type content.

XSD Schema provides three flavors of simple types:

1. Atomic types
2. List types
3. Union types

Each of these is discussed in the paragraphs that follow. XSD Schema simple types will be discussed in detail in Chapter 4, "Applying Datatypes."

Simple types can be either those simple types, such as xsd:string, built into the XML Schema language or can be simple types created by a schema author by using techniques which we will describe later. All simple types created by a schema author are *derived* datatypes. Those datatypes built into XSD Schema include both *primitive* datatypes and *derived* datatypes. Those datatypes are fully described in Part 2 of the W3C XML Schema Recommendation.

Atomic (Simple) Types

Let's assume that we wanted to describe the title and authors of this book in XML. A first, crude attempt at an instance document might look like the following (SimpleBook01.xml).

As you can see, the structure of the document is poor, but a schema for such an instance document could be created by only declaring a single element of simple type, as shown in Listing 1.5 (SimpleBook01.xsd). This code *declares* an element <Book> whose type is one of the built-in primitive types of XSD Schema, xsd:string.

```
<?xml version='1.0'?>
<Book>
XML Schema Essentials, R. Allen Wyke, Andrew Watt, Wiley, USA
</Book>
```

Listing 1.4 A first attempt at an instance document (SimpleBook01.xml).

```
<?xml version="1.0" encoding="UTF-8"?>
<xsd:schema xmlns:xsd="http://www.w3.org/2001/XMLSchema" >
 <xsd:element name="Book" type="xsd:string"/>
</xsd:schema>
```

Listing 1.5 A schema for Listing 1.4 (SimpleBook01.xsd).

You will recognize the XML declaration and the <xsd:schema> element. To declare an element with simple type content, we simply use an <xsd:element>. The name attribute and the type attribute on the <xsd:element> serve to associate the *element type name* of the <Book> element in an instance document and its permitted datatype, xsd:string. We will go on to further develop the structure of an instance document later in the chapter.

From the point of view of XSD Schema, an atomic simple type is indivisible. An xsd:string, as far as XSD Schema is concerned, cannot be split into simpler types. Such indivisibility applies to both in-built simple types and to derived simple types.

Let's suppose that we have a European-based e-commerce operation that sells to the United Kingdom, France, and Germany only. The shipping address part of an invoice or purchase order might look like Listing 1.6.

A schema for the code from Listing 1.6 is shown in Listing 1.7. The point of interest relating to atomic simple types relates to the <xsd:simpleType name="CountryType"> element towards the end of the following schema.

In the declaration for the <CountryType> element, we indicate that the datatype is a named type that is defined by using the <xsd:simpleType> element. The value of the CountryType contained in the <Country> element in the instance document is "DE", meaning Deutschland (Germany). This type is atomic because we cannot take one of its constituent letters and maintain some of the meaning. The meaning is related to the two-letter code for Germany in this example.

List (Simple) Types

A list type in XSD Schema is made up of a sequence of atomic types. There are no built-in list types in XSD Schema, so we must define a list type if we wish to

```
<ShippingAddress type="EUAddress">
<Name>
<FirstName>Hans</FirstName>
<LastName>Schmidt</LastName>
</Name>
<Address>
<Street>123 Hallgarten</Street>
<City>Berlin</City>
<PostalCode>12345</PostalCode>
<Country>DE</Country>
</Address>
</ShippingAddress>
```

Listing 1.6 Shipping address part of invoice (ShippingAddress.xml).

```
<?xml version='1.0'?>
<xsd:schema xmlns:xsd="http://www.w3.org/2001/XMLSchema">
<xsd:element name="ShippingAddress">
<xsd:complexType>
<xsd:sequence>
<xsd:element name="Name" type="NameType"/>
<xsd:element name="Address" type="AddressType"/>
</xsd:sequence>
<xsd:attribute name="type" type="xsd:string"/>
</xsd:complexType>
</xsd:element>

<xsd:complexType name="NameType">
<xsd:sequence>
<xsd:element name="FirstName" type="xsd:string"/>
<xsd:element name="LastName" type="xsd:string"/>
</xsd:sequence>
</xsd:complexType>

<xsd:complexType name="AddressType">
<xsd:sequence>
<xsd:element name="Street" type="xsd:string"/>
<xsd:element name="City" type="xsd:string"/>
<xsd:element name="PostalCode" type="PostalCodeType"/>
<xsd:element name="Country" type="CountryType"/>
</xsd:sequence>
</xsd:complexType>

<xsd:simpleType name="PostalCodeType">
<xsd:restriction base="xsd:integer">
<xsd:length value="5" />
</xsd:restriction>
</xsd:simpleType>

<xsd:simpleType name="CountryType">
<xsd:restriction base="xsd:string">
<xsd:length value="2"/>
</xsd:restriction>
</xsd:simpleType>
</xsd:schema>
```

Listing 1.7 A schema for Listing 1.7 (ShippingAddress.xsd).

use one. For example, we could define a list type called SouthEastStatesType, which is a list type consisting of the values "FL LA GA SC." The list type has four string values (each of which happens to be two characters long) that are separated by a space.

So, we could have an element <SouthEastStates> as follows:

```
<SouthEastStates>FL LA GA SC</SouthEastStates>
```

This element uses the SouthEastStatesType simple type. If we wanted to *define* a new simple type, we could use the following code:

```
<xsd:simpleType name="SouthEastStatesType">
 <xsd:list itemType="xsd:string"/>
</xsd:simpleType>
```

A simple instance document is shown in Listing 1.8.

An XSD schema for Listing 1.8 is shown in Listing 1.9.

The <xsd:element> element is the *declaration* that associates the <SouthEastStates> element with the datatype SouthEastStatesType. The <xsd:simpleType> element is the *definition* of the datatype SouthEastStatesType. In order to create a list simple type, we need to nest an <xsd:list> element within the <xsd:simpleType> element. The base type for a list is known as its itemType.

NOTE It is possible to define list types based on the xsd:string type. The xsd:string type might contain space characters or other whitespace characters, however, which are the separators for the individual items in a list type. So, you

```
<?xml version='1.0'?>
<SouthEastStates>
 FL LA GA SC
</SouthEastStates>
```

Listing 1.8 Simple instance document for four southeastern states (SouthEasternStates.xml).

```
<?xml version="1.0" encoding="UTF-8"?>
<xsd:schema xmlns:xsd="http://www.w3.org/2001/XMLSchema" >
<xsd:element name="SouthEastStates" type="SouthEastStatesType"/>

<xsd:simpleType name="SouthEastStatesType">
 <xsd:list itemType="xsd:string"/>
</xsd:simpleType>
</xsd:schema>
```

Listing 1.9 A schema for Listing 1.8 (SouthEasternStates.xsd).

should be careful when attempting to use the xsd:string type as the base type for a list simple type.

Let's look briefly at the kind of problems that can arise when using strings that include whitespace. For example, if we had a simple list datatype NorthAmericanCountriesType defined as follows,

```
<xsd:simpleType name="NorthAmericanCountriesType">
 <xsd:list itemType="xsd:string"/>
</xsd:simpleType>
```

and we had an element, <NorthAmericanCountries>, which used the NorthAmericanCountriesType datatype with content like the following,

```
<NorthAmericanCountries>United States of America Canada
Mexico</NorthAmericanCountries>
```

this code would be treated in XSD Schema as a list of six items, not as three countries as you might expect. The first item in the list would be the string "United," followed by a whitespace character. The second item in the list would be "States," again separated from the third item, "of," by a whitespace character (and so on). To avoid this type of problem, avoid the use of spaces if you are using the xsd:string datatype, or use more appropriate datatypes as list members. Simple datatypes are discussed further in Chapter 4.

Union (Simple) Types

Union datatypes are always derived datatypes. In XSD Schema, there are no built-in union datatypes. The maxOccurs attribute uses a union simple datatype, however, as shown in the following code snippet:

```
<xsd:attribute name="maxOccurs">
 <xsd:simpleType>
  <xsd:union>
   <xsd:simpleType>
    <xsd:restriction base='xsd:nonNegativeInteger'/>
   </xsd:simpleType>
   <xsd:simpleType>
    <xsd:restriction base='xsd:string'>
      <xsd:enumeration value='xsd:unbounded'/>
    </xsd:restriction>
   </xsd:simpleType>
  </xsd:union>
 </xsd:simpleType>
</xsd:attribute>
```

The permitted values of the maxOccurs attribute are any non-negative integer (in other words, any value of type of xsd:nonNegativeInteger) unioned with the string value of "unbounded."

A union datatype has memberTypes. In the example you have just seen for the maxOccurs attribute, the memberTypes are xsd:nonNegativeInteger and the anonymous datatype derived from xsd:string by restriction.

The default evaluation of memberTypes is that they are evaluated in the order given in the schema. Evaluation ceases once a first matching memberType is found. The order of evaluation can be overridden by the xsi:type attribute.

Having looked at how we can define the available simple types and use them in element declarations, let's move on to look at the situation where an element might have simple type content but also possesses an attribute.

Simple Type Content and an Attribute

Strictly speaking, we are straying into the territory of complex types—because in XSD Schema terminology, an element possesses an attribute that by definition makes it a complex type in XSD Schema. Thus, if we wanted to create an element that would reflect a selling price for a particular locality, perhaps including local sales tax (Value Added Tax in the European Union, for example), we would need to be able to create an element like the following:

```
<UKPrice currency="GBP">199.99</UKPrice>
```

The content of the <UKPrice> element is simply of xsd:decimal type. To express that notion, we can use the <xsd:simpleContent> element and then use the <xsd:extension> element with the base type xsd:decimal within which we nest an <xsd:attribute> element to define the currency attribute:

```
<xsd:element name="UKPrice">
 <xsd:complexType>
  <xsd:simpleContent>
   <xsd:extension base="xsd:decimal">
    <xsd:attribute name="currency" type="xsd:string"/>
   </xsd:extension>
  </xsd:simpleContent>
 </xsd:complexType>
</xsd:element>
```

What we have done with this fairly verbose syntax is to derive a new complex type from the built-in simple type of xsd:decimal. The <xsd:complexType> element is anonymous, but a named complex type could have been used if, for example, similar prices in local currency were to be added for a number of European Union countries.

If we apply this scenario to our simple book instance document so that it has a PubCountry attribute of the <Book> element, we see the result in Listing 1.10.

Adding the PubCountry attribute means that the content of <Book> element is now of complex type. Listing 1.11 shows a schema to describe our modified instance document.

As you can see, the mechanism of adding a single attribute to an element that has simple type content is pretty verbose in XSD Schema. If you follow the nesting within the <xsd:element>, you should grasp the logic. Because an attribute is present, the content in XSD Schema is complex type; therefore, we use the <xsd:complexType> element. The content of the <Book> element is a simple datatype, and therefore we use the <xsd:simpleContent> element. As well as the simple type content, however, an attribute is also present. Thus, the simple type content is extended, which is shown by the presence of the <xsd:extension> element. The specific nature of the extension is an attribute signaled by the presence of an <xsd:attribute> element nested within the <xsd:extension> element.

```
<?xml version='1.0'?>
<Book PubCountry="USA">
 XML Schema Essentials, R. Allen Wyke, Andrew Watt, Wiley
</Book>
```

Listing 1.10 Adding an attribute to the <Book> element (SimpleBook02.xml).

```
<?xml version="1.0" encoding="UTF-8"?>
<xsd:schema xmlns:xsd="http://www.w3.org/2001/XMLSchema" >
 <xsd:element name="Book">
  <xsd:complexType>
   <xsd:simpleContent>
    <xsd:extension base="xsd:string">
     <xsd:attribute name="PubCountry" type="xsd:string"/>
    </xsd:extension>
   </xsd:simpleContent>
  </xsd:complexType>
 </xsd:element>
</xsd:schema>
```

Listing 1.11 A schema to reflect the added PubCountry attribute (SimpleBook02.xsd).

This example is a special case of a complex type. Let's move on to introduce how to define complex types.

Defining Complex Types

In the terminology of XML Schema, an element that either has child elements (sometimes called subelements) or that possesses attributes is termed a *complex type*. A type that possesses neither child elements nor attributes is termed a simple type.

A complex type definition will typically contain one or more element declarations, element references, and/or attribute declarations. Elements are declared by using the <xsd:element> element, and attributes are declared by using the <xsd:attribute> element.

A declaration, whether of an element or of an attribute, is not (strictly speaking) a type but is an association between a name and a set of constraints on the appearance of that name in the XML document governed by the relevant schema that contains the name.

XSD Schema provides mechanisms for us to define anonymous and named complex types. First, let's take a look at how we define anonymous complex types.

Anonymous Complex Types

Anonymous complex types, as you might guess, are complex types that have no name. In creating an anonymous complex type, typically an <xsd:complexType> element will be nested within an <xsd:element> element.

For example, in an invoice we might typically specify each line item which was purchased and which is being billed. Listing 1.12 shows a simplified invoice.

The schema that corresponds to SimpleInvoice.xml is shown in Listing 1.13. The schema contains both anonymous and named complex types, but we will focus on the anonymous types in the meantime.

The declaration for the <SimpleInvoice> element has nested within it the definition of an anonymous complex type as shown here:

```
<xsd:element name="SimpleInvoice">
 <xsd:complexType>
  <xsd:sequence>
   <xsd:element name="Customer" type="CustomerType"/>
   <xsd:element name="LineItems" type="LineItemsType"/>
  </xsd:sequence>
 </xsd:complexType>
</xsd:element>
```

```
<?xml version='1.0'?>
<SimpleInvoice>
 <Customer>
  <CustomerName>XMML.com</CustomerName>
 </Customer>
 <LineItems>
  <LineItem quantity="2">Mandrake Linux version 8</LineItem>
  <LineItem quantity="1">IBM WebSphere Studio Workbench version
4</LineItem>
 </LineItems>
</SimpleInvoice>
```

Listing 1.12 A simple invoice (SimpleInvoice.xml).

Notice that we declare an element named "SimpleInvoice." We define the type for a <SimpleInvoice> element in an anonymous complex type by means of a nested anonymous <xsd:complexType> element; that is, an <xsd:complexType> element that lacks a name attribute. The complex type is defined by means of an <xsd:sequence> element as a sequence of <Customer> and <LineItems> elements.

The declaration of the <LineItem> element also contains an anonymous complex type definition. You will perhaps recognize this definition as similar to the book example shown in Listing 1.11. The <LineItem> element, too, has a single attribute and xsd:string content.

Named Complex Types

You have seen the anonymous complex type demonstrated. In many uses of XML documents, however, you might well want to use a complex type more than once, for two different purposes, in the same XML document. In an invoice or purchase order, for example, you might want to define and/or declare a complex type for an address structure that can be used both for the billing address and the shipping address. There is unlikely to be any useful purpose served by creating two separate but essentially identical address structures. Reuse of type definitions makes practical sense.

XML Schema enables us to create complex types that can be used in the same XML document for more than one purpose by means of the *named complex type*.

If you are creating an invoice or purchase order, you are likely to include addresses for the purchaser and the billing party. To create a complex type that would describe such an address, you could use code like that in Listing 1.14.

```
<?xml version='1.0'?>
<xsd:schema xmlns:xsd="http://www.w3.org/2001/XMLSchema">
<xsd:element name="SimpleInvoice">
 <xsd:complexType>
  <xsd:sequence>
   <xsd:element name="Customer" type="CustomerType"/>
   <xsd:element name="LineItems" type="LineItemsType"/>
  </xsd:sequence>
 </xsd:complexType>
</xsd:element>

<xsd:complexType name="CustomerType">
 <xsd:sequence>
  <xsd:element name="CustomerName" type="xsd:string"/>
 </xsd:sequence>
</xsd:complexType>

<xsd:complexType name="LineItemsType">
 <xsd:sequence>
  <xsd:element ref="LineItem" minOccurs="1"
maxOccurs="unbounded"/>
 </xsd:sequence>
</xsd:complexType>

<xsd:element name="LineItem">
 <xsd:complexType>
  <xsd:simpleContent>
   <xsd:extension base="xsd:string">
    <xsd:attribute name="quantity" type="xsd:string"/>
   </xsd:extension>
  </xsd:simpleContent>
 </xsd:complexType>
</xsd:element>

</xsd:schema>
```

Listing 1.13 A schema for Listing 1.12 (SimpleInvoice.xsd).

The <xsd:complexType> element contains the information that defines the complex type named "USAddressType." The element content is defined as a sequence (note the <xsd:sequence> element) of elements with element type names of Name, Street, City, State, and Zip—each having simple type content. We will see in Chapter 8, "Deriving Types," how we can create new datatypes that constrain the content of the <State> and <Zip> elements to appropriate

```
<?xml version="1.0" encoding="UTF-8"?>
<xsd:schema xmlns:xsd="http://www.w3.org/2001/XMLSchema" >
<!-- NOTE - This is NOT a complete schema! -->

<xsd:element name="BillingAddress" type="USAddressType"/>
<xsd:element name="ShippingAddress" type="USAddressType"/>

<xsd:complexType name="USAddressType" >
<xsd:sequence>
<xsd:element name="Name" type="xsd:string"/>
<xsd:element name="Street" type="xsd:string"/>
<xsd:element name="City" type="xsd:string"/>
<xsd:element name="State" type="xsd:string"/>
<xsd:element name="Zip" type="xsd:decimal"/>
</xsd:sequence>
<xsd:attribute name="country" type="xsd:NMTOKEN" fixed="USA"/>
</xsd:complexType>
</xsd:schema>
```

Listing 1.14 A partial schema with a named complex type (USAddress.xsd).

derived datatypes. The <xsd:attribute> element indicates the presence on an element of USAddressType of a country attribute.

Notice that there are two element declarations declared to be of type USAddressType: the declarations for the <BillingAddress> element and the <ShippingAddress> element. The type attribute of the <xsd:element> references the appropriate named complex type.

Notice that the type of the country attribute is "xsd:NMTOKEN," which has a fixed value of "USA." An xsd:NMTOKEN is a *derived datatype* that is derived from the datatype *xsd:token* (all lower case). The token derived datatype is itself derived from the normalizedString derived data type. In XML Schema terminology, normalizedString is said to be the *base type* of token.

Let's get a little more into the jargon of XML Schema. The xsd:token derived type has the *value space* that is the set of strings that does not contain a line feed (character #xA) or a tab (character #x9), nor is there any leading space or a sequence of two or more spaces within the string. The xsd:NMTOKEN type constrains the allowed characters further because all whitespace characters are disallowed.

NOTE The NMTOKEN attribute type is defined in the XML 1.0 (Second Edition) Recommendation.

If you wanted to further refine the definition of the USAddressType complex type, you might want to ensure that you only allow five-digit zip codes. You could go partway toward achieving that goal by using the code shown here:

```
<xsd:element name="Zip" type="xsd:decimal" minLength="5" maxLength="5"/>
```

Two named complex types are shown in Listing 1.13 which you saw earlier. The complex datatypes CustomerType and LineItemsType are used in the type attributes of the declaration of the <Customer> element and the <LineItems> element.

We can use complex type definitions to add more structure to the simple book example. Listing 1.15 shows a further refinement of the structure of the instance document.

You might instantly recognize the content of the <Book> element as being a complex type. We can use an XSD schema as shown in Listing 1.16 to describe the instance document.

The schema demonstrates several of the kinds of declarations and definitions that you have already seen. The <Book> element is of complex type and makes use of an anonymous complex type definition. The <Title>, <Author>, and <Publisher> elements use element declarations that use the predefined xsd:string simple type. The definition of the <Authors> element again uses an anonymous complex type definition.

Using Anonymous or Named Complex Types

You might already have grasped the issues involved with choosing when to use an anonymous complex type or a named complex type, but these will be briefly summarized here. There is no rule that says you must use either an anonymous or named complex type in any particular situation. Whether you

```
<?xml version="1.0"?>
<Book pubCountry="USA">
 <Title>XML Schema Essentials</Title>
  <Authors>
   <Author>R. Allen Wyke</Author>
   <Author>Andrew Watt</Author>
  </Authors>
 <Publisher>John Wiley</Publisher>
</Book>
```

Listing 1.15 Adding element content to the simple book (SimpleBook03.xml).

```
<?xml version="1.0" encoding="UTF-8"?>
<xsd:schema xmlns:xsd="http://www.w3.org/2001/XMLSchema" >

<xsd:annotation>
    <xsd:documentation>
     This is a sample XML Schema for Chapter 1 of XML Schema
Essentials.
    </xsd:documentation>
</xsd:annotation>

<xsd:element name="Book">
  <xsd:complexType>
   <xsd:sequence>
    <xsd:element name="Title" ref="Title"/>
    <xsd:element name="Authors" ref="Authors"/>
    <xsd:element name="Publisher" ref="Publisher"/>
   </xsd:sequence>
   <xsd:attribute name="PubCountry" type="xsd:string"/>
  </xsd:complexType>
</xsd:element>

<xsd:element name="Title" type="xsd:string"/>

<xsd:element name="Authors">
  <xsd:complexType>
   <xsd:sequence>
    <xsd:element name="Author" ref="Author" minOccurs="1"
maxOccurs="unbounded"/>
   </xsd:sequence>
  </xsd:complexType>
</xsd:element>

<xsd:element name="Author" type="xsd:string"/>

<xsd:element name="Publisher" type="xsd:string"/>
</xsd:schema>
```

Listing 1.16 A schema containing simple and complex types (SimpleBook03.xsd).

use an anonymous complex type or a named complex type is a matter of convenience and efficiency.

If you plan to use a structure more than once in an instance document—for example, an address structure in both the billing address and shipping address part of an invoice—then it makes sense to avoid duplication of declarations, declare a named complex type once, and then reference it twice by using the type attribute of the <xsd:element> element.

In Chapter 10, "Bringing the Parts Together,"we will look at how we can reuse derived types from other schema documents. In order to be able to reference those type definitions, they must be named. As you will see later, we can also import element declarations that always include a name attribute on the <xsd:element>.

If you plan to use a structure only once, then you need to define the structure once in any case. If you have no plans to use that structure on multiple occasions in an instance document, then little useful purpose is served by naming the complex type, declaring it globally, and then referencing it by name. In that situation, you would almost certainly use an anonymous complex type.

Mixed Content

You might be aware that when using a DTD (which defines a mixed content model), little worthwhile validation can be carried out on an instance document. The instance document, or a selected part of it that contains mixed content, is allowed to contain both elements and character content—but the DTD cannot say anything about which elements are to be allowed in the mixed content, what order they might be in, or whether there should be any restrictions on where character content is to be allowed. XSD Schema can improve significantly on what is a significant weakness of the DTD.

Let's suppose that we want routinely to send out a letter to customers, created from XML, which thanks the customer for an order, details the items purchased, and informs the customer of any special offers that we might have available at the time that the letter is sent. An outline of a possible instance document might look like that in Listing 1.17.

A full version showing mixed content is shown in Listing 1.18. We needn't concern ourselves with where, from, or how the information contained in the document was assembled; rather, we simply accept it as an approximation of a finished document.

If we were using a DTD as a schema for our instance document, we could say little more than that mixed content was to be allowed. XSD Schema gives

```
<?xml version='1.0'?>
<CustomerLetter>
<CustomerAddress></CustomerAddress>
<Salutation></Salutation>
<Thanks></Thanks>
<ItemsOrdered></ItemsOrdered>
<SpecialOffers></SpecialOffers>
</CustomerLetter>
```

Listing 1.17 The skeleton of a customer letter (CustomerLetter01.xml).

```
<?xml version='1.0'?>
<CustomerLetter>
 <CustomerAddress>
  <Customer>Siegried Idylls</Customer>
  <Street>WagnerStrasse 88</Street>
  <City>Bayreuth</City>
  <Country>Germany</Country>
 </CustomerAddress>
Dear <Salutation>Richard</Salutation>,
 <Thanks>XMML.com is grateful to you for the order detailed
below and hope that all parts of the order will prove
satisfactory.</Thanks>
 <ItemsOrdered>
  <Item quantity="2">Some item</Item>
  <Item quantity="4">Some other item</Item>
 </ItemsOrdered>
We would like to introduce you to some special offers we are currently
making available to selected customers only.
 <SpecialOffers>
  <SpecialOffer specialPrice="99">Some great bargain</SpecialOffer>
  <SpecialOffer specialPrice="250">Some other great
bargain</SpecialOffer>
 </SpecialOffers>
These very special offers are available only until October 31st, so if
you want to take
advantage of these contact us immediately to secure this special
pricing.
</CustomerLetter>
```

Listing 1.18 An instance document illustrating the customer letter (CustomerLetter02.xml).

us significantly more control over element content and ordering. Listing 1.19 shows an XSD Schema for the customer letter.

The key part of the schema, as far as understanding how to control mixed content by using XSD Schema, is the declaration of the <CustomerLetter> element:

```
<xsd:element name="CustomerLetter" >
 <xsd:complexType mixed="true">
  <xsd:sequence>
    <xsd:element name="CustomerAddress" type="CustomerAddressType"/>
    <xsd:element name="Salutation" type="xsd:string"/>
    <xsd:element name="Thanks" type="xsd:string"/>
    <xsd:element name="ItemsOrdered" type="ItemsOrderedType"/>
    <xsd:element name="SpecialOffers" type="SpecialOffersType"/>
  </xsd:sequence>
 </xsd:complexType>
</xsd:element>
```

```
<?xml version="1.0" encoding="UTF-8"?>
<xsd:schema xmlns:xsd="http://www.w3.org/2001/XMLSchema" >

<xsd:element name="CustomerLetter" >
 <xsd:complexType mixed="true">
  <xsd:sequence>
    <xsd:element name="CustomerAddress" type="CustomerAddressType"/>
    <xsd:element name="Salutation" type="xsd:string"/>
    <xsd:element name="Thanks" type="xsd:string"/>
    <xsd:element name="ItemsOrdered" type="ItemsOrderedType"/>
    <xsd:element name="SpecialOffers" type="SpecialOffersType"/>
  </xsd:sequence>
 </xsd:complexType>
</xsd:element>

<xsd:complexType name="CustomerAddressType">
 <xsd:sequence>
  <xsd:element name="Customer" type="xsd:string"/>
  <xsd:element name="Street" type="xsd:string"/>
  <xsd:element name="City" type="xsd:string"/>
  <xsd:element name="Country" type="xsd:string"/>
 </xsd:sequence>
</xsd:complexType>

<xsd:complexType name="ItemsOrderedType">
 <xsd:sequence>
  <xsd:element name="Item" minOccurs="1" maxOccurs="unbounded">
   <xsd:complexType>
    <xsd:simpleContent>
     <xsd:extension base="xsd:string">
      <xsd:attribute name="quantity" type="xsd:decimal"/>
     </xsd:extension>
    </xsd:simpleContent>
   </xsd:complexType>
  </xsd:element>
 </xsd:sequence>
</xsd:complexType>

<xsd:complexType name="SpecialOffersType">
 <xsd:sequence>
   <xsd:element name="SpecialOffer" minOccurs="2"
maxOccurs="unbounded">
   <xsd:complexType>
    <xsd:simpleContent>
     <xsd:extension base="xsd:string">
      <xsd:attribute name="specialPrice" type="xsd:decimal"/>
     </xsd:extension>
```

continues

Listing 1.19 An XSD Schema for the customer letter (CustomerLetter02.xsd).

```
      </xsd:simpleContent>
    </xsd:complexType>
   </xsd:element>
  </xsd:sequence>
 </xsd:complexType>

 </xsd:schema>
```

Listing 1.19 An XSD Schema for the customer letter (CustomerLetter02.xsd). (Continued)

Notice in the anonymous <complexType> element that a mixed attribute is present and has a value of true. This situation indicates that mixed content (elements and text) is permitted within the <CustomerLetter> element. Unlike a DTD, however, where we could then not constrain the element content in any way, the declaration of the <CustomerLetter> element goes on to specify that there is a specific sequence of elements that are permitted. The permitted sequence of elements is <CustomerAddress>, <Salutation>, <Thanks>, <ItemsOrdered>, and <SpecialOffers>. In addition, we can specify the allowed datatypes for each of those elements. For example, the <SpecialOffers> element must conform to the constraints of the SpecialOffersType datatype. Thus, using XSD Schema, we can permit the flexibility of mixed content while at the same time constraining the element structure and defining the permitted datatypes within that element structure. This combination of flexibility with control is a major improvement over the mixed content mechanisms available with a DTD.

Declarations

A declaration in XSD Schema, whether a global declaration or a local declaration, is the association of a name—either of an element or an attribute—with a datatype. Thus, if we see code such as

```
<xsd:element name="FirstName" type="xsd:string"/>
```

we know that an element <FirstName> is constrained to have content that corresponds to the XSD Schema xsd:string datatype.

Let's move on to examine what the characteristics are of global element declarations and local element declarations.

Global Element Declarations

A global element is declared as the immediate child of an <xsd:schema> element. A global element declaration consists of declarations of an element whose content is a simple type or complex type but must not reference another global declaration. In addition, a global element must not contain the cardinality constraints minOccurs or maxOccurs, although those can be used in local element declarations that reference the global element. Translating those restrictions to specific syntax requirements, a global element declaration can contain a type attribute but not a ref attribute. Additionally, a global element declaration must not contain minOccurs, maxOccurs, or use attributes.

Declaring an element globally can be more efficient than a local element declaration, particularly if it is to be reused within a schema. Suppose that we wish to hold information about both billing and shipping addresses for each order that our company processes. An instance document is shown in Listing 1.20.

```
<?xml version='1.0'?>
<Invoice>
<BillingInfo>
 <Address>
  <Company></Company>
  <FAO></FAO>
  <Street1></Street1>
  <Street2></Street2>
  <City></City>
  <State></State>
  <PostalCode></PostalCode>
  <Country></Country>
  <Date>2001-08-31</Date>
 </Address>
</BillingInfo>
<ShippingInfo>
 <Address>
  <Company></Company>
  <FAO></FAO>
  <Street1></Street1>
  <Street2></Street2>
  <City></City>
  <State></State>
  <PostalCode></PostalCode>
  <Country></Country>
  <Date>2001-09-25</Date>
 </Address>
</ShippingInfo>
<!-- Item information would go here. -->
</Invoice>
```

Listing 1.20 An invoice using two addresses (TwoAddresses.xml).

It is clear that the structure of information that we need for the <Billing-Info> element is the same as the structure of the <ShippingInfo> element. XSD Schema enables us to declare the required structure once in a global element declaration and use it more than once by means of a ref attribute in the element declarations for the <BillingInfo> and <ShippingInfo> elements, as you can see in Listing 1.21.

The first part of the schema is the global declaration of the Address element. That declaration is then referenced from within the declaration of the <Invoice> element by the following code:

```
<xsd:element ref="Address" minOccurs="1" maxOccurs="1"/>
```

(both within the declaration of the <BillingInfo> element and of the <Shipping-Info> element). Because the declaration of the <Address> element is global, it can be referenced from anywhere within the schema for reuse. That is achieved by using an <xsd:element> that possesses a ref attribute. Additionally, we can specify the permitted cardinality of the referenced element by using the minOccurs and maxOccurs attributes. In the earlier code, we explicitly stated values for the minOccurs and maxOccurs attributes but did not need to do that, because the value of "1" is the default for each of those attributes.

An element that is declared as a global element in an XSD schema can be used as the element root in the corresponding XML instance document. Thus, by declaring more than one element globally, substantial flexibility in the allowed structure of instance documents is possible.

It is possible to declare all elements within a schema as global elements if the elements so declared are unique within their namespace.

Local Element Declarations

An element declared in an <xsd:element> element that is the child of an <xsd:schema> element, in the manner you saw in the previous section, is globally declared. All other element declarations are local.

Listing 1.22 illustrates an instance document that requires comments within certain elements.

Notice that a <comment> element is located within a <Food> element and within a <Drink> element.

Listing 1.23 shows a schema to describe this document.

Notice in the definition of the complex type FoodType that a declaration for a <comment> element is present. That declaration can only be used within the FoodType complex type definition. We could not, for example, have a reference to that element declaration within the DrinkType complex type definition. The first element declaration for a <comment> element is locally declared and is therefore not accessible globally.

```
<?xml version='1.0'?>
<xsd:schema xmlns:xsd="http://www.w3.org/2001/XMLSchema">

<xsd:element name="Address">
 <xsd:complexType>
  <xsd:sequence>
   <xsd:element name="Company" type="xsd:string"/>
   <xsd:element name="FAO" type="xsd:string"/>
   <xsd:element name="Street1" type="xsd:string"/>
   <xsd:element name="Street2" type="xsd:string"/>
   <xsd:element name="City" type="xsd:string"/>
   <xsd:element name="State" type="xsd:string" />
   <xsd:element name="PostalCode" type="xsd:decimal"/>
   <xsd:element name="Country" type="xsd:string"/>
   <xsd:element name="Date" type="xsd:date"/>
  </xsd:sequence>
 </xsd:complexType>
</xsd:element>

<xsd:element name="Invoice">
 <xsd:complexType>
  <xsd:sequence>   <xsd:element name="BillingInfo">
    <xsd:complexType>
     <xsd:sequence>
      <xsd:element ref="Address" minOccurs="1" maxOccurs="1"/>
     </xsd:sequence>
    </xsd:complexType>
   </xsd:element>

   <xsd:element name="ShippingInfo">
    <xsd:complexType>
     <xsd:sequence>
      <xsd:element ref="Address" minOccurs="1" maxOccurs="1"/>
     </xsd:sequence>
    </xsd:complexType>
   </xsd:element>

  </xsd:sequence>
 </xsd:complexType>
</xsd:element>

</xsd:schema>
```

Listing 1.21 An XSD Schema showing reuse of a globally declared element (TwoAddresses.xsd).

```
<?xml version='1.0'?>
<FoodAndDrink>
<Food>
 <comment>Many children like eating hamburgers.</comment>
 <FoodName>Hamburgers</FoodName>
</Food>
<Drink>
 <comment>Many children like drinking cola drinks.</comment>
 <DrinkName>A proprietary cola drink</DrinkName>
</Drink>
</FoodAndDrink>
```

Listing 1.22 An XML document containing two <comment> elements (FoodAndDrink.xml).

```
<?xml version="1.0" encoding="UTF-8"?>
<xsd:schema xmlns:xsd="http://www.w3.org/2001/XMLSchema" >

<xsd:element name="FoodAndDrink">
 <xsd:complexType>
  <xsd:sequence>
  <xsd:element name="Food" type="FoodType" maxOccurs="unbounded"/>
  <xsd:element name="Drink" type="DrinkType" maxOccurs="unbounded"/>
  </xsd:sequence>
 </xsd:complexType>
</xsd:element>

<xsd:complexType name="FoodType">
 <xsd:sequence>
  <xsd:element name="comment" type="xsd:string"/>
  <xsd:element name="FoodName" type="xsd:string"/>
 </xsd:sequence>
</xsd:complexType>

<xsd:complexType name="DrinkType">
 <xsd:sequence>
  <xsd:element name="comment" type="xsd:string"/>
  <xsd:element name="DrinkName" type="xsd:string"/>
 </xsd:sequence>
</xsd:complexType>

</xsd:schema>
```

Listing 1.23 An XSD Schema with local declaration of <comment> elements (FoodAnd-Drink.xsd).

Global Attribute Declarations

Like global elements, global attributes are created by declarations that are children of the <xsd:schema> element. Once declared, a global attribute can be referenced in other declarations by means of the ref attribute.

Fixed and Default Values for Elements and Attributes

An XSD schema can specify values for the content of an element or attribute in an instance document by means of default or fixed attributes. First, let's look at how default values are specified in XSD Schema and what effect the default attribute in an XSD schema has on an XML instance document.

The descriptions that follow, of course, only apply to processing by XSD Schema-aware processors. Other processors can be expected to be unable to access and apply default values of either elements or attributes.

Default Values of Elements

If a default attribute is present on an <xsd:element> element in an XSD schema, then three possible situations might arise:

1. If the element is present in the instance document and contains content, then the default value in the XSD schema is not used.
2. If the element is present in the instance document and is empty, then the default value of the element content defined in the XSD schema is used.
3. If the element is absent from the instance document, then no element is inserted.

In summary, the value contained in a default attribute of an <xsd:element> element is applied to an element in the instance document only when the element is present in the instance document and is an empty element.

Default Values of Attributes

An attribute of an XML element can occur only zero or one time. It is an error, according to the XML 1.0 Recommendation, if an attribute is duplicated on an element. Therefore, XML Schema makes provision only for zero or one attributes of any specified name to be present on an XML element.

If a default attribute is present in an XSD schema for an attribute in the instance document, there are three possible behaviors depending on what is or is not present in the instance document. A default value for an attribute only makes sense where use of the attribute is optional in the instance document.

The first possibility is that the attribute is present in the instance document and has some content. In that case, the value provided in the instance document overrides the default content provided in the default attribute of the <xsd:attribute> element in the schema.

The second possibility is that the attribute is present in the instance document but has no content provided by the author of the instance document. In that situation, the value contained in the default attribute of the <xsd:attribute> element in the schema is not used to create the content of the attribute in the instance document.

The third possibility is that the attribute, for which a default attribute exists in the XSD schema, is absent from the instance document. In that situation, the attribute is added to the instance document together with its default content.

In summary, the value contained in a default attribute of an <xsd:attribute> element is applied to an attribute in the instance document only when the attribute is absent in the instance document. An error occurs if a default value is specified for an attribute and the use attribute has a value other than optional.

Fixed Values of Elements

XSD Schema enables us to define a fixed value for one or more elements in an instance document. In the instance document in the following code (CurrentMembers.xml), all three elements are valid against the schema in Listing 1.24.

```
<?xml version='1.0'?>
<CurrentMembers>
<Member>
<FirstName>Carl</FirstName>
<LastName>Brandt</LastName>
<Membership>Current</Membership>
</Member>
<Member>
<FirstName>Pierre</FirstName>
<LastName>Dumas</LastName>
<Membership></Membership>
</Member>
<Member>
<FirstName>Anna</FirstName>
<LastName>Verova</LastName>
<Membership/>
</Member>
</CurrentMembers>
```

Listing 1.24 Instance document (CurrentMembers.xml).

```
<?xml version='1.0'?>
<xsd:schema xmlns:xsd="http://www.w3.org/2001/XMLSchema">
<xsd:element name="CurrentMembers">
 <xsd:complexType>
  <xsd:sequence>
   <xsd:element name="Member" type="MemberType" minOccurs="0"
maxOccurs="unbounded"/>
  </xsd:sequence>
 </xsd:complexType>
</xsd:element> <!-- End tag for <CurrentMembers> element. -->

<xsd:complexType name="MemberType">
 <xsd:sequence>
  <xsd:element name="FirstName"/>
  <xsd:element name="LastName"/>
  <xsd:element name="Membership" fixed="Current"/>
 </xsd:sequence>
</xsd:complexType>
</xsd:schema>
```

Listing 1.25 An XSD Schema that provides a fixed value for the <Membership> element (CurrentMembers.xsd).

Listing 1.25 is a schema that will define the <Membership> element as having a fixed value of "Current."

The line of code that defines the value of the <Membership> element in the instance document as having the value of "Current" is as follows:

```
<xsd:element name="Membership" fixed="Current"/>
```

Let's consider why each of the three <Membership> elements in the instance document in Listing 1.24 are considered valid. The first <Membership> element,

```
<Membership>Current</Membership>
```

is valid because it corresponds exactly to the fixed value defined for the <Membership> element. The second <Membership> element,

```
<Membership></Membership>
```

is considered valid because when an element is empty for which a fixed value is defined, then a validating processor processes the element as if that fixed value is present in the empty element. The third <Membership> element,

```
<Membership/>
```

is also an empty element—and, as with the second element in the instance document, an XSD Schema-aware validating processor will treat that element as if the value "Current" were its text content.

Both default and fixed values will often be used in conjunction with specifying the occurrence (cardinality) of an element in an instance document. Combining the use of the default and fixed attributes with XSD Schema's cardinality operators is described later in this chapter.

Fixed Values of Attributes

When a fixed attribute is present on an <xsd:attribute> element, then the effect is very similar to that just described for fixed values of elements.

If the attribute is present in the instance document, then its value must correspond to the value of the fixed attribute on the <xsd:attribute> element. If the attribute is absent from the instance document, then an attribute will be added to the instance document by an XSD Schema-aware processor with the fixed value specified for the attribute in the schema.

Annotations in Schema

Documentation of any code is a valuable resource when a new user begins to use a schema or when the time comes for maintenance of the schema code to be carried out. XML Schema is no exception. Similarly, if you want to create a schema that is to be used by other parties, then full and expressive documentation improves the likelihood that others will quickly assimilate your intentions and thus make it more likely that the desired schema is accepted. Viewed from the other angle, if your company decides to adopt an external schema of some sort—perhaps a budding industry or sector standard—then full internal documentation makes it much easier for you and your colleagues to produce the code to support the schema and to communicate any constraints to other staff who perhaps have to modify how they enter data into instance documents.

Good documentation helps everybody who is using a schema for XML instance documents. The options for documentation in XSD Schema follow.

Standard XML Comments

An XSD schema is an XML document; therefore, standard XML comments can be used within the schema. One limitation of typical XML comments is that they are intended solely for human consumption. The XML processing instruction applies to information intended to be machine readable.

XSD Schema provides an <xsd:annotation> element that can contain information intended to be human readable, machine readable, or both, however.

The <annotation> Element

The <xsd:annotation> element is the main annotation element in XSD Schema. The other annotation elements, <xsd:documentation> and <xsd:appinfo>, are nested within an <xsd:annotation> element.

The <xsd:annotation> element can be used at the beginning of many XSD Schema constructs. For example, in a simple schema to define the structure of a name, we could insert an <xsd:annotation> element together with an <xsd:documentation> element within the <xsd:annotation> element, as shown in Listing 1.26.

Notice that the <xsd:annotation> element is a child element of the <xsd:element> that it is describing and is the first child element. The nested <xsd:documentation> element carries an xml:lang attribute that defines the language of the documentation that is contained within the <xsd:documentation> element. An alternative approach is to place the xml:lang attribute in the start tag of the <xsd:schema> element as follows:

```
<xsd:schema xmlns:xsd="http://www.w3.org/2001/XMLSchema"
xml:lang="en">
```

The corresponding instance document could look like that in Listing 1.27.

An <xsd:annotation> element can similarly occur as the first child of the <xsd:schema> element as you saw in Listing 1.2.

```
<?xml version="1.0" encoding="UTF-8"?>
<xsd:schema xmlns:xsd="http://www.w3.org/2001/XMLSchema">
 <xsd:element name="Name">
  <xsd:annotation>
   <xsd:documentation xml:lang="en">This schema provides a simply
structured
   definition of a name consisting of first name, middle initial(s)
and last
   name.
   </xsd:documentation>
  </xsd:annotation>
  <xsd:complexType>
   <xsd:sequence>
    <xsd:element name="FirstName" type="xsd:string"/>
    <xsd:element name="MiddleInitials" type="xsd:string"/>
    <xsd:element name="LastName" type="xsd:string"/>
    </xsd:sequence>
  </xsd:complexType>
 </xsd:element>
</xsd:schema>
```

Listing 1.26 A schema that includes annotation (NameAnnotation.xsd).

```
<?xml version='1.0'?>
<Name>
<FirstName>Janet</FirstName>
<MiddleInitials>D</MiddleInitials>
<LastName>Middlebush</LastName>
</Name>
```

Listing 1.27 Corresponding instance document (NameAnnotation.xml).

The <xsd:documentation> Element

The <xsd:documentation> element is intended for human-readable documentation, such as that shown in Listing 1.26. It can be used, nested within an <xsd:annotation> element, in multiple places within an XSD schema. It can also be placed as a child of the <xsd:schema> element or nested within an element declaration or within a complex type definition.

A more fully documented version of Listing 1.26 is shown in Listing 1.28.

The <appinfo> Element

The <xsd:appinfo> element is used to contain information to be used by XML tools, stylesheets, or other applications. The <xsd:appinfo> element is nested within an <xsd:annotation> element.

Self-Documenting Annotations

XSD Schema annotations provide an opportunity to create documentation for XSD schemas by creating an XSLT stylesheet that extracts the content of <xsd:annotation> elements, and their nested <xsd:documentation> elements, to create a standalone documentation file for each of your XSD schemas.

We will use Listing 1.28, NameAnnotation02.xsd, as the source document for the XSLT transformation shown in Listing 1.29.

The XSLT stylesheet in Listing 1.29 produces an HTML file that contains the content of all the <xsd:documentation> elements in Listing 1.28. The HTML output is shown in Listing 1.30.

The on-screen output of the XSLT transformation is shown in Figure 1.7.

Creating documentation in this way demands some discipline in the use of <xsd:documentation> to make sense when read in a standalone HTML document. But if that discipline is followed, it makes training of new members of staff and maintenance of code a significantly easier exercise.

```
<?xml version="1.0" encoding="UTF-8"?>
<xsd:schema xmlns:xsd="http://www.w3.org/2001/XMLSchema">
 <xsd:element name="Name">
  <xsd:annotation>
   <xsd:documentation xml:lang="en">This schema provides a simply
structured
   definition of a name consisting of first name, middle initial(s)
and last
   name.
   </xsd:documentation>
  </xsd:annotation>
  <xsd:complexType>
  <xsd:annotation>
   <xsd:documentation>The element &lt;Name&gt; is an XSD Schema
complex type, since
   it has multiple child elements.</xsd:documentation>
  </xsd:annotation>
   <xsd:sequence>

    <xsd:element name="FirstName" type="xsd:string">
     <xsd:annotation>
      <xsd:documentation>The &lt;FirstName&gt; element has simple type
content of type
      xsd:string.</xsd:documentation>
     </xsd:annotation>
    </xsd:element>

    <xsd:element name="MiddleInitials" type="xsd:string">
     <xsd:annotation>
      <xsd:documentation>The &lt;MiddleInitials&gt; element also has
simple type content
      of type xsd:string.</xsd:documentation>
     </xsd:annotation>
    </xsd:element>

    <xsd:element name="LastName" type="xsd:string"/>

    </xsd:sequence>
  </xsd:complexType>
 </xsd:element>
</xsd:schema>
```

Listing 1.28 A more fully annotated schema (NameAnnotation02.xsd).

Empty Element Declaration

It is sometimes necessary to be able to declare elements that have no content (in other words, empty elements). In practice, empty elements are (in XSD

```
<?xml version='1.0'?>
<xsl:stylesheet version="1.0"
                xmlns:xsl="http://www.w3.org/1999/XSL/Transform"
                xmlns:xsd="http://www.w3.org/2001/XMLSchema">

<xsl:output
   method="html"
   indent="yes"/>
<xsl:strip-space elements="*"/>

<xsl:template match="/">
<html>
<head>
<title>Extracting content of &lt;xsd:annotation&gt; elements using
XSLT.</title>
</head>
<body>
<h3>This documentation has been created using an XSLT stylesheet to
process &lt;xsd:annotation&gt;
and &lt;xsd:documentation&gt; elements in an XSD Schema document.</h3>
<xsl:apply-templates select="//xsd:documentation"/>
</body>
</html>
</xsl:template>

<xsl:template match="xsd:documentation">
<xsl:choose>
<xsl:when test="ancestor::*[position()=2]/@name">
<p><b>Documentation for the &lt;<xsl:value-of
select="ancestor::*[position()=2]/@name"/>&gt; element.</b><br />
<xsl:value-of select="."/></p>
</xsl:when>
<xsl:otherwise>
<p><b>Documentation for the anonymous &lt;<xsl:value-of
select="name(ancestor::*[position()=2])"/>&gt; element.</b><br />
<xsl:value-of select="."/></p>
</xsl:otherwise>
</xsl:choose>
</xsl:template>
</xsl:stylesheet>
```

Listing 1.29 An XSLT stylesheet to create HTML documentation from <xsd:annotation> elements (NameAnnotation02.xsl).

Schema terminology) complex types because they would typically have attributes. There would be little point in declaring a simple type empty element, which would have no attributes or text content.

```
<html xmlns:xsd="http://www.w3.org/2001/XMLSchema">
   <head>
      <meta http-equiv="Content-Type" content="text/html; charset=utf-
8">

      <title>Extracting content of &lt;xsd:annotation&gt; elements
using XSLT.</title>
   </head>
   <body>
      <h3>This documentation has been created using an XSLT stylesheet
to process &lt;xsd:annotation&gt; and &lt;xsd:documentation&gt;
elements in an XSD Schema document.
      </h3>
      <p><b>Documentation for the &lt;Name&gt; element.</b><br>This
schema provides a simply structured
definition of a name consisting of first name, middle initial(s) and
last name.
      </p>
      <p><b>Documentation for the anonymous &lt;xsd:complexType&gt;
element.</b>
<br>The element &lt;Name&gt; is an XSD Schema complex type, since it
has multiple child elements.
      </p>
      <p><b>Documentation for the &lt;FirstName&gt;
element.</b><br>The &lt;FirstName&gt; element has simple type content
of type xsd:string.
      </p>
      <p><b>Documentation for the &lt;MiddleInitials&gt;
element.</b><br>The &lt;MiddleInitials&gt; element also has simple
type content of type xsd:string.
      </p>
   </body>
</html>
```

Listing 1.30 HTML output using the content of <xsd:annotation> elements (NameAnnotationOut.html).

Let's suppose that in a purchase order, you choose to create line items with all the relevant information contained in attributes but with no text content. An instance document might look like that in Listing 1.31.

The corresponding XSD schema is shown in Listing 1.32.

The important part of the schema is contained in the definition for the LineItemType:

```
<xsd:complexType name="LineItemType">
 <xsd:complexContent>
  <xsd:restriction base="xsd:anyType">
```

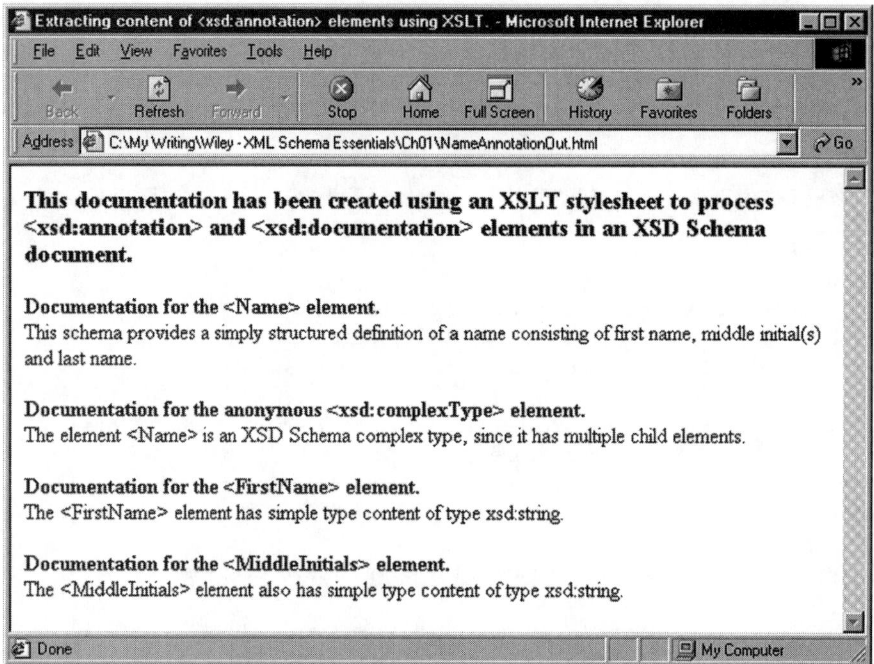

Figure 1.7 Self-documentation of XSD Schemas created by using an XSLT transformation.

```
<?xml version='1.0'?>
<PurchaseOrder>
<Customer>
 <CustomerName></CustomerName>
</Customer>
<LineItems>
 <LineItem price="99.99" quantity="5" description="widget"/>
 <LineItem price="24.99" quantity="3" description="whotsit"/>
</LineItems>
</PurchaseOrder>
```

Listing 1.31 An instance document with empty <LineItem> elements (EmptyElement.xml).

```
    <xsd:attribute name="price" type="xsd:decimal"/>
    <xsd:attribute name="quantity" type="xsd:nonNegativeInteger"/>
    <xsd:attribute name="description" type="xsd:string"/>
   </xsd:restriction>
  </xsd:complexContent>
</xsd:complexType>
```

```
<?xml version='1.0'?>
<xsd:schema xmlns:xsd="http://www.w3.org/2001/XMLSchema">
<xsd:element name="PurchaseOrder">
 <xsd:complexType>
  <xsd:sequence>
   <xsd:element name="Customer" type="CustomerType"/>
   <xsd:element name="LineItems" type="LineItemsType"/>
  </xsd:sequence>
 </xsd:complexType>
</xsd:element> <!-- End tag for the <PurchaseOrder> element. -->

<xsd:complexType name="CustomerType">
 <xsd:sequence>
  <xsd:element name="CustomerName" type="xsd:string"/>
 </xsd:sequence>
</xsd:complexType> <!-- End tag for <complexType> element named
"CustomerType" -->

<xsd:complexType name="LineItemsType">
 <xsd:sequence>
  <xsd:element name="LineItem" type="LineItemType"
maxOccurs="unbounded"/>
 </xsd:sequence>
</xsd:complexType> <!-- End tag for <complexType> element named
"LineItemsType" -->

<xsd:complexType name="LineItemType">
 <xsd:complexContent>
  <xsd:restriction base="xsd:anyType">
   <xsd:attribute name="price" type="xsd:decimal"/>
   <xsd:attribute name="quantity" type="xsd:nonNegativeInteger"/>
   <xsd:attribute name="description" type="xsd:string"/>
  </xsd:restriction>
 </xsd:complexContent>
</xsd:complexType> <!-- End tag for <complexType> element named
"LineItemType" -->
</xsd:schema>
```

Listing 1.32 XSD schema corresponding to Listing 1.31 (EmptyElement.xsd).

The <xsd:complexContent> element is used. The <xsd:restriction> element (which is nested within it) has a base type of xsd:anyType that is then restricted, with respect to allowed content, to the three attributes defined in the <xsd:attribute> elements.

The definition of LineItemType in this example is pretty verbose, so XSD Schema provides an abbreviated syntax for such situations shown in Listing 1.33.

```
<?xml version='1.0'?>
<xsd:schema xmlns:xsd="http://www.w3.org/2001/XMLSchema">
<xsd:element name="PurchaseOrder">
 <xsd:complexType>
  <xsd:sequence>
   <xsd:element name="Customer" type="CustomerType"/>
   <xsd:element name="LineItems" type="LineItemsType"/>
  </xsd:sequence>
 </xsd:complexType>
</xsd:element> <!-- End tag for the <PurchaseOrder> element. -->

<xsd:complexType name="CustomerType">
 <xsd:sequence>
  <xsd:element name="CustomerName" type="xsd:string"/>
 </xsd:sequence>
</xsd:complexType> <!-- End tag for <complexType> element named
"CustomerType" -->

<xsd:complexType name="LineItemsType">
 <xsd:sequence>
  <xsd:element name="LineItem" type="LineItemType"
maxOccurs="unbounded"/>
 </xsd:sequence>
</xsd:complexType> <!-- End tag for <complexType> element named
"LineItemsType" -->

<xsd:complexType name="LineItemType">
   <xsd:attribute name="price" type="xsd:decimal"/>
   <xsd:attribute name="quantity" type="xsd:nonNegativeInteger"/>
   <xsd:attribute name="description" type="xsd:string"/>
</xsd:complexType> <!-- End tag for <complexType> element named
"LineItemType" -->
</xsd:schema>
```

Listing 1.33 Abbreviated syntax for LineItemType (EmptyElementAbbrev.xsd).

The anyType Type

In the previous section, the base type for the <xsd:restriction> element in Listing 1.32 was "xsd:anyType." The xsd:anyType type is an abstract type that places no constraints on allowed content; in other words, the type(s) it contains can be of any type, including a mixture of elements and other content, hence the name. The xsd:anyType type is the default type for XSD Schema when a type is not otherwise specified. Hence, writing

```
<xsd:element name="MyElement">
```

is equivalent to

```
<xsd:element name="MyElement" type="anyType">
```

because the anyType type is the default. In practice, you will likely want to avoid using the anyType type other than as a base type for the <xsd:restriction> element or as a placeholder until you finalize the design of some part of a schema and define an appropriate type for a particular part of the content.

Occurrence Constraints

One of the ways in which an XML Schema schema constrains the content of an instance document is with respect to the number of times that an element can occur in a document. In order to understand how XSD Schema has improved our control over cardinality, let's first briefly look at cardinality in DTDs.

Cardinality in DTDs

In the DTDs that are part of XML 1.0, the capability to define cardinality is useful but limited. DTDs provide cardinality constraints that are particularly relevant to document-centric use but that fall short for data-centric applications. A DTD provides ways to express the following:

- Optional occurrence of an element; in other words, zero or one occurrences expressed by the question mark (?) operator
- Zero or more occurrences expressed by the asterisk (*) operator
- One or more occurrences expressed by the plus sign (+) operator

If, for example, you wanted to state that a book must have a minimum of two authors and a maximum of four authors, DTDs provide no way to express this information. But XSD schemas do.

minOccurs and maxOccurs

XML Schema provides functionality that permits the occurrence constraints provided in DTDs and also adds control over cardinality, which a DTD is unable to provide.

The minOccurs and maxOccurs attributes of an <xsd:element> element provide a mechanism to define permitted cardinality. Because the minimum permitted occurrence specified by the minOccurs attribute and the maximum permitted occurrence specified by the maxOccurs attribute are defined separately, we can create any arbitrary cardinality constraints that we might want.

```
<?xml version="1.0"?>
<Book>
  <Title>The book title</Title>
  <Author>Author's Name</Author>
  <Publisher>John Wiley</Publisher>
</Book>
```

Listing 1.34 Constraining cardinality to exactly 1: The instance document (BookCardin01.xml).

Let's suppose that in a book catalog we want to constrain the number of authors for a book to be exactly one, similar to the structure shown in Listing 1.34.

One way to express a schema for this structure is shown in Listing 1.35.

In Listing 1.35, we make it explicit that the minimum number of occurrences of, for example, the <Title> element is 1, as is its maximum number of occurrences. There is no real need for us to express that in this way, however. In W3C XML Schema, the default for both minOccurs and maxOccurs is 1; therefore, we can omit both the minOccurs and maxOccurs attributes so we can express the same constraints (of one and only one occurrence of each element) by using the schema shown in Listing 1.36.

```
<?xml version="1.0" encoding="UTF-8"?>
<xsd:schema xmlns:xsd="http://www.w3.org/2001/XMLSchema" >

<xsd:element name="Book">
  <xsd:complexType>
   <xsd:sequence>
    <xsd:element name="Title" ref="Title" minOccurs="1"
maxOccurs="1"/>
    <xsd:element name="Author" ref="Author" minOccurs="1"
maxOccurs="1"/>
    <xsd:element name="Publisher" ref="Publisher" minOccurs="1"
maxOccurs="1"/>
   </xsd:sequence>
  </xsd:complexType>
 </xsd:element>

<xsd:element name="Title" type="xsd:string"/>
<xsd:element name="Author" type="xsd:string"/>
<xsd:element name="Publisher" type="xsd:string"/>
</xsd:schema>
```

Listing 1.35 Constraining cardinality to exactly 1: The XSD schema (BookCardin01.xsd).

```
<?xml version="1.0" encoding="UTF-8"?>
<xsd:schema xmlns:xsd="http://www.w3.org/2001/XMLSchema" >

<xsd:element name="Book">
  <xsd:complexType>
   <xsd:sequence>
    <xsd:element name="Title" ref="Title"/>
    <xsd:element name="Author" ref="Author"/>
    <xsd:element name="Publisher" ref="Publisher"/>
   </xsd:sequence>
  </xsd:complexType>
 </xsd:element>

<xsd:element name="Title" type="xsd:string"/>
<xsd:element name="Author" type="xsd:string"/>
<xsd:element name="Publisher" type="xsd:string"/>
</xsd:schema>
```

Listing 1.36 A more succinct syntax to define a cardinality of exactly 1 (BookCardin02.xsd).

The default value for both minOccurs and maxOccurs is 1. Thus, Listing 1.36 specifies that the instance documents, to be valid, must have exactly one <Book> element and exactly one of each of the subelements <Title>, <Author>, and <Publisher>.

Of course in practice, real life is typically not as tidy and consistent as to have all books with exactly one author. For example, the book you are reading has more than one author, and to include it in the book catalog we would have to modify both the instance document and the schema that constrains it.

Listing 1.37 shows an instance document that would appropriately describe this book in the book catalog.

```
<?xml version="1.0"?>
<Book>
  <Title>The book title</Title>
  <Authors>
   <Author>Author's Name</Author>
   <Author>Another author</Author>
  </Authors>
  <Publisher>John Wiley</Publisher>
</Book>
```

Listing 1.37 A book with more than one author (BookCardin03.xml).

```
<?xml version="1.0" encoding="UTF-8"?>
<xsd:schema xmlns:xsd="http://www.w3.org/2001/XMLSchema" >

<xsd:element name="Book">
  <xsd:complexType>
   <xsd:sequence>
    <xsd:element name="Title" ref="Title"/>
    <xsd:element name="Authors" type="AuthorsType"/>
    <xsd:element name="Publisher" ref="Publisher"/>
   </xsd:sequence>
  </xsd:complexType>
 </xsd:element>

<xsd:element name="Title" type="xsd:string"/>

<xsd:complexType name="AuthorsType">
<xsd:sequence>
<xsd:element name="Author" type="xsd:string" minOccurs="1"
maxOccurs="unbounded"/>
</xsd:sequence>
</xsd:complexType>

<xsd:element name="Author" type="xsd:string"/>
<xsd:element name="Publisher" type="xsd:string"/>
</xsd:schema>
```

Listing 1.38 A schema to allow a cardinality of more than 1 (BookCardin03.xsd).

To be able to validate that instance document, we would need to adapt the XSD schema as shown in Listing 1.38.

Within the <complexType> element for the <Book> element, we simply replace the declaration of the <Author> element with

```
<xsd:element name="Authors" type="AuthorsType"/>
```

and then add an AuthorsType <complexType> element

```
<xsd:complexType name="AuthorsType">
<xsd:sequence>
<xsd:element name="Author" type="xsd:string" minOccurs="1"
maxOccurs="unbounded"/>
</xsd:sequence>
</xsd:complexType>
```

to the XSD schema.

For instance, for the documents such as the book examples that we have looked at so far, it is pretty much essential that there be at least one author for a book. After all, I can testify that books don't write themselves. In the schema shown earlier, the maxOccurs attribute has the value unbounded. We could specify any suitable value of type xsd:nonNegativeInteger for the maxOccurs attribute, however.

In other situations, we might want to have an optional occurrence of an element. First, let's look at the situation where we want an element to occur optionally—and, if it does occur, it might only occur once. That is something that a DTD can also express.

For example, if we want a list of <Item> elements on which a comment is optional, similar to the instance document shown in Listing 1.39, we can use an XSD schema like that shown in Listing 1.40.

As you can see, some <Item> elements contain a <comment> element while others do not. In other words, the <comment> element is optional.

To define optional elements, we use the minOccurs attribute with a value of zero and a maxOccurs attribute with a value of one. If we wish to allow an element to occur a specified number of times, then we can simply set the value of the maxOccurs attribute to the desired number. Another possibility is that we wish an element to occur optionally but to occur an unlimited number of times. In that case, we can set the value of the maxOccurs attribute to "unbounded" with the minOccurs attribute having a value of zero.

```
<?xml version='1.0'?>
<StockKeepingUnits>
 <Item>
  <ItemName>Alpha</ItemName>
  <ItemCode>A123</ItemCode>
 </Item>
 <Item>
  <comment>Beta is really great!</comment>
  <ItemName>Beta</ItemName>
  <ItemCode>B123</ItemCode>
 </Item>
 <Item>
  <comment>Gamma is the pits!</comment>
  <ItemName>Gamma</ItemName>
  <ItemCode>C123</ItemCode>
 </Item>
</StockKeepingUnits>
```

Listing 1.39 A list of items (StockKeepingUnits.xml).

```
<?xml version="1.0" encoding="UTF-8"?>
<xsd:schema xmlns:xsd="http://www.w3.org/2001/XMLSchema" >

<xsd:element name="StockKeepingUnits">
 <xsd:complexType>
  <xsd:sequence>
   <xsd:element name="Item" type="ItemType" maxOccurs="unbounded"/>
  </xsd:sequence>
 </xsd:complexType>
</xsd:element>

<xsd:complexType name="ItemType">
 <xsd:sequence>
  <xsd:element name="comment" type="xsd:string" minOccurs="0"
maxOccurs="1"/>
  <xsd:element name="ItemName" type="xsd:string" />
  <xsd:element name="ItemCode" type="xsd:string" />
 </xsd:sequence>
</xsd:complexType>

</xsd:schema>
```

Listing 1.40 A schema to allow for optional <comment> elements (StockKeepingUnits.xsd).

Defining Your Own Simple Type

As well as its built-in primitive and derived simple types, XSD Schema enables schema authors to create new simple types (for example, by restriction). We might, for example, want to create a five-character string simple type. We could do so by using the following code:

```
<xsd:simpleType name="FiveCharacterStringType">
 <xsd:restriction base="xsd:string">
  <xsd:length value="5"/>
 </xsd:restriction>
</xsd:simpleType>
```

The facility in XSD Schema to derive new datatypes from those defined in the W3C XML Schema Recommendation or derived types created by ourselves or other schema authors is an immensely powerful tool. It is a great improvement over the very limited support for datatyping in XML 1.0 DTDs. The length facet, which you have just seen, and other facets will be discussed in detail in Chapters 5, "Data Facets," and 6, "More about Data Facets." Deriving new datatypes will be discussed in greater detail in Chapter 8.

Model Groups in Schema

XSD Schema enables us to group elements in order to use them in a number of different ways. In this section, we will introduce the use of the <xsd:group> element.

If we have created a named group, we can reference that group and reuse it by inserting code like

```
<xsd:group ref="GroupNameGoesHere" />
```

within a type definition.

Sequence Group

In many earlier examples, you have seen the use of the <xsd:sequence> element to group sequences of element declarations. The <xsd:group> element enables us to group such sequences of element declarations and name them for reuse. This process is demonstrated in the following example (SoccerPlayers.xml), which also illustrates choice groups.

Choice Group

A choice group in XSD schemas permits a choice to be made in the structure of an instance document. Choice groups can be named or unnamed.

There are differences in how names are structured internationally. In the United States and the United Kingdom, for example, the structure is typically first name, middle initial(s) (optional), and last name. In some countries, for example Brazil, names can consist of a single name. We will illustrate how a schema could be constructed to cope with this necessary choice of structure, using Listing 1.41 as an instance document.

The XSD schema in Listing 1.42 shows how we can allow for the difference in structure of the soccer players' names by using a choice group.

The interesting part of SoccerPlayers.xsd is shown here:

```
<xsd:choice>
 <xsd:group ref="ThreePartName"/>
 <xsd:element name="SingleName" type="xsd:string"/>
</xsd:choice>
```

The <xsd:choice> element enables only one of its child elements to apply to the relevant part of the instance document. In this instance (forgive the pun), the choice is either the group represented by the <xsd:group> element

```
<?xml version='1.0'?>
<SoccerPlayers>
<Player>
<FirstName>David</FirstName>
<MiddleInitials></MiddleInitials>
<LastName>Beckham</LastName>
</Player>
<Player>
<SingleName>Pele</SingleName>
</Player>
<Player>
<SingleName>Ronaldo</SingleName>
</Player>
<Player>
<FirstName>Franz</FirstName>
<MiddleInitials></MiddleInitials>
<LastName>Beckenbauer</LastName>
</Player>
</SoccerPlayers>
```

Listing 1.41 An instance document with two name structures (SoccerPlayers.xml).

with name equal to "ThreePartName," which is referenced from within the <xsd:choice> element:

```
<xsd:group name="ThreePartName">
 <xsd:sequence>
  <xsd:element name="FirstName" type="xsd:string"/>
  <xsd:element name="MiddleInitials" type="xsd:string"/>
  <xsd:element name="LastName" type="xsd:string"/>
 </xsd:sequence>
</xsd:group>
```

or the single element

```
<xsd:element name="SingleName" type="xsd:string"/>
```

which is permitted as the content of a <Player> element.

All Group

XSD Schema provides a further type of grouping indicated by the <xsd:all> element. When an <xsd:all> element is present the content of the <xsd:all> element is either applicable in its entirety or not at all.

```
<?xml version='1.0'?>
<xsd:schema xmlns:xsd="http://www.w3.org/2001/XMLSchema">

<xsd:element name="SoccerPlayers">
 <xsd:complexType>
  <xsd:sequence>
   <xsd:element name="Player" maxOccurs="unbounded">
    <xsd:complexType>
     <xsd:sequence>
      <xsd:choice>
       <xsd:group ref="ThreePartName"/>
       <xsd:element name="SingleName" type="xsd:string"/>
      </xsd:choice>
     </xsd:sequence>
    </xsd:complexType>
   </xsd:element>
  </xsd:sequence>
 </xsd:complexType>
</xsd:element> <!-- End tag for <SoccerPlayers> element. -->

<xsd:group name="ThreePartName">
 <xsd:sequence>
  <xsd:element name="FirstName" type="xsd:string"/>
  <xsd:element name="MiddleInitials" type="xsd:string"/>
  <xsd:element name="LastName" type="xsd:string"/>
 </xsd:sequence>
</xsd:group>
</xsd:schema>
```

Listing 1.42 A schema to allow a choice between two structure options (SoccerPlayers.xsd).

Listing 1.43 provides a fictional listing of persons who are either law-abiding or who have a criminal record. Those with a criminal record must have a Web-based DNA and fingerprint profile. Those with no criminal record likely have no such profiles on record.

The following schema in Listing 1.44 uses the <xsd:all> element to apply either all (in this case, both) the profiles or none of them.

The definition of the ProfilesType complex type has an <xsd:all> element. Thus, the corresponding individual records in an instance document must have both a <DNAProfile> element and a <FingerPrint> element. If the instance document contained a record with only one of these two elements, then an XSD Schema-aware processor would report an error. If you want to permit such an occurrence, then the <xsd:all> element is unsuitable for that

```
<?xml version='1.0'?>
<Persons>
<Person status="lawabiding">
<Name>
<FirstName>Phoebe</FirstName>
<MiddleInitials>Z</MiddleInitials>
<LastName>Kruschev</LastName>
</Name>
</Person>
<Person status="criminalrecord">
<Name>
<FirstName>Patrick</FirstName>
<MiddleInitials>Q</MiddleInitials>
<LastName>O'Mahoney</LastName>
</Name>
<Profiles>
<DNAProfile>http://www.criminalrecords.gov/DNA2348899.html</DNAProfile
>
<FingerPrint>http://www.criminalrecords.gov/FP2348899.html</FingerPrin
t>
</Profiles>
</Person>
<Person status="criminalrecord">
<Name>
<FirstName>Cyril</FirstName>
<MiddleInitials>Y</MiddleInitials>
<LastName>Pinkerton</LastName>
</Name>
<Profiles>
<DNAProfile>http://www.criminalrecords.gov/DNA2948899.html</DNAProfile
>
<FingerPrint>http://www.criminalrecords.gov/FP2948899.html</FingerPrin
t>
</Profiles>
</Person>
</Persons>
```

Listing 1.43 A list of persons (Persons.xml).

purpose. One solution would be to use <xsd:sequence> with each of the element declarations indicating optional elements:

```
<xsd:complexType name = "ProfilesType">
 <xsd:sequence>
  <xsd:element name="DNAProfile" minOccurs="0" maxOccurs="1"
type=xsd:anyURI"/>
  <xsd:element name="FingerPrint" minOccurs="0" maxOccurs="1"
type=xsd:anyURI"/>
```

```
<?xml version='1.0'?>
<xsd:schema xmlns:xsd="http://www.w3.org/2001/XMLSchema">
<xsd:element name="Persons">
<xsd:complexType>
<xsd:sequence>
<xsd:element ref="Person" maxOccurs="unbounded"/>
</xsd:sequence>
</xsd:complexType>
</xsd:element> <!-- End tag of <Persons> element. -->

<xsd:element name="Person">
<xsd:complexType>
<xsd:sequence>
<xsd:element name="Name" type="NameType"/>
<xsd:element name="Profiles" type="ProfilesType" minOccurs="0"
maxOccurs="1"/>
</xsd:sequence>
<xsd:attribute name="status" type="xsd:string"/>
</xsd:complexType>
</xsd:element> <!-- End tag of <Person> element. -->

<xsd:complexType name="NameType">
<xsd:sequence>
<xsd:element name="FirstName" type="xsd:string"/>
<xsd:element name="MiddleInitials" type="xsd:string"/>
<xsd:element name="LastName" type="xsd:string"/>
</xsd:sequence>
</xsd:complexType>

<xsd:complexType name="ProfilesType">
<xsd:all>
<xsd:element name="DNAProfile" type="xsd:anyURI"/>
<xsd:element name="FingerPrint" type="xsd:anyURI"/>
</xsd:all>
</xsd:complexType>

</xsd:schema>
```

Listing 1.44 A schema to demonstrate the <xsd:all> element (Persons.xsd).

```
  </xsd:sequence>
</xsd:complexType>
```

Attribute Groups

Just as XSD Schema provides functionality to group elements, it also provides a means to group attributes. An attribute group provides an alternate way to express, and of course group, a number of attributes that have something in common—typically being used on more than one particular element in an instance document. If an attribute group is declared as a child of the <xsd:schema> element, then the attribute group can be referenced in the definition of more than one element in a schema as appropriate.

Suppose we had a clothing catalog where the information about each garment was held in the attributes of elements in an instance document, such as that shown in Listing 1.45.

We could declare each attribute individually, as in Listing 1.46.

Notice that within the <xsd:complexType> element for GarmentType that three individual attributes are nested within the <xsd:extension> element. In Listing 1.47 we see the same attributes declared by means of an <xsd:attributeGroup> element.

More about the XML 1.0 DTD Content Model

Now that you have seen a number of examples of W3C XML Schema in action, let's compare how a DTD and an XSD schema constrain a fairly typical simple instance document. The instance document, BookCatalog.xml, is shown in Listing 1.48.

We can create a DTD, BookCatalog.dtd, as shown in Listing 1.49.

It isn't the purpose of this chapter to teach you about DTDs if you are not already familiar with them. Notice, however, that for each element that does not have child elements, that the content is defined as #PCDATA. There is no way directly to constrain the text content further, although it is possible to add

```
<?xml version='1.0'?>
<ClothingCatalog>
<Garment size="S" color="aquamarine" manufacturer="XMML">
T-shirt
</Garment>
<Garment size="XL" color="navy" manufacturer="XMML">
Skirt
</Garment>
<Garment size="M" color="green" manufacturer="XMML">
T-shirt
</Garment>
<Garment size="L" color="cerise" manufacturer="XMML">
Sweat shirt
</Garment>
</ClothingCatalog>
```

Listing 1.45 A simple clothing catalog (ClothingCatalog.xml).

```
<?xml version='1.0'?>
<xsd:schema xmlns:xsd="http://www.w3.org/2001/XMLSchema">
<xsd:element name="ClothingCatalog">
<xsd:complexType>
<xsd:sequence>
<xsd:element name="Garment" type="GarmentType" minOccurs="1"
maxOccurs="unbounded"/>
</xsd:sequence>
</xsd:complexType>
</xsd:element> <!-- End tag for <ClothingCatalog> element. -->

<xsd:complexType name="GarmentType">
<xsd:simpleContent>
<xsd:extension base="xsd:string">
<xsd:attribute name="size" type="xsd:string"/>
<xsd:attribute name="color" type="xsd:string"/>
<xsd:attribute name="manufacturer" type="xsd:string"/>
</xsd:extension>
</xsd:simpleContent>
</xsd:complexType>

</xsd:schema>
```

Listing 1.46 A schema without grouped attributes (ClothingCatalog01.xsd).

type attributes to elements that describe the type of data that they contain, but that approach, while helpful, is very much a workaround of intrinsic limitations of the DTD.

An XSD schema provides us with better datatyping facilities such as those illustrated in Listing 1.50.

You need not attempt to grasp all the detail of this schema. It is there to give you an impression of the richness of the datatyping structures that XSD Schema can provide. We will discuss many of the options for datatyping of both simple types and complex types in later chapters.

Validation in XSD Schema

XSD Schema has two processes that are carried out by an XSD Schema validating processor:

- Determining local schema validity
- Assessment

Let's examine and compare validation and assessment.

```
<?xml version='1.0'?>
<xsd:schema xmlns:xsd="http://www.w3.org/2001/XMLSchema">
<xsd:element name="ClothingCatalog">
<xsd:complexType>
<xsd:sequence>
<xsd:element name="Garment" type="GarmentType" minOccurs="1"
maxOccurs="unbounded"/>
</xsd:sequence>
</xsd:complexType>
</xsd:element> <!-- End tag for <ClothingCatalog> element. -->

<xsd:complexType name="GarmentType">
<xsd:simpleContent>
<xsd:extension base="xsd:string">
<xsd:attributeGroup ref="GarmentGroup"/>
</xsd:extension>
</xsd:simpleContent>
</xsd:complexType>

<xsd:attributeGroup name="GarmentGroup">
<xsd:attribute name="size" type="xsd:string"/>
<xsd:attribute name="color" type="xsd:string"/>
<xsd:attribute name="manufacturer" type="xsd:string"/>
</xsd:attributeGroup>

</xsd:schema>
```

Listing 1.47 A schema to demonstrate grouping of attributes (ClothingCatalog02.xsd).

Validation versus Assessment

Validation is the simpler of the two concepts to understand because it has many similarities to validation (which is carried out against a DTD). What the XSD Schema specification refers to as local schema validity corresponds closely to the validity of an instance document validated against a DTD. If an element or attribute is local schema valid, then that element or attribute in the instance document (or more strictly, the corresponding information item in the XML information set) corresponds to the relevant definition or declaration in the appropriate XSD schema.

The W3C XML Schema Recommendation expresses the notion of "determining local schema-validity" as determining "whether an element or attribute information item satisfies the constraints embodied in the relevant components of an XML Schema."

We need to remember that element declarations and type definitions are *schema components* in XSD Schema jargon. Also, an XSD Schema-validating processor operates on the abstract XML information set, not directly on the

```
<?xml version="1.0"?>
<BookCatalog>
<Book pubCountry="USA">
  <Title series="XML Essentials">XML Schema Essentials</Title>
  <Authors>
   <Author>R. Allen Wyke</Author>
   <Author>Andrew Watt</Author>
  </Authors>
  <Publisher>John Wiley</Publisher>
  <ISBN>0471412597</ISBN>
  <DatePublished>2002-02</DatePublished>
  <Price>44.99</Price>
</Book>
<Book pubCountry="USA">
  <Title series="XML Essentials">XPath Essentials</Title>
  <Authors>
   <Author>Andrew Watt</Author>
  </Authors>
  <Publisher>John Wiley</Publisher>
  <ISBN>0471205486
</ISBN>
  <DatePublished>2001-10</DatePublished>
  <Price>44.99</Price>
</Book>
</BookCatalog>
```

Listing 1.48 A simple book catalog (BookCatalog.xml).

```
<!ELEMENT BookCatalog (Book)*>
<!ELEMENT Book (Title, Authors, Publisher, ISBN, DatePublished,
Price)>
<!ATTLIST Book pubCountry CDATA #IMPLIED >
<!ELEMENT Title (#PCDATA)>
<!ATTLIST Title series CDATA #IMPLIED>
<!ELEMENT Authors (Author)+>
<!ELEMENT Author (#PCDATA)>
<!ELEMENT Publisher (#PCDATA) >
<!ELEMENT ISBN (#PCDATA) >
<!ELEMENT DatePublished (#PCDATA) >
<!ELEMENT Price (#PCDATA) >
```

Listing 1.49 A Document Type Definition for the book catalog (BookCatalog.dtd).

serialized version of an instance document. Putting those ideas together, all that this definition is saying is that the structure and content of an element or attribute (as represented by the corresponding element information item or

```
<?xml version='1.0'?>
<xsd:schema xmlns:xsd="http://www.w3.org/2001/XMLSchema">
<xsd:element name="BookCatalog">
<xsd:complexType>
<xsd:sequence>
<xsd:element name="Book" type="BookType" minOccurs="0"
maxOccurs="unbounded"/>
</xsd:sequence>
</xsd:complexType>
</xsd:element>

<xsd:complexType name="BookType">
<xsd:sequence>
<xsd:element name="Title" type="TitleType"/>
<xsd:element name="Authors" type="AuthorsType"/>
<xsd:element name="Publisher" type="xsd:string"/>
<xsd:element name="ISBN" type="ISBNType"/>
<xsd:element name="DatePublished" type="DatePubType"/>
<xsd:element name="Price" type="xsd:decimal"/>
</xsd:sequence>
<xsd:attribute name="pubCountry" type="xsd:string"/>
</xsd:complexType>

<xsd:complexType name="TitleType">
<xsd:simpleContent>
<xsd:extension base="xsd:string">
<xsd:attribute name="series" type="xsd:string"/>
</xsd:extension>
</xsd:simpleContent>
</xsd:complexType>

<xsd:complexType name="AuthorsType">
<xsd:sequence>
<xsd:element name="Author" type="xsd:string" maxOccurs="unbounded"/>
</xsd:sequence>
</xsd:complexType>

<xsd:simpleType name="ISBNType">
 <xsd:restriction base="xsd:string">
  <xsd:length value="10"/>
 </xsd:restriction>
</xsd:simpleType>

<xsd:simpleType name="DatePubType">
<xsd:restriction base="xsd:string">
<xsd:pattern value="\d{4}-\d{2}"/>
</xsd:restriction>
</xsd:simpleType>
</xsd:schema>
```

Listing 1.50 An XSD schema for the book catalog (BookCatalog.xsd).

attribute information item) corresponds to the structure and content allowed by the corresponding part of an XSD schema.

So, what is "assessment"? The XSD Schema Recommendation defines assessment as "synthesizing an overall validation outcome for the item, combining local schema validity with the results of schema-validity assessments of its descendants, if any, and adding appropriate augmentations to the infoset to record this outcome."

Let's take that one part at a time. The first of the three parts is local schema validation, which we have just discussed: establishing whether or not an element or attribute satisfies the constraints of the corresponding part of the XSD schema. The second part of assessment is putting together the result of that local schema validation with the local schema validation of its descendant elements or attributes (if it has any). Thirdly, the information set might have information added to it to record the outcome of the first two aspects of this three-part *assessment* process.

The XML information set has been mentioned in passing, so let's go on to take a brief look at what the XML Information Set actually is.

XML Information Set

The W3C has produced three distinct models of XML documents: the Document Object Model, the DOM (in its various Levels), the XPath data model, and the XML Information Set. It is the XML Information set, sometimes termed the infoset, which is particularly relevant to XML Schema. In addition, XPath is used in certain parts of XSD Schema; for example, in identity-constraint definitions (see Chapter 9, "Uniqueness and Keys in XSD Schema").

Introduction to the XML Information Set

The XML Information Set specification was conceived at a time when XSD Schema was at an early stage of development and the XML 1.0 Recommendation (the original 1998 version) and its associated DTDs were stable and increasingly being widely implemented. Thus, the XML Information Set, when any type of schema is mentioned within the specification, is expressed in relation to well-formed XML documents that have a DTD (rather than a W3C XML Schema).

The W3C XML Information Set specification, sometimes called the infoset, is a W3C recommendation. W3C XML Schema made use of the infoset, although at the time that the W3C XML Schema Recommendation was finalized, the XML Information Set specification had not been finished.

NOTE **The full XML Information Set Recommendation is located at www.w3.org/TR/xml-infoset.**

The XML Information Set specification views the information contained within a well-formed XML document as being represented by the XML Information Set. The information set consists of a set of *information items*. Each information item has associated with it a number of *properties*. Broadly, the information set can be looked on as a tree and an information item as a node in that tree. The XML Information Set specification is careful to state that implementation detail need not make use of a tree or nodes, however.

The XML Information Set and XSD Schema

Earlier in the chapter, we touched on the concept that an XSD schema-validating parser can process an instance document and add default attributes, for example. In reality, the XSD schema-validating processor makes use of an information set, and the default attribute (or more precisely, the corresponding information item) is added to the information set that the XSD schema validating processor is using.

NOTE While both the XML Information Set specification and the W3C XML Schema specification refer to properties, the XML Information Set specification uses square brackets ([and]) to refer to the properties of an information item and the XSD Schema specification uses curly braces ({ and }) to refer to the properties of schema components.

Required Infoset Support

A validating processor that supports XSD Schema must provide a specified minimum support for parts of the XML information set. The following information items and properties must be supported:

- Attribute Information Item
  - [local name] property
  - [namespace name] property
  - [normalized value] property
- Character information item
  - [character code] property
- Element Information Item
  - [attributes] property
  - [children] property
  - [local name] property
  - [namespace name] property

and either

- [in-scope namespaces] property

or

- [namespace attributes] property

- Namespace Information Item
  - [namespace name] property
  - [prefix] property

Post-Schema Validation Infoset

The document information item in an XML infoset has a property called [all declarations processed] which, strictly speaking, is not part of the XML infoset at all. Instead, it records whether or not processing of the document (for example, retrieval of external entities) has been achieved or not. Such a property is useful, however, because it provides a record of the processing of the infoset corresponding to a particular XML source document.

Similarly, it is useful for applications (and human beings) to be aware of how processing of an XSD schema and the corresponding instance documents has progressed. The [all declarations processed] information item is pretty simple—it can take a boolean value, either true or false.

After validation an XSD Schema processor can add information to the infoset to indicate the result of the validation processing. That augmented information set is termed the post-schema validation infoset, which in a way is similar to the [all declarations processed] property records within the augmented information set information about the validation process itself.

Summary

The preceding paragraphs have introduced many of the concepts and elements of XSD Schema in a single chapter in order to give you a broad view of what W3C XML Schema is and a hint of what it can do.

We have seen how an XSD schema document contains element and attribute declarations, associating a name with the appearance of an element or attribute in an instance document. We have also seen how simple types and complex types are defined in a schema document.

The following chapters show in more detail many of the aspects of XSD Schema that we have already touched upon in this introduction. In Chapter 2, "XSD Elements," we will go on to examine in more detail the <xsd:element> element.

CHAPTER

2

XSD Elements

Elements represent what many consider to be the most important features of any XML-based language. They enable us to encapsulate data and provide a home for attributes. They are used as wrappers around the data payload that we wish to describe, and the attributes within them provide additional metadata about that payload. The combination of these two items enables users to easily mark up their content and exchange information.

One of the few features that help XSD in simplicity is its use of elements to define the language. As we saw in Chapter 1, "Elementary XML Schema," defining an XSD-based language is accomplished through the use of applying XML 1.0-defined elements. In other words, if we are building an XSD-defined language that has an element called <customer>, then we actually use an XSD element called <xsd:element> to define the <customer> element. This concept of using elements to define elements might seem a little strange at first, but this approach will be revealed as a means to simplify the XSD structure, core language semantics, and syntax.

This chapter focuses on elements in general and the <xsd:element> element in particular. This element is used to define language elements to be used in XML instance documents. Other elements will be examined as well, because XSD has several other elements that can be child elements of <xsd:element>.

For that reason, this chapter also explores how to create what is known as complex content and how to apply attributes and datatypes to our definitions. Ways of grouping elements, and even ways of importing them from other schemas, are also shown. The chapter finishes with an example that uses most of what has been learned in these pages.

XML Elements

Elements are used to wrap most all content, so they are extremely important. Before XSD elements are examined in detail, a little background on XML 1.0 element definitions will be provided, which should help whoever is making the transition from XML DTDs to XSD schemas. Both the syntax and a quick example will be shown, which will enable us to then build the XSD-equivalent example. This information will help you better understand the XML 1.0 DTD-to-XSD schema transformation and how the syntax differs.

NOTE For more information about XML-based structure languages, check out the W3C XML Working Group page at www.w3.org/XML. At this site, you will find lots of information about both XML and XSD.

Defining within a DTD

When defining new elements with the XML 1.0 language, we use the <!ELEMENT> declaration. This declaration is followed by the name of the element being defined and information about the element. The information could include a list of child elements, or it could specify that the element contains text or other data. Using this declaration, we are able to define the overall structure of our markup language, which represents an element's position in relation to other elements.

For example, suppose that we have to define an XML 1.0 representation of the visual model in Figure 2.1. In this model, there is a <parent> name object with child objects of <first>, <middle>, and <last>. As the figure shows, it is important to be able to represent the structure of the four elements—because without the structure, the implied context of the child elements is no longer there. What does <first> mean as a root element? First what?

Because we want to start with XML 1.0 syntax, let's look at how you would define the <name> element with <first>, <middle>, and <last> child elements. The <name> element itself is defined, followed by the inclusion (or referencing) of the child elements. The following syntax would be used to accomplish this goal:

```
<!ELEMENT name (first , middle , last)>
```

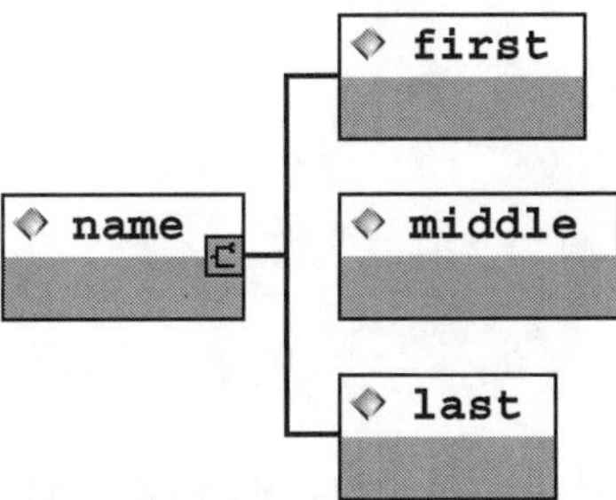

Figure 2.1 A visual representation of a simple model.

This syntax only defines the <name> element and not the <first>, <middle>, and <last> elements. Just like <name>, each of these elements will have to have their own corresponding <!ELEMENT> declaration followed by a content description. Let's assume that they will only contain text for this simple example, defined by using the #PCDATA type, which yields the following code used to define these elements:

```
<!ELEMENT first (#PCDATA)>
<!ELEMENT middle (#PCDATA)>
<!ELEMENT last (#PCDATA)>
```

That is all that is required. If we pull these lines together and add the <?xml?> directive line, then we have successfully created an XML 1.0 DTD that models our data in Figure 2.1. In Listing 2.1, the entire file is shown.

Once the model has been defined, an instance document can be created to reference the model (which contains data wrapped with the new elements). Listing 2.2 shows the new DTD to describe data by placing it within the body of the <first>, <middle>, and <last> elements:

```
<?xml version='1.0' encoding='UTF-8' ?>

<!ELEMENT name (first, middle, last)>
<!ELEMENT first (#PCDATA)>
<!ELEMENT middle (#PCDATA)>
<!ELEMENT last (#PCDATA)>
```

Listing 2.1 Schema for our <name> element (name.dtd).

```
<?xml version = "1.0" encoding = "UTF-8"?>
<!DOCTYPE name SYSTEM "file://S:/name.dtd">
<name>
  <first>Robert</first>
  <middle>Allen</middle>
  <last>Wyke</last>
</name>
```

Listing 2.2 DTD description of <first>, <middle>, and <last> elements (allenwyke.xml).

NOTE The presence of the file:// protocol identifier indicates that the governing DTD is located on the s: drive of the filesystem. If you want the instance document to reside in a different directory or even at a given URL, you must include the full path to the DTD.

This example is very simple, but it certainly does not represent everything that XML 1.0 can do. For example, XML DTD has the capability to represent people's many varieties of names. Many people have more than one middle name while others have none. So, an instance document that includes a person's name will have zero to many middle names. Also, a person might have more than one last name; perhaps the name is hyphenated. So, how can we represent this factor in our XML DTD?

The <!ELEMENT> declaration has a means by which you can specify whether an element is optional or not. For example, to specify a middle name, the ? character can be used after the <middle> declaration in the <name> content model. Additionally, the + character can be used to specify whether an element can occur more than one time (that is, *repeatable*). If your element is optional *and* repeatable, as with our <middle> element, then you use the * character to signify that both apply.

To allow a DTD to have zero or more <middle> element instances and one or more <last> element instances, simply change the <name> definition to the following:

```
<!ELEMENT name (first, middle*, last+)>
```

Notice the presence of the * and + characters, because they change the meaning of the <name> content model. Now that the <name> content has been defined, which is put in a new file called name_v2.dtd, let's look at a couple examples. First, there is Listing 2.3 (johndoe.xml), which contains no middle name. This situation demonstrates the ability to define the <middle> element as being optional.

```
<?xml version = "1.0" encoding = "UTF-8"?>
<!DOCTYPE name SYSTEM "file://S:/name_v2.dtd">
<name>
  <first>John</first>
  <last>Doe</last>
</name>
```

Listing 2.3 File that contains no middle name (johndoe.xml).

NOTE **Be sure to include the version number of your DTD or XSD schema either in the name of your definition file or in the directory or URI path to it. You will then be able to tell quickly on which version you are building an instance document. Having that number there is also necessary when different namespaces are being defined for different versions of your schemas.**

The next example, Listing 2.4 (reallylongname.xml), contains both multiple <middle> and <last> element instances. This example demonstrates our ability to mark an element as repeatable. You can see a copy of this document loaded into Microsoft's Internet Explorer browser, which has a built-in XML parser called MSXML, in Figure 2.2.

These previous definitions are fairly simple ones, and while that simplicity might make things easier, it could also be restrictive when you need more flexibility. The amount of control that you have as a schema developer might not be as great as you would like it to be or as your application would demand.

```
<?xml version = "1.0" encoding = "UTF-8"?>
<!DOCTYPE name SYSTEM "file://S:/name_v2.dtd">
<name>
  <first>John</first>
  <middle>Smith</middle>
  <middle>Franklin</middle>
  <last>Doe</last>
  <last>Ray</last>
  <last>Me</last>
</name>
```

Listing 2.4 File with multiple <middle> and <last> element instances (reallylongname.xml).

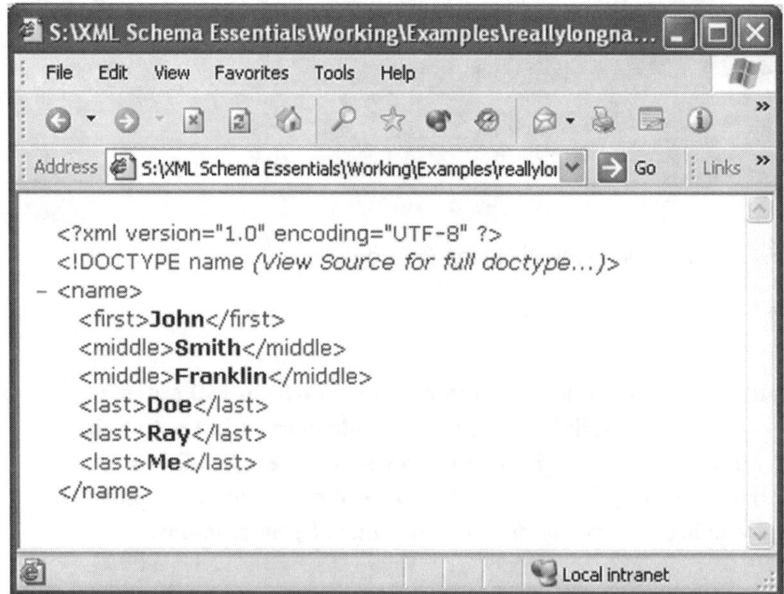

Figure 2.2 Internet Explorer displaying the long-name example.

Limitations

XML 1.0 element definitions have several limitations, most of which have been taken care of in the XSD Recommendations. Note that there is a fundamental difference between an enhancement and a limitation. For example, one of the big native limitations of XML 1.0 is its inability to have datatypes applied to it. An enhancement, on the other hand, that XSD brings to the table is its capability to pull in elements defined in other files and restrict or redefine their models. Several enhancements will be explored later in this chapter, but for now we are going to look into the two main limitations of XML 1.0 DTDs.

The first limitation of XML 1.0 is its inability to also define the datatype for a given element. Some standards such as *Datatypes for DTDs* (DT4DTD) can be included, but not all parsers support this specification. Using it, however, enables one to define datatypes such as strings, integers, dates, times, and others. For example, we can apply the DT4DTDs specification to our name_v2.dtd data model and explicitly define <first>, <middle>, and <last> as *string* types. We have saved this for the following code (name_v3.dtd), Listing 2.5, and the complete file is as follows.

NOTE For more information about DT4DTDs, read the official W3C Note at www.w3.org/TR/dt4dtd.

```
<?xml version='1.0' encoding='UTF-8' ?>

<!ELEMENT name (first , middle* , last+)>

<!ELEMENT first (#PCDATA)>
<!ATTLIST first  e-dtype NMTOKEN  #FIXED 'string' >

<!ELEMENT middle (#PCDATA)>
<!ATTLIST middle  e-dtype NMTOKEN  #FIXED 'string' >

<!ELEMENT last (#PCDATA)>
<!ATTLIST last  e-dtype NMTOKEN  #FIXED 'string' >
```

Listing 2.5 Complete file for our <name> example (name_v3.dtd).

The need for datatypes can clearly be seen when considering defining an XML DTD to represent a set of database tables. The database schema might specify that a given element should be an integer; however, there is no way to represent that in XML 1.0. Of course, DT4DTDs could be used for this purpose, but a problem might occur—especially if you were exchanging these documents with third parties that might not use a parser that supports this specification.

A second limitation of XML 1.0 is its inability to define how often an element is present as anything other than 0, 1, or unlimited (optional and/or repeatable). Let's say, for example, that you wanted to limit the number of last names that a person could have in the name_v2.dtd example to 2. In XML 1.0, this task cannot be accomplished. Someone could pass 3, 4, or more and the instance document would still validate successfully against our DTD.

These are just a couple of the limitations we might run up against if we are using XML 1.0 to define our schemas. These two have been mentioned here specifically, because XSD addresses both of them directly.

Moving On to XSD Elements

With the inherent limitations present in XML 1.0 and how it can be used to define elements, along with the overall desire by developers for XML-related languages to be more *object-oriented* (OO), it was only a matter of time before new standards emerged. *Schema for Object-Oriented XML* (SOX), which heavily influenced XSD, was one of the first standards to begin adding needed enhancements. The last subsection of this chapter introduces XML elements and discusses XSD's <xsd:element> element. Let's first look at the simple syntax for this element.

The <xsd:element> element, as defined in the XML Schema Part 1: Structures Recommendation, has a basic syntax that looks like the following:

```
<element
  abstract = boolean : false
  block = (#all | List of (extension | restriction | substitution))
  default = string
  final = (#all | List of (extension | restriction))
  fixed = string
  form = (qualified | unqualified)
  id = ID
  maxOccurs = (nonNegativeInteger | unbounded)  : 1
  minOccurs = nonNegativeInteger : 1
  name = NCName
  nillable = boolean : false
  ref = QName
  substitutionGroup = QName
  type = QName
  {any attributes with non-schema namespace . . .}>
  Content: (annotation?, ((simpleType | complexType)?, (unique | key |
keyref)*))
</element>
```

As you can see, the attributes in this element enable you to really control the definition of your elements. Note that the *#all* reference means that all of the items after the OR (| symbol) are present.

NOTE "Any attributes with non-schema namespace" simply refers to the capability of non-XSD-defined attributes to be included through the use of namespaces in XML. So, for example, if we were to create our own attribute definition language but we only wanted to extend the XSD method of attributes, then we would declare a namespace for our language and include our attributes (with prefix) in this designated location.

This element has a set of attributes as well as rules for the use of these attributes. Table 2.1 shows a list of the attributes that can be used in the <xsd:element> element. Within the definition, you will also notice that the <xsd:element> element can in fact contain content in the form of an <xsd:annotation>, <xsd:simpleType>, <xsd:complexType>, <xsd:unique>, <xsd:key>, or <xsd:keyref>. Some of these were discussed in Chapter 1, and others are covered later in this chapter.

All of this new information might seem a bit alien to you, because some of the settings (like abstract, block, or nillable) might not make sense without an example. One will follow (see the next code example, name.xsd). But for now, let's begin our learning of <xsd:element> by looking at an XSD version of the XML 1.0 DTD in the previous example (name_v3.xsd).

Table 2.1 Attributes of the <xsd:element> Tag

ATTRIBUTE	DESCRIPTION
abstract	Boolean value that requires the use of a substitution group
block	Allows you to control replacement by restriction, extension, or both derived types
default	Default value for the element
final	Allows you to prevent derivations by restriction, extension, or both
fixed	A default, but unchangeable, value for the element
form	Used to specify if the qualification of an element is to be done by a local or global declaration
id	Unique identifier
maxOccurs	Maximum number of times the element can occur within the parent element
minOccurs	Minimum number of times the element can occur within the parent element
name	The name of the attribute being created
nillable	Used to specify if an element can contain a nil value (which is different than not being present)
ref	Allows you to reference a global element declaration, and therefore inherit some of its settings
substitutionGroup	Allows you to assign the element to a group whereby any one element of the group can be substituted for another element instance
type	The datatype of the value of the element being created

As related in Chapter 1, the first thing we need to have is the presence of an <?xml?> declaration and <xsd:schema> element defining both the start of our XSD schema and declaring the anxsd: namespace. The code for this looks like the following:

```
<?xml version = "1.0" encoding = "UTF-8"?>
<xsd:schema xmlns:xsd = "http://www.w3.org/2001/XMLSchema"
```

The next thing needed is an <xsd:element> instance that creates the <name> element. Because there are subelements and <name> contains no content other than these elements, there is no use for the type attribute. In fact, for this simple example, we are only going to use the name attribute:

```
<xsd:element name = "name">
```

NOTE The fact that our element is named <name> here is completely coincidental. If it were named something else, such as <reference>, then we would have name="reference" in our <xsd:element> instance.

At this point, the defining gets a little tricky: How are the <first>, <middle>, and <last> child elements of our <name> parent element defined? Recall the discussion of the <xsd:simpleType> and <xsd:complexType> elements in Chapter 1. There, it was shown that <xsd:simpleType> can only carry content and that if you have attributes or other elements as part of the definition of an element, that element must be a <xsd:complexType>. Here is where we apply that knowledge.

In this situation, we do have child elements of the <name> element, so we will be using <xsd:complexType>. Additionally, because we want our child elements to appear in a specific order, we will also use a new element called <xsd:sequence> in our definition. This element will appear as a child element of the <xsd:complexType> instance. (See the following section, "Using a Sequence," for more detail about <xsd.sequence> instances.)

With <xsd:complexType> and <xsd:sequence> attended to, we can get to the definitions of the <first>, <middle>, and <last> elements. Recall that the <name> document in the previous example (name_v3.dtd) used DT4DTDs to specify datatypes for our elements. Because it did so, and because we should do it anyway, we will use the type attribute within the definition of these three elements and specify the type as xsd:string. (For more information about datatypes, see the detailed discussion in Chapter 4, "Applying Datatypes," and Appendix A, "Datatypes." Also, refer to the "XML Schema, Part 2: Datatypes" document, which is part of the XSD Recommendation.)

Additionally, we not only specified that <middle> is optional but that it and <last> could also repeat. We accommodate these settings by using the minOccurs and maxOccurs attributes of <xsd:element>. These attributes enable us to specify zero or an integer value to restrict the number of occurrences that can appear, or we can specify unbounded for maxOccurs if there is no limit. According to our needs, we will define these three elements as follows:

```
<xsd:element name = "first" type = "xsd:string"/>
<xsd:element name = "middle" type = "xsd:string" minOccurs = "0"
maxOccurs = "unbounded"/>
<xsd:element name = "last" type = "xsd:string" maxOccurs = "unbounded"/>
```

That will suffice for a direct conversion from XML 1.0 DTD to XSD Schema. The complete, final file will look like Listing 2.6.

The type of file shown in Listing 2.6 is quite simple. But this method is not the only way to declare child elements for a parent element. They can be

```
<?xml version = "1.0" encoding = "UTF-8"?>
<xsd:schema xmlns:xsd = "http://www.w3.org/2001/XMLSchema">
  <xsd:element name = "name">
    <xsd:complexType>
      <xsd:sequence>
        <xsd:element name = "first" type = "xsd:string"/>
        <xsd:element name = "middle" type = "xsd:string" minOccurs =
"0" maxOccurs = "unbounded"/>
        <xsd:element name = "last" type = "xsd:string" maxOccurs =
"unbounded"/>
      </xsd:sequence>
    </xsd:complexType>
  </xsd:element>
</xsd:schema>
```

Listing 2.6 Complete schema for <name> file from Listing 2.5 (name.xsd).

declared globally and referenced locally. This task is accomplished by using the ref attribute of the <xsd:element> element. When this approach is taken, as shown in Listing 2.7 , items like the type attribute are defined in the global definition while any constraining attributes (such as minOccurs and maxOccurs) are used in the local reference.

Defining elements as we did in the previous two examples is a relatively straightforward procedure, but there are many other things we can do with XSD-defined elements. Not only can they be defined in different ways, but there are a variety of ways in which they can be used as well. Let's now take a more detailed move past this simple example and take a harder look at <xsd:element> and what it can do for you.

<xsd:element>: A Closer Examination

Simply converting our simple example to its XSD representation does not exhibit the power of the <xsd:element> element and its child elements. It does not fully demonstrate how we can define complex content and apply attributes and datatypes, nor does it show how to enforce restrictions or define extensions. XSD even has the capability to both import elements from other locations and redefine both elements and attributes when imported.

NOTE **Because the id attribute is simply a unique identifier for most all XSD elements, we will not explicitly cover it in this chapter for the <xsd:element> element. You will see its usage in various places throughout the book, however.**

```
<?xml version = "1.0" encoding = "UTF-8"?>
<xsd:schema xmlns:xsd = "http://www.w3.org/2001/XMLSchema">
  <xsd:element name = "name">
    <xsd:complexType>
      <xsd:sequence>

        <!-- local references -->
        <xsd:element ref = "first" />
        <xsd:element ref = "middle" minOccurs = "0" maxOccurs =
"unbounded"/>
        <xsd:element ref = "last" maxOccurs = "unbounded"/>

      </xsd:sequence>
    </xsd:complexType>
  </xsd:element>

  <!-- defining our elements globally -->
  <xsd:element name = "first" type = "xsd:string"/>
  <xsd:element name = "middle" type = "xsd:string" minOccurs = "0"
maxOccurs = "unbounded"/>
  <xsd:element name = "last" type = "xsd:string" maxOccurs =
"unbounded"/>

</xsd:schema>
```

Listing 2.7 Declaring elements globally and referencing them locally (name-ref.xsd).

Take our minOccurs and maxOccurs attributes for <xsd:element> and our name.xsd schema as an example. Is it really realistic for a person to have an unlimited number of <middle> and <last> names? It is possible, but given that the data contained in a document referencing name.xsd will most likely be stored in a database or some other repository, it might be wise to limit the number of <middle> and <last> instances. For example, we would guess that a limit of three <middle> instances and two <last> instances would suffice for most all applications. Redefining this factor in our schema, which is not possible when using XML 1.0 DTDs, would look like Listing 2.8 (name_v2.xsd).

NOTE **When minOccurs and maxOccurs are not specified in a schema, the default values are 1. So, an element without these attributes can occur once and only once within an instance document.**

Up to this point, the topic of moving from XML 1.0 to XSD schemas has been discussed in general terms. Over the next few sections, we are going to delve deeper into the <xsd:element> element and its usage.

```
<?xml version = "1.0" encoding = "UTF-8"?>
<xsd:schema xmlns:xsd = "http://www.w3.org/2001/XMLSchema">
  <xsd:element name = "name">
    <xsd:complexType>
      <xsd:sequence>
        <xsd:element name = "first" type = "xsd:string"/>
        <xsd:element name = "middle" type = "xsd:string" minOccurs =
"0" maxOccurs = "3"/>
        <xsd:element name = "last" type = "xsd:string" maxOccurs =
"2"/>
      </xsd:sequence>
    </xsd:complexType>
  </xsd:element>
</xsd:schema>
```

Listing 2.8 Controlling elements through options and repeatability (name_v2.xsd).

Default Values

Default values are a crucial aspect of the <xsd:element>. It is important to learn how default values are set and to have a full understanding of how conforming processors handle default values for elements, because default *values* do differ from default *attributes*. With attributes, *if* the attribute is missing in an instance document, the value of the default attribute automatically appears when being processed. An element, on the other hand, also has a default value but that value *only* appears when the element has no content. If the element is missing from the document, then the default value is not automatically inserted. Let's look at a short example to see how this method works.

Let's build a data model that represents all the actions from which one might have to select when having their car washed at Joe's Car Wash. At Joe's, there are two categories of service for cars: interior and exterior. For the interior, Joe can vacuum and/or shampoo the carpet and seats, he can clean the windows, and he can clean the dashboard. For the exterior, he can wash, wax, and/or detail the car as well as perform a thorough cleaning of the tires. A visual representation of what Joe can perform is found in Figure 2.3.

To build the XSD Schema representation of this model, we must first create a <carwash> element. As you can see in Figure 2.3, this element must have <interior> and <exterior> elements. Because they are not used anywhere else in the schema, let's define those locally. Before moving on to the <exterior> child elements, let's first finish the definition of all child elements of the <interior> element.

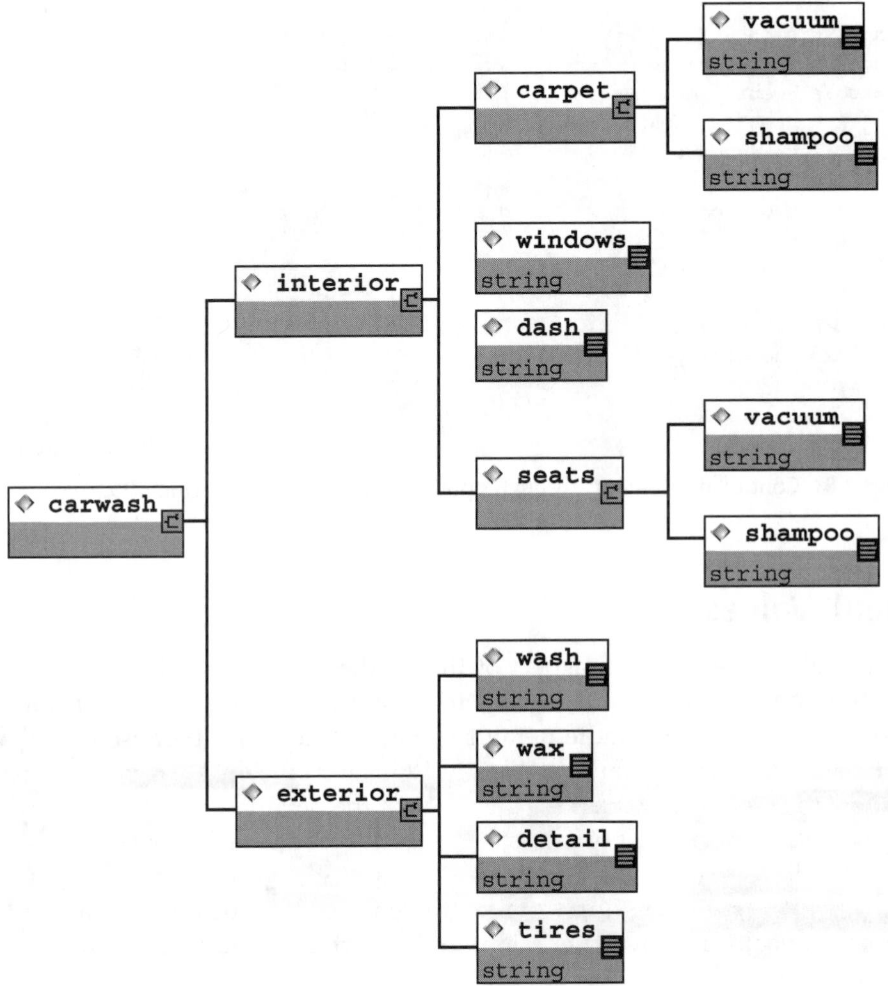

Figure 2.3 Service at Joe's Car Wash.

Within <interior>, we must define a <carpet>, <windows>, <dash>, and <seats> set of elements. Additionally, both <carpet> and <seats> have a <vacuum> and <shampoo> child element. Because they both have this element, let's declare it globally and declare all the others local to <interior>. If we now look at <exterior>, we can see that it is very simple. It only includes a <wash>, <wax>, <detail>, and <tires> set of child elements, which we will declare locally. At this point, we have outlined the basic structure of what we need to represent our XSD schema, but we are not finished.

One other major point is that all child elements are optional. This feature will enable us to set the proper minOccurs attributes, and because it is not repeatable, we will not include a maxOccurs attribute. Why is that? Because the default value for maxOccurs when it is not present in a schema definition is equal to 1, which is what we want. Our final bit of information will use the default attribute. For <dash> and <windows> of the <interior> element, <detail>, <tires>, <wash>, and <wax> of the <exterior> element, and all instances of the <vacuum> and <shampoo> elements, we will set the default attribute equal to the string "Yes." We will talk more about why a bit later.

Everything with our schema has been defined in a human-readable form. Our final XSD schema, shown in Listing 2.9 (carwash.xsd), includes our final schema representation.

```
<?xml version = "1.0" encoding = "UTF-8"?>
<xsd:schema xmlns:xsd = "http://www.w3.org/2001/XMLSchema"
            elementFormDefault = "qualified">
  <xsd:element name = "carwash">
    <xsd:complexType>
      <xsd:sequence>

        <!-- define our interior services -->
        <xsd:element name = "interior" minOccurs = "0">
          <xsd:complexType>
            <xsd:sequence minOccurs = "0">

              <!-- define our carpet options -->
              <xsd:element name = "carpet" minOccurs = "0">
                <xsd:complexType>
                  <xsd:sequence>

                    <!-- reference our global elements -->
                    <xsd:element ref = "vacuum" minOccurs = "0"/>
                    <xsd:element ref = "shampoo" minOccurs = "0"/>

                  </xsd:sequence>
                </xsd:complexType>
              </xsd:element>

              <xsd:element name = "windows" type = "xsd:string"
default = "Yes" minOccurs = "0"/>
              <xsd:element name = "dash" type = "xsd:string" default =
"Yes" minOccurs = "0"/>

              <!-- define our seats options -->
              <xsd:element name = "seats">
                <xsd:complexType>
                  <xsd:sequence>
```

Listing 2.9 Schema for our carwash example (carwash.xsd).

```
                    <!-- reference our global elements -->
                    <xsd:element ref = "vacuum" minOccurs = "0"/>
                    <xsd:element ref = "shampoo" minOccurs = "0"/>

                  </xsd:sequence>
                </xsd:complexType>
              </xsd:element>

            </xsd:sequence>
          </xsd:complexType>
        </xsd:element>

        <!-- define our exterior services -->
        <xsd:element name = "exterior" minOccurs = "0">
          <xsd:complexType>
            <xsd:sequence>
              <xsd:element name = "wash" type = "xsd:string" default =
"Yes" minOccurs = "0"/>
              <xsd:element name = "wax" type = "xsd:string" default =
"Yes" minOccurs = "0"/>
              <xsd:element name = "detail" type = "xsd:string" default
= "Yes" minOccurs = "0"/>
              <xsd:element name = "tires" type = "xsd:string" default
= "Yes" minOccurs = "0"/>
            </xsd:sequence>
          </xsd:complexType>
        </xsd:element>
      </xsd:sequence>
    </xsd:complexType>
  </xsd:element>

  <!-- we have some global elements, so define them here -->
  <xsd:element name = "vacuum" type = "xsd:string" default = "Yes"/>
  <xsd:element name = "shampoo" type = "xsd:string" default = "Yes"/>

</xsd:schema>
```

Listing 2.9 Schema for our carwash example (carwash.xsd). (Continued)

At Joe's, the software applications that process car wash orders use this data model for two things. First, it represents an order form: what the customer ordered. The presence of an element means that the customer wishes to have that particular service. Second, this model enables customers to include specific directions in their requests for services. For instance, let's say that a customer with a Toyota wanted to have her carpet shampooed, windows washed, dash cleaned, seats vacuumed, and the exterior washed and waxed. Let's also say that she had special instructions to not use glossy protectant on the dash. Listing 2.10 (toyota.xml) shows the document that represents this order.

The customer order in Listing 2.10 explicitly specifies a "Yes" value for several of the elements and special instructions for <dash>. But this example does not demonstrate how the default values work. To show this process, let's look at an equivalent document in Listing 2.11. In this document, the "Yes" values for the elements are not specified; instead, empty elements are included.

```
<?xml version = "1.0" encoding = "UTF-8"?>
<carwash xmlns:xsi = "http://www.w3.org/2001/XMLSchema-instance"
        xsi:noNamespaceSchemaLocation = "file:///S:/carwash.xsd">
  <interior>
    <carpet>
      <shampoo>Yes</shampoo>
    </carpet>
    <windows>Yes</windows>
    <dash>Please do not use glossy protectant</dash>
    <seats>
      <vacuum>Yes</vacuum>
    </seats>
  </interior>
  <exterior>
    <wash>Yes</wash>
    <wax>Yes</wax>
  </exterior>
</carwash>
```

Listing 2.10 A sample car wash order (toyota.xml).

```
<?xml version = "1.0" encoding = "UTF-8"?>
<carwash xmlns:xsi = "http://www.w3.org/2001/XMLSchema-instance"
        xsi:noNamespaceSchemaLocation = "file:///S:/carwash.xsd">
  <interior>
    <carpet>
      <shampoo></shampoo>
    </carpet>
    <windows></windows>
    <dash>Please do not use glossy protectant</dash>
    <seats>
      <vacuum></vacuum>
    </seats>
  </interior>
  <exterior>
    <wash></wash>
    <wax></wax>
  </exterior>
</carwash>
```

Listing 2.11 Using default values (toyota-defaults.xml).

Because the processor will insert the default values for <shampoo>, <windows>, <vacuum>, <wash>, and <wax>, both examples are essentially the same. But what if you want to specify a default and not allow it to be changed? Is that possible? The answer is yes.

Using our same example here, let's say that Joe is running a special in which every customer gets a free car wash when he or she comes in. Additionally, because the wash is free, Joe is not allowing customers to specify any special instructions. XSD has an attribute for <xsd:element>, called fixed, that enables us to perform this task. Rather than say default="Yes" in our definition of <wash>, as we did in Listing 2.9, we say fixed="Yes." In Listing 2.12, this change has been made.

```
<?xml version = "1.0" encoding = "UTF-8"?>
<xsd:schema xmlns:xsd = "http://www.w3.org/2001/XMLSchema"
            elementFormDefault = "qualified">
  <xsd:element name = "carwash">
    <xsd:complexType>
      <xsd:sequence>

        <!-- define our interior services -->
        <xsd:element name = "interior" minOccurs = "0">
          <xsd:complexType>
            <xsd:sequence minOccurs = "0">

              <!-- define our carpet options -->
              <xsd:element name = "carpet" minOccurs = "0">
                <xsd:complexType>
                  <xsd:sequence>

                    <!-- reference our global elements -->
                    <xsd:element ref = "vacuum" minOccurs = "0"/>
                    <xsd:element ref = "shampoo" minOccurs = "0"/>

                  </xsd:sequence>
                </xsd:complexType>
              </xsd:element>

              <xsd:element name = "windows" type = "xsd:string"
default = "Yes" minOccurs = "0"/>
              <xsd:element name = "dash" type = "xsd:string" default =
"Yes" minOccurs = "0"/>
```

continues

Listing 2.12 Using fixed default values (carwash-promo.xsd).

```
            <!-- define our seats options -->
            <xsd:element name = "seats">
              <xsd:complexType>
                <xsd:sequence>

                  <!-- reference our global elements -->
                  <xsd:element ref = "vacuum" minOccurs = "0"/>
                  <xsd:element ref = "shampoo" minOccurs = "0"/>

                </xsd:sequence>
              </xsd:complexType>
            </xsd:element>

          </xsd:sequence>
        </xsd:complexType>
      </xsd:element>

      <!-- define our exterior services -->
      <xsd:element name = "exterior" minOccurs = "0">
        <xsd:complexType>
          <xsd:sequence>

            <!-- wash can only be "Yes" now
<xsd:element name = "wash" type = "xsd:string" fixed = "Yes" minOccurs
= "0"/>

            <xsd:element name = "wax" type = "xsd:string" default =
"Yes" minOccurs = "0"/>
            <xsd:element name = "detail" type = "xsd:string" default
= "Yes" minOccurs = "0"/>
            <xsd:element name = "tires" type = "xsd:string" default
= "Yes" minOccurs = "0"/>
          </xsd:sequence>
        </xsd:complexType>
      </xsd:element>
    </xsd:sequence>
  </xsd:complexType>
</xsd:element>

<!- we have some global elements, so define them here -->
<xsd:element name = "vacuum" type = "xsd:string" default = "Yes"/>
<xsd:element name = "shampoo" type = "xsd:string" default = "Yes"/>

</xsd:schema>
```

Listing 2.12 Using fixed default values (carwash-promo.xsd). (Continued)

Now, when an instance document shows anything other than the presence of the string "Yes," an error will result. Setting an unchangeable default value can be useful in certain circumstances, so be sure to remember that it is there.

Substitution Groups

The <xsd:element> includes many interesting attributes other than the ones mentioned thus far. The abstract and substitutionGroup attributes are particularly notable because they control element substitutions.

To understand how they are used, suppose that we want to make a list of items that define a new schema for items that you own, called mythings.xsd, shown in Listing 2.12. Within this schema are two child elements, <house> and <vehicle>, both capable of holding xsd:string datatypes. Let's also set a minimum of zero for both elements and a maximum of 2 for <house> and 3 for <vehicle>. At this point, which is not our final schema, we have the following:

```
<?xml version = "1.0" encoding = "UTF-8"?>
<xsd:schema xmlns:xsd = "http://www.w3.org/2001/XMLSchema">
  <xsd:element name = "mythings">
    <xsd:complexType>
      <xsd:sequence>
        <xsd:element name = "house" type = "xsd:string" minOccurs = "0"
maxOccurs = "2"/>
        <xsd:element name = "vehicle" type = "xsd:string" minOccurs =
"0" maxOccurs = "3"/>
      </xsd:sequence>
    </xsd:complexType>
  </xsd:element>
</xsd:schema>
```

To make things interesting, suppose that we are not really expecting a <vehicle> to be contained in the instance document but rather a specific vehicle, like a car, motorcycle, or bicycle. In this case, <vehicle> is really functioning just like a placeholder for us. With XSD, individual elements can be used in this manner by means of substitution groups. Why would we set up elements this way? The answer is, because we are able to control the overall use of a defined group within a single element definition—<vehicle>, in this instance.

For setting up substitution groups, we must first define three new global elements called <car>, <motorcycle>, and <bicycle>. Next, we must assign them to the vehicle group by using the substitutionGroup attribute. Code would look like the following:

```
<xsd:element name = "car" type = "xsd:string"
substitutionGroup="vehicle"/>
<xsd:element name = "motorcyle" type = "xsd:string"
```

```
substitutionGroup="vehicle"/>
<xsd:element name = "bicycle" type = "xsd:string"
substitutionGroup="vehicle"/>
```

But this step is only part of the process. Up to this point, we have only defined the group, not specified that one of these elements should be used instead of our <vehicle> element. To do that, we need to add a single attribute to the <vehicle> element: the abstract attribute. Because the default value of this Boolean attribute is False, we must assign it a value of True to enable the group to represent the attribute. Our final document would look like Listing 2.13.

Now that our schema has been defined, we can create an instance document based on it. Because of our specifications, we can have 0, 1, or 2 houses and 0, 1, 2, or 3 vehicles, and our vehicles must be either car(s), motorcycle(s), or bicycle(s). Listing 2.14 shows a sample document in which the <vehicle> element cannot be used explicitly, but the <car> element can be used more than once.

Null Values

As you begin to design schemas and use them within your enterprise, there might be times where you need to define and specify null values. What is meant by null? Let's say that you had created a schema that represented the shipment of a product to a consumer (Listing 2.15). During the fulfillment

```
<?xml version = "1.0" encoding = "UTF-8"?>
<xsd:schema xmlns:xsd = "http://www.w3.org/2001/XMLSchema">
  <xsd:element name = "mythings">
    <xsd:complexType>
      <xsd:sequence>
        <xsd:element name = "house" type = "xsd:string" minOccurs =
"0" maxOccurs = "2"/>
        <xsd:element name = "vehicle" type = "xsd:string" abstract =
"true" minOccurs = "0" maxOccurs = "3"/>
      </xsd:sequence>
    </xsd:complexType>
  </xsd:element>
  <xsd:element name = "car" type = "xsd:string" substitutionGroup =
"vehicle"/>
  <xsd:element name = "motorcyle" type = "xsd:string"
substitutionGroup = "vehicle"/>
  <xsd:element name = "bicycle" type = "xsd:string" substitutionGroup
= "vehicle"/>
</xsd:schema>
```

Listing 2.13 Our final schema for list of your things (mythings.xsd).

```
<?xml version = "1.0" encoding = "UTF-8"?>
<mythings xmlns:xsi = "http://www.w3.org/2001/XMLSchema-instance"
         xsi:noNamespaceSchemaLocation = "file:///S:/mythings.xsd">
  <house>traditional style</house>
  <car>Toyota</car>
  <car>Ford</car>
  <motorcyle>Honda</motorcyle>
</mythings>
```

Listing 2.14 Sample document with multiple vehicles (allensthings.xml).

```
<?xml version = "1.0" encoding = "UTF-8"?>
<order>
  <name>
    <first>Robert</first>
    <middle>Allen</middle>
    <last>Wyke</last>
  </name>
  <item>Windows XP Professional</item>
</order>
```

Listing 2.15 Using null values (processing.xml).

process of taking the order and shipping it, your XML-based shipping document might or might not be able to include certain items. For instance, you might be able to include the customer's name, address, and item selected but not have the date that the item ships.

The document in Listing 2.15 is intended to serve as a snapshot of the order at a certain point in the process. But at that point in time, there might not be a ship date available. So, how do we define a schema that states that there needs to be a ship date and no data is available for that date yet?

This need is fulfilled by specifying an element as nillable. This concept is like that of NULL values in a database. The column/placeholder is there for data, but the value is zero or blank—it is null. If we apply this concept to our example, it implies that if we have an item, say <shipdate>, that is not present in an instance document, it doesn't mean that it doesn't exist—only that there is no data for it yet. It would be like having an empty element, as in the following:

```
<shipdate></shipdate>
```

To specify that a given element is nillable, we set the nillable attribute of the <xsd:element> element to True. So, if we build an XSD schema for Listing 2.15, we would have a schema as shown in Listing 2.16.

There is one last requirement for null values to work. In our instance document, we will actually include the <shipdate> element, but we will have to use the null attribute of the XMLSchema-instance namespace (commonly referred to as the xsi namespace) within the body of the element. The following document (Listing 2.17) shows how that is done.

```
<?xml version = "1.0" encoding = "UTF-8"?>
<xsd:schema xmlns:xsd = "http://www.w3.org/2001/XMLSchema">
  <xsd:element name = "order">
    <xsd:complexType>
      <xsd:sequence>
        <xsd:element name = "name">
          <xsd:complexType>
            <xsd:sequence>
              <xsd:element name = "first" type = "xsd:string"/>
              <xsd:element name = "middle" type = "xsd:string"
minOccurs = "0" maxOccurs = "3"/>
              <xsd:element name = "last" type = "xsd:string" maxOccurs
= "2"/>
            </xsd:sequence>
          </xsd:complexType>
        </xsd:element>
        <xsd:element name = "item" type = "xsd:string"/>
        <xsd:element name = "shipdate" type = "xsd:date" nillable =
"true"/>
      </xsd:sequence>
    </xsd:complexType>
  </xsd:element>
</xsd:schema>
```

Listing 2.16 Schema for our order processing (order.xsd).

```
<?xml version = "1.0" encoding = "UTF-8"?>
<order xmlns:xsi = "http://www.w3.org/2001/XMLSchema-instance"
       xsi:noNamespaceSchemaLocation = "file:///S:/order.xsd">
  <name>
    <first>Robert</first>
    <middle>Allen</middle>
    <last>Wyke</last>
  </name>
  <item>Windows XP Professional</item>
  <shipdate xsi:null = "true"/>
</order>
```

Listing 2.17 Final touch on our instance document to ensure null values work correctly (processing2.xml).

Attributes

Until now, none of the elements that we have defined in our example schemas have included *attributes*. Attributes represent a very important function when markup languages are created, because they enable you to specify additional information about the elements. This meta-information can be used for a variety of purposes, like for the inclusion of parameters or processing instructions for an application parsing the document.

Suppose, for example, that we needed to define a data model that contained a root <person> element. Let's also say that there are the following different kinds of people:

- Customer
- Employee
- Family
- Friend

Finally, let's say that a given person of a given type has a name (first, middle, and last), address, phone number, and an e-mail address. These are all optional and can only have a maximum of one occurrence. You can see a model of the <person> element in Figure 2.4.

When we create the XSD schema that represents the model shown in Figure 2.4, we will end up declaring our <name>, <address>, <phone>, and <email> elements globally so that they all can be referenced by <customer>, <employee>, <family>, and <friend>. Although the main definition of these elements is global, they still require a line of XSD to reference the global instance. This function creates a rather long schema, which you can see in Listing 2.18.

This schema is very verbose. A better way to express it would be through the use of attributes. A look at our model reveals that the different types of people could be best represented as attributes and not as elements. In this case, an element forces us to re-reference other elements over and over. A better approach would be to have a solid data model and use an attribute to augment the information and apply the context that we need to distinguish the type of user.

In XSD, the addition of an attribute is handled by the <xsd:attribute> element. Taking our example, we are able to remove the <employee>, <customer>, <friend>, and <family> elements and replace them with a single attribute called type that will be present in the <person> element. Because XSD enables us to specify a list of values that must be used, we are also able to explicitly say that the type can only equal the terms employee, customer, friend, and family.

To use the <xsd:attribute> element, we will specify both the name of the attribute and the fact that it is a required element by assigning the use

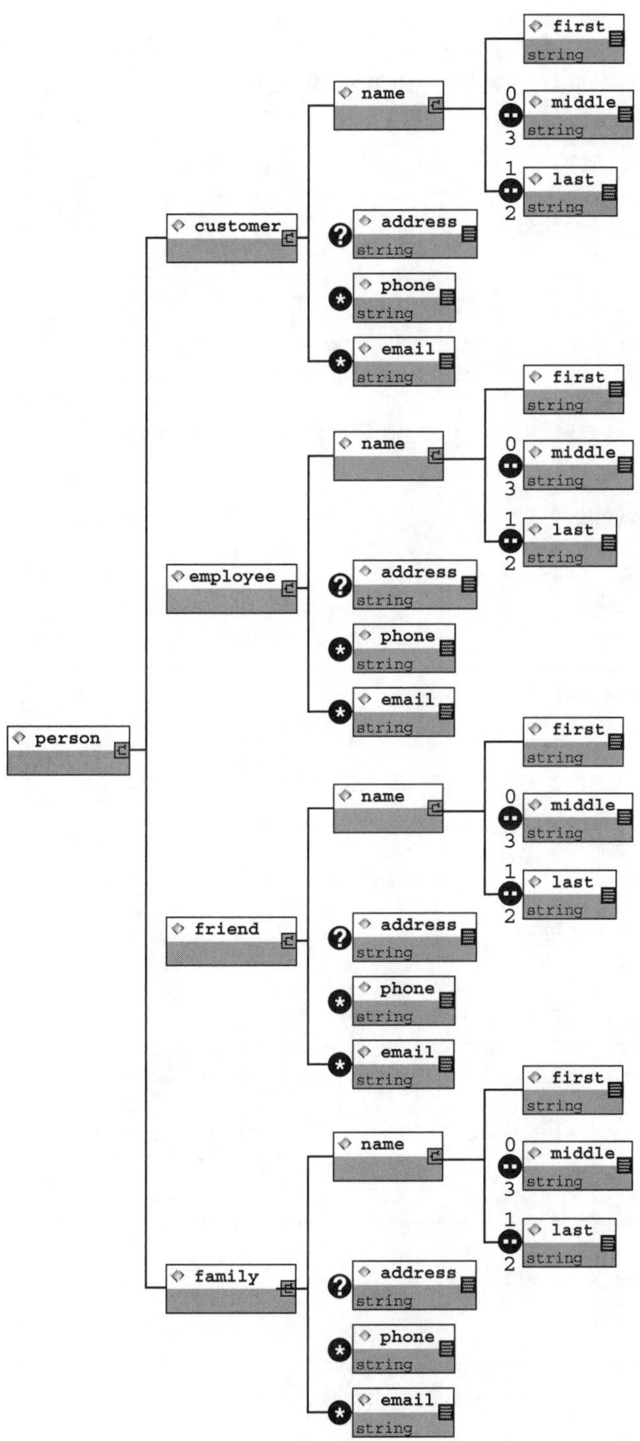

Figure 2.4 Our <person> element.

```
<?xml version = "1.0" encoding = "UTF-8"?>
<xsd:schema xmlns:xsd = "http://www.w3.org/2001/XMLSchema"
   elementFormDefault = "qualified">
  <xsd:element name = "person">
    <xsd:complexType>
      <xsd:sequence>
        <xsd:element name = "customer">
          <xsd:complexType>
            <xsd:sequence>
              <xsd:element ref = "name"/>
              <xsd:element ref = "address" minOccurs = "0"/>
              <xsd:element ref = "phone" minOccurs = "0" maxOccurs =
"unbounded"/>
              <xsd:element ref = "email" minOccurs = "0" maxOccurs =
"unbounded"/>
            </xsd:sequence>
          </xsd:complexType>
        </xsd:element>
        <xsd:element name = "employee">
          <xsd:complexType>
            <xsd:sequence>
              <xsd:element ref = "name"/>
              <xsd:element ref = "address" minOccurs = "0"/>
              <xsd:element ref = "phone" minOccurs = "0" maxOccurs =
"unbounded"/>
              <xsd:element ref = "email" minOccurs = "0" maxOccurs =
"unbounded"/>
            </xsd:sequence>
          </xsd:complexType>
        </xsd:element>
        <xsd:element name = "friend">
          <xsd:complexType>
            <xsd:sequence>
              <xsd:element ref = "name"/>
              <xsd:element ref = "address" minOccurs = "0"/>
              <xsd:element ref = "phone" minOccurs = "0" maxOccurs =
"unbounded"/>
              <xsd:element ref = "email" minOccurs = "0" maxOccurs =
"unbounded"/>
            </xsd:sequence>
          </xsd:complexType>
        </xsd:element>
        <xsd:element name = "family">
          <xsd:complexType>
            <xsd:sequence>
              <xsd:element ref = "name"/>
              <xsd:element ref = "address" minOccurs = "0"/>
```

Listing 2.18 Schema for <person> element (person.xsd).

```
              <xsd:element ref = "phone" minOccurs = "0" maxOccurs =
"unbounded"/>
              <xsd:element ref = "email" minOccurs = "0" maxOccurs =
"unbounded"/>
            </xsd:sequence>
          </xsd:complexType>
        </xsd:element>
      </xsd:sequence>
    </xsd:complexType>
  </xsd:element>
  <xsd:element name = "name">
    <xsd:complexType>
      <xsd:sequence>
        <xsd:element name = "first" type = "xsd:string"/>
        <xsd:element name = "middle" type = "xsd:string" minOccurs =
"0" maxOccurs = "3"/>
        <xsd:element name = "last" type = "xsd:string" maxOccurs =
"2"/>
      </xsd:sequence>
    </xsd:complexType>
  </xsd:element>
  <xsd:element name = "address" type = "xsd:string"/>
  <xsd:element name = "phone" type = "xsd:string"/>
  <xsd:element name = "email" type = "xsd:string"/>
</xsd:schema>
```

Listing 2.18 Schema for <person> element (person.xsd). (Continued)

attribute of <xsd:attribute> to required. The choices of this attribute will be restricted to person, employee, friend, and family. This restriction is accomplished by using the <xsd:restriction> element. The final segment of code that enables us to define this attribute is as follows:

```
<xsd:attribute name = "type" use = "optional">
  <xsd:simpleType>
    <xsd:restriction base = "xsd:string">
      <xsd:enumeration value = "person"/>
      <xsd:enumeration value = "employee"/>
      <xsd:enumeration value = "friend"/>
      <xsd:enumeration value = "family"/>
    </xsd:restriction>
  </xsd:simpleType>
</xsd:attribute>
```

Do not worry too much about the details of some of these elements, like <xsd:enumeration>. We will cover those later. In Listing 2.19, a modified version of our schema is shown that represents this change in its entirety.

```
<?xml version = "1.0" encoding = "UTF-8"?>
<xsd:schema xmlns:xsd = "http://www.w3.org/2001/XMLSchema"
            elementFormDefault = "qualified">
  <xsd:element name = "person">
    <xsd:complexType>
      <xsd:sequence>
        <xsd:element ref = "name"/>
        <xsd:element ref = "address" minOccurs = "0"/>
        <xsd:element ref = "phone" minOccurs = "0" maxOccurs =
"unbounded"/>
        <xsd:element ref = "email" minOccurs = "0" maxOccurs =
"unbounded"/>
      </xsd:sequence>
      <xsd:attribute name = "type" use = "required">
        <xsd:simpleType>
          <xsd:restriction base = "xsd:string">
            <xsd:enumeration value = "person"/>
            <xsd:enumeration value = "employee"/>
            <xsd:enumeration value = "friend"/>
            <xsd:enumeration value = "family"/>
          </xsd:restriction>
        </xsd:simpleType>
      </xsd:attribute>
    </xsd:complexType>
  </xsd:element>
  <xsd:element name = "name">
    <xsd:complexType>
      <xsd:sequence>
        <xsd:element name = "first" type = "xsd:string"/>
        <xsd:element name = "middle" type = "xsd:string" minOccurs =
"0" maxOccurs = "3"/>
        <xsd:element name = "last" type = "xsd:string" maxOccurs =
"2"/>
      </xsd:sequence>
    </xsd:complexType>
  </xsd:element>
  <xsd:element name = "address" type = "xsd:string"/>
  <xsd:element name = "phone" type = "xsd:string"/>
  <xsd:element name = "email" type = "xsd:string"/>
</xsd:schema>
```

Listing 2.19 Restricting our type attribute to a list of choices (person-attri.xsd).

Listing 2.19 is much cleaner than Listing 2.20. Figure 2.5 shows the visual representation of this approach.

Listing 2.20 shows how the use of this schema might look.

Chapter 3, "Adding Attributes," will discuss attributes in detail. After you have completed that chapter, you will have more than enough information to begin using attributes.

```
<?xml version = "1.0" encoding = "UTF-8"?>
<person xmlns:xsi = "http://www.w3.org/2001/XMLSchema-instance" xsi:
        noNamespaceSchemaLocation = "file:///S:/person-attri.xsd"
        type = "friend">
  <name>
    <first>Chad</first>
    <last>Walsh</last>
  </name>
  <address>123 Anywhere, Chapel Hill NC</address>
  <phone>999.555.1212</phone>
  <email>chad@anywhere.com</email>
</person>
```

Listing 2.20 Using our newly restricted type attribute (friend.xml).

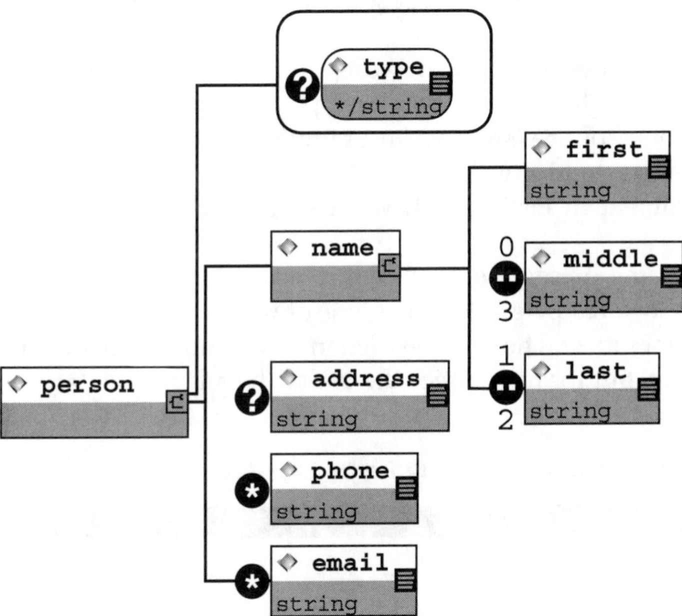

Figure 2.5 Our cleaner schema using an attribute.

Complex Content

Another very important element in XSD is the <xsd:complexContent> element. This element can be used as a child element of the <xsd:complexType>, which is discussed in Chapter 1, but it can only contain other elements. It cannot contain any character data.

The <xsd:complexContent> element is used to restrict or extend the content model of a complex type. Unlike simple content, which can contain *character data* (CDATA) and attributes, complex content can only contain elements or no content at all. The following is the full definition of the element (Table 2.2 shows the attributes for this element):

```
<complexContent
  id = ID
  mixed = boolean
  {any attributes with non-schema namespace . . .}>
  Content: (annotation?, (restriction | extension))
</complexContent>
```

As Table 2.2 and the description reveal, <xsd:complexType> is a relatively simple element. It has the now-common id attribute and one other: mixed. The mixed attribute contains a boolean value that specifies whether or not an element contains mixed content. Let's look at some examples to see how this feature works.

If we wanted to create an element called <computer>, that would require both a type and speed attribute. Let's say that the type of computer can either be eMachines, Dell, Compaq, or Gateway. An example usage of this model might look like the one shown Listing 2.21.

In the instance document in Listing 2.21, we referenced a schema called computer.xsd.

Notice in Listing 2.22 the presence of our <xsd:complexContent> element. Within this element are two restricted attributes, one of which is restricted to a list of four computer types itself. The <xsd:restriction> element is discussed in detail in the next section, but for now notice the use of the anyType datatype

Table 2.2 Attributes of the <xsd:complexContent> Tag

ATTRIBUTE	DESCRIPTION
id	Unique identifier
mixed	Boolean item that specifies whether an element contains mixed content or not

```
<?xml version = "1.0" encoding = "UTF-8"?>
<computer type = "emachines" speed = "1GHz"
        xmlns:xsi = "http://www.w3.org/2001/XMLSchema-instance"
        xsi:noNamespaceSchemaLocation = "file:///S:/computer.xsd"/>
```

Listing 2.21 Sample instance document for <computer> (emachines.xml).

```
<?xml version = "1.0" encoding = "UTF-8"?>
<xsd:schema xmlns:xsd = "http://www.w3.org/2001/XMLSchema">
  <xsd:element name = "computer">
    <xsd:complexType>
      <xsd:complexContent>
        <xsd:restriction base = "anyType">

          <!-- lets define our first attribute -->
          <xsd:attribute name = "type" use = "required">
            <xsd:simpleType>
              <xsd:restriction base = "xsd:string">
                <xsd:enumeration value = "emachines"/>
                <xsd:enumeration value = "dell"/>
                <xsd:enumeration value = "compaq"/>
                <xsd:enumeration value = "gateway"/>
              </xsd:restriction>
            </xsd:simpleType>
          </xsd:attribute>

          <!-- lets define our second attribute -->
          <xsd:attribute name = "speed" use = "required" type =
"xsd:string"/>
        </xsd:restriction>
      </xsd:complexContent>
    </xsd:complexType>
  </xsd:element>
</xsd:schema>
```

Listing 2.22 Schema for our computer element (computer.xsd).

for the restriction. Essentially, the anyType datatype means that any type of data can occur here. Listing 2.22 shows an example with an empty element. With this schema, we are able to create a shorthand version. Because our <xsd:complexType> element is defined without any <xsd:simpleContent>, the default is to assume <xsd:complexContent> that restricts anyType. The result is that we do not have to include the <xsd:restriction> or <xsd:complexContent> elements in our definition. Listing 2.23 illustrates what the short version would look like.

Now that we have an understanding of what the <xsd:complexContent> element is used for, let's look at how both <xsd:restriction> and <xsd:extension> are used within the context of <xsd:complexContent>. These elements are used in other places as well, but for now the discussion is limited to their use with <xsd:complexContent>.

```
<?xml version = "1.0" encoding = "UTF-8"?>
<xsd:schema xmlns:xsd = "http://www.w3.org/2001/XMLSchema">
  <xsd:element name = "computer">
    <xsd:complexType>
      <xsd:attribute name = "type" use = "required">
        <xsd:simpleType>
          <xsd:restriction base = "xsd:string">
            <xsd:enumeration value = "emachines"/>
            <xsd:enumeration value = "dell"/>
            <xsd:enumeration value = "compaq"/>
            <xsd:enumeration value = "gateway"/>
          </xsd:restriction>
        </xsd:simpleType>
      </xsd:attribute>
      <xsd:attribute name = "speed" use = "required" type =
"xsd:string"/>
    </xsd:complexType>
  </xsd:element>
</xsd:schema>
```

Listing 2.23 Shorthand version of our schema (computer-short.xsd).

Restrictions of Complex Types

In previous codes, we saw how the <xsd:restriction> element is used to restrict the content model of an element being defined. In Chapter 1, we learned about simple types in XSD, which can be restricted. Unlike restricting simple types, complex types do not limit you to simply restricting a range of values. To understand this concept, one might certainly ask what "restrict" is relative to. In other words, what makes it a restriction?

The following is a formal definition of a restriction and its attributes:

```
<restriction
  base = QName
  id = ID
  {any attributes with non-schema namespace . . .}>
  Content: (annotation?, (group | all | choice | sequence)?, ((attribute
| attributeGroup)*, anyAttribute?))
</restriction>
```

The definition shows <xsd:restriction> to contain two attributes that are described in Table 2.3: the id attribute, already described, and the base attribute, which will require further explanation.

The <xsd:restriction> must be relative to the element referenced by the base attribute. That element might or might not contain a namespace prefix, depending on whether or not the element is in another schema. What the

Table 2.3 Attributes of the <xsd:restriction> Tag

ATTRIBUTE	DESCRIPTION
base	Base item on which you wish to restrict based
id	Unique identifier

<xsd:restriction> element does is enable you to build a new element that is a subset of another element, located at the base. All you do is change the information that needs to be different and then cut and paste in the rest of the definition. So, why is this feature valuable? The value is that parsers then check to make sure the new element is actually a subset of the original element and not a superset.

For example, suppose that we have a model with a parent element called <policecar> that contains child elements of <body>, <wheels>, <engine>, and <gear>. Also, the <gear> element has child elements of <siren>, <lights>, and <radio>—all things specific to police cars. Figure 2.6 is a representation of this model.

The following is the definition of the XSD version of the policecar element, with all of our child elements (except <gear>) defined globally:

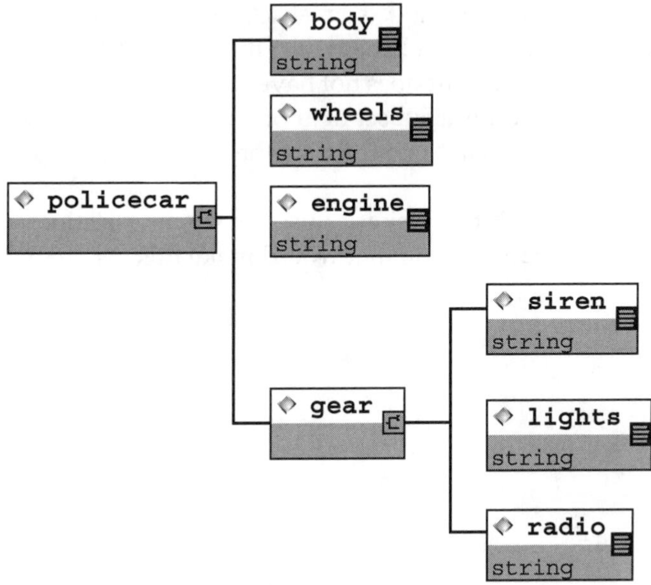

Figure 2.6 Representation of our <policecar> model.

```
<xsd:element name = "policecar">
  <xsd:complexType>
    <xsd:sequence>

      <!-- referencing child elements defined globally -->
      <xsd:element ref = "body"/>
      <xsd:element ref = "wheels"/>
      <xsd:element ref = "engine"/>

      <!-- defining police-specific information -->
      <xsd:element name = "gear">
        <xsd:complexType>
          <xsd:sequence>
            <xsd:element name = "siren" type = "xsd:string"/>
            <xsd:element name = "lights" type = "xsd:string"/>
            <xsd:element name = "radio" type = "xsd:string"/>
          </xsd:sequence>
        </xsd:complexType>
      </xsd:element>

    </xsd:sequence>
  </xsd:complexType>
</xsd:element>

<!-- global declarations of some elements -->
<xsd:element name = "body" type = "xsd:string"/>
<xsd:element name = "wheels" type = "xsd:string"/>
<xsd:element name = "engine" type = "xsd:string"/>
```

Now, we need to tap into the power of the <xsd:restriction> element. Let's say that we need to define a new top-level element, but this element (<car>) has all the child elements of <policecar> but does not have <gear> or any of its child elements. Because what we want is a subset of another element, it is the perfect time to use a restriction approach to defining the new element (as shown in Figure 2.7).

The key to being able to accomplish this task is to use the <xsd:restriction> within this complex type. The snippet of code that would make this task happen is as follows:

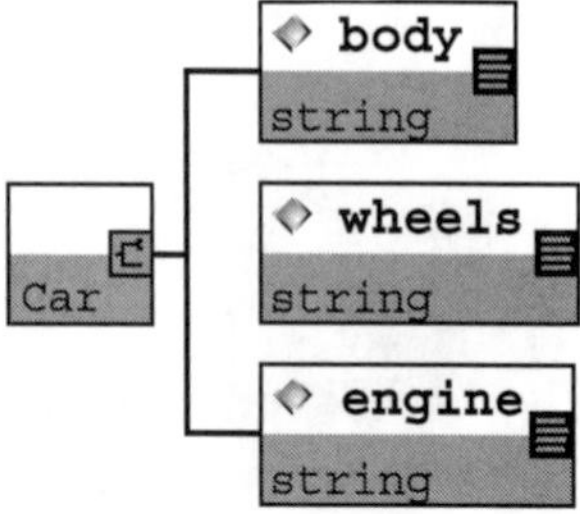

Figure 2.7 A look at our new <car> element.

```
<xsd:complexType name = "car">
  <xsd:complexContent>
    <xsd:restriction base = "policecar">
      <xsd:sequence>
        <xsd:element ref = "body"/>
        <xsd:element ref = "wheels"/>
        <xsd:element ref = "engine"/>
      </xsd:sequence>
    </xsd:restriction>
  </xsd:complexContent>
</xsd:complexType>
```

NOTE In this snippet, both the <car> and <policecar> elements are assumed to be defined in the same document.

As you can see, we use the <xsd:restriction> element to base our <car> element on the <policecar> element. We are even able to use the same globally declared elements by referencing them in our <car> model. And, because we use <xsd:restriction>, we can be assured that this element is actually a subset of <policecar>.

We have included the entire schema in Listing 2.24.

```
<?xml version = "1.0" encoding = "UTF-8"?>
<!-- Generated by XML Authority. Conforms to w3c
http://www.w3.org/2001/XMLSchema -->
<xsd:schema xmlns:xsd = "http://www.w3.org/2001/XMLSchema"
            elementFormDefault = "qualified">

  <xsd:element name = "policecar">

  <!-- defining police-specific information -->
    <xsd:complexType>
      <xsd:sequence>
        <xsd:element ref = "body"/>
        <xsd:element ref = "wheels"/>
        <xsd:element ref = "engine"/>

        <!-- this element and its children are specific to it -->
        <xsd:element name = "gear">
          <xsd:complexType>
            <xsd:sequence>
              <xsd:element name = "siren" type = "xsd:string"/>
              <xsd:element name = "lights" type = "xsd:string"/>
              <xsd:element name = "radio" type = "xsd:string"/>
```

continues

Listing 2.24 Schema for our <policecar> element (cars.xsd).

```
            </xsd:sequence>
          </xsd:complexType>
        </xsd:element>

      </xsd:sequence>
    </xsd:complexType>
  </xsd:element>

  <!-- defining our car element that is a subset of policecar -->
  <xsd:complexType name = "car">
    <xsd:complexContent>
      <xsd:restriction base = "policecar">
        <xsd:sequence>
          <xsd:element ref = "body"/>
          <xsd:element ref = "wheels"/>
          <xsd:element ref = "engine"/>
        </xsd:sequence>
      </xsd:restriction>
    </xsd:complexContent>
  </xsd:complexType>

  <!-- global declarations of some elements -->
  <xsd:element name = "body" type = "xsd:string"/>
  <xsd:element name = "wheels" type = "xsd:string"/>
  <xsd:element name = "engine" type = "xsd:string"/>

</xsd:schema>
```

Listing 2.24 Schema for our <policecar> element (cars.xsd). (Continued)

Extensions

Suppose that we want to create a superset rather than a subset. A superscript can be created with the <xsd:extension> element like the way the subset was created.

For example, suppose that we have our <name> element , used previously, but it only has <first> and <last> as the content model. This simple model might be defined as follows:

```
<xsd:element name = "name">
  <xsd:complexType>
    <xsd:sequence>
      <xsd:element ref = "first"/>
      <xsd:element ref = "last" maxOccurs = "2"/>
    </xsd:sequence>
  </xsd:complexType>
</xsd:element>
```

```
<xsd:element name = "first" type = "xsd:string"/>
<xsd:element name = "last" type = "xsd:string"/>
```

This model might work for a lot of instances, but it does not work for us. We need a <middle> name. Rather than build our own, new data model that fits our needs, let's use the <xsd:extension> element to create a new element called <myname> by extending the <name> element. The extension would add the <middle> element that we need. The syntax for doing so is much the same as using <xsd:restriction>, except we only need to include a definition for the new element (we do not have to include the previously defined content model). This definition would look as follows:

```
<xsd:complexType name = "myname">
  <xsd:complexContent>
    <xsd:extension base = "name">
      <xsd:sequence>
        <xsd:element name = "middle" type = "xsd:string" minOccurs = "0"
maxOccurs = "3"/>
      </xsd:sequence>
    </xsd:extension>
  </xsd:complexContent>
</xsd:complexType>
```

As you can see in the code snippet, just as with <xsd:restriction>, we use the base element to reference a base content model. We then add the definition for the new <middle> element. Table 2.4 shows attributes of the <xsd:extension> tag. The following code (extension.xsd, Listing 2.25) shows the entire source code for this example.

Because we are sure you are interested, we have included the official definition of the <xsd:extension> element here and described the two attributes of this element in Table 2.4.

```
<extension
  base = QName
  id = ID
  {any attributes with non-schema namespace . . .}>
  Content: (annotation?, ((group | all | choice | sequence)?,
((attribute | attributeGroup)*, anyAttribute?)))
</extension>
```

Table 2.4 Attributes of the <xsd:extension> Tag

ATTRIBUTE	DESCRIPTION
base	Base item off of which that you want to extend
id	Unique identifier

```
<?xml version = "1.0" encoding = "UTF-8"?>
<xsd:schema xmlns:xsd = "http://www.w3.org/2001/XMLSchema"
   elementFormDefault = "qualified">
  <xsd:element name = "name">
    <xsd:complexType>
      <xsd:sequence>
        <xsd:element ref = "first"/>
        <xsd:element ref = "last" maxOccurs = "2"/>
      </xsd:sequence>
    </xsd:complexType>
  </xsd:element>
  <xsd:complexType name = "myname">
    <xsd:complexContent>
      <xsd:extension base = "name">
        <xsd:sequence>
          <xsd:element name = "middle" type = "xsd:string" minOccurs =
"0" maxOccurs = "3"/>
        </xsd:sequence>
      </xsd:extension>
    </xsd:complexContent>
  </xsd:complexType>
  <xsd:element name = "first" type = "xsd:string"/>
  <xsd:element name = "last" type = "xsd:string"/>
</xsd:schema>
```

Listing 2.25 Schema for <name> element (extension.xsd).

Importing Elements from Other Locations

The last section explored the ability to extend and restrict elements. In the examples, an element was both extended and restricted within the same document. It would be convenient if we could extend and restrict elements that were originally defined in other schemas. We can. That can be accomplished with a couple of elements within the XSD language: namely, <xsd:import> and <xsd:include>. Recall the example in Listing 2.25 in which we created a <myname> element that extended a <name> element. Let's redo this example by breaking it into two different schema files to illustrate how <xsd:import> and <xsd:include> work.

Before we examine how these two elements work in an example, we need to know what these two elements are. The first element, <xsd:include>, is used to import (or reference) another schema. This feature is a very powerful piece of functionality, because it means that you can literally build new schemas that are nothing more than a collection of other schemas. For example, you might take one schema that defines vehicles, another that defines property, and another that defines boats and pull them all together in a single schema that represents your assets.

The <xsd:include> element is a very simple element with only two attributes. The definition of this element is as follows:

```
<include
  id = ID
  schemaLocation = anyURI
  {any attributes with non-schema namespace . . .}>
  Content: (annotation?)
</include>
```

Table 2.5 identifies each of these attributes and describes what they do. Pay particular attention to the schemaLocation attribute, which is what is used to reference (include) additional schemas.

Another schema can be imported into your working schema by using the <xsd:import> element. Including a schema is only half the battle; you must now *import* the definitions and declarations of the imported schema. This process includes specifying the location of the schema you are importing, which *must* be the same as the schemaLocation attribute value used in <xsd:include>, and the declaration of a target namespace. Other than that, this element is pretty simple to use. The following is the official definition of the <xsd:import> element:

```
<import
  id = ID
  namespace = anyURI
  schemaLocation = anyURI
  {any attributes with non-schema namespace . . .}>
  Content: (annotation?)
</import>
```

This element contains three attributes detailed in Table 2.6. Familiarize yourself with this information.

To build different schemas by using the <xsd:import> and the <xsd:include> tags, the first thing to do is build our <name> element in a new file. We have performed this action several times in several examples, so we

Table 2.5 Attributes of the <xsd:include> Tag

ATTRIBUTE	DESCRIPTION
id	Unique identifier.
schemaLocation	Specifies location of the schema you wish to include.

Table 2.6 Attributes of the <xsd:import> Tag

ATTRIBUTE	DESCRIPTION
id	Unique identifier
namespace	Specifies target namespace for imported schema
schemaLocation	Specifies location of the schema you wish to include

```
<?xml version = "1.0" encoding = "UTF-8"?>
<xsd:schema xmlns:xsd = "http://www.w3.org/2001/XMLSchema"
   elementFormDefault = "qualified">
  <xsd:element name = "name">
    <xsd:complexType>
      <xsd:sequence>
        <xsd:element name = "first" type = "xsd:string"/>
        <xsd:element name = "last" type = "xsd:string" maxOccurs =
"2"/>
      </xsd:sequence>
    </xsd:complexType>
  </xsd:element>
</xsd:schema>
```

Listing 2.26 Schema for our <name> element (simple-name.xsd).

will spare you the extra description of the process. Listing 2.26 gives the source code for this schema.

Now, let's turn our attention to including this schema and importing its elements into our new schema. The first part of the process is to include our schema. This job can be accomplished by using the following line of code.

```
<xsd:include schemaLocation = "file:///S:/simple-name.xsd"/>
```

Once the schema has been included, we now need to import its definitions and declarations. We use the <xsd:import> element in the following manner:

```
<xsd:import namespace = "file:///S:/simple-name.xsd" schemaLocation =
"file:///S:/simple-name.xsd""/>
```

Before we are able to use these definitions and declarations and now that they are imported, we must define a namespace prefix for this schema. We are going to add the following attribute to our <xsd:schema> element:

```
xmlns:sname = "file:///S:/simple-name.xsd"
```

This addition will enable us to reference the newly imported definitions and declarations by using the name prefix. Now, we are ready to build the schema. All we have to do is define our new <myname> element with the desired <middle> element, which will act as an extension to the <name> element defined in Listing 2.26. This definition is almost the same as our example in the last section; however, the reference to the base element must contain the namespace prefix name. You can see that in the following snippet:

```
<xsd:complexType name = "myname">
  <xsd:complexContent>
    <xsd:extension base = "sname:name">
      <xsd:sequence>
        <xsd:element name = "middle" type = "xsd:string" minOccurs = "0"
maxOccurs = "3"/>
      </xsd:sequence>
    </xsd:extension>
  </xsd:complexContent>
</xsd:complexType>
```

Notice that this definition is almost exactly the same as the definition for the <name> element in the previous section. Listing 2.27 shows the complete schema in which both the declarations and definitions are included and imported and the new <myname> element (<middle>) is defined.

```
<?xml version = "1.0" encoding = "UTF-8"?>
<xsd:schema xmlns:sname = "file:///S:/simple-name.xsd"
            xmlns:xsd = "http://www.w3.org/2001/XMLSchema"
            elementFormDefault = "qualified">
  <xsd:import namespace = "file:///S:/simple-name.xsd" schemaLocation
= "file:///S:/simple-name.xsd"/>
  <xsd:include schemaLocation = "file:///S:/simple-name.xsd"/>
  <xsd:complexType name = "myname">
    <xsd:complexContent>
      <xsd:extension base = "sname:name">
        <xsd:sequence>
          <xsd:element name = "middle" type = "xsd:string" minOccurs =
"0" maxOccurs = "3"/>
        </xsd:sequence>
      </xsd:extension>
    </xsd:complexContent>
  </xsd:complexType>
</xsd:schema>
```

Listing 2.27 Final schema with included schema reference and imported declarations (myname.xsd).

Table 2.7 Attributes of the <xsd:redefine> Tag

ATTRIBUTE	DESCRIPTION
id	Unique identifier
schemaLocation	Specifies location of the schema you wish to include

Redefining Elements

The definition of an imported element can be changed without extending it. To do so, we use the <xsd:redefine> element. That element is defined as follows:

```
<redefine
  id = ID
  schemaLocation = anyURI
  {any attributes with non-schema namespace . . .}>
  Content: (annotation | (simpleType | complexType | group |
attributeGroup))*
</redefine>
```

A description of the <xsd:redefine> attributes is given in Table 2.7.

The <xsd:redefine> element is very much like the <xsd:import> element, except that with <xsd:redefine> we are able to redefine an item that was previously defined. This capability might not seem beneficial when the included schema only has one or two items defined in it. But it can be extremely powerful if many items are being defined.

For example, let's say that we had a large schema that defines the content model for shipping out goods to a consumer. The business has prospered, and the company has now decided to expand into international markets. Because international addresses, phone numbers, and other contact information are slightly different from domestic ones, we really need to have a different schema for international orders. Rather than create a new schema with many of the same and previously defined elements, attributes, and datatypes, we can simply redefine the ones we want to change.

If we were to take this approach with Listing 2.27, the result would be that contained in Listing 2.28 (myname-redefine.xsd).

More on <xsd:complexType>

By this point, we have seen how the <xsd:complexType> type is used on many different occasions. Because it is such an import element in the XSD language, we should examine it in further detail now and give additional examples of how it is used. The following is a definition of <xsd:complexType>:

```
<?xml version = "1.0" encoding = "UTF-8"?>
<xsd:schema xmlns:sname = "file:///S:/simple-name.xsd"
   xmlns:xsd = "http://www.w3.org/2001/XMLSchema"
   elementFormDefault = "qualified">
  <xsd:import namespace = "file:///S:/simple-name.xsd" schemaLocation
= "file:///S:/simple-name.xsd"/>
  <xsd:redefine schemaLocation = "file:///S:/simple-name.xsd"/>
  <xsd:complexType name = "myname">
    <xsd:complexContent>
      <xsd:extension base = "sname:name">
        <xsd:sequence>
          <xsd:element name = "middle" type = "xsd:string" minOccurs =
"0" maxOccurs = "3"/>
        </xsd:sequence>
      </xsd:extension>
    </xsd:complexContent>
  </xsd:complexType>
</xsd:schema>
```

Listing 2.28 Redefining <myname> (myname-redefine.xsd).

```
<complexType
  abstract = boolean : false
  block = (#all | List of (extension | restriction))
  final = (#all | List of (extension | restriction))
  id = ID
  mixed = boolean : false
  name = NCName
  {any attributes with non-schema namespace . . .}>
  Content: (annotation?, (simpleContent | complexContent | ((group | all
| choice | sequence)?, ((attribute | attributeGroup)*, anyAttribute?))))
</complexType>
```

This element shares many of the same attributes as the <xsd:element> element, as shown in Table 2.8.

As we learned in Chapter 1, complex types (items defined by using the <xsd:complexType> element) represent elements that have child elements and attributes in their definition as well as potentially carry character data in their instance documents. In this respect, they differ from simple types (items defined by using the <xsd:simpleType> element), which cannot have character data or attributes.

The definition of <xsd:complexType> reveals that the element can have several different child elements. Over the next few pages, we are going to look specifically at the elements that enable us to control how a content model is defined.

Table 2.8 Attributes of the <xsd:complexType> Tag

ATTRIBUTE	DESCRIPTION
abstract	Boolean value that requires the use of a substitution group
block	Allows you to control replacement by restriction, extension, or both derived types
final	Allows you to prevent derivations by restriction, extension, or both
id	Unique identifier
mixed	Boolean item that specifies if an element contains mixed content or not
name	The name of the attribute you are creating

Using a Sequence

Within XSD, there is an <xsd:sequence> element that enables us to define a series of elements called a *sequence*. A sequence is a series of child elements that are supposed to appear within a content model of a parent element. Most of our examples thus far have used sequences; refer back to them for an illustration of how they are to appear. The following is the definition of the <xsd:sequence> element:

```
<sequence
  id = ID
  maxOccurs = (nonNegativeInteger | unbounded)  : 1
  minOccurs = nonNegativeInteger : 1
  {any attributes with non-schema namespace . . .}>
  Content: (annotation?, (element | group | choice | sequence | any)*)
</sequence>
```

The attributes of <xsd:sequence> should look very familiar, as they have been used often throughout the book. See Table 2.9 for a brief description of each. Keep in mind that the order of a sequence is important. So, for example, if you have a <first> element defined in a sequence before a <last> element, then an instance document should reflect that same order.

Grouping

On many occasions when defining schemas, you will find it necessary, or at least desirable, to group elements together. You might want to do so for organizational reasons, or perhaps you might want to have a means to more accurately define your content model. For example, suppose that you had a root <address> element, and within this element you could either have a <work> or <home> child element to signify a work or home address. The ability to restrict the presences of only one of these child elements, a concept that was also present in XML 1.0, is needed to force the user to enter only one or the other.

ACCOMPLISHED LIST.

Much more gratifying than a to-do list, don't you think?

IDA Intelligent Data

Accession

courtyard.com

Table 2.9 Attributes of the <xsd:sequence> Tag

ATTRIBUTE	DESCRIPTION
id	Unique identifier
maxOccurs	Maximum number of occurrences the element can appear within the parent element
minOccurs	Minimum number of occurrences the element can appear within the parent element

This situation is just one simple example of how one might group elements, or choices in this sample, together within an XML-based schema definition. This section of the chapter explores three specific XSD elements that provide a means to group elements: <xsd:group>, <xsd:choice>, and <xsd:all>. The use of each of these will be briefly explored as well.

Group

When building schemas, we might run across times when we want to define reusable groups of elements. For example, if a set of elements is used often, then it would be to our advantage to group them together and reference the entire group instead of each element individually. To perform this task, we can use the <xsd:group> element, which has the following definition:

```
<group
  name = NCName>
  Content: (annotation?, (all | choice | sequence))
</group>
```

Within this element, there is only a single attribute shown in Table 2.10.

To illustrate how this technique would be used, suppose that we wanted to build a model based on the names of several people. The purpose of this model, when used in an instance document, would be to outline each person's role. For example, if we define an <allen> element for a role-player named Allen, it might have the following instance when used in the context of Allen's role as an employee:

```
<allen>Hard worker</allen>
```

Table 2.10 Attributes of the <xsd:group> Tag

ATTRIBUTE	DESCRIPTION
name	Name of the group being created

On the other hand, it might have the following instance when used in the context of Allen's role among friends:

```
<allen>Has good parties</allen>
```

Our model for people's roles in a group needs to encompass five people, each of whom should be listed: <allen>, <andrew>, <donald>, <frank>, and <john>. Additionally, each person needs to be defined in the context of being an employee, friend, or both—potential <employees> and <friends> parent elements. Because <allen>, <andrew>, and <donald> are both <employees> and <friends>, we are going to pull them together using <xsd:group> into a group called "thegang." The grouping aspect is actually very easy to do because it only requires a parent <xsd:group> element with a name. The following code shows us how to perform this task:

```
<xsd:group name = "thegang">
  <xsd:sequence>
    <xsd:element name = "allen" type = "xsd:string"/>
    <xsd:element name = "andrew" type = "xsd:string"/>
    <xsd:element name = "donald" type = "xsd:string"/>
  </xsd:sequence>
</xsd:group>
```

To reference this group in our <employees> and <friends> models, we simply include the following:

```
<xsd:group ref = "thegang"/>
```

For a complete example, see Listing 2.29, which includes not only this grouping but also how we would build both the <employees> and <friends> models that used this group.

```
<?xml version = "1.0" encoding = "UTF-8"?>
<xsd:schema xmlns:xsd = "http://www.w3.org/2001/XMLSchema"
   elementFormDefault = "qualified">
  <xsd:group name = "thegang">
    <xsd:sequence>
      <xsd:element name = "allen" type = "xsd:string"/>
      <xsd:element name = "andrew" type = "xsd:string"/>
      <xsd:element name = "donald" type = "xsd:string"/>
    </xsd:sequence>
  </xsd:group>
  <xsd:element name = "friends">
    <xsd:complexType>
```

Listing 2.29 Using <xsd:group> groups (people.xsd).

```
      <xsd:sequence>
        <xsd:group ref = "thegang"/>
      </xsd:sequence>
    </xsd:complexType>
  </xsd:element>
  <xsd:element name = "employees">
    <xsd:complexType>
      <xsd:sequence>
        <xsd:group ref = "thegang"/>
        <xsd:element ref = "frank"/>
        <xsd:element ref = "john"/>
      </xsd:sequence>
    </xsd:complexType>
  </xsd:element>
  <xsd:element name = "frank" type = "xsd:string"/>
  <xsd:element name = "john" type = "xsd:string"/>
</xsd:schema>
```

Listing 2.29 Using <xsd:group> groups (people.xsd). (Continued)

Choices

Another important method of defining content models is through the use of <xsd:choice>, which is defined as follows:

```
<choice
  id = ID
  maxOccurs = (nonNegativeInteger | unbounded)  : 1
  minOccurs = nonNegativeInteger : 1
  {any attributes with non-schema namespace . . .}>
  Content: (annotation?, (element | group | choice | sequence | any)*)
</choice>
```

This element enables us to specify a list of elements where only one can appear in an instance document. Table 2.11 gives the attributes of this element.

A good example of how one might use this code is to modify Listing 2.29 and say that there can only be one employee. We change our <xsd:sequence> within our <employees> definition to an <xsd:choice>. The result is found in Listing 2.30.

Table 2.11 Attributes of the <xsd:choice> Tag

ATTRIBUTE	DESCRIPTION
id	Unique identifier
maxOccurs	Maximum number of occurrences the element can appear within the parent element
minOccurs	Minimum number of occurrences the element can appear within the parent element

```
<?xml version = "1.0" encoding = "UTF-8"?>
<xsd:schema xmlns:xsd = "http://www.w3.org/2001/XMLSchema"
   elementFormDefault = "qualified">
  <xsd:group name = "thegang">
    <xsd:sequence>
      <xsd:element name = "allen" type = "xsd:string"/>
      <xsd:element name = "andrew" type = "xsd:string"/>
      <xsd:element name = "donald" type = "xsd:string"/>
    </xsd:sequence>
  </xsd:group>
  <xsd:element name = "friends">
    <xsd:complexType>
      <xsd:sequence>
        <xsd:group ref = "thegang"/>
      </xsd:sequence>
    </xsd:complexType>
  </xsd:element>
  <xsd:element name = "employees">
    <xsd:complexType>
      <xsd:choice>
        <xsd:group ref = "thegang"/>
        <xsd:element ref = "frank"/>
        <xsd:element ref = "john"/>
      </xsd:choice>
    </xsd:complexType>
  </xsd:element>
  <xsd:element name = "frank" type = "xsd:string"/>
  <xsd:element name = "john" type = "xsd:string"/>
</xsd:schema>
```

Listing 2.30 Using <xsd:choice> groups (people-choice.xsd).

Using <xsd:all>

The final type of grouping that we can do in XSD revolves around the use of the <xsd:all> element. This element is defined as follows:

```
<all
  id = ID
  maxOccurs = 1 : 1
  minOccurs = (0 | 1) : 1
  {any attributes with non-schema namespace . . .}>
  Content: (annotation?, element*)
</all>
```

This element provides a simplified version of the SGML &- connector. The attributes of this element, which are described in Table 2.12, are the same as

Table 2.12 Attributes of the <xsd:all> Tag

ATTRIBUTE	DESCRIPTION
id	Unique identifier
maxOccurs	Maximum number of occurrences the element can appear within the parent element
minOccurs	Minimum number of occurrences the element can appear within the parent element

we saw in <xsd:choice>. You have the ability to control how many occurrences are in instance documents.

Using the <xsd:all> group, you are limited to it being at the top level of any content model. In addition, there can be no <xsd:group> instances within <xsd:all>, only individual <xsd:element> elements. There is also a restriction on the <xsd:element> elements defined in that they can be optional but they cannot be repeatable (that is, maxOccurs cannot be greater than 1, which is the default when not specified otherwise). So, what can <xsd:all> be used for?

Recall that an <xsd:sequence> has to appear in a specific order. That type of ordering makes complete sense when we are referring to things like <name>. But suppose that we were defining something that had no specific order, like a day planner. One day, a person might exercise before breakfast while on other days she might do it after dinner. Using the <xsd:all> element, we would be able to specify that an instance of <exercise> would occur within an instance of <day>, but it might not be before <breakfast>.

Listing 2.31 shows what the XSD schema for this very scenario would look like.

```
<?xml version = "1.0" encoding = "UTF-8"?>
<xsd:schema xmlns:xsd = "http://www.w3.org/2001/XMLSchema"
   elementFormDefault = "qualified">
  <xsd:complexType name = "day">
    <xsd:all>
      <xsd:element name = "breakfast" type = "xsd:string"/>
      <xsd:element name = "lunch" type = "xsd:string"/>
      <xsd:element name = "dinner" type = "xsd:string"/>
      <xsd:element name = "exercise" type = "xsd:string"/>
    </xsd:all>
  </xsd:complexType>
</xsd:schema>
```

Listing 2.31 Schema for our day planner (day.xsd).

Summary

This chapter has explored the concept of <xsd:element> in terms of its many uses as well as some of the child elements it can contain. Complex content has been examined in detail, as has the topic of adding attributes, which is covered in detail Chapter 3. We have investigated how to apply datatypes, restrict them, and extend them, and we have been introduced to the concept of importing elements and attributes from other XSD schemas. Also, the use of sequences and various types of groups within complex element types has been discussed. The final few sections of the chapter have taken us through a quick example of applying what we have learned.

Elements have been shown to be key in the success of using XML-based languages to exchange data. This chapter has laid the foundation for using <xsd:element> to define elements—a portion of the XML Schema Recommendation that is used often throughout the rest of the book.

Chapter 3 augments the information discussed thus far with coverage of <xsd:attribute> and other attribute-related XSD elements. The next chapter goes beyond what was covered in this chapter and shows how attributes can be used to supply all types of additional information about the data being defined.

CHAPTER

3

Adding Attributes

In Chapter 2, "XSD Elements,"we got into the details of defining XSD elements by using the <xsd:element> element. We learned that XSD differs from XML 1.0 in that XSD actually uses elements to define elements versus using an SGML-based language to define elements. But elements do not represent everything that is needed when it comes to defining and describing data. On most every occasion, there is a need for attributes as well.

Attributes are more or less metadata about a given element's meaning or content. They are there to provide additional information about that element or even its uses. For example, an attribute can be used to provide the language used for the text content wrapped with an element, or maybe it defines an encryption method for the data that will be used by the receiving application to decrypt. While elements often get credited with describing data and their structure, in actuality attributes often provide the real description of the data, leaving the structure to elements.

The paragraphs that follow discuss attributes and how they are used. XML attributes are explored first, followed by XSD attributes and how they represent a new generation in attribute abilities. Also examined are how attributes are declared, their scope, and common practices. Throughout the chapter, examples are included to help better your understanding.

To fully understand how attributes are defined and then used in an instance, one must have a clear technical understanding of what attributes really are and how they can be used to help describe data.

What Are Attributes?

What do attributes represent? That is, what is attribute data really for? Does it hold content, or does it hold additional descriptors about the content described by a beginning and ending set of tags? And what uses this information—parsers, applications, or processors? Most everyone has a different opinion as to what attributes are and how they are used.

Unfortunately (or fortunately, depending on how you look at it), none of these opinions are always wrong or always right. How attributes are used, like many methods of programming, varies. It's more of a convention on how they are used. Like programming guidelines, entire XML-based systems should at least attempt to utilize attributes in a similar manner, which enables schema developers to have a common set of rules to adhere to. It also enables applications to have certain expectations about what to expect for new XML documents.

Essentially, attributes can be pared down to three main uses. The first usage is as metadata that further describes the data the element is carrying—for example, the width of an image or the color of text. The second is information-specific as to how an application is supposed to use the data, like the parameters that should be passed for authenticating processing. The first two are related because, like the mention of text color, this metadata could be about the text, but it also represents information on how an application might use the data. Finally, attributes have been known to hold the actual data.

The pages that follow examine these uses and show you how an XML document might look for them. The objective is not to push you toward one method versus another but rather to expose you to different methodologies of approaching the use of attributes.

At this point, you will see how attributes look in XML documents and learn how they can be used. Later, this chapter will cover the syntax for creating attributes in schemas. For now, just focus on why attributes are needed.

Additional Metadata

Metadata refers to attributes that are used to further describe the data being transported in the element, be it empty or open. This method is the most common way that attributes are used. At the very least, even hybrid approaches use this method. Using attributes in this manner can be one of the most powerful uses for many reasons.

```
<?xml version="1.0" encoding="UTF-8"?>
<contact>
  <name>
    <first>R.</first>
    <middle>Allen</middle>
    <last>Wyke</last>
  </name>
  <address>
    <street>123 Somestreet</street>
    <city>Anytown</city>
    <state_province>NC</state_province>
    <postalcode>55555</postalcode>
    <country>USA</country>
  </address>
  <phone>999-555-1212</phone>
</contact>
```

Listing 3.1 A simple document for exchanging contact information between applications (simple.xml).

Suppose, for example, that we are exchanging contact information between applications and have used XML to mark up the data. Listing 3.1 shows what this document might look like.

The document includes a parent <contact> element that contains <name>, <address>, and <phone> child elements. This document certainly provides us with the ability to exchange a single contact record, but it does not really provide the flexibility to include multiple information sets for a given contact person. For example, let's say that our applications have the ability to also exchange work-contact information as well. One approach would be to define a set of tags that would signify that part of the contact information was home or work, as shown in Listing 3.2.

But, is the type of document shown in Listing 3.2 really the best way to accomplish this goal? An application now has to look for the "home" or "work" sections to perform its processing, when in reality most applications would just consider this a different "type" of address or phone number versus a completely new record for an individual. Would it not be best to include a *type* attribute within the <address> and <phone> element, as is shown in Listing 3.3?

The <name> element in the document does not change, so with a type attribute specified, the amount of data that would have to be sent back and forth would be minimized because the need for the <home> and <work> tags has been removed. The amount of data exchange in this simple example would be minimal, but imagine sending 1,000 or a million contact records between the servers. The number adds up fast. More importantly, a methodology is adopted that is easy to understand and follow as developers begin building integrations with these systems.

```
<?xml version="1.0" encoding="UTF-8"?>
<contact>
  <name>
    <first>R.</first>
    <middle>Allen</middle>
    <last>Wyke</last>
  </name>
  <home>
    <address>
      <street>123 Somestreet</street>
      <city>Anytown</city>
      <state_province>NC</state_province>
      <postalcode>55555</postalcode>
      <country>USA</country>
    </address>
    <phone>999-555-1212</phone>
  </home>
  <home>
    <address>
      <street>ABC Avenue</street>
      <city>Somecity</city>
      <state_province>NC</state_province>
      <postalcode>88888</postalcode>
      <country>USA</country>
    </address>
    <phone>999-777-8989</phone>
  </home>
</contact>
```

Listing 3.2 A document showing addresses with no attributes (noattribs.xml).

NOTE For structural reasons, <addressGroup> and <phoneGroup> elements are defined the way they are in the document shown in Listing 3.3. Defining elements in this way enables a limitless number of <address> and <phone> instances to be added, described by their type, to this <contact>. The same thing could be done by wrapping the entire <contact> element structure with an element like <contactGroup>, which would enable many different contact records to be sent.

This example of a simple document listing addresses points out the power of using attributes to define additional metadata about data—in this case, <address> and <phone>. Defining additional metadata in this manner enables programmers to incorporate better design practices while at the same time conforming to a common structure differentiated by the type value. Now, let's examine how applications can use attributes.

```
<?xml version="1.0" encoding="UTF-8"?>
<contact>
  <name>
    <first>R.</first>
    <middle>Allen</middle>
    <last>Wyke</last>
  </name>
  <addressGroup>
    <address type="work">
      <street>123 Somestreet</street>
      <city>Anytown</city>
      <state_province>NC</state_province>
      <postalcode>55555</postalcode>
      <country>USA</country>
    </address>
    <address type="home">
      <street>ABC Avenue</street>
      <city>Somecity</city>
      <state_province>NC</state_province>
      <postalcode>88888</postalcode>
     <country>USA</country>
    </address>
  </addressGroup>
  <phoneGroup>
    <phone type="work">999-555-1212</phone>
    <phone type="home">999-777-8989</phone>
  </phoneGroup>
</contact>
```

Listing 3.3 Document using attributes (withattribs.xml).

Application Uses

A second method of using attributes is strictly for application purposes. For example, you could use the value of an attribute to pass in a parameter or other bit of information that is agnostic—that is, unrelated—to the data but that is important to the application processing the data. Although this action could cause interoperability problems with third parties with whom you might be exchanging data, it can be very helpful if your system is entirely internal. To maintain the flexibility and integration promises of XML, you are advised, if you do use attributes for this method, not to make it a requirement. It is more of a hint mechanism to the application processing the data. One could certainly argue that the line between metadata and application uses of attributes is blurred. For instance, consider the document shown in Listing 3.4. In this example, a <comments> element is declared that contains the name

```
<?xml version="1.0" encoding="UTF-8"?>
<comments>
  <from>
    <name>
      <first>R.</first>
      <middle>Allen</middle>
      <last>Wyke</last>
    </name>
  </from>
  <comment type="complaint" priority="high">
    I really wish you would fix your application problem!!!
  </comment>
</comments>
```

Listing 3.4 Using attributes as metadata (comment.xml).

and a particular comment from a person. You should focus on the <comment> element and its attributes.

As seen in Listing 3.4, a type attribute (metadata) is used that defines the type of comment it is. The value is set to "complaint," but it could have been a suggestion or compliment. The priority attribute, however, is there because we want the system to know that it should process quickly and properly route the message to the appropriate application or person to respond.

In this example, the priority does not really describe the data. Priority is a relative piece of information. A high-priority thing to one person might be a low-priority thing to another. The document in Listing 3.4, however, contains a priority because the system knows that it should use that information in its processing. Again, it would quickly route the complaint instead of waiting 24 hours to process, as it might do for a suggestion or compliment. This example is very simple, but it certainly illustrates the point of including application-specific information in attributes.

Storing Data

Although the use of metadata is almost always a given when attributes are used, its use in storing data is almost guaranteed to cause heated discussions. The advantages of using metadata to store data include smaller file sizes, because you are not including extraneous tags, as well as a single programmatic approach to accessing all information in a given XML document. You can simply look for attribute values and not the content contained within an element. The main disadvantage is that you lose the structure of your data and therefore lose some inherent readability.

For example, suppose that you wanted to pass a customer list from one application to another. In this document, all you would need to pass are the

```
<?xml version="1.0" encoding="UTF-8"?>
<customers>
  <user id="1">
    <name>
      <first>
        Allen
      </first>
      <last>
        Wyke
      </last>
    </name>
    <postalcode>
      55555
    </postalcode>
  </user>
  <user id="2">
    <name>
      <first>
        Andrew
      </first>
      <last>
        Watt
      </last>
    </name>
    <postalcode>
      87878
    </postalcode>
  </user>
  <user id="3">
    <name>
      <first>
        Bob
      </first>
      <last>
        Kern
      </last>
    </name>
    <postalcode>
      35476
    </postalcode>
  </user>
</customers>
```

Listing 3.5 Customer list with information to be passed included in elements and attributes (inelements.xml).

customers' IDs, their first and last names, and their postal codes. If you included this information in a combination of elements and attributes, you might have a document that looks like Listing 3.5.

```
<?xml version="1.0" encoding="UTF-8"?>
<customers>
  <user id="1" firstname="Allen" lastname="Wyke" postalcode="55555" />
  <user id="2" firstname="Andrew" lastname="Watt" postalcode="87878"
/>
  <user id="3" firstname="Bob" lastname="Kern" postalcode="35476" />
</customers>
```

Listing 3.6 Customer list with items stored in single element per user and all data as values of attributes (inattributes.xml).

As you can see from Listing 3.5, this document is a little long and most of the actual characters in the file are used in the tag names; they are not the data itself. In contrast, look at the document in Listing 3.6. In that document, items are stored in a single element per user and all the data as values of attributes. Notice that the number of characters in the file have substantially decreased.

Now, here is where the arguments begin. File size has been reduced, but there is very little or no structure, which goes against many of XML's basic principles. XML is suppose to be verbose, while at the same time larger files can be directly tied to the speed in processing data as well as the cost for transmitting it between locations.

This book will avoid recommendations as to whether or not to use metadata to store data. To decide, you must fully evaluate what you are using XML for and even more importantly what you might use it for in the long run. You should also take into account the types of machines that you have available and ensure that whatever decision you make does not cause bottlenecks in your processing.

Hybrid Approaches

A hybrid approach to adding attributes can be found within the HTML and XHTML languages. XHTML, and its predecessor HTML, both define an <img> tag. This empty tag has five attributes in addition to the *common* attributes. These attributes, whether or not they are required, and a brief description of each, are shown in Table 3.1.

NOTE **For more information about the common attributes, see them defined in the Modularization of XHTML Recommendation at www.w3.org/TR/xhtml-modularization/abstract_modules.html#s_common_collection.**

To see this tag in action, look at the following one-line example. Each of these attributes has been utilized to its fullest potential:

```
<img src="/images/companyinfo.gif"
        alt="Company Information"
        longdesc="This image contains detailed information about our
company, where we do business, and
                          how to contact us."
        height="500"
        width="200"
        />
```

Looking at Table 3.1 and our example, you can see that with the exception of src, these attributes represent metadata about the image. The height, width, alt, and longdesc attributes all further provide information about the image that is specified by the src attribute. So, in this example we not only have the data (in other words, the src), but we also have metadata (in other words, all other attributes).

Taking this one step further, let's assume that there is an onclick attribute, which is one of the common attributes. And let's say that it contains the necessary JavaScript code to pop up an alert box. With this example, which we have included here, you now have application usage information. We have included code that causes the rendering application to perform a specific function of the user clicks on the image, which is not part of the data or any other description of it. It is information targeted more to the environment using the data.

```
<img src="/images/companyinfo.gif"
        alt="Company Information"
        longdesc="This image contains detailed information about our
company, where we do business, and
                          how to contact us."
        height="500"
        width="200"
        onclick="javascript:alert('Obtain more information by calling
999-555-1212')"
        />
```

Table 3.1 The Non-Common Attributes of the <img> Tag in XHTML

ATTRIBUTE	REQUIREMENTS	DESCRIPTION
alt	Required	Contains alternate text that should be used to describe the image. This is especially useful in non-image-supporting user agents.
height	Optional	Provides the height, in pixels, of the image.

continues

Table 3.1 The Non-Common Attributes of the <img> Tag in XHTML. (Continued)

ATTRIBUTE	REQUIREMENTS	DESCRIPTION
longdesc	Optional	Similar to the alt attribute, this attribute contains text that further describes the image. The alt is sometimes displayed when you hold your mouse pointer over an image, or if you have images turned off.
src	Required	Contains a URI pointing to the location of the image resource.
width	Optional	Provides the width, in pixels, of the image.

Considerations for Using Attributes

There is no "right" answer to the question of how to use attributes. At this point, you have been exposed to two main approaches to using them, including a third hybrid approach. This information should provide you with enough information to make your own assumptions and decisions.

In the next section, we are going to look at how attributes were used in XML 1.0 and then how XSD attributes have redefined and extended that model.

XML Attributes Foundation

XSD essentially reconstructs, and then extends, XML 1.0. So, the attributes in XML 1.0 need to be understood before XSD can be used properly. The following discussion of XML 1.0 is, by necessity, brief. But the overview should help you to familiarize yourself with the appropriate syntax and capabilities of XML attributes. Understanding how they operate will help you understand how XSD relates to XML, and it will help you make better decisions about whether to implement XML schemas or XSD schemas.

Syntax

Attributes are fairly easy to add to XML DTDs, and can also be shared across elements. This feature enables us to define an attribute, or set of attributes, in a common place and then reference and use them in several locations. This approach is used heavily in standards like XHTML, where attributes such as the common attributes are defined in groups and then shared. The following is the basic syntax used for adding attributes (the grouping of attributes will be discussed in detail in Chapter 7, "Grouping Elements and Attributes"):

```
<!ATTLIST element  name datatype #use >
```

In this syntax definition, *element* refers to the element with which the attribute is associated. The *name* is the name you give the attribute, such as type or id. In document instances, such as the ones shown throughout this chapter, a *name="value"* pair is used to assign attribute values. The *datatype*, at least in XML 1.0, can be one of three types. It can be a string (CDATA), a set of tokenized types (ID, IDREF, IDREFS, ENTITY, ENTITIES, NMTOKEN, or NMTOKENS), or enumerated types. The string type can take any literal string while the tokenized types have varying lexical and semantic constraints. Enumerated types can take one of a list of possible values. (Datatypes are covered in detail in Chapter 4, "Applying Datatypes,"and both the primitive and derived datatypes in XSD are explored in Appendix A, "Datatypes.") Finally, the *#use* is a method of specifying whether the attribute is required or optional or has a default value. If it is required, *#use* will contain #REQUIRED; if optional, it will contain #IMPLIED; and if there is a default value, it will contain #FIXED. It is also worth noting that an element can have more than one attribute, so you can repeat this syntax within the same <!ATTLIST> instance.

NOTE If the use of the attribute is #FIXED, then another parameter is passed after the #use that specifies the default value.

Let's look at the syntax that would be required to add our type attribute to our <address> element earlier in the chapter. Suppose that we want the attribute to be required, and we want it to contain either home or work as possible values. The syntax would look as follows:

```
<!ATTLIST address  type (home | work) #REQUIRED >
```

Capabilities

The capabilities of XML 1.0 to define attributes are quite good. Not only can one reference attributes for different elements and group them together, but one can also force them to be present or to contain a default value to represent valid data. Let's say, for instance, that we were defining a method attribute for an <HttpTransmission> element and that our implementation required the method to equal a value of POST. This situation might look like the following:

```
<!ATTLIST HttpTransmission  method CDATA #FIXED "POST" >
```

It would also be possible to give the system a choice of POST or GET but default to POST. This definition would look as follows:

```
<!ATTLIST HttpTransmission  method (POST | GET) "POST" >
```

Several combinations can be devised and used in your XML DTDs, which ultimately gives you great control over the data you are accepting and processing. Because these are inherent checks in an XML 1.0 supporting parser, you do not have to write the necessary code to ensure that documents contain all the correct data. If it passes the parser (assuming that you have it checking for validity), then you only have to act as you see fit on the data.

XSD Attributes: The Next Generation

XSD introduces new enhancements and features to the use of attributes. As shown in Chapters 1, "Elementary XML Schema," and 2, "XSD Elements," XSD schemas are actually defined by using elements and attributes. Just as the <xsd:element> tag is used to create elements in schemas, an <xsd:attribute> tag can be used to create attributes. Does this situation change how instance documents use attributes or represent them? Do our previous examples change in any way? The answer is, absolutely not.

NOTE To help avoid confusion, elements defined in the XSD Recommendation are being prefixed with xsd—for example, <xsd:attribute>. This situation will prevent you from thinking that the reference is to an element defined in an example.

XSD provides means by which you can further define and have greater control over your attributes, which furthers the efforts to allow parsers to do much of the work. You are able to enforce a greater array of datatypes and place more conditions on the use of attributes. XSD-defined attributes provide a lot of power, and if you come to know and use them correctly, they can save you a lot of time and programming in the long run.

The paragraphs that follow examine some of the basic syntax and capabilities of XSD, and further information about XSD attributes is put to use. Here, we will look at the scope of attributes, their Qualification, and how to control defaults.

NOTE Qualification, with a capital letter Q, refers to an attribute or element needing to be qualified by a particular namespace.

Syntax Changes

The <xsd:attribute> element, as defined in the XML Schema Part 1: Structures Recommendation, has a basic syntax that includes the following:

```
<attribute
  default = string
```

```
    fixed = string
    form = (qualified | unqualified)
    id = ID
    name = NCName
    ref = QName
    type = QName
    use = (optional | prohibited | required) : optional
    {any attributes with non-schema namespace . . .}>
    Content: (annotation?, (simpleType?))
</attribute>
```

As you can see, the attributes in this element enable you to control the definition of your attributes. In Table 3.2, we have listed these attributes alone with a brief description.

NOTE Any attributes with non-schema namespace simply refers to the ability of non-XSD-defined attributes to be included through the use of namespaces in XML. So, for instance, if we were to create our own attribute definition language, but we only wanted to extend the XSD method of attributes, then we would declare a namespace for our language and include our attributes (with prefix) in this designated location.

This tag has a set of attributes as well as rules for the use of these attributes. Table 3.2 gives a list of the attributes that can be used in the <xsd:attribute> tag. Within the definition, notice that the <xsd:attribute> element can contain

Table 3.2 Attributes of the <xsd:attribute> Tag

ATTRIBUTE	DESCRIPTION
default	Default value for the attribute
fixed	A default, but unchangeable value for the attribute
form	Used to specify if the qualification of an attribute is to be done by a local or global declaration
id	Unique identifier
name	The name of the attribute being created
ref	Allows you to reference a global attribute declaration and therefore inherit some of its settings
type	The datatype of the value of the attribute you are creating
use	Optional item that allows you to specify whether the attribute is optional, prohibited, or required

content in the form of an <xsd:annotation> or <xsd:simpleType>, which were discussed in Chapters 1 and 2.

As an example, let's look at the required line of code that would add the type attribute to our <address> element earlier in the chapter. If all we wanted to do was include the attribute with a default value of home, then we would have the following in our XSD schema. Of course, it would be contained in the appropriate location, which is inside the <xsd:complexType> child of our <xsd:element name="address"> definition.

```
<xsd:attribute name="type" default="home" type="xsd:string" />
```

That looks simple, but one thing was forgotten. We wanted to further define that the value of type had to be either home or work and nothing else. To accomplish this task, we have to change our approach slightly. We have to declare a <xsd:simpleType> within the content model of <xsd:attribute>, and within it we will use <xsd:restriction> to limit our choices to those defined in child <xsd:enumeration> elements. The following is the markup:

```
<xsd:attribute name = "type" default = "home">
  <xsd:simpleType>
    <xsd:restriction base = "xsd:string">
      <xsd:enumeration value = "home"/>
      <xsd:enumeration value = "work"/>
    </xsd:restriction>
  </xsd:simpleType>
</xsd:attribute>
```

In this example, notice that the type attribute of the <xsd:attribute> element has been removed and the type of content expected has been defined by using the base attribute of <xsd:restriction>. The attributes of the <xsd:attribute> element will be examined in detail later.

Further Capabilities

XSD attribute definitions provide several enhancements over XML 1.0 attribute definitions: datatyping, the ability to specify default or fixed values, and the ability to apply namespace Qualification—all mentioned in the previous paragraphs. But these are not the only enhancements that have been added or at least improved upon.

Another feature that should please many programmers is the ref attribute of the <xsd:attribute> element. This attribute enables you to, more or less, declare an attribute in the appropriate place within your schema *but* define it elsewhere. So, for example, you could define a type attribute at the bottom of your schema and then locally declare that attribute within the element or elements in which you wish to use it.

For example, let's say that we have a schema with two global elements: <car> and <radio>. Let's also say that both elements need a type attribute that contains nothing more than a string—no enumerated list. Let's also say that we think our schema is going to grow significantly over time, so we want to organize it so that common attributes and elements are defined at the bottom of the schema while instances of these items occur within their proper structure at the top of the schema. For many programmers, this process no doubt sounds like defining classes or objects and then instances of those classes or objects. And so it is.

Following these basic guidelines, we end up with the schema defined in Listing 3.7. (car-radio.xsd). As you can see, the type attribute is defined at the bottom of the schema while it is referenced from both the <car> and <radio> elements. As you probably have guessed, we could have taken the same approach with the elements (in other words, define at the bottom but declare at the top).

```
<?xml version="1.0" encoding="UTF-8"?>
<xsd:schema xmlns:xsd="http://www.w3.org/2001/XMLSchema">

  <!-- define car element -->
  <xsd:element name="car">
    <xsd:complexType>
      <xsd:sequence>
        <xsd:element name="make" type="xsd:string"/>
        <xsd:element name="model" type="xsd:string"/>
        <xsd:element name="year" type="xsd:gYear"/>
      </xsd:sequence>

      <!-- reference type defintion at bottom of schema -->
      <xsd:attribute ref="type" />

    </xsd:complexType>
  </xsd:element>

  <!-- define radio element -->
  <xsd:element name="radio">
    <xsd:complexType>
      <xsd:sequence>
        <xsd:element name="brand" type="xsd:string"/>
        <xsd:element name="model" type="xsd:string"/>
        <xsd:element name="year" type="xsd:gYear"/>
      </xsd:sequence>
```

continues

Listing 3.7 Schema for two global elements: <car> and <radio> (car-radio.xsd).

```
        <!-- reference type defintion at bottom of schema -->
        <xsd:attribute ref="type" />

      </xsd:complexType>
    </xsd:element>

    <!-- attribute definitions here -->
    <xsd:attribute name="type" use="required" type="xsd:string" />

  </xsd:schema>
```

Listing 3.7 Schema for two global elements: <car> and <radio> (car-radio.xsd). (Continued)

The schema in Listing 3.7 is just one simple example of some of the extended functionality present in XSD attribute definitions. The remainder of the chapter will cover some other features and talk further about local-versus-global attribute declarations.

Using Attributes

Now is the time to actually define XSD attributes and show how they are used. Previous paragraphs of this chapter alluded to a few more advanced features present when XSD is used to define schemas, and those features are covered in this section of the chapter. First, scope is examined, as are ways in which you can create both local and global attributes and reference them appropriately. This discussion naturally leads into a discussion of Qualification and how to specify defaults. Shown are ways to properly document and annotate your <xsd:attribute> definitions so that others can understand your objective.

Scope

Programmers who work with a particular language, be it C, Java, or JavaScript, no doubt are familiar with the scope of variables. Scope refers to when and where variables can be accessed from a given location in a program. For example, if a variable is defined *locally* within a function, then that variable will not be accessible outside of that function. If the variable is defined *globally*, then the variable is accessible everywhere in the program.

Scope is an important concept, because failure to adhere to the proper rules can cause collision. For example, suppose that you defined a global counter variable that you used in one function to count the number of times it has been accessed. Suppose, too, that that same variable was used to count the number of times the other function had been called. Then, one definition of the variable would overwrite the other. If these variables were declared local to the function, however, you would achieve the desired results of counting access individually.

This section examines how scope applies to attributes defined in XSD. The paragraphs that follow also discuss Qualification, which refers to an additional level of control over what can be accessed and where and how it can be accessed.

Local Attributes

Locally declared attributes, like the locally declared elements discussed in Chapter 2, are attributes that are defined locally to an element versus globally to a schema. When attributes are defined locally, the scope of the attribute is confined to that of the element within which it is defined.

For example, if we build a schema for our inattributes.xml document (see Listing 3.6, where we stored all data as values in attributes), then we need to define a root <customers> element that contains one or more <user> elements. Within the <user> element, there are four locally declared attributes: id, firstname, lastname, and postalcode. Both the id and postalcode attributes need to be positive integers, while we will want to enforce an additional constraint on postalcode to be no more than 99999. The firstname and lastname attributes, on the other hand, are simply strings.

We have defined all of these functions in the schema shown in Listing 3.8. Notice how attributes are defined locally to the <user> element definition.

```
<?xml version="1.0" encoding="UTF-8"?>
<xsd:schema xmlns:xsd="http://www.w3.org/2001/XMLSchema">

  <!-- define our root customers element -->
  <xsd:element name="customers">
    <xsd:complexType>
      <xsd:sequence>

        <!-- reference our user element which we defined elsewhere -->
        <xsd:element ref="user" minOccurs="1" maxOccurs="unbounded" />

      </xsd:sequence>
    </xsd:complexType>
  </xsd:element>
```

continues

Listing 3.8 Schema with locally declared elements (customers.xsd).

```
  <!-- user element definition -->
  <xsd:element name="user">
    <xsd:complexType>
      <xsd:attribute name="id" type="xsd:positiveInteger"/>
      <xsd:attribute name="firstname" type="xsd:string"/>
      <xsd:attribute name="lastname" type="xsd:string"/>

      <!-- postalcode has additional restriction, so we must further
           define elsewhere under the name postal_zip -->
      <xsd:attribute name="postalcode" type="postal_zip"/>

    </xsd:complexType>
  </xsd:element>

  <!-- define our postal_zip derived datatype that must have a max
value -->
  <xsd:simpleType name="postal_zip">
    <xsd:restriction base="xsd:positiveInteger"/>
  </xsd:simpleType>
</xsd:schema>
```

Listing 3.8 Schema with locally declared elements (customers.xsd). (Continued)

And if you want to apply the schema in Listing 3.8 to govern our instance document, simply replace the beginning <customers> element with the following element:

```
<customers xmlns:xsi="http://www.w3.org/2001/XMLSchema-instance"
                  xsi:noNamespaceSchemaLocation="file://customers.xsd">
```

This new element now specifies the appropriate namespace.

Locally declared attributes are not the only way to declare attributes, as shown in the schema in Listing 3.7 (car-radio.xsd).

Global Attributes

Global attributes are attributes that are declared outside any parent element definition. In other words, they have no specific parent elements. Your first question might be, "Why would we do such a thing? Why would we define an attribute at all if there were no element for it to go in?" In actuality, there is an element, but we are not restricting it at the point of definition to a specific element. A reference to this definition, however, will be local to an element definition.

One reason to define an attribute in this way, as we saw in Listing 3.7, is if we wanted to reference that attribute in multiple elements. We are able to define a common attribute, or group of attributes (see Chapter 7 for more on grouping of attributes), globally to the XSD schema and then use it over and over. The benefit of doing so is that we minimize our chance of errors for elements with this attribute. If we had to redefine an attribute several times, we would introduce the chance of inadvertently defining them with different datatypes or other properties. Having a common attribute avoids such a risk. With global attributes, we still have the ability, at the element definition level, to set aspects such as minimum and maximum occurrences.

Qualification

Another important aspect of <xsd:attribute> scope is Qualification, which refers to whether or not locally declared attributes or elements need to be qualified by a namespace. How Qualification pertains to XSD elements has already been discussed in Chapter 2, but now let's explore how it applies to XSD attributes. Many of the same concepts apply to both XSD elements and attributes. For example, a namespace qualification can occur through either an explicit prefix or an implicit prefix. But, for the sake of brevity, the discussion that follows will pertain only to attributes.

NOTE What does Qualification mean within the overall context of XSD? In general, it refers to a requirement that locally defined attributes and elements require or do not require an explicit namespace.

To globally qualify local attributes, which is handled syntactically as one would when globally qualifying local elements, one would use the attributeFormDefault attribute of the <xsd:schema> element and set it either to *qualified* or *unqualified*. When this task is done, all locally declared attributes inherit this setting. Optionally, Qualification can be applied on each local declaration by using the form attribute in the <xsd:attribute> element. For example, the following <xsd:schema> element would define, globally, that all attributes should in fact be qualified to the targetNamespace:

```
<xsd:schema xmlns:xsd="http://www.w3.org/2001/XMLSchema"
                  xmlns:sample="http://www.wiley.com/xml/sample"
                  targetNamespace="http://www.wiley.com/xml/sample"
                  attributeFormDefault="qualified">
```

NOTE By default, the absence of attributeFormDefault has the same meaning as attributeFormDefault="unqualified".

In this example, if we refer to our previous examples where we have a type attribute declared for our <address> element, then specifying that it had to be qualified would mean that we would have to prefix the attribute with a namespace. Further assuming, for this example, that our namespace prefix was simple, the relevant snippet of our instance document would look like the following:

```
<!-- start of document -->
<address sample:type="home">
<!-- rest of document -->
```

On the other hand, if we had specified the type attribute to be unqualified, as we have done locally to the attribute definition, effectively overriding the attributeFormDefault setting, we would not have to include the namespace prefix:

```
<xsd:attribute name="type" default="home" type="xsd:string"
form="unqualified" />
```

NOTE Qualification in this manner applies only to locally declared attributes. If the author of the schema declared all attributes global to the schema, then Qualification has no meaning and therefore the attributeFormDefault is irrelevant.

Defaults

Default values in attributes are often very important because they will remove a level of ambiguity. We can state, for example, that by default the content of a conforming XML instance document is written in U.S. English versus U.K. English unless otherwise specified. We could also make assumptions about the type of data, such as our assumption that an address sent in our contact example would default to home:

```
<xsd:attribute name="type" default="home" type="xsd:string" />
```

This situation enables us to impose some rules on users of the schema when it comes to implementation.

Simply specifying a default value for an XSD attribute is not all that needs to be done with defaults. In addition, the following rules also apply to defaults, which you should be familiar with and act upon to have valid XSD schemas:

- When the default attribute is specified in an <xsd:attribute> definition, you *cannot* use the fixed attribute at the same time.
- If both use and default attributes are included in an <xsd:attribute> definition, then the value of use must be "optional."

These rules are fairly simple and sensible. For the first one, if an attribute value is fixed, that implies that there is only one possible value. For example, suppose we wanted to set our type attribute to a fixed value of home. We would include the following:

```
<xsd:attribute name="type" fixed="home" type="xsd:string" />
```

For the second rule, if use is required, that would imply that the setting is fixed or prohibited. One way to use the use attribute would be not to specify a default value. If we looked at an example that required the type attribute, this type of definition would look like the following:

```
<xsd:attribute name="type" use="required" type="xsd:string" />
```

Let's assume that there is a default setting, but it is optional. Now, our example becomes:

```
<xsd:attribute name="type" use="optional" default="home"
type="xsd:string" />
```

Again, these are just a couple of very simple rules that you will need to follow when creating default attribute values.

Grouping

XSD has another element called <xsd:attributeGroup>. (Groupings of attitudes will be discussed in detail in Chapter 7, but at this point you should be aware of the existence of this other element and familiarize yourself with its overall function.) This element enables you to group together a set of attributes which then can be used within multiple <xsd:element> instances. This feature not only improves the organization and readability of many schemas, but also enables you to import the group into another schema. (Importation into other schema will be discussed in detail in Chapter 9, "Uniqueness and Keys in XSD Schema.")

Suppose, for example, that we had an element called <radio> that had attributes for the types of media it played, the number of speakers, treble, base, and volume settings. Because treble, base, and volume have to do with the sound level and quality, we might wish to group them together. A snippet of XSD code defining this element might look like the following:

```
<xsd:attributeGroup name="sound">
  <xsd:attribute name="treble" type="xsd:integer"/>
  <xsd:attribute name="base" type="xsd:integer"/>
  <xsd:attribute name="volume" type="xsd:integer"/>
</xsd:attributeGroup>
```

Now, if we wanted to reference this group within our <radio> element, we would use the following syntax:

```
<!-- define radio element -->
<xsd:element name="radio">
  <xsd:complexType>
    <xsd:sequence>
      <xsd:element name="brand" type="xsd:string"/>
      <xsd:element name="model" type="xsd:string"/>
      <xsd:element name="year" type="xsd:gYear"/>
    </xsd:sequence>

    <!-- begin defining attributes -->
    <xsd:attribute name="mediaType" type="xsd:string"/>
    <xsd:attribute name="speakers" type="xsd:integer"/>

    <!-- reference our sound attribute group -->
    <xsd:attributeGroup ref="sound" />

  </xsd:complexType>
</xsd:element>
```

This approach can provide a very powerful mechanism when XSD schemas are being defined. Common attributes can be encapsulated while at the same time the ability to modularize one's programmatic approach is increased.

Inclusion of Other Attributes

The last section mentioned the ability to import parts of an XSD schema (in this case, attribute groups) into other XSD schemas. That subject will be discussed in detail in Chapter 9, but here you should be aware of an attribute-specific element called <xsd:anyAttribute> that enables any attribute defined at the referenced namespace to be used within the current scope of the XSD schema by using the <xsd:anyAttribute> element.

For example, let's say that we defined a language that allowed us to mark up content to be displayed at a money-machine kiosk. With the release of XHTML 1.1, and specifically with the Modularization of XHTML Recommendation on which it relies heavily, building an XHTML-based language to accomplish this task would be fairly easy. But for argument's sake, let's assume that we had to develop our own language with our own tags. Let's also say that in doing so, we found that we were going to have to define many of the same attributes that have already been defined in XHTML, which would seem rather pointless. In a situation like this one, the <xsd:anyAttribute> element shines.

Rather than define every attribute again, we can simply add the following line to our schema:

```
<xsd:anyAttribute namespace="http://www.w3.org/1999/xhtml"/>
```

Inclusion of this line essentially enables an instance document of our schema to use any of the attributes within the XHTML 1.0 Recommendation without their having to be defined again. And because the <xsd:anyAttribute> element can occur with the body of defining elements in XSD or at a top level, we can control when and where those imported attributes can be used.

Summary

By this point, you should have a new respect for attributes. If used properly, they can be extremely powerful and useful. Not only do they provide us with a mechanism to better describe our data, but they also force better integration among applications. By providing the extra information contained in attributes, applications are better able to understand and utilize the actual data and therefore they can create more complete and comprehensive solutions.

This chapter has defined what attributes are and has shown how they fit into the big picture. XML attributes have been discussed, as have XSD attributes and how they differ and offer more flexibility. Effective use of attributes in XSD schemas has been explored, and some common practices have been suggested. Finally, the elements that enable you to group attributes or reference already-defined attributes present in another schema have been introduced.

Chapter 4 goes beyond XML DTDs and discusses how you can apply XSD datatypes to elements. Throughout Chapters 4 to 8, which form Part Two of this book, we learn about both primitive and derived datatypes, data facets, and how to group elements and attributes.

Going Beyond DTDs

CHAPTER

4

Applying Datatypes

In the first three chapters, we examined the rudiments of XSD and focused on two of the most important aspects of defining a schema: the use of elements and attributes. There is, however, one additional portion of XSD that is extremely important when an XSD-based language is defined: the ability to apply datatypes to elements and attributes. On several occasions thus far, datatypes have been discussed and used. With the knowledge of elements and attributes in hand, now is the time for a full explanation of what datatypes are and how they can be used.

This chapter also explores a number of tangential topics related to the use of datatypes, including defining your own datatypes and constraining how a datatype can be used.

What Are Datatypes?

Recall that XML 1.0 DTDs have very little, if any, datatyping abilities without the help of DT4DTDs. So, what are datatypes really? A simple, if incomplete, definition is that datatypes specify whether a piece of data is a string, number, boolean value, or any other type of data that might not necessarily be a concrete binary type. For example, what makes a Toyota vehicle a Toyota? Is it because it has different wheels, number of doors, or basic components from other cars? Not really. When it comes right down to it, the name—the *maker* of vehicle—is what makes a Toyota a Toyota. Let's use this information to define a schema for Toyotas. Before we define the schema, however, let's look at what an instance document might look like (see Listing 4.1).

In Listing 4.1, we see that a <vehicle> is defined as being of maker="toyota" and that it has four wheels and two doors. But what is a "toyota"? What does that really mean? To understand, we must look at the schema, which appears in Listing 4.2.

In Listing 4.2, we can see that <vehicle> and its two child elements, <wheels> and <doors>, are defined in the same manner that we always do. We can also see that the type attribute is defined by using the <xsd:attribute> element as normal. The first hint that there is more to this schema than first meets the eye is that the datatype (specified by the type attribute of the <xsd:attribute> element) of the <vehicle> element says the type is car. But what is car?

Glance down at the final section of the vehicle.xsd file and notice the presence of a section starting with the <xsd:simpleType> element. Here, car is defined within the context of this schema. Within the definition of car, you can see that we are *deriving* this new datatype from the xsd:string datatype, which is defined in the XML Schema Part 2: Datatypes Recommendation (www.w3.org/TR/xmlschema-2). This task is accomplished with the <xsd:restriction> element. Next, we have a set of <xsd:enumeration> instances that list the possible values (toyota, ford, chevy, and nissan) of the car datatype. See Chapter 8, "Deriving Types," for more information about <xsd:enumeration> instances.

NOTE Like XSD element references in the book, XSD-defined datatypes will be signified with the xsd: namespace prefix. For example, xsd:string refers to the string datatype defined within the XML Schema Recommendation.

The definition of <vehicle>—the Toyota—in Listing 2 pointed out that we can define our own datatypes, but core datatypes can also be defined by the XML Schema Recommendation. The remainder of this chapter explores these datatypes as well as means for deriving datatypes of your own.

```
<?xml version = "1.0" encoding = "UTF-8"?>
<vehicle xmlns:xsi = "http://www.w3.org/2001/XMLSchema-instance"
         xsi:noNamespaceSchemaLocation = "file:///S:/vehicle.xsd"
         maker = "toyota">
  <wheels>4</wheels>
  <doors>2</doors>
</vehicle>
```

Listing 4.1 Instance document for a Toyota (mycar.xml).

```
<?xml version = "1.0" encoding = "UTF-8"?>
<xsd:schema xmlns:xsd = "http://www.w3.org/2001/XMLSchema"
   elementFormDefault = "qualified">

  <!-- define our vehicle element and child elements -->
  <xsd:element name = "vehicle">
    <xsd:complexType>
      <xsd:sequence>
        <xsd:element name = "wheels" type = "xsd:string"/>
        <xsd:element name = "doors" type = "xsd:string"/>
      </xsd:sequence>
      <xsd:attribute name = "maker" use = "required" type = "car"/>
    </xsd:complexType>
  </xsd:element>

  <!-- define our car datatype -->
  <xsd:simpleType name = "car">
    <xsd:restriction base = "xsd:string">
      <xsd:enumeration value = "toyota"/>
      <xsd:enumeration value = "ford"/>
      <xsd:enumeration value = "chevy"/>
      <xsd:enumeration value = "nissan"/>
    </xsd:restriction>
  </xsd:simpleType>
</xsd:schema>
```

Listing 4.2 Schema for our <vehicle> element (vehicle.xsd).

Primitive Datatypes

The first set of datatypes to be examined is *primitive datatypes*. These represent the core datatypes that lay the foundation for all other datatypes within the XSD language, including xsd:anyURI, xsd:date, xsd:decimal, xsd:string, and xsd:time. There are 19 primitive datatypes in all, as shown in Table 4.1—three of which were first defined in XML 1.0.

Table 4.1 Primitive Datatypes Present in XSD

DATATYPE	ORIGINALLY DEFINED IN XML 1.0	DESCRIPTION
anyURI	No	Represents an absolute or relative URI
baseBinary	No	Represents Base64-encoded arbitrary binary data
boolean	No	Represents the ability for an item to be valued as true or false

continues

Table 4.1 Primitive Datatypes Present in XSD. (Continued)

DATATYPE	ORIGINALLY DEFINED IN XML 1.0	DESCRIPTION
date	No	Represents a given day in a given month in a given year, regardless of time, in the Gregorian calendar as defined by ISO 8601
dateTime	No	Represents a given day in a given month in a given year at a given time (hour, minute, seconds) in the Gregorian calendar as defined by ISO 8601
decimal	No	Represents arbitrary precision decimal numbers that can be either positive or negative
double	No	Consists of the values m x 2^e, where m is an integer whose absolute value is less than 2^{53}, and e is an integer between -1075 and 970, inclusively
duration	No	Represents a duration of time made up of a year, month, day, hour, minute, second within a Gregorian calendar
float	No	Consists of the values m x 2^e, where m is an integer whose absolute value is less than 2^{24} and e is an integer between -149 and 104 inclusively
gDay	No	Represents a recurring day in a given month in the Gregorian calendar as defined by ISO 8601
gMonth	No	Represents a reoccurring month every year in the Gregorian calendar as defined by ISO 8601
gMonthDay	No	Represents a recurring day every year in the Gregorian calendar as defined by ISO 8601
gYear	No	Represents a given year in the Gregorian calendar as defined by ISO 8601
gYearMonth	No	Represents a specific month in a specific year in the Gregorian calendar as defined by ISO 8601
hexBinary	No	Represents binary data that has been hex-encoded
NOTATION	Yes	Represents a NOTATION attribute type as defined in XML 1.0
QName	Yes	Represents qualified names. These names are broken into a Prefix, which represents the appropriate namespace, and a LocalPart, which defines the local part, or name, of the qualified name.
string	Yes	Represents a finite-length sequence of characters
time	No	Represents an instance in time in a given day, with values ranging from 00:00:00 (midnight) to 23:59:59

NOTE **For more information on ISO 8601, go to www.iso.ch and search on this particular ISO Number to find the specification. Note that there is a substantial charge to download the document from that site, so you might wish to search the Web for the specific information you are looking for.**

What are these datatypes, and how are they used? Earlier chapters have shown datatypes to provide the ability to define the type of data that should be present within an instance document. Most of the primitive datatypes are numeric or date/time-related, with a few exceptions. The best way to understand this concept is to see it in action. See Listing 4.3, which utilizes several of these primitive datatypes. To help you understand the same, look at Figure 4.1.

```
<?xml version = "1.0" encoding = "UTF-8"?>
<xsd:schema xmlns:xsd = "http://www.w3.org/2001/XMLSchema"
   elementFormDefault = "qualified">
  <xsd:element name = "sampleData">
    <xsd:complexType>
      <xsd:sequence>
        <xsd:element name = "url" type = "xsd:anyURI"/>
        <xsd:element name = "numeric">
          <xsd:complexType>
            <xsd:sequence>
              <xsd:element name = "decimal" type = "xsd:decimal"/>
              <xsd:element name = "double" type = "xsd:double"/>
              <xsd:element name = "float" type = "xsd:float"/>
            </xsd:sequence>
          </xsd:complexType>
        </xsd:element>
        <xsd:element name = "detailedDate">
          <xsd:complexType>
            <xsd:sequence>
              <xsd:element name = "day" type = "xsd:gDay"/>
              <xsd:element name = "month" type = "xsd:gMonth"/>
              <xsd:element name = "date" type = "xsd:gMonthDay"/>
              <xsd:element name = "year" type = "xsd:gYear"/>
            </xsd:sequence>
          </xsd:complexType>
        </xsd:element>
        <xsd:element name = "time" type = "xsd:time"/>
      </xsd:sequence>
    </xsd:complexType>
  </xsd:element>
</xsd:schema>
```

Listing 4.3 Schema using primitive datatypes (primitivesamples.xsd).

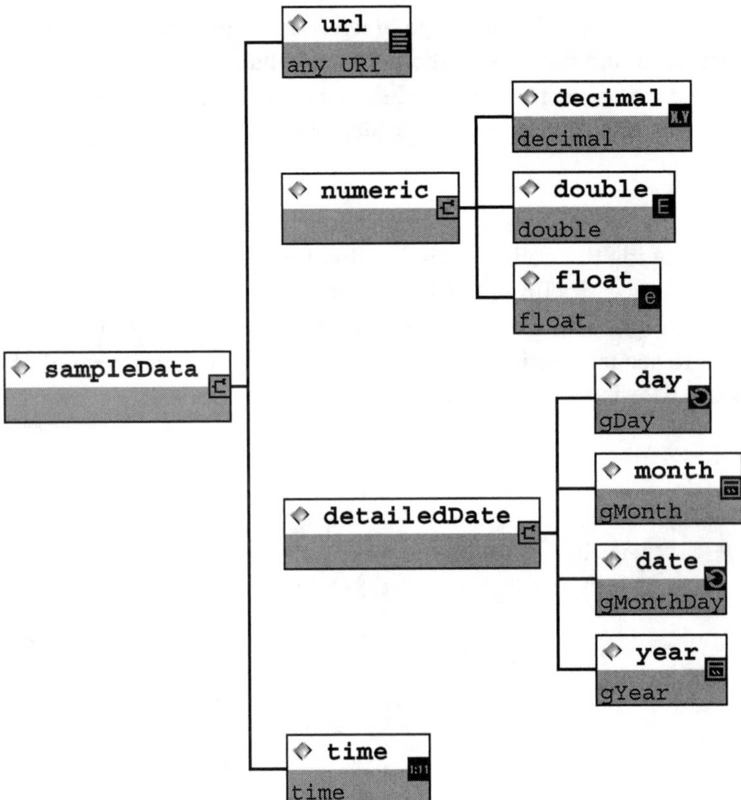

Figure 4.1 Data model of a sample using several of the primitive datatypes.

Now that our data model is defined, let's look at a quick example in Listing 4.4 (primitive.xml).

The first thing that grabs our attention are the <day>, <month>, and <date> elements. These are all defined within the ISO 8601 standard from the *International Organization for Standards* (ISO).

```
<?xml version = "1.0" encoding = "UTF-8"?>
<sampleData xmlns:xsi = "http://www.w3.org/2001/XMLSchema-instance"
            xsi:noNamespaceSchemaLocation =
"file:///S:/primitivesamples.xsd">
  <url>http://www.wiley.com</url>
  <numeric>
    <decimal>0.98</decimal>
    <double>-0829082907423</double>
    <float>987892340892374</float>
```

Listing 4.4 Example XML document using our primitive datatypes schema (primitive.xml).

```
  </numeric>
  <detailedDate>
    <day>---23</day>
    <month>--10--</month>
    <date>--10--23</date>
    <year>2002</year>
  </detailedDate>
  <time>06:30:00</time>
</sampleData>
```

Listing 4.4 Example XML document using our primitive datatypes schema (primitive.xml). (Continued)

Now that we see what primitive datatypes are and how they can be used, let's move on to other datatypes predefined within XML Schema: derived datatypes.

Derived Datatypes

Other datatypes are included within the XSD specification that are equally as important as primitive datatypes. These datatypes are, by necessity, derived from the primitive datatypes. Table 4.2 shows some of the more commonly used derived datatypes.

Many of the data types shown in Table 4.2 will help us control our element definitions, as shown in the following paragraphs. Datatypes like xsd:positiveInteger or xsd:language provide a level of detail not present in the primitive datatypes. As with our definition in Listing 4.3, which uses primitive datatypes, Listing 4.5 contains a data model (shown in Figure 4.2) that will enable us to create an instance document utilizing some datatypes.

With our schema built, let's look at Listing 4.6 for samples that correspond to these datatypes.

Primitive and derived datatypes are the only official datatypes defined in XML Schema Part 2: Datatypes. They certainly are not the only choices for using datatypes within your schemas. You can also define your own.

Defining Our Own Datatypes

Deriving your own new datatypes from other datatypes is done in much the same manner as the derived datatypes are derived from the primitive datatypes. If you really plan on using XML Schema to its fullest potential, then you will find that many of the datatypes you use will be ones that you defined yourself. Why? Because your company, own personal usage, or whatever personal reason will be what drives your use of XSD. Because of that, you will desire to use the language in a manner that best reflects your needs.

Table 4.2 Derived Datatypes Present in XSD

DATATYPE	ORIGINALLY DEFINED IN XML 1.0	DERIVED FROM	DESCRIPTION
byte	No	short	Represents a value between −128 and 127
ENTITIES	Yes	ENTITY	A finite, nonzero length sequence of ENTITY datatype instances that have been declared as unparsed entities in a DTD
ENTITY	Yes	NCName	Set of all strings that match the NCName production in namespaces in XML and that have been declared as unparsed entities in a DTD
ID	Yes	NCName	Set of all strings that match the NCName production in Namespaces in XML
IDREF	Yes	NCName	Set of all strings that match the NCName production in Namespaces in XML
IDREFS	Yes	IDREF	Set of finite, nonzero-length sequences of IDREFs
int	No	long	Represents a value between −2147483648 and 2147483647
integer	No	decimal	Represents a whole number, with no decimal places (e.g., equivalent to all values after the decimal equal to 0)
language	No	token	Represents natural language identifiers as defined in RFC 1766
long	No	integer	Represents a value between −9223372036854775808 and 9223372036854775807
Name	Yes	token	Represents Names as defined in XML 1.0
NCName	Yes	Name	Represents "noncolonized" names as defined in XML 1.0
negativeInteger	No	nonPositiveInteger	Represents any negative integer. Remember that an integer is defined as a whole number, with no decimal values.

continues

Table 4.2 Derived Datatypes Present in XSD (Continued)

DATATYPE	ORIGINALLY DEFINED IN XML 1.0	DERIVED FROM	DESCRIPTION
NMTOKEN	Yes	token	Represents the NMTOKEN attribute as defined in XML 1.0
NMTOKENS	Yes	NMTOKEN	Set of finite, nonzero-length sequences of NMTOKENs
nonNegativeInteger	No	integer	Represents any positive integer. Remember that an integer is defined as a whole number, with no decimal values.
nonPositiveInteger	No	integer	Represents any negative integer. Remember that an integer is defined as a whole number, with no decimal values
normalizedString	No	string	Represents whitespace normalized strings, which do not carry a carriage return, line feed, or tab character
positiveInteger	No	nonNegativeInteger	Represents any positive integer. Remember that an integer is defined as a whole number, with no decimal values
short	No	int	Represents a value between -32768 and 32767. The byte datatype is derived off the short datatype
token	No	normalizedString	Set of strings that do not contain a line feed or tab character and that have no leading or trailing spaces
unsignedByte	No	unsignedShort	Represents a number with an upperbound of 255
unsignedInt	No	unsignedLong	Represents a number with an upperbound of 4294967295
unsignedLong	No	nonNegativeInteger	Represents a number with an upperbound of 18446744073709551615
unsignedShort	No	unsignedInt	Represents a number with an upperbound of 65535

```
<?xml version = "1.0" encoding = "UTF-8"?>
<xsd:schema xmlns:xsd = "http://www.w3.org/2001/XMLSchema"
   elementFormDefault = "qualified">
  <xsd:element name = "sampleData">
    <xsd:complexType>
      <xsd:sequence>
        <xsd:element name = "numeric">
          <xsd:complexType>
            <xsd:sequence>
              <xsd:element name = "negInt" type =
"xsd:negativeInteger"/>
              <xsd:element name = "posInt" type =
"xsd:positiveInteger"/>
              <xsd:element name = "integer" type = "xsd:integer"/>
              <xsd:element name = "unsignedInt" type =
"xsd:unsignedInt"/>
            </xsd:sequence>
          </xsd:complexType>
        </xsd:element>
        <xsd:element name = "strings">
          <xsd:complexType>
            <xsd:sequence>
              <xsd:element name = "normalized" type =
"xsd:normalizedString"/>
              <xsd:element name = "string" type = "xsd:string"/>
            </xsd:sequence>
          </xsd:complexType>
        </xsd:element>
      </xsd:sequence>
    </xsd:complexType>
  </xsd:element>
</xsd:schema>
```

Listing 4.5 Schema using derived datatypes (derivedsamples.xsd).

For example, let's say that we are defining a simple schema that would allow us to track item expenses. The schema would include the type of expense, what it was, and the cost. The model for this information would look like that of Figure 4.3.

One of the first things that stand out in this model is the fact that we need to define the type of expense. For our example, we are going to define it as a *personal* type of expense, which would include mortgage, car payment, or bill. The definition of this type is pretty simple and is as follows:

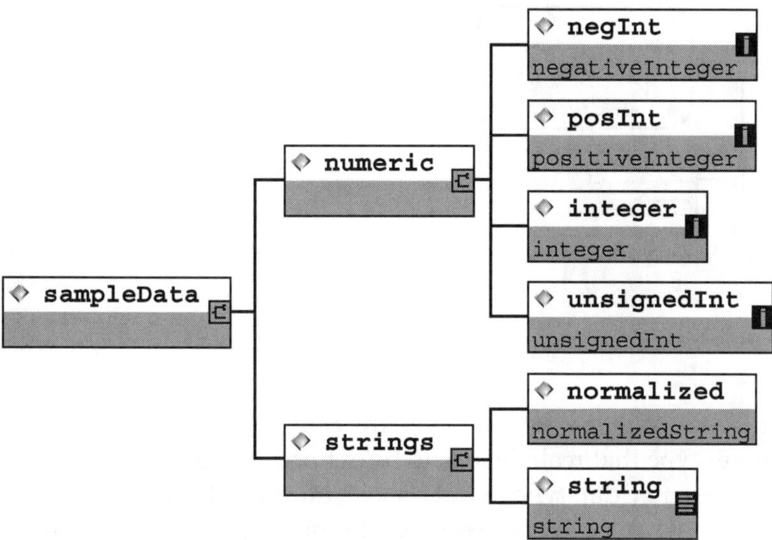

Figure 4.2 Data model of a sample using several of the derived datatypes.

```
<?xml version = "1.0" encoding = "UTF-8"?>
<sampleData xmlns:xsi = "http://www.w3.org/2001/XMLSchema-instance"
        xsi:noNamespaceSchemaLocation =
"file:///S:/derivedsamples.xsd">
  <numeric>
    <negInt>-68756</negInt>
    <posInt>7654</posInt>
    <integer>-8736</integer>
    <unsignedInt>23432</unsignedInt>
  </numeric>
  <strings>
    <normalized>here is a string with carriage returns</normalized>
    <string>here is a string</string>
  </strings>
</sampleData>
```

Listing 4.6 Schema that corresponds to derived datatypes from Listing 4.5 (derived.xml).

```
<xsd:simpleType name = "personal">
  <xsd:restriction base = "xsd:string">
    <xsd:enumeration value = "mortgage"/>
    <xsd:enumeration value = "car"/>
    <xsd:enumeration value = "bill"/>
  </xsd:restriction>
</xsd:simpleType>
```

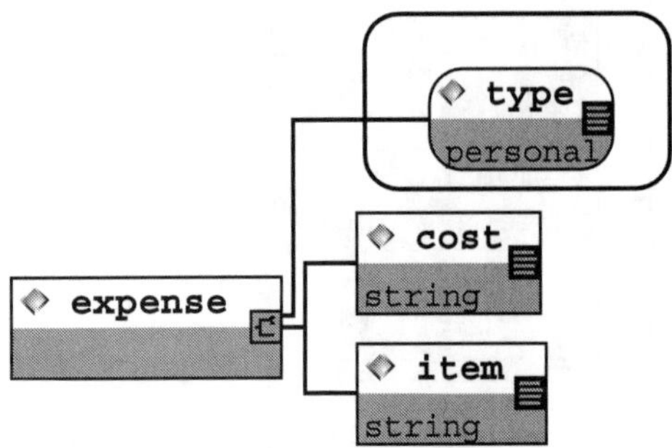

Figure 4.3 Our expense model.

As you can see, this code is very much like the car type we defined in Listing 4.3. But another type that really needs to be defined is <cost>. As we now know, there is no currency datatype in XSD, so we must create one.

If you break down what a currency really is, it is nothing more than a number that has a maximum of two digits after the decimal point. Because we have a decimal datatype, let's derive our current datatype from it. At the same time, we want to make sure that it has no more than two digits after the decimal. We can apply the fractionDigits facet to accomplish this task. Finally, one more thing needs to be done. We want to make sure that the lowest value of our currency type is 0.00. To perform this action, we can use the minInclusive facet and set it equal to 0. The end result is as follows:

```
<xsd:simpleType name = "currency">
  <xsd:restriction base = "xsd:decimal">
    <xsd:minInclusive value = "0"/>
    <xsd:fractionDigits value = "2"/>
  </xsd:restriction>
</xsd:simpleType>
```

And now, we have both of our derived types defined. Now, all we need to do is define our elements and specify the types appropriately. Listing 4.7 shows the final XSD schema with all the elements and datatypes defined.

```
<?xml version = "1.0" encoding = "UTF-8"?>
<xsd:schema xmlns:xsd = "http://www.w3.org/2001/XMLSchema"
   elementFormDefault = "qualified">
  <xsd:element name = "expense">
    <xsd:complexType>
```

Listing 4.7 Final XSD schema for expense model, with all elements and datatypes defined (expense.xsd).

```
        <xsd:sequence>
          <xsd:element name = "cost" type = "xsd:string"/>
          <xsd:element name = "item" type = "xsd:string"/>
        </xsd:sequence>
        <xsd:attribute name = "type" use = "required" type =
"personal"/>
      </xsd:complexType>
    </xsd:element>
    <xsd:simpleType name = "personal">
      <xsd:restriction base = "xsd:string">
        <xsd:enumeration value = "mortgage"/>
        <xsd:enumeration value = "car"/>
        <xsd:enumeration value = "bill"/>
      </xsd:restriction>
      </xsd:simpleType>
    <xsd:simpleType name = "currency">
      <xsd:restriction base = "xsd:decimal">
        <xsd:minInclusive value = "0"/>
        <xsd:fractionDigits value = "2"/>
      </xsd:restriction>
    </xsd:simpleType>
</xsd:schema>
```

Listing 4.7 Final XSD schema for expense model, with all elements and datatypes defined (expense.xsd). (Continued)

```
<?xml version = "1.0" encoding = "UTF-8"?>
<expense xmlns:xsi = "http://www.w3.org/2001/XMLSchema-instance"
         xsi:noNamespaceSchemaLocation = "file:///S:/expense.xsd"
         type = "bill">
  <cost>76.89</cost>
  <item>April 2002</item>
</expense>
```

Listing 4.8 Sample document showing how the schema from Listing 4.7 can be used (electricity.xml).

Listing 4.8 , is an example document that shows how this schema can be used.

In the following section, the <xsd:simpleType> element is reintroduced and covered in detail. Also, some more facets will be introduced and information will be given on how to control datatypes.

More on Simple Types

Recall that simple types refer to the definition of elements that have no child elements as part of their content model (see Chapter 1). Simple types are extremely useful when your own datatypes are being defined, which might not necessary be "true" datatypes as much as certain *types of data*. For example, we could define a simple type called friends and then apply that type to a list of names to specify who is a friend and who is not.

The <xsd:simpleType> element is used to define simple data types. The definition for this element is as follows:

```
<simpleType
  final = (#all | (list | union | restriction))
  id = ID
  name = NCName
  {any attributes with non-schema namespace . . .}>
  Content: (annotation?, (restriction | list | union))
</simpleType>
```

The attributes of the <xsd:simpleType> are listed and described in Table 4.3.

In addition to being able to give it a name, ID, and control its derivations, we are able to use child elements to define and describe how the new type is to function. This action is either done by restriction, as we have used several times before, or by lists or unions, which we discuss in the following sections.

Defining Lists

There are several ways to define lists within XSD. First, there are the primitive list types NMTOKENS, IDREFS, and ENTITIES, which constitute a list of NMTOKEN, IDREF, and ENTITY instances, respectively. In addition to these built-in types, you can also create your own lists by using the <xsd:list> element, which is defined as follows:

Table 4.3 Attributes of the <xsd:simpleType> Tag

ATTRIBUTE	DESCRIPTION
Final	Enables you to prevent derivations by lists, unions, restriction, or all
Id	Unique identifier
Name	The name of the simple type you are creating

Table 4.4 Attributes of the <xsd:list> Tag

ATTRIBUTE	DESCRIPTION
id	Unique identifier
itemType	References the list type

```
<list
  id = ID
  itemType = QName
  {any attributes with non-schema namespace . . .}>
  Content: (annotation?, (simpleType?))
</list>
```

As we see in the definition, there are only two attributes to this element. Both are defined in Table 4.4.

When can <xsd:list> be used, and when is it helpful? Suppose, for example, that we wanted to call three different painters to get estimates for painting a house. Let's limit it to three for now because we have only a limited amount of time to be at the house with them during the estimations.

In defining this schema, the first thing we need to do is create an enumeration of all the painters' phone numbers. We will call this type numbers, and it is defined as follows:

```
<xsd:simpleType name = "numbers">
  <xsd:restriction base = "xsd:positiveInteger">
    <xsd:enumeration value = "9195551212"/>
    <xsd:enumeration value = "9195551213"/>
    <xsd:enumeration value = "9195551214"/>
    <xsd:enumeration value = "9195551215"/>
    <xsd:enumeration value = "9195551216"/>
    <xsd:enumeration value = "9195551217"/>
    <xsd:enumeration value = "9195551218"/>
  </xsd:restriction>
</xsd:simpleType>
```

The next thing we need to do is create our list from these phone numbers as follows:

```
<xsd:simpleType name = "house">
  <xsd:list itemType = "numbers"/>
</xsd:simpleType>
```

Once the list has been created, we can derive a new datatype from it called threeHousePainters and restrict the length to 3:

```
<xsd:simpleType name = "threeHousePainters">
  <xsd:restriction base = "house">
    <xsd:length value = "3"/>
  </xsd:restriction>
</xsd:simpleType>
```

We won't concern ourselves with the length facet just yet. (See the following section, "Specifying Lengths," for more about length facets.)

At this point, we have defined all of our datatypes as needed. The final XSD schema is defined in Listing 4.9.

```
<?xml version = "1.0" encoding = "UTF-8"?>
<xsd:schema xmlns:xsd = "http://www.w3.org/2001/XMLSchema"
   elementFormDefault = "qualified">

  <!- single element that is of type threeHousePainters ->
  <xsd:element name = "painters" type = "threeHousePainters"/>

  <!- define all possible phone numbers ->
  <xsd:simpleType name = "numbers">
    <xsd:restriction base = "xsd:positiveInteger">
      <xsd:enumeration value = "9195551212"/>
      <xsd:enumeration value = "9195551213"/>
      <xsd:enumeration value = "9195551214"/>
      <xsd:enumeration value = "9195551215"/>
      <xsd:enumeration value = "9195551216"/>
      <xsd:enumeration value = "9195551217"/>
      <xsd:enumeration value = "9195551218"/>
    </xsd:restriction>
  </xsd:simpleType>

  <!- create a list out of the phone numbers ->
  <xsd:simpleType name = "house">
    <xsd:list itemType = "numbers"/>
  </xsd:simpleType>

  <!- define a new datatype from the list and limit to 3 ->
  <xsd:simpleType name = "threeHousePainters">
    <xsd:restriction base = "house">
      <xsd:length value = "3"/>
    </xsd:restriction>
  </xsd:simpleType>

</xsd:schema>
```

Listing 4.9 Final schema for house painters (painters.xsd).

```
<?xml version = "1.0" encoding = "UTF-8"?>
<painters xmlns:xsi = "http://www.w3.org/2001/XMLSchema-instance"
        xsi:noNamespaceSchemaLocation = "file:///S:/painters.xsd">
  9195551214 9195551217 9195551212
</painters>
```

Listing 4.10 Instance document for house painters (threepainters.xml).

We can now create an instance document listing all three phone numbers to be called, which is shown in Listing 4.10. Notice that the order of the list does not matter, but if a fourth number is added, we will get an error.

Lists can be extremely useful when creating schemas, but that it is not the only method of creating a set of constraining choices for content.

Creating a Union

When defining your own datatypes or even referencing previously defined datatypes, you are sure to come across instances where you want some new data to be one of two (or more) types. For instance, if you wanted only a type="new" <customer> to be able to purchase a given <item>, *or* if they were your type="friend", then you would want to be able to define that as part of your <customer> element. This type of functionality is accomplished through the use of unions and the <xsd:union> element, which is defined as follows:

```
<union
  id = ID
  memberTypes = List of QName
  {any attributes with non-schema namespace . . .}>
  Content: (annotation?, (simpleType*))
</union>
```

The <xsd:union> element only has a couple of attributes, which are defined in Table 4.5.

One of the best ways to see how <xsd:union> can work is through an example. In our example, we are going to define an <employee> element that has <name>, <gender>, and <age> as child elements. With the <age> element, we

Table 4.5 Attributes of the <xsd:union> Tag

ATTRIBUTE	DESCRIPTION
id	Unique identifier
memberTypes	Space separated list of datatypes that the union can be made up of

are going to specify that it must contain a positive integer number that is greater than 0 and that <gender> must take on values of male or female:

```
<!-- only allow male and female as genders -->
<xsd:element name = "gender">
  <xsd:simpleType>
    <xsd:restriction base = "xsd:string">
      <xsd:enumeration value = "male"/>
      <xsd:enumeration value = "female"/>
    </xsd:restriction>
  </xsd:simpleType>
</xsd:element>

<!-- specify that age must be greater than 0 -->
<xsd:element name = "age">
  <xsd:simpleType>
    <xsd:restriction base = "xsd:positiveInteger">
      <xsd:minExclusive value = "0"/>
    </xsd:restriction>
  </xsd:simpleType>
</xsd:element>
```

The <employee> element, on the other hand, has a required reference attribute that represents the employee's ID number. Because instance documents can contain both current and previous employees, we are going to define datatypes (with a list of IDs) for *previous* and *current* employees as follows:

```
<!-- id list of current employees -->
<xsd:simpleType name = "current">
  <xsd:restriction base = "xsd:decimal">
    <xsd:enumeration value = "17242"/>
    <xsd:enumeration value = "13456"/>
    <xsd:enumeration value = "13456"/>
    <xsd:enumeration value = "34566"/>
    <xsd:enumeration value = "28766"/>
  </xsd:restriction>
</xsd:simpleType>

<!-- id list of previous employees -->
<xsd:simpleType name = "previous">
  <xsd:restriction base = "xsd:decimal">
    <xsd:enumeration value = "25643"/>
    <xsd:enumeration value = "56890"/>
    <xsd:enumeration value = "36478"/>
    <xsd:enumeration value = "34784"/>
    <xsd:enumeration value = "49905"/>
  </xsd:restriction>
</xsd:simpleType>
```

There is nothing complex here, just the definition of two new datatypes and a list of possible values. But how do we specify that the reference attribute of the <employee> element is to use either of these? Here is where <xsd:union> comes into play. By using <xsd:union>, we are able to create a grouping whereby either values of current or previous can be included as the value of the reference attribute, as shown in the following example:

```
<xsd:attribute name = "reference" use = "required">
  <xsd:simpleType>

    <!-- create list of all employees by including current and previous -->
    <xsd:union memberTypes = "current previous"/>

  </xsd:simpleType>
</xsd:attribute>
```

In the previous code, we use the memberTypes attribute of the <xsd:union> element to specify a space-separated list of possible datatypes. Listing 4.11 shows the complete code listing.

```
<?xml version = "1.0" encoding = "UTF-8"?>
<xsd:schema xmlns:xsd = "http://www.w3.org/2001/XMLSchema">
  <xsd:element name = "employee">
    <xsd:complexType>
      <xsd:sequence>
        <xsd:element name = "name" type = "xsd:string"/>

        <!-- only allow male and female as genders -->
        <xsd:element name = "gender">
          <xsd:simpleType>
            <xsd:restriction base = "xsd:string">
              <xsd:enumeration value = "male"/>
              <xsd:enumeration value = "female"/>
            </xsd:restriction>
          </xsd:simpleType>
        </xsd:element>

        <!-- specify that age must be greater than 0 -->
        <xsd:element name = "age">
          <xsd:simpleType>
            <xsd:restriction base = "xsd:positiveInteger">
              <xsd:minExclusive value = "0"/>
            </xsd:restriction>
```

continues

Listing 4.11 Complete schema for list of employees (employee.xsd).

```
          </xsd:simpleType>
        </xsd:element>

      </xsd:sequence>
      <xsd:attribute name = "reference" use = "required">
        <xsd:simpleType>

          <!-- create list of all employees by including current and
previous -->
          <xsd:union memberTypes = "current previous"/>

        </xsd:simpleType>
      </xsd:attribute>
    </xsd:complexType>
  </xsd:element>

  <!-- id list of current employees -->
  <xsd:simpleType name = "current">
    <xsd:restriction base = "xsd:decimal">
      <xsd:enumeration value = "17242"/>
      <xsd:enumeration value = "13456"/>
      <xsd:enumeration value = "13456"/>
      <xsd:enumeration value = "34566"/>
      <xsd:enumeration value = "28766"/>
    </xsd:restriction>
  </xsd:simpleType>

  <!—- id list of previous employees —->
  <xsd:simpleType name = "previous">
    <xsd:restriction base = "xsd:decimal">
      <xsd:enumeration value = "25643"/>
      <xsd:enumeration value = "56890"/>
      <xsd:enumeration value = "36478"/>
      <xsd:enumeration value = "34784"/>
      <xsd:enumeration value = "49905"/>
    </xsd:restriction>
  </xsd:simpleType>

</xsd:schema>
```

Listing 4.11 Complete schema for list of employees (employee.xsd). (Continued)

We see this schema in action in Listing 4.12.

Note that in this example, we set the reference attribute to 28766, which was one of the enumerations within the current datatype. If we were to change this value to a value that is not part of the current or previous datatypes, then the parser would output an error as shown within the XML Instance (from TIBCO Extensibility) application in Figure 4.4.

```
<?xml version = "1.0" encoding = "UTF-8"?>
<employee xmlns:xsi = "http://www.w3.org/2001/XMLSchema-instance"
          xsi:noNamespaceSchemaLocation = "file:///S:/employee.xsd"
          reference = "28766">
  <name>Allen Wyke</name>
  <gender>male</gender>
  <age>29</age>
</employee>
```

Listing 4.12 Instance document for list of employees (28766.xml).

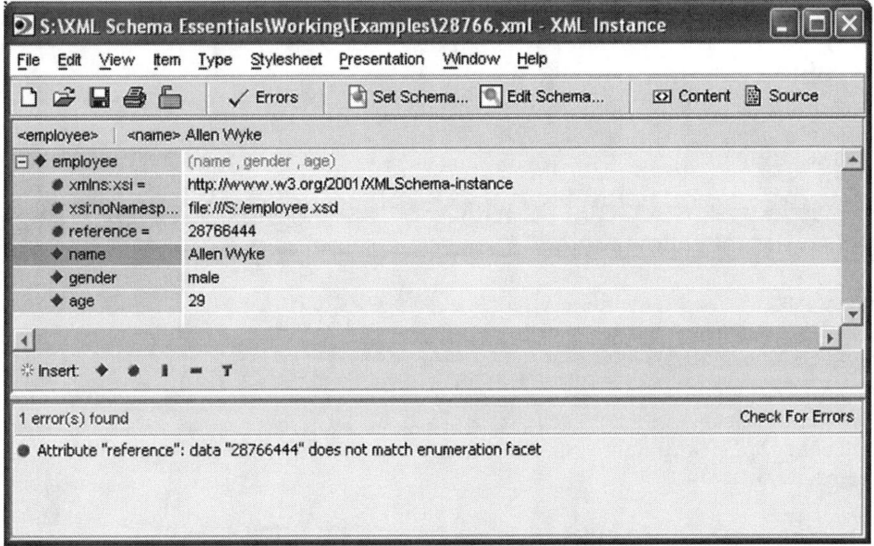

Figure 4.4 Getting an error with a value not defined in one of our datatypes.

Constraining Type Definitions

On many occasions when schemas are defined, we often find that we want more control over how things appear and in what context. Elements, for example, have the minOccurs and maxOccurs attributes that enable one to have greater control over how often an element can appear within an instance document. The need to constrain datatypes is no different. At times, we might want to both specify that the content of an element can have a string and limit things like the number of characters that the string can contain. For example, if that data were to be placed in a database, there would probably be limits as to how long it could be.

Datatypes can definitely be constrained in this manner through the use of facets (a concept we briefly introduced in Chapter 1). Facets themselves warrant more than just a few pages of coverage because they are not only incredibly powerful but a major aspect of defining schemas. For that reason, several facets are introduced in this section of the chapter, and there will be more complete coverage in Chapters 5 and 6 (which deal with specifying lengths).

It is just as important to provide boundaries for datatype types as it is to have the types defined. Being able to limit the number of items in a list or the maximum value of an integer is very important. This section covers several of the facets that control datatypes and shows you how they differ according to the context in which they are placed (for example, the length of a string and an integer are different). The following are the facets covered in this chapter:

- length
- minLength
- maxLength

The first facet is <xsd:length>, which is used to control the length of a datatype. It has the following definition:

```
<length
  fixed = boolean : false
  id = ID
  value = nonNegativeInteger
  {any attributes with non-schema namespace . . .}>
  Content: (annotation?)
</length>
```

The <xsd:length> element has three attributes, all listed in Table 4.6. One of them specifies whether or not the value can be changed; another is the unique identifier; and a third contains the number of items that represent the length we are trying to enforce on the datatype.

For example, suppose that we wanted to define a schema that would describe an address. This <address> contains a <street>, <city>, <state>, <postalcode>, and <country> and is shown in Figure 4.5.

Table 4.6 Attributes of the <xsd:length> Tag

ATTRIBUTE	DESCRIPTION
fixed	A default, but unchangeable value for the element
id	Unique identifier
value	Number of items that represent the length

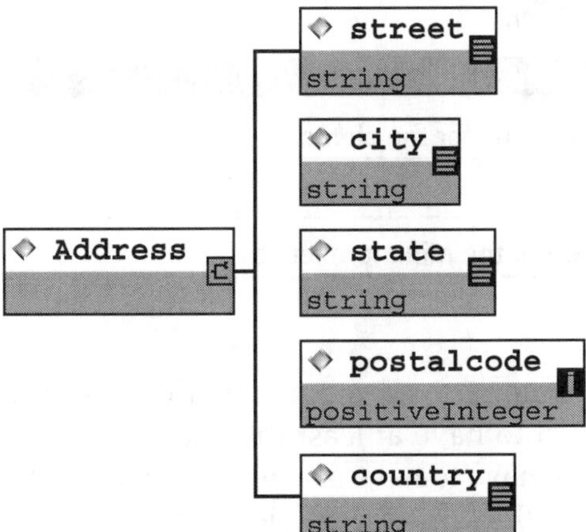

Figure 4.5 Our address data model.

The element that we are going to apply the <xsd:length> facet to is <state>. It will be limited to the two-character abbreviation that is commonly used. To perform this task, we need to define <state> as we normally would with <xsd:element> and then restrict it to two characters. The following will accomplish this task:

```
<xsd:element name = "state">
  <xsd:simpleType>
    <xsd:restriction base = "xsd:string">
      <xsd:length value = "2"/>
    </xsd:restriction>
  </xsd:simpleType>
</xsd:element>
```

This particular example is going to be a work in progress, so the complete code will not be given at this point. Over the next few sections, however, we will arrive at a completed XSD schema.

The <xsd:length> facet is not the only one that enables us to control the length of an item. The <xsd:minLength> facet also enables us to specify a minimum length. It is defined as follows:

```
<minLength
  fixed = boolean : false
  id = ID
  value = nonNegativeInteger
  {any attributes with non-schema namespace . . .}>
  Content: (annotation?)
</minLength>
```

Table 4.7 Attributes of the <xsd:minLength> Tag

ATTRIBUTE	DESCRIPTION
fixed	A default, but unchangeable value for the element
id	Unique identifier
value	Number of items that represent the minimum length

This element, unlike <xsd:length>, is not a fixed requirement on instance documents. It only states that "you need to have at least this many" characters, where <xsd:length> states that "you have to have exactly this many." The attributes, as you can see in Table 4.7, are the same as <xsd:length>.

A good place to use <xsd:minLength> is for our definitions of <city>, <street>, and <country>. We want to make sure that the users at least pass in one character for each of these, which might not be as practical as in other examples, but it will serve our purpose. We are able to enforce this requirement by using the following code:

```
<xsd:element name = "street">
  <xsd:simpleType>
    <xsd:restriction base = "xsd:string">
      <xsd:minLength value = "1"/>
    </xsd:restriction>
  </xsd:simpleType>
</xsd:element>
<xsd:element name = "city">
  <xsd:simpleType>
    <xsd:restriction base = "xsd:string">
      <xsd:minLength value = "1"/>
    </xsd:restriction>
  </xsd:simpleType>
</xsd:element>
<xsd:element name = "country">
  <xsd:simpleType>
    <xsd:restriction base = "xsd:string">
      <xsd:minLength value = "1"/>
    </xsd:restriction>
  </xsd:simpleType>
</xsd:element>
```

Is a minimum length really everything we need for these elements, however? It is not, especially if we are going to insert this data into a database. More important than a minimum set of information is a maximum set. Conveniently, XSD also has a <xsd:maxLength> facet. It has the following definition:

Table 4.8 Attributes of the <xsd:maxLength> Tag

ATTRIBUTE	DESCRIPTION
fixed	A default but unchangeable value for the element
id	Unique identifier
value	Number of items that represent the maximum length

```
<maxLength
  fixed = boolean : false
  id = ID
  value = nonNegativeInteger
  {any attributes with non-schema namespace . . .}>
  Content: (annotation?)
</maxLength>
```

Like <xsd:length> and <xsd:minLength>, <xsd:maxLength> has three attributes that are defined in Table 4.8.

In our use of <xsd:maxLength>, we are going to put a cap on the number of characters, including white space, that can occur within our <city>, <street>, and <country> elements. For <city> and <country>, we are going to limit it to 15. The <street> element might need to hold more information, so we are going to set it to 25. To perform this task, we only need to add the following line as part of the <xsd:restriction> definition to each of the <city>, <street>, and <country> elements:

```
<xsd:maxLength value = "25"/>
```

The ability to enforce restrictions on strings is not the only type of control you have over instance documents. In addition, you can also control digits.

Controlling Digits

There are several constraining facets that enable you to specify how you want digit-based datatypes handled, two of which will be discussed here:

- totalDigits
- fractionDigits

The first one of these facets we are going to look at is the <xsd:totalDigits> element, which has the following definition:

```
<totalDigits
  fixed = boolean : false
  id = ID
  value = positiveInteger
  {any attributes with non-schema namespace . . .}>
  Content: (annotation?)
</totalDigits>
```

This element enables us to specify the maximum number of digits that are to appear in an instance document. We like to compare this element to <xsd:maxLength>, because it is to numerical values what <xsd: maxLength > is to string values. Like so many of the other facets, it has three attributes, which are defined in Table 4.9.

In what situation would a person use this facet? Our <postalcode> element is a great example. A postal code (in the United States, at least) is positive integer of five digits. Using this facet, we can impose this restriction on our element. The definition for this element, which will be derived from the postiveInteger datatype, is as follows:

```
<xsd:element name = "postalcode">
  <xsd:simpleType>
    <xsd:restriction base = "xsd:positiveInteger">
      <xsd:totalDigits value = "5"/>
    </xsd:restriction>
  </xsd:simpleType>
</xsd:element>
```

The complete schema for the <postalcode> element, with restrictions, is shown in Listing 4.13.

Now that we have our schema defined, we can create an instance document that uses it, as shown in Listing 4.14. Notice that all of the content conforms to the schema that we have defined. If we were to change parts of this schema, such as making a 16-digit <city>, three-digit <state>, or six-digit <postalcode>, we would get an error like that shown in Figure 4.6.

Table 4.9 Attributes of the <xsd:totalDigits> Tag

ATTRIBUTE	DESCRIPTION
fixed	A default but unchangeable value for the element
id	Unique identifier
value	Number of items that represent the total number of digits

```
<?xml version = "1.0" encoding = "UTF-8"?>
<xsd:schema xmlns:xsd = "http://www.w3.org/2001/XMLSchema"
   elementFormDefault = "qualified">
  <xsd:element name = "address">
    <xsd:complexType>
      <xsd:sequence>

        <!-- street should be more than 1, less than 25 -->
        <xsd:element name = "street">
          <xsd:simpleType>
            <xsd:restriction base = "xsd:string">
              <xsd:maxLength value = "25"/>
              <xsd:minLength value = "1"/>
            </xsd:restriction>
          </xsd:simpleType>
        </xsd:element>

        <!-- city should be more than 1, less than 15 -->
        <xsd:element name = "city">
          <xsd:simpleType>
            <xsd:restriction base = "xsd:string">
              <xsd:maxLength value = "15"/>
              <xsd:minLength value = "1"/>
            </xsd:restriction>
          </xsd:simpleType>
        </xsd:element>

        <!-- state should be 2 characters -->
        <xsd:element name = "state">
          <xsd:simpleType>
            <xsd:restriction base = "xsd:string">
              <xsd:length value = "2"/>
            </xsd:restriction>
          </xsd:simpleType>
        </xsd:element>

        <!-- postalcode should be less than 5 -->
        <xsd:element name = "postalcode">
          <xsd:simpleType>
            <xsd:restriction base = "xsd:positiveInteger">
              <xsd:totalDigits value = "5"/>
            </xsd:restriction>
          </xsd:simpleType>
        </xsd:element>
```

continues

Listing 4.13 Schema for the <postalcode> element with restrictions (address.xsd).

```
        <!- country should be more than 1, less than 15 ->
        <xsd:element name = "country">
          <xsd:simpleType>
            <xsd:restriction base = "xsd:string">
              <xsd:maxLength value = "15"/>
              <xsd:minLength value = "1"/>
            </xsd:restriction>
          </xsd:simpleType>
        </xsd:element>

      </xsd:sequence>
    </xsd:complexType>
  </xsd:element>
</xsd:schema>
```

Listing 4.13 Schema for the <postalcode> element with restrictions (address.xsd) (Continued).

```
<?xml version = "1.0" encoding = "UTF-8"?>
<address xmlns:xsi = "http://www.w3.org/2001/XMLSchema-instance"
        xsi:noNamespaceSchemaLocation = "file:///S:/address.xsd">
  <street>123 Anystreet</street>
  <city>Some City</city>
  <state>NC</state>
  <postalcode>27665</postalcode>
  <country>USA</country>
</address>
```

Listing 4.14 Instance document for restricted <postalcode> element (123Anystreet.xml).

Another important facet for controlling digits is <xsd:fractionDigits>. This facet enables us to specify the number of digits that are to occur after the decimal point of a positive or negative numerical value. It has the following definition:

```
<fractionDigits
  fixed = boolean : false
  id = ID
  value = nonNegativeInteger
  {any attributes with non-schema namespace . . .}>
  Content: (annotation?)
</fractionDigits>
```

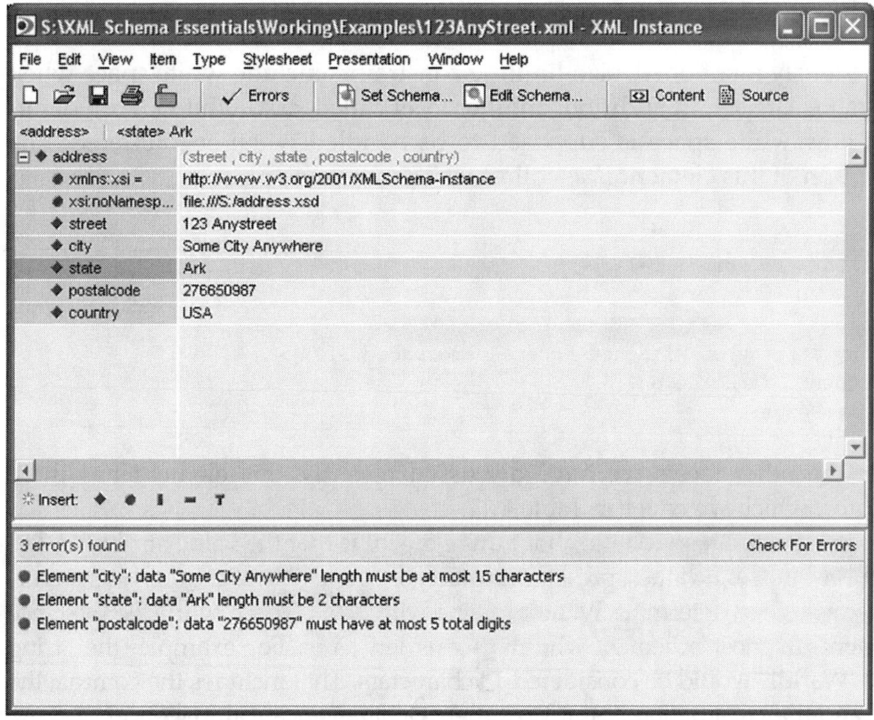

Figure 4.6 Errors from not conforming to our <city>, <state>, and <postalcode> definitions.

Table 4.10 Attributes of the <xsd:fractionDigits> Tag

ATTRIBUTE	DESCRIPTION
fixed	A default but unchangeable value for the element
id	Unique identifier
value	Number of items that represent the total number of fractional digits

This facet can be extremely useful when we want to limit the accuracy of data coming into our system. Definitions of the attributes of this element are given in Table 4.10.

Refer to the section, "Defining Your Own Datatypes," particularly Listing 4.7, for an example of how to use <xsd:fractionDigits>. Just remember that it represents the number of digits to the right of the decimal point.

Handling White Space

As previously mentioned, size-limiting constraints include white space when their values are set. In addition, another facet called <xsd:whiteSpace> determines how white space is supposed to be handled when encountered. The description of this element is as follows.

```
<whiteSpace
  fixed = boolean : false
  id = ID
  value = (collapse | preserve | replace)
  {any attributes with non-schema namespace . . .}>
  Content: (annotation?)
</whiteSpace>
```

Like the other facets we have discussed recently, this element has three attributes, which we cover in Table 4.11.

One interesting thing to note about this element is that the value attribute takes one of three possible values: preserve, replace, or collapse. These values are important because they determine what happens with white space within an instance document. In most schemas, white space is left as is. For example, the string "Hello, World!" would be considered 13 characters. That includes the comma, the space, and the exclamation point. The other 10 characters are alphabetical.

The preserve setting tells the schema processors to perform no normalization on the data—to leave it exactly as it was passed. So, for instance, let's examine the simple schema defined in Listing 4.15.

Table 4.11 Attributes of the <xsd:whiteSpace> Tag

ATTRIBUTE	DESCRIPTION
fixed	A default but unchangeable value for the element
id	Unique identifier
value	Contains a value of collapse, preserve, or replace to signify how white space is supposed to be handled when encountered

```
<?xml version = "1.0" encoding = "UTF-8"?>
<xsd:schema xmlns:xsd = "http://www.w3.org/2001/XMLSchema"
            elementFormDefault = "qualified">
  <xsd:element name = "someText">
    <xsd:simpleType>
```

Listing 4.15 Simple schema using preserve value (preserve.xsd).

```
        <xsd:restriction base = "xsd:string">
          <xsd:whiteSpace value = "preserve"/>
        </xsd:restriction>
      </xsd:simpleType>
    </xsd:element>
</xsd:schema>
```

Listing 4.15 Simple schema using preserve value (preserve.xsd). (Continued)

If we had Listing 4.16 passed to a processor, all tabs, line feeds, and carriage returns would be left in.

If, however, we wanted to replace all tabs, line feeds, and carriage returns with space characters, then we could change our <xsd:whiteSpace> definition. Listing 4.17 shows an example of defining this element for a sample e-mail data model. We specifically do not want these characters in our e-mails for this example.

```
<?xml version = "1.0" encoding = "UTF-8"?>
<someText xmlns:xsi = "http://www.w3.org/2001/XMLSchema-instance"
          xsi:noNamespaceSchemaLocation =
"file:///S:/preserve.xsd">Here is some data followed by a carriage
returns

Another return before this line starts and a last return before the
ending of the element occurs.
</someText>
```

Listing 4.16 Instance document using the preserve value (preserve.xml).

```
<?xml version = "1.0" encoding = "UTF-8"?>
<xsd:schema xmlns:xsd = "http://www.w3.org/2001/XMLSchema"
            elementFormDefault = "qualified">
  <xsd:element name = "email">
    <xsd:complexType>
      <xsd:sequence>
        <xsd:element name = "header">
          <xsd:complexType>
            <xsd:sequence>
              <xsd:element name = "to" type = "xsd:string"/>
              <xsd:element name = "cc" type = "xsd:string" minOccurs =
"0" maxOccurs = "unbounded"/>
```

continues

Listing 4.17 Schema using the replace value (email.xsd).

```
                <xsd:element name = "bcc" type = "xsd:string" minOccurs
= "0" maxOccurs = "unbounded"/>
                <xsd:element name = "from" type = "xsd:string"/>
                <xsd:element name = "date" type = "xsd:date"/>
                <xsd:element name = "subject" type = "xsd:string"
minOccurs = "0"/>
              </xsd:sequence>
            </xsd:complexType>
          </xsd:element>
          <xsd:element name = "body">
            <xsd:simpleType>
              <xsd:restriction base = "xsd:string">

                <!- replace tabs, line feeds, and carriage returns with
spaces ->
                <xsd:whiteSpace value = "replace"/>

              </xsd:restriction>
            </xsd:simpleType>
          </xsd:element>
        </xsd:sequence>
      </xsd:complexType>
  </xsd:element>
</xsd:schema>
```

Listing 4.17 Schema using the replace value (email.xsd). (Continued)

In the schema in Listing 4.17, we have specified that we want our <body> element to have its tabs, line feeds, and carriage returns replaced with spaces. The resulting instance document would look like Listing 4.18.

```
<?xml version = "1.0" encoding = "UTF-8"?>
<email xmlns:xsi = "http://www.w3.org/2001/XMLSchema-instance"
       xsi:noNamespaceSchemaLocation = "file:///S:/email.xsd">
  <header>
    <to>support@wiley.com</to>
    <cc>myself@home.com</cc>
    <bcc/>
    <from/>
    <date>2002-05-30</date>
    <subject>Great Book!</subject>
  </header>
```

continues

Listing 4.18 Instance document using the replace value (email_support.xml).

```
  <body>Just wanted to send you guys a note to say how much I have
enjoyed your Essential series. I already have read the XHTML and XPath
books, and am now finishing the one on XML Schema - love them!

Thanx a ton - John
</body>
</email>
```

Listing 4.18 Instance document using the replace value (email_support.xml) (Continued).

Taking the instance document from Listing 4.18, we would end up with a <body> that looks like the following:

```
<body>Just wanted to send you guys a note to say how much I have enjoyed
your Essential series. I already have read the XHTML and XPath books,
and am now finishing the one on XML Schema - love them! Thanx a ton -
John </body>
```

Our last option is to use collapse. When this option is used, it not only performs the replace operation but also collapses contiguous sequences of spaces into a single space. It will also remove any leading and trailing spaces.

As an example, let's build a schema to represent a search. It will contain a <site> and <phrase> element that provides the URI of the search site as well as the phrase you want to search. We are going to use the collapse option to remove all the extra characters in the <phrase> so that we can pass it to the search engine. In Listing 4.19, we have defined our schema.

```
<?xml version = "1.0" encoding = "UTF-8"?>
<xsd:schema xmlns:xsd = "http://www.w3.org/2001/XMLSchema"
            elementFormDefault = "qualified">
  <xsd:element name = "search">
    <xsd:complexType>
      <xsd:sequence>
        <xsd:element name = "site" type = "xsd:anyURI"/>
        <xsd:element name = "phrase">
          <xsd:simpleType>
            <xsd:restriction base = "xsd:string">
              <xsd:whiteSpace value = "collapse"/>
            </xsd:restriction>
          </xsd:simpleType>
        </xsd:element>
      </xsd:sequence>
    </xsd:complexType>
  </xsd:element>
</xsd:schema>
```

Listing 4.19 Schema using the collapse value (search.xsd).

```
<?xml version = "1.0" encoding = "UTF-8"?>
<search xmlns:xsi = "http://www.w3.org/2001/XMLSchema-instance"
        xsi:noNamespaceSchemaLocation = "file:///S:/search.xsd">
  <site>http://www.google.com</site>
  <phrase>computer hardware
misc items    as well as other things


</phrase>
</search>
```

Listing 4.20 Instance document using the collapse value (googlesearch.xml).

Listing 4.20 shows a sample instance document for this model. Extra carriage returns and spaces are included so that you can see what the document will look like after processing with our collapse setting in place.

In this example, our <phrase> element has a lot of extra trash in it—everything from carriage returns after hardware as well as two extra ones creating blank lines before our ending </phrase> element. There are even have some extra spaces between the words items. If we ran this example through a parser, our resulting <phrase> element would resemble something like the following:

```
<phrase>computer hardware misc items as well as other things</phrase>
```

This code is a little more manageable and does not necessarily detract from our meaning. This situation might not always be the case for your schemas, so make sure that the removal of these extraneous characters will not have any impact on your applications.

Pattern Matching

The facets used thus far have done such things as defined limitations or specified how certain content should be handled. Another type of facet, <xsd:pattern>, takes a different approach. This facet has the following definition:

```
<pattern
  id = ID
  value = anySimpleType
  {any attributes with non-schema namespace . . .}>
  Content: (annotation?)
</pattern>
```

Attributes of this facet, which are defined in Table 4.12, enable you to apply constraint through regular expression pattern matching. For anyone who is

Table 4.12 Attributes of the <xsd:pattern> Tag

ATTRIBUTE	DESCRIPTION
id	Unique identifier
value	Regular expression pattern

familiar with scripting languages like Perl or JavaScript, regular expression pattern matching has probably been used before, so the concept should be familiar.

Recall the restriction of our <state> element to two characters in Listing 4.13. Suppose that we wanted to restrict it to two capitalized characters. We could do that by using the <xsd:pattern> element as follows:

```
<xsd:element name = "state">
  <xsd:simpleType>
    <xsd:restriction base = "xsd:string">
      <xsd:pattern value="[A-Z]{2}"/>
    </xsd:restriction>
  </xsd:simpleType>
</xsd:element>
```

The expression "[A-Z]{2}" essentially reads "two upper-case ASCII letters." Many other types of expressions enable us to search for digits, vary cases, and all sorts of combinations therein. For example, we could have used <xsd:pattern> in our currency datatype to ensure that it had the proper currency symbol (such as $ or £). More detailed information about the <xsd:pattern> element can be found in Chapter 8.

NOTE **Regular expressions can be very powerful, but they are beyond the scope of this book. If you are not familiar with them, the authors highly recommend that you review Appendix D of the *XML Schema Part 0: Primer Recommendation* located at www.w3.org/TR/xmlschema-0#regexAppendix.**

Applicability of Facets

Table 4.13 gives an overview of facets and lists to which datatypes they apply. For more complete coverage of facets, see Chapters 5 and 6.

Table 4.13 summarizes the information about datatypes, constraints, and facets covered in this chapter. For more detail about how these operate, see Chapters 5 and 6.

Table 4.13 Datatypes to Which Each Facet Applies

FACET	APPLIES TO DATATYPE LIST
enumeration	ENTITIES, ENTITY, ID, IDREF, IDREFS, NCName, NMTOKEN, NMTOKENS, NOTATION, Name, QName, anyURI, base64Binary, byte, date, dateTime, decimal, double, duration, float, gDay, gMonth, gMonthDay, gYear, gYearMonth, hexBinary, int, integer, language, long, negativeInteger, nonNegativeInteger, nonPositiveInteger, normalizedString, positiveInteger, short, string, time, token, unsignedByte, unsignedInt, unsignedLong, unsignedShort
fractionDigits	byte, decimal, int, integer, long, negativeInteger, nonNegativeInteger, nonPositiveInteger, positiveInteger, short, unsignedByte, unsignedInt, unsignedLong, unsignedShort
length	ENTITIES, ENTITY, ID, IDREF, IDREFS, NCName, NMTOKEN, NMTOKENS, NOTATION, Name, QName, anyURI, base64Binary, hexBinary, language, normalizedString, string, token
maxExclusive	byte, date, dateTime, decimal, double, duration, float, gDay, gMonth, gMonthDay, gYear, gYearMonth, int, integer, long, negativeInteger, nonNegativeInteger, nonPositiveInteger, positiveInteger, short, time, unsignedByte, unsignedInt, unsignedLong, unsignedShort
maxInclusive	byte, date, dateTime, decimal, double, duration, float, gDay, gMonth, gMonthDay, gYear, gYearMonth, int, integer, long, negativeInteger, nonNegativeInteger, nonPositiveInteger, positiveInteger, short, time, unsignedByte, unsignedInt, unsignedLong, unsignedShort
maxLength	ENTITIES, ENTITY, ID, IDREF, IDREFS, NCName, NMTOKEN, NMTOKENS, NOTATION, Name, QName, anyURI, base64Binary, hexBinary, language, normalizedString, string, token
minExclusive	byte, date, dateTime, decimal, double, duration, float, gDay, gMonth, gMonthDay, gYear, gYearMonth, int, integer, long, negativeInteger, nonNegativeInteger, nonPositiveInteger, positiveInteger, short, time, unsignedByte, unsignedInt, unsignedLong, unsignedShort
minInclusive	byte, date, dateTime, decimal, double, duration, float, gDay, gMonth, gMonthDay, gYear, gYearMonth, int, integer, long, negativeInteger, nonNegativeInteger, nonPositiveInteger, positiveInteger, short, time, unsignedByte, unsignedInt, unsignedLong, unsignedShort
minLength	ENTITIES, ENTITY, ID, IDREF, IDREFS, NCName, NMTOKEN, NMTOKENS, NOTATION, Name, QName, anyURI, base64Binary, hexBinary, language, normalizedString, string, token

continues

Table 4.13 Datatypes to Which Each Facet Applies (Continued)

FACET	APPLIES TO DATATYPE LIST
pattern	ENTITY, ID, IDREF, NCName, NMTOKEN, NOTATION, Name, QName, anyURI, base64Binary, boolean, byte, date, dateTime, decimal, double, duration, float, gDay, gMonth, gMonthDay, gYear, gYearMonth, hexBinary, int, integer, language, long, negativeInteger, nonNegativeInteger, nonPositiveInteger, normalizedString, positiveInteger, short, string, time, token, unsignedByte, unsignedInt, unsignedLong, unsignedShort
totalDigits	byte, decimal, int, integer, long, negativeInteger, nonNegativeInteger, nonPositiveInteger, positiveInteger, short, unsignedByte, unsignedInt, unsignedLong, unsignedShort
whiteSpace	ENTITIES, ENTITY, ID, IDREF, IDREFS, NCName, NMTOKEN, NMTOKENS, NOTATION, Name, QName, anyURI, base64Binary, boolean, byte, date, dateTime, decimal, double, duration, float, gDay, gMonth, gMonthDay, gYear, gYearMonth, hexBinary, int, integer, language, long, negativeInteger, nonNegativeInteger, nonPositiveInteger, normalizedString, positiveInteger, short, string, time, token, unsignedByte, unsignedInt, unsignedLong, unsignedShort

Summary

This chapter rounds out the core aspects of the XSD language, also covered at length in Chapters 1 and 2. Now that we have familiarized ourselves with the concepts of <xsd:element>, <xsd:attribute>, and datatypes and have seen many examples of how they are used, the foundation has been laid for us to really start exploring how to apply XSD. It is time for us to examine in detail how these elements can be used.

The preceding paragraphs have covered datatypes and how they are applied to elements and attributes; they also touched on other important points such as facets and deriving your own datatypes. The next few chapters delve into more information about these two items and show how to use them in our schemas.

CHAPTER

5

Data Facets

In this chapter and in Chapter 6, "More about Data Facets," we are going to examine how to use the data facets that W3C XML Schema provides in order to specifically constrain the permitted content of XML elements in the instance documents that we wish to create or make use of.

First, before considering facets in detail, let's briefly revisit the setting in which facets exist. An XSD Schema datatype is a *3-tuple* consisting of the following:

- A set of distinct values, which is the datatype's *value space*
- A set of lexical representations called the datatype's *lexical space*
- A set of *facets* that characterize properties of the datatype's value space, individual values, or lexical items

An xsd:float type would include the value of 100 in its value space. Each value in the value space of a datatype is designated by one or more representations of that value in the lexical space of the datatype. For example, the lexical space for that same xsd:float datatype could have included 100 or 1.0E2, as well as other possibilities, as representations in the lexical space of the datatype of the value 100.

It is important for you to understand the distinction between the value space of a datatype and the same datatype's lexical space. It is the value space that is constrained by facets of the datatype. When the value space is constrained, however, there is a corresponding (although not necessarily one-to-one) constraint on the lexical space. If we were to exclude the xsd:float of 100 from the value space, then the two representations 100 and 1.0E2, as well as other possibilities, would be excluded from the lexical space.

For datatypes of xsd:string, the value space and lexical space correspond one-to-one.

Fundamental and Constraining Facets

Part 2 of the W3C XML Schema Recommendation refers to two types of facets in XSD Schema: *fundamental facets* and *constraining facets*. This chapter and the next will primarily be concerned with constraining facets.

A fundamental facet is, essentially, the definition of a datatype. Such fundamental facets can be difficult to express in words because the basis for them is, practically speaking, axiomatic. It is quite obvious that the value ABC is not of the type xsd:integer, for example.

A constraining facet takes the datatype defined by a fundamental facet and constrains the possible values. For example, XSD Schema enables us to constrain the length of types that are of the xsd:string type, and other types, to being a certain number of characters in length. When constraining (for example, the xsd:integer type) to be of length 4, we are essentially constraining the permitted integer values to be between 1,000 and 9,999, inclusive.

Now, let's take an overview of all the constraining facets that are available in version 1.0 of W3C XML Schema.

Constraining Facets in XSD Schema

The W3C XML Schema Recommendation lists 12 constraining facets that are, in alphabetical order:

- enumeration
- fractionDigits
- length
- maxExclusive
- maxInclusive
- maxLength
- minExclusive

- minInclusive
- minLength
- pattern
- totalDigits
- whiteSpace

Each of these facets will be discussed in detail, and many examples of how they are used will be given in this chapter and in the next. First, let's look at the three facets that relate to the length of a datatype: *length, minLength,* and *maxLength.*

The length Element

It is not uncommon for us to want a datatype to be of a particular length. For example, a U.S. zip code of three digits would be pretty much meaningless as would a credit card number that is seven digits in length. Similarly, a code for a U.S. state that had one, three, four, or more characters might be interpretable by a human reader. "Wyom" is pretty unmistakable, for example, but an application that expects a two-character description of a U.S. state might well struggle to interpret a state code of non-standard length.

So, clearly at times we need to define exactly the length that the character content of an element or the value of an attribute can have. In this section, we will look at a situation in which the content must be of a fixed length.

The *length* facet is defined as the number of units of length of the datatype to which it is being applied. The units of length used vary with the base type from which a datatype is derived. For example, when a datatype is an xsd:string or is derived from xsd:string, the units of length are the number of characters in the string. When a datatype is xsd:hexBinary or base64Binary or a datatype derived from those types, then the unit of length is an octet, which is eight bits of binary data. When a list datatype is constrained by the length facet, it is the number of list items to which we are referring.

The value of the length facet must be a *nonNegativeInteger*. That is pretty much common sense. A string, for example, can be of zero length or any arbitrary length greater than zero, depending on the number of characters it contains. A string of length −2, however, makes no sense—nor does a string of length 3.5. Thus, the length facet must be an integer and must not be negative.

Let's look at the simple situation in which you must create a schema—for example, one describing a collection of addresses for individual customers. A possible instance document is shown in Listing 15.1.

The XSD schema for much of that document is straightforward, with a <CustomerAddress> element being a complex type having <Name> and <Address> elements as content, each of which contains also a complex type.

```
<?xml version='1.0'?>
<CustomerAddresses>
 <CustomerAddress>
  <Name>
   <FirstName>Patrick</FirstName>
   <MiddleInitials>Z</MiddleInitials>
   <LastName>Belladonna</LastName>
  </Name>
  <Address>
   <Street1>999 Calamity Jane Street</Street1>
   <Street2></Street2>
   <City>Seattle</City>
   <State>WA</State>
   <PostalCode>98765</PostalCode>
   <Country>USA</Country>
  </Address>
 </CustomerAddress>
<!-- More <CustomerAddress> elements would go here. -->
</CustomerAddresses>
```

Listing 5.1 List of addresses for individual customers (CustAddresses.xml).

There are two parts for which we might well want to limit the permitted length of data, however. The data to be entered as content in the <State> element should be exactly two characters in length. The <PostalCode> element, if one assumes that the application only stores U.S. zip codes, should be exactly five digits in length (assuming that one is not wanting to collect extended zip codes). Listing 5.2 shows the schema in which, using the length facet, we can constrain the length of the content of the <State> element to two characters and the length of the content of the <PostalCode> element to five digits.

Let's look at the two parts of the code that define the two elements of interest to us as far as the length facet is concerned. The <State> element is declared to be of type "StateList2letter":

```
<xsd:element name="State" type="StateList2letter"/>
```

which is defined as follows:

```
<xsd:simpleType name="StateList2letter">
  <xsd:restriction base="xsd:string">
    <xsd:length value="2"/>
  </xsd:restriction>
</xsd:simpleType>
```

The base type for the StateList2letter datatype is xsd:string. We want to restrict allowable strings to a length of two characters. That base datatype is

```
<?xml version='1.0'?>
<xsd:schema xmlns:xsd="http://www.w3.org/2001/XMLSchema">

<xsd:element name="CustomerAddresses">
 <xsd:complexType>
  <xsd:sequence>
   <xsd:element name="CustomerAddress">
    <xsd:complexType>
     <xsd:sequence>
      <xsd:element name="Name">
       <xsd:complexType>
        <xsd:sequence>
         <xsd:element name="FirstName" type="xsd:string"/>
         <xsd:element name="MiddleInitials" type="xsd:string"/>
         <xsd:element name="LastName" type="xsd:string"/>
        </xsd:sequence>
       </xsd:complexType>
      </xsd:element> <!-- End of the <Name> element. -->
      <xsd:element name="Address">
       <xsd:complexType>
        <xsd:sequence>
         <xsd:element name="Street1" type="xsd:string"/>
         <xsd:element name="Street2" type="xsd:string"/>
         <xsd:element name="City" type="xsd:string"/>
         <xsd:element name="State" type="StateList2letter"/>
         <xsd:element name="PostalCode" type="ZipCode5digit"/>
         <xsd:element name="Country" type="xsd:string"/>
        </xsd:sequence>
       </xsd:complexType>
      </xsd:element><!-- End of the <Address> element. -->
     </xsd:sequence>
    </xsd:complexType>
   </xsd:element> <!-- End of the <CustomerAddress> element. -->
  </xsd:sequence>
 </xsd:complexType>
</xsd:element> <!-- End of the <CustomerAddresses> element. -->

<xsd:simpleType name="StateList2letter">
 <xsd:restriction base="xsd:string">
  <xsd:length value="2"/>
 </xsd:restriction>
</xsd:simpleType>

<xsd:simpleType name="ZipCode5digit">
 <xsd:restriction base="xsd:decimal">
  <xsd:length value="5"/>
```

Listing 5.2 Schema with length of content of <State> element limited to two characters and <PostalCode> limited to five digits (CustAddresses.xsd).

```
    </xsd:restriction>
  </xsd:simpleType>

  </xsd:schema>
```

Listing 5.2 Schema with length of content of <State> element limited to two characters and <PostalCode> limited to five digits (CustAddresses.xsd). (continued)

restricted to a permitted length of two characters by using the <xsd:length> element nested within an <xsd:restriction> element, as shown earlier. Using this technique, we can exclude content of the <State> element that is of inappropriate length. When we come later to consider the enumeration facet, we will show you how to make sure that only legitimate two character strings are allowed.

Similarly, the <PostalCode> element is, for the purposes of this example, declared to be of type "ZipCode5digit":

```
<xsd:element name="PostalCode" type="ZipCode5digit"/>
```

which is defined as follows:

```
<xsd:simpleType name="ZipCode5digit">
  <xsd:restriction base="xsd:decimal">
    <xsd:length value="5"/>
  </xsd:restriction>
</xsd:simpleType>
```

The base type for the ZipCode5digit datatype is xsd:decimal. That base datatype is restricted to a length of exactly five digits by means of an <xsd:length> element nested within an <xsd:restriction> element. Alternative base datatypes that could have been used are <xsd:nonNegativeInteger> or <xsd:PositiveInteger>.

Another situation in which the length facet might supply us with a solution would be if we wanted to store U.S. *Social Security numbers* (SSNs) for individuals. An SSN has nine meaningful numeric digits commonly displayed as a ddd-dd-dddd format. Let's suppose that we wanted, for some reason, to create an XML-based data store that also could handle data from U.K. citizens, who also have a personal identifier that takes the form AB123456C, that is two characters followed by six numeric digits followed by a single character. We need to create two different lengths of number, depending on the citizenship of the individual. We can use the <xsd:length> element to constrain the length of each of the two elements representing the U.S. and U.K. SSNs to 11 and 9, respectively. To allow the choice between those two elements, each with a defined length, we can use an XSD choice group in combination with the length facet.

If we make the simplifying assumption that an individual can have citizenship in only one of the two countries of interest, then an instance document showing a listing of U.S. and U.K. identifiers could look like that in Listing 5.3.

```
<?xml version='1.0'?>
<PersonsWithSSN>
<Person>
 <Name>
  <FirstName>George</FirstName>
  <MiddleNames>Walker</MiddleNames>
  <LastName>Bush</LastName>
 </Name>
 <Address>
  <Street1>1600 Pennsylvania Avenue</Street1>
  <Street2></Street2>
  <City>Washington</City>
  <State>DC</State>
  <Country>USA</Country>
 </Address>
 <Status>
  <Citizenship>US</Citizenship>
  <USSSN>123-45-6789</USSSN>
 </Status>
</Person>
<Person>
 <Name>
  <FirstName>Anthony</FirstName>
  <MiddleNames></MiddleNames>
  <LastName>Blair</LastName>
 </Name>
 <Address>
  <Street1>10 Downing Street</Street1>
  <Street2>Westminster</Street2>
  <City>London</City>
  <State>England</State>
  <Country>UK</Country>
 </Address>
 <Status>
  <Citizenship>UK</Citizenship>
  <UKSSN>AB123456C</UKSSN>
 </Status>
</Person>

</PersonsWithSSN>
```

Listing 5.3 A listing of U.S. and U.K. citizens with personal identifiers (SSN01.xml).

The XSD schema to describe such an instance document is shown in Listing 5.4.

The interesting part of Listing 5.4 as far as constraining length is concerned is in the declaration of the <StatusType> element:

```
<xsd:complexType name="StatusType">
 <xsd:sequence>
  <xsd:element name="Citizenship" type="xsd:string"/>
  <xsd:group ref="SSNChoiceGroup" />
 </xsd:sequence>
</xsd:complexType>
```

The permitted content of the <StatusType> element is a <Citizenship> element followed by a group named SSNChoiceGroup. That group is defined by using the <xsd:group> element within which is nested an <xsd:choice> element:

```
<xsd:group name="SSNChoiceGroup">
 <xsd:choice>
  <xsd:element name="USSSN" type="USSSNType"/>
  <xsd:element name="UKSSN" type="UKSSNType"/>
 </xsd:choice>
</xsd:group>
```

The choice available is between a <USSSN> element and a <UKSSN> element. The permitted length of the content of those elements is constrained within the definitions of the USSSNType and UKSSNType types to be 11 characters and nine characters, respectively.

When we consider simple list datatypes and apply the length facet to them, then we see that length, in that context, is interpreted as the number of list items. For example, Listing 5.5 is a schema that includes a list datatype, named MyListType.

The definition for the simple type MyListType is as follows:

```
<xsd:simpleType name="MyListType">
  <xsd:list itemType="xsd:string">
   <xsd:simpleType>
    <xsd:restriction base="xsd:string">
     <xsd:length value="3"/>
    </xsd:restriction>
   </xsd:simpleType>
  </xsd:list>
 </xsd:simpleType>
```

The definition uses the <xsd:list> element, with itemType of xsd:string, to indicate that it is a list simple type. The <xsd:restriction> element has a nested <xsd:length> element that defines the length as "3." As mentioned earlier, that means a length of three list items.

```
<?xml version="1.0" encoding="UTF-8"?>
<xsd:schema xmlns:xsd="http://www.w3.org/2001/XMLSchema" >

<xsd:element name="PersonsWithSSN">
 <xsd:complexType>
  <xsd:sequence>
   <xsd:element name="Person" type="PersonType" minOccurs="0"
maxOccurs="unbounded"/>
  </xsd:sequence>
 </xsd:complexType>
</xsd:element>

<xsd:complexType name="PersonType">
 <xsd:sequence>
  <xsd:element name="Name" type="NameType"/>
  <xsd:element name="Address" type="AddressType"/>
  <xsd:element name="Status" type="StatusType"/>
 </xsd:sequence>
</xsd:complexType>

<xsd:complexType name="NameType">
 <xsd:sequence>
  <xsd:element name="FirstName" type="xsd:string"/>
  <xsd:element name="MiddleNames" type="xsd:string"/>
  <xsd:element name="LastName" type="xsd:string"/>
 </xsd:sequence>
</xsd:complexType>

<xsd:complexType name="AddressType">
 <xsd:sequence>
  <xsd:element name="Street1" type="xsd:string"/>
  <xsd:element name="Street2" type="xsd:string"/>
  <xsd:element name="City" type="xsd:string"/>
  <xsd:element name="State" type="xsd:string"/>
  <xsd:element name="Country" type="xsd:string"/>
 </xsd:sequence>
</xsd:complexType>

<xsd:complexType name="StatusType">
 <xsd:sequence>
  <xsd:element name="Citizenship" type="xsd:string"/>
  <xsd:group ref="SSNChoiceGroup" />
 </xsd:sequence>
</xsd:complexType>
```

Listing 5.4 A schema using the length facet to control SSN length (SSN01.xsd).

```
<xsd:group name="SSNChoiceGroup">
 <xsd:choice>
  <xsd:element name="USSSN" type="USSSNType"/>
  <xsd:element name="UKSSN" type="UKSSNType"/>
 </xsd:choice>
</xsd:group>

<xsd:simpleType name="USSSNType">
 <xsd:restriction base="xsd:string">
  <xsd:length value="11"/>
 </xsd:restriction>
</xsd:simpleType>

<xsd:simpleType name="UKSSNType">
 <xsd:restriction base="xsd:string">
  <xsd:length value="9"/>
 </xsd:restriction>
</xsd:simpleType>

</xsd:schema>
```

Listing 5.4 A schema using the length facet to control SSN length (SSN01.xsd). (continued)

```
<?xml version='1.0'?>
<xsd:schema xmlns:xsd="http://www.w3.org/2001/XMLSchema">
 <xsd:element name="MyLists">
  <xsd:complexType>
   <xsd:sequence>
    <xsd:element name="MyList" type="MyListType" minOccurs="1"
maxOccurs="unbounded"/>
   </xsd:sequence>
  </xsd:complexType>
 </xsd:element>

 <xsd:simpleType name="MyListType">
  <xsd:list itemType="xsd:string">
   <xsd:simpleType>
    <xsd:restriction base="xsd:string">
     <xsd:length value="3"/>
    </xsd:restriction>
   </xsd:simpleType>
  </xsd:list>
 </xsd:simpleType>
</xsd:schema>
```

Listing 5.5 A schema using a list simple type with <xsd:length> (MyLists.xsd).

```
<?xml version='1.0'?>
<MyLists>
<MyList>A B C</MyList>
<MyList>ABC DEF GHI</MyList>
<MyList>ABCD EFGH IJKL</MyList>
<MyList>ALongItem ALongerItem ALongerItemStill</MyList>
</MyLists>
```

Listing 5.6 An instance document using a list type of Length 3 (MyLists.xml).

The instance document in Listing 5.6 would validate against the schema in Listing 5.5, because the number of items in each <MyList> element is exactly three, although the length of the text content in a <MyList> element varies considerably among <MyList> elements.

Remember that if you are using strings of type xsd:string in a list simple type, you must avoid the use of space separators. In place of the xsd:string type, you might be better to use the xsd:NMTOKEN type. If you tried to use "My String" as a string in a list type, then that would be treated as two lists items with the first list item, "My," separated by a space character from the second list item, "String."

As we have seen, the length facet can be used to define content of specific length. Often, however, we might want more flexibility in permitted length, and for example, we might want to constrain the length of the content of an element to specified minimum and maximum lengths. The minLength and maxLength facets enable us to achieve that.

The minLength Element

The minLength facet is defined as the minimum number of units of length permitted for a value. As with the length facet, the units of length vary with the datatype of the value and/or the datatype from which it is derived.

One use of the minLength facet might be for the (partial) validation of credit card numbers. Major credit card numbers are at least 13 digits in length. Therefore, as a partial validation of a credit card number, we could make the simple check that the number entered as the credit card number was a number and was at least 13 digits long. In the remainder of this example, we will assume that users have followed instructions to enter their credit card number without including spaces. A simple listing for purchase details is shown in Listing 5.7.

As you can see in Listing 5.7, the content of the <CardNumber> element is entered as a sequence of numeric digits without spaces or other separators. An XSD schema that defines the instance document is shown in Listing 5.8.

```
<?xml version='1.0'?>
<PurchaseDetails>
 <Name>
  <FirstNameInitials>John B</FirstNameInitials>
  <LastName>Smith</LastName>
 </Name>
 <CreditCard>
  <Company>Mastercard</Company>
  <CardNumber>1234567890123456</CardNumber>
  <ExpiryDate>05/03</ExpiryDate>
 </CreditCard>
</PurchaseDetails>
```

Listing 5.7 An XML document describing a purchase using a credit card (PurchaseDetails.xml).

The focus of our interest in this example is the declaration of the <CardNumber> element,

```
<xsd:element name="CardNumber" type="CardNumberType"/>
```

which references a named simple type definition named CardNumberType.

```
<xsd:simpleType name="CardNumberType">
 <xsd:restriction base="xsd:decimal">
  <xsd:minLength value="13"/>
 </xsd:restriction>
</xsd:simpleType>
```

The base type for the CardNumberType datatype is xsd:decimal, arbitrary precision numerical values. Again, the types xsd:nonNegativeInteger, xsd: positiveInteger, or xsd:unsignedLong would be suitable alternatives. The <xsd:minLength> element implements the minLength facet and ensures, with the use of suitable validation, that all values entered into the <CreditCardNumber> element's content are numerical values with a length of at least 13 digits. Of course, that is far from a complete validation of a credit card number, because we might also want to restrict the maximum length of any credit card number to 16 digits—something that we can achieve by using the maxLength facet.

We could also use the minLength facet to check that data has been entered for a particular item. Suppose that we had an XML pizza ordering service, and we might want to ensure that the customer had not inadvertently forgotten to choose a topping. An instance document might look like Listing 5.9.

A schema for Listing 5.9 is shown in Listing 5.10.

```
<?xml version='1.0'?>
<xsd:schema xmlns:xsd="http://www.w3.org/2001/XMLSchema">
<xsd:element name="PurchaseDetails">
 <xsd:complexType>
  <xsd:sequence>
   <xsd:element name="Name" type="CreditCardName"/>
   <xsd:element name="CreditCard" type="CreditCardDetails"/>
  </xsd:sequence>
 </xsd:complexType>
</xsd:element>

<xsd:complexType name="CreditCardName">
 <xsd:sequence>
  <xsd:element name="FirstNameInitials" type="xsd:string"/>
  <xsd:element name="LastName" type="xsd:string"/>
 </xsd:sequence>
</xsd:complexType>

<xsd:complexType name="CreditCardDetails">
 <xsd:sequence>
  <xsd:element name="Company" type="xsd:string"/>
  <xsd:element name="CardNumber" type="CardNumberType"/>
  <xsd:element name="ExpiryDate" type="xsd:string"/>
 </xsd:sequence>
</xsd:complexType>

<xsd:simpleType name="CardNumberType">
 <xsd:restriction base="xsd:decimal">
  <xsd:minLength value="13"/>
 </xsd:restriction>
</xsd:simpleType>

</xsd:schema>
```

Listing 5.8 A schema to constrain the minimum length of the content of <CardNumber> (PurchaseDetails.xsd).

The <xsd:minLength> element is used within the named simple type definition of ToppingsType towards the end of the schema. On this occasion, the xsd:NMTOKEN type has been used to avoid the potential for ambiguous entries when using xsd:string types in a list. Notice that we can specify that the minimum length of the list is one item, that is the list of toppings cannot be empty, by specifying the value of the value attribute of the <xsd:minLength> element. If a customer consciously wanted no topping, he or she could enter "none" as a permitted value.

Often, we might want to specify a maximum length for the content of an element, either as an alternative to specifying a minimum length or in conjunction

```
<?xml version='1.0'?>
<PizzaOrders>
<PizzaOrder DateOrdered="2002-05-30T22:18:23">
 <Name>John Doe</Name>
 <Address>123 Pennsylvania Avenue</Address>
 <Telephone>123 456 7890</Telephone>
 <PaymentMethod>COD</PaymentMethod>
 <TotalCost>14.00</TotalCost>
 <PizzasOrdered>
  <Pizza>
   <Type>Pepperoni</Type>
   <Toppings>Ham Anchovies</Toppings>
  </Pizza>
 </PizzasOrdered>
</PizzaOrder>
<PizzaOrder DateOrdered="2003-01-31T21:02:45">
 <Name>Jane Doe</Name>
 <Address>987 5th Avenue</Address>
 <Telephone>123 789 0123</Telephone>
 <PaymentMethod>CC Mastercard</PaymentMethod>
 <TotalCost>12.50</TotalCost>
 <PizzasOrdered>
  <Pizza>
   <Type>Chocolate</Type>
   <Toppings>Pepperoni Ham</Toppings>
  </Pizza>
 </PizzasOrdered>
</PizzaOrder>
</PizzaOrders>
```

Listing 5.9 A pizza order in XML (PizzaOrders.xml).

with the specification of a minimum length. To specify a maximum length, we use the maxLength facet.

The maxLength Element

The maxLength facet defines the maximum permitted length of the content of an element or attribute in an instance document.

We saw in our consideration of the minLength facet how we could ensure a minimum length for the credit card number entered. We can use the maxLength facet to similarly determine a maximum length for the credit card number. We will again use Listing 5.7 as the instance document.

```
<?xml version="1.0" encoding="UTF-8"?>
<xsd:schema xmlns:xsd="http://www.w3.org/2001/XMLSchema" >

<xsd:element name="PizzaOrders">
 <xsd:complexType>
  <xsd:sequence>
   <xsd:element name="PizzaOrder" type="PizzaOrderType"
    minOccurs="0" maxOccurs="unbounded"/>
  </xsd:sequence>
 </xsd:complexType>
</xsd:element>

<xsd:complexType name="PizzaOrderType">
 <xsd:sequence>
  <xsd:element name="Name" type="xsd:string"/>
  <xsd:element name="Address" type="xsd:string"/>
  <xsd:element name="Telephone" type="xsd:string"/>
  <xsd:element name="PaymentMethod" type="xsd:string"/>
  <xsd:element name="TotalCost" type="xsd:decimal"/>
  <xsd:element name="PizzasOrdered" type="PizzasOrderedType"/>
 </xsd:sequence>
 <xsd:attribute name="DateOrdered" type="xsd:dateTime"/>
</xsd:complexType>

<xsd:complexType name="PizzasOrderedType">
  <xsd:sequence>
   <xsd:element name="Pizza" type="PizzaType"/>
  </xsd:sequence>
</xsd:complexType>

<xsd:complexType name="PizzaType">
  <xsd:sequence>
   <xsd:element name="Type" type="xsd:string"/>
   <xsd:element name="Toppings" type="ToppingsType"/>
  </xsd:sequence>
</xsd:complexType>

<xsd:simpleType name="ToppingsType">
 <xsd:restriction base="xsd:NMTOKEN">
  <xsd:simpleType>
   <xsd:list itemType="xsd:NMTOKEN">
    <xsd:simpleType>
     <xsd:restriction base="xsd:NMTOKEN">
      <xsd:minLength value="1"/>
     </xsd:restriction>
    </xsd:simpleType>
```

Listing 5.10 An XSD schema using the <xsd:minLength> element on a list type (PizzaOrders.xsd).

```
    </xsd:list>
   </xsd:simpleType>
  </xsd:restriction>
 </xsd:simpleType>

</xsd:schema>
```

Listing 5.10 An XSD schema using the <xsd:minLength> element on a list type (PizzaOrders.xsd). (continued)

We need to modify the definition of the CardNumberType <xsd:simpleType> element, as shown here:

```
<xsd:simpleType name="CardNumberType">
 <xsd:restriction base="xsd:decimal">
  <xsd:minLength value="13"/>
  <xsd:maxLength value="16"/>
 </xsd:restriction>
</xsd:simpleType>
```

As before, the minLength facet defines a minimum length of 13 for the <CardNumber> element, and the maxLength facet defines a maximum length of 16 digits.

The modified schema is shown in Listing 5.11.

The length, minLength, and maxLength facets enable us to constrain the length of content of an element or attribute but do nothing to define detail of, for example, the types of character that might occur in an xsd:string type. The *pattern* facet gives us such control.

The pattern Element

The <xsd:pattern> element is one of the most powerful of the XSD Schema facets and also potentially one of the most complex. The three facets that deal with the length of a value can be very useful but are pretty straightforward. The pattern facet offers very precise control of the content of an element, but particularly if you are not familiar with regular expressions, it can seem pretty complex and impenetrable (at least, at first sight). So, we will look at several examples of using the <xsd:pattern> element in this section.

In Listings 5.3 and 5.4, we looked at ways to provide some control over the information contained in U.S. and U.K. SSNs. The length facet enabled us to check for entries that are too short or too long but do not prevent entries such as "123ABC456789," which of course would not be a valid SSN. Simi-

```
<?xml version='1.0'?>
<xsd:schema xmlns:xsd="http://www.w3.org/2001/XMLSchema">

<xsd:element name="PurchaseDetails">
 <xsd:complexType>
  <xsd:sequence>
   <xsd:element name="Name" type="CreditCardName"/>
   <xsd:element name="CreditCard" type="CreditCardDetails"/>
  </xsd:sequence>
 </xsd:complexType>
</xsd:element>

<xsd:complexType name="CreditCardName">
 <xsd:sequence>
  <xsd:element name="FirstNameInitials" type="xsd:string"/>
  <xsd:element name="LastName" type="xsd:string"/>
 </xsd:sequence>
</xsd:complexType>

<xsd:complexType name="CreditCardDetails">
 <xsd:sequence>
  <xsd:element name="Company" type="xsd:string"/>
  <xsd:element name="CardNumber" type="CardNumberType"/>
  <xsd:element name="ExpiryDate" type="xsd:string"/>
 </xsd:sequence>
</xsd:complexType>

<xsd:simpleType name="CardNumberType">
 <xsd:restriction base="xsd:decimal">
  <xsd:minLength value="13"/>
  <xsd:maxLength value="16"/>
 </xsd:restriction>
</xsd:simpleType>

</xsd:schema>
```

Listing 5.11 A schema to specify both minimum and maximum length of a simple type (PurchaseDetails02.xsd).

larly, the U.K. SSN could be entered as "12ABCDEF3," which also is an invalid structure.

The <xsd:pattern> element enables us to achieve much greater control over content. For the U.S. SSN, we can specify that the only allowed structure of the content is three numeric digits followed by a dash followed by two numeric digits followed by a dash followed by four numeric digits.

Similarly for the U.K. SSN, we can specify that the allowed structure is two upper-case letters followed by six numeric digits followed by one numeric digit. The schema shown in Listing 5.12 enables us to achieve such precise control.

The <xsd:pattern> elements are used in the two simple type definitions towards the end of the schema. The reason why we use a pattern facet is to restrict the allowed entries of type xsd:string. The fact that we intend a restriction is expressed by using the <xsd:restriction> element within which we nest the <xsd:pattern> element. The value of the value attribute of each <xsd:pattern> element is a regular expression. Regular expressions used in XSD Schema use Perl regular expressions as their basis but apply to Unicode characters (because XSD Schema is expressed in XML 1.0) rather than to ASCII characters.

The type definition for the USSSNType simple type contains an <xsd:pattern> element that defines the pattern facet:

```
<xsd:simpleType name="USSSNType">
 <xsd:restriction base="xsd:string">
  <xsd:pattern value="[0-9]{3}-[0-9]{2}-[0-9]{4}"/>
 </xsd:restriction>
</xsd:simpleType>
```

The characters [0-9]{3} mean that three digits from 0 to 9 inclusive is the only pattern of characters permitted at the beginning of the USSSNType. That is followed by a literal dash. The pattern [0-9]{2} indicates that following the dash, two digits in the range 0 to 9 inclusive are allowed. That is followed by a literal dash. Finally, the pattern [0-9]{4} indicates that the pattern must finish with four digits in the range 0 to 9, inclusive.

The <xsd:pattern> element shown as follows represents the pattern facet for a U.K. SSN:

```
<xsd:pattern value="[A-Z]{2}[0-9]{6}[A-Z]{1}"/>
```

The first part of the pattern [A-Z]{2} indicates that exactly two upper-case characters in the range A to Z inclusive are allowed. If we wanted also to allow exactly two lower-case characters from A to Z, as well as the upper-case characters, we would have written [A-Za-z]{2}. Following the initial two alphabetic characters, the pattern [0-9]{6} indicates that the alphabetic characters must be followed by exactly six digits in the range 0 to 9, inclusive. The final part of the pattern [A-Z]{1} indicates that a single upper-case alphabetic character completes the pattern.

Parts Catalog Example

Let's suppose that as part of an XML-based warehouse stock application, we have a particular structure to the part numbers of individual *stock keeping units* (SKUs). An XML instance document might look like the code in Listing 5.13.

```
<?xml version="1.0" encoding="UTF-8"?>
<xsd:schema xmlns:xsd="http://www.w3.org/2001/XMLSchema" >

<xsd:element name="PersonsWithSSN">
 <xsd:complexType>
  <xsd:sequence>
   <xsd:element name="Person" type="PersonType" minOccurs="0"
maxOccurs="unbounded"/>
  </xsd:sequence>
 </xsd:complexType>
</xsd:element>

<xsd:complexType name="PersonType">
 <xsd:sequence>
  <xsd:element name="Name" type="NameType"/>
  <xsd:element name="Address" type="AddressType"/>
  <xsd:element name="Status" type="StatusType"/>
 </xsd:sequence>
</xsd:complexType>

<xsd:complexType name="NameType">
 <xsd:sequence>
  <xsd:element name="FirstName" type="xsd:string"/>
  <xsd:element name="MiddleNames" type="xsd:string"/>
  <xsd:element name="LastName" type="xsd:string"/>
 </xsd:sequence>
</xsd:complexType>

<xsd:complexType name="AddressType">
 <xsd:sequence>
  <xsd:element name="Street1" type="xsd:string"/>
  <xsd:element name="Street2" type="xsd:string"/>
  <xsd:element name="City" type="xsd:string"/>
  <xsd:element name="State" type="xsd:string"/>
  <xsd:element name="Country" type="xsd:string"/>
 </xsd:sequence>
</xsd:complexType>

<xsd:complexType name="StatusType">
 <xsd:sequence>
  <xsd:element name="Citizenship" type="xsd:string"/>
  <xsd:group ref="SSNChoiceGroup" />
 </xsd:sequence>
</xsd:complexType>
```

Listing 5.12 Using the pattern facet to define Social Security numbers (SSN02.xsd).

```
<xsd:group name="SSNChoiceGroup">
 <xsd:choice>
  <xsd:element name="USSSN" type="USSSNType"/>
  <xsd:element name="UKSSN" type="UKSSNType"/>
 </xsd:choice>
</xsd:group>

<xsd:simpleType name="USSSNType">
 <xsd:restriction base="xsd:string">
  <xsd:pattern value="[0-9]{3}-[0-9]{2}-[0-9]{4}"/>
 </xsd:restriction>
</xsd:simpleType>

<xsd:simpleType name="UKSSNType">
 <xsd:restriction base="xsd:string">
  <xsd:pattern value="[A-Z]{2}[0-9]{6}[A-Z]{1}"/>
 </xsd:restriction>
</xsd:simpleType>

</xsd:schema>
```

Listing 5.12 Using the pattern facet to define Social Security numbers (SSN02.xsd). (Continued)

```
<?xml version='1.0'?>
<PartsCatalog>
<SKU PartNo="81-ADL">5</SKU>
<SKU PartNo="38-LHM">18</SKU>
<SKU PartNo="19-DAG">21</SKU>
<SKU PartNo="27-HCB">88</SKU>
<SKU PartNo="44-EFI">40</SKU>
</PartsCatalog>
```

Listing 5.13 A parts catalog expressed in XML (PartsCatalog.xml).

The parts catalog consists of a sequence of <SKU> elements, each of which possess a PartNo attribute that consists of two numeric digits, a dash, and three upper-case characters from A to M inclusive, as in the following:

```
<SKU PartNo="38-ABC">12</SKU>
```

To constrain the values of the PartNo attribute to the values just mentioned, we again need to use the pattern facet, as shown in Listing 5.14.

```
<?xml version='1.0'?>
<xsd:schema xmlns:xsd="http://www.w3.org/2001/XMLSchema">
<xsd:element name="PartsCatalog">
 <xsd:complexType>
  <xsd:sequence>
   <xsd:element name="SKU" type="SKUType" minOccurs="1"
maxOccurs="unbounded"/>
  </xsd:sequence>
 </xsd:complexType>
</xsd:element>

<xsd:complexType name="SKUType">
 <xsd:simpleContent>
  <xsd:extension base="xsd:string">
   <xsd:attribute name="PartNo" type="PartNoType"/>
  </xsd:extension>
 </xsd:simpleContent>
</xsd:complexType>

<xsd:simpleType name="PartNoType">
 <xsd:restriction base="xsd:string">
  <xsd:pattern value="\d{2}-[A-M]{3}"/>
 </xsd:restriction>
</xsd:simpleType>

</xsd:schema>
```

Listing 5.14 An XSD schema to describe the parts catalog (PartsCatalog.xsd).

The part of the XSD schema that is used to constrain the content of the PartNo attribute in an instance document such as Listing 5.13 makes use of the <xsd:pattern> element:

```
<xsd:simpleType name="PartNoType">
 <xsd:restriction base="xsd:string">
  <xsd:pattern value="\d{2}-[A-M]{3}"/>
 </xsd:restriction>
</xsd:simpleType>
```

The <xsd:restriction> element indicates that a base type of xsd:string is to be constrained in some way. The <xsd:pattern> element defines exactly which constraints are to be applied to the PartNo attribute of the <SKU> element. The value of the <xsd:pattern> element indicates that the structure of the text content of the PartNo attribute is two numerical digits (the characters \d indicate that it is a numeric digit, and {2} indicates that there are two) followed by a dash which, in turn, is followed by three upper-case letters between A and M, inclusive (the [A-M] gives the range of permitted characters and {3} indicates that there are three such characters). To define the pattern for the first two characters, we could equally have used [0-9]{2}.

Postal Code Examples

In this section, we will look at how we can use the <xsd:pattern> element to create types that conform to the requirements of U.S. zip codes and U.K. postal codes. First, let's take a look at how we could create a schema to require a strictly conforming short form of a U.S. zip code.

U.S. Zip Code Examples

We will first look at how we can require a U.S. zip code in the five-digit form. A simple instance document containing billing information for U.S. customers is shown in Listing 5.15.

The XSD schema that describes such an instance document is shown in Listing 5.16.

Within the definition of the USAddressType complex type, there is a declaration for the <ZipCode> element that is defined to be of type USZipCodeType. The definition for the USZipCodeType indicates that we want to restrict the permitted values of type xsd:positiveInteger by using a pattern facet. The value of the <xsd:pattern> element indicates that we are to expect numeric digits, indicated by the \d characters, of which there are to be five, as indicated by the {5} characters. An alternative approach would be to define the

```
<?xml version='1.0'?>
<USBillingInfo>
 <Customer>Peter Pan Products</Customer>
 <Address>
  <Street1>1234 Hamlyn Street</Street1>
  <Street2>Fantasy Technology Park</Street2>
  <City>New York</City>
  <State>NY</State>
  <ZipCode>12345</ZipCode>
  <Country></Country>
 </Address>
</USBillingInfo>
```

Listing 5.15 Billing information expressed as XML (USBillingInfo.xml).

```
<?xml version='1.0'?>
<xsd:schema xmlns:xsd="http://www.w3.org/2001/XMLSchema">

<xsd:element name="USBillingInfo">
 <xsd:complexType>
  <xsd:sequence>
   <xsd:element name="Customer" type="xsd:string"/>
   <xsd:element name="Address" type="USAddressType"/>
  </xsd:sequence>
 </xsd:complexType>
</xsd:element>

<xsd:complexType name="USAddressType">
 <xsd:sequence>
  <xsd:element name="Street1" type="xsd:string"/>
  <xsd:element name="Street2" type="xsd:string"/>
  <xsd:element name="City" type="xsd:string"/>
  <xsd:element name="State" type="xsd:string"/>
  <xsd:element name="ZipCode" type="USZipCodeType"/>
  <xsd:element name="Country" type="xsd:string" minOccurs="0"
maxOccurs="1"/>
 </xsd:sequence>
</xsd:complexType>

<xsd:simpleType name="USZipCodeType">
 <xsd:restriction base="xsd:positiveInteger">
  <xsd:pattern value="\d{5}"/>
 </xsd:restriction>
</xsd:simpleType>

</xsd:schema>
```

Listing 5.16 An XSD schema to describe the billing information (USBillingInfo.xsd).

base attribute on the <xsd:restriction> element to be of type xsd:string and to set the value of the value attribute of the <xsd:pattern> element to [0-9]{5}.

Next, let's extend that example to allow for codes to be entered in either the five-digit zip code format or the zip+4 extended zip code format. Listing 5.17 includes an extended zip code, in the format of five numeric digits followed by a dash followed by four numeric digits.

The following XSD schema, Listing 5.18, can be used to validate either Listing 5.17 (extended zip code) or Listing 5.15 (standard zip code). It allows both five-digit and extended zip codes.

The changes that are necessary are to be found in the final simple type definition of the schema. Because we are using the extended zip code format, we

```
<?xml version='1.0'?>
<USBillingInfo>
 <Customer>Peter Pan Products</Customer>
 <Address>
 <Street1>1234 Hamlyn Street</Street1>
 <Street2>Fantasy Technology Park</Street2>
 <City>New York</City>
 <State>NY</State>
 <ZipCode>12345-6789</ZipCode>
 <Country></Country>
 </Address>
</USBillingInfo>
```

Listing 5.17 A billing document in XML including extended zip code (USBillingInfo02.xml).

include a dash (hyphen) that is no longer of the datatype xsd:positiveInteger that we used in Listing 5.16. So, the base type for the <xsd:restriction> element has been changed to xsd:string to accommodate the necessary dash. The regular expression contained in the value element of the <xsd:pattern> element means that two structures are allowed. The | character, sometimes called a pipe, means the same as logical OR. The leftmost option consists of numeric digits (shown by \d), of which there are five (shown by {5}). The rightmost option, following the pipe, is for the extended zip code and consists first of numeric digits (shown by \d") of which there are five (shown by {5}) followed by a literal dash, then numeric digits (shown by \d) of which there are four (shown by {4}).

Be very careful that you do not include any white space on either side of the pipe character. If you do include white space, then validation will likely fail because you are telling the schema processor to expect a literal space character as part of the value of the zip code. Including a space character inadvertently can also cause problems if you specify a numeric type such as xsd:integer, because the space character is not permitted.

U.K. Postal Code Example

Postal codes in the United Kingdom have a more complex structure than U.S. zip codes. U.K. postal codes have a mixture of digits and characters, and at least as written by humans also include a space character to separate the first group of digits and characters and numbers from a second group of characters and numbers.

```
<?xml version='1.0'?>
<xsd:schema xmlns:xsd="http://www.w3.org/2001/XMLSchema">

<xsd:element name="USBillingInfo">
 <xsd:complexType>
  <xsd:sequence>
   <xsd:element name="Customer" type="xsd:string"/>
   <xsd:element name="Address" type="USAddressType"/>
  </xsd:sequence>
 </xsd:complexType>
</xsd:element>

<xsd:complexType name="USAddressType">
 <xsd:sequence>
  <xsd:element name="Street1" type="xsd:string"/>
  <xsd:element name="Street2" type="xsd:string"/>
  <xsd:element name="City" type="xsd:string"/>
  <xsd:element name="State" type="xsd:string"/>
  <xsd:element name="ZipCode" type="USZipCodeType"/>
  <xsd:element name="Country" type="xsd:string" minOccurs="0"
maxOccurs="1"/>
 </xsd:sequence>
</xsd:complexType>

<xsd:simpleType name="USZipCodeType">
 <xsd:restriction base="xsd:string">
  <xsd:pattern value="\d{5}|\d{5}-\d{4}"/>
 </xsd:restriction>
</xsd:simpleType>

</xsd:schema>
```

Listing 5.18 An XSD Schema allowing standard and extended zip code formats (USBillingInfo02.xsd).

A U.K. postal code can take forms such as EC1W 8DD or AB33 9UV. So, our <xsd:pattern> element must have flexibility built in to allow for the considerable variations that exist. There are other variants that we won't cover in our example.

The instance document for the U.K. postal code example is shown in Listing 5.19.

An XSD schema to describe such an instance document is shown in Listing 5.20.

The final simple type definition for the UKPostalCodeType type includes the pattern for U.K. postal codes. The regular expression is a little more complex than those you have seen so far. The part [A-Z]{2} means that the U.K.

```
<?xml version='1.0'?>
<UKBillingInfo>
 <Customer>Peter Pan Products</Customer>
 <Address>
 <Street1>1234 Regent Street</Street1>
 <Street2></Street2>
 <City>London</City>
 <County></County>
 <PostalCode>WC1E 8XX</PostalCode>
 <Country>England</Country>
 </Address>
</UKBillingInfo>
```

Listing 5.19 Billing information in XML for a U.K. customer (UKBillingInfo.xml).

postal code begins with two upper-case characters from A to Z. As mentioned earlier, if you wished to also allow lower-case characters, you would use the pattern [A-Za-z]{2} to express that. This pattern is followed by one or two numeric digits. The \d indicates the requirements for numeric digits, and the {1,2} indicates that either one or two digits are acceptable. The digit before the comma within the curly braces indicates the minimum number of digits, and the digit following the comma indicates the maximum permitted number of digits. Similarly [A-Z]{0,1} indicates an optional upper case character, followed by a literal space character. Finally, we have one numeric digit followed by two upper-case letters.

XML Schema regular expressions provide very powerful techniques to precisely define allowed text content. In fact, it can be used as an alternate technique to define enumerations by simply using the | symbol. Thus, if we wanted to allow the sizes Small, Medium, and Large as the only sizes allowed for a clothing catalog, we could do so by using a simple type similar to the following:

```
<xsd:simpleType name="SizeType">
 <xsd:restriction base="xsd:string">
  <xsd:pattern value="Small|Medium|Large"/>
 </xsd:restriction>
</xsd:simpleType>
```

Again, in such situations you must be careful to avoid including a space character within the pattern. If you inadvertently put a space character, then (for example) "Medium" will not be accepted if the option within the <xsd:pattern> element indicates that only " Medium" (beginning with a space character) is acceptable as a pattern.

```
<?xml version='1.0'?>
<xsd:schema xmlns:xsd="http://www.w3.org/2001/XMLSchema">

<xsd:element name="UKBillingInfo">
 <xsd:complexType>
  <xsd:sequence>
   <xsd:element name="Customer" type="xsd:string"/>
   <xsd:element name="Address" type="UKAddressType"/>
  </xsd:sequence>
 </xsd:complexType>
</xsd:element>

<xsd:complexType name="UKAddressType">
 <xsd:sequence>
  <xsd:element name="Street1" type="xsd:string"/>
  <xsd:element name="Street2" type="xsd:string" minOccurs="0"
maxOccurs="1"/>
  <xsd:element name="City" type="xsd:string"/>
  <xsd:element name="County" type="xsd:string" minOccurs="0"
maxOccurs="1"/>
  <xsd:element name="PostalCode" type="UKPostalCodeType"/>
  <xsd:element name="Country" type="xsd:string" minOccurs="0"
maxOccurs="1"/>
 </xsd:sequence>
</xsd:complexType>

<xsd:simpleType name="UKPostalCodeType">
 <xsd:restriction base="xsd:string">
  <xsd:pattern value="[A-Z]{2}\d{1,2}[A-Z]{0,1} \d{1}[A-Z]{2}"/>
 </xsd:restriction>
</xsd:simpleType>

</xsd:schema>
```

Listing 5.20 An XSD schema to describe U.K. billing information (UKBillingInfo.xsd).

XSD Schema also provides a facet designed specifically to create enumerated types.

The Enumeration Element

The enumeration facet constrains a simple type to a set of defined values. The permitted values must each be listed within the XSD schema. For lengthy lists of permitted values, creating the schema can, at times, become a little tedious.

Using enumerations can often be very useful, however. First, let's look at a very simple example.

Simple Enumeration Example

For example, suppose that you were conducting an XML-based online survey and part of your instance document looked like the following:

```
<Gender>Male
</Gender>
```

Then, you could constrain the permitted responses by using the following code:

```
<xsd:simpleType name="Gender">
  <xsd:restriction base="xsd:string">
    <xsd:enumeration value="Male"/>
    <xsd:enumeration value="Female"/>
  </xsd:restriction>
</xsd:simpleType>
```

Each of the enumerated values must have its own <xsd:enumeration> element nested within an <xsd:restriction> element.

An alternative approach to produce such a simple enumeration is a pattern facet of the following pattern:

```
<xsd:pattern value="Male|Female"/>
```

If we wanted to recreate the size example shown earlier when using <xsd:-pattern> by using the enumeration facet, we could do so using code like the following:

```
<xsd:simpleType name="ClothingSizeType">
  <xsd:restriction base="xsd:string">
    <xsd:enumeration value="Small"/>
    <xsd:enumeration value="Medium"/>
    <xsd:enumeration value="Large"/>
  </xsd:restriction>
</xsd:simpleType>
```

The <xsd:pattern> approach is a little more succinct, but the <xsd:enumeration> approach is more readable at the expense of slightly longer code.

U.S. States Example

The *United States Postal Service* (USPS) has a standard abbreviation for each of the 50 states of the United States, as well as equivalent abbreviations for some military "states." In this example, we will focus only on the 50 states, but if you want the full USPS list, visit www.usps.gov/ncsc/lookups/usps_abbreviations.html#states.

As our instance document, we will use the addresses of some well-known corporations, as shown in Listing 5.21.

The schema shown in Listing 5.22 provides an enumeration of all 50 U.S. states (plus the District of Columbia) and also checks that zip codes conform

```
<?xml version='1.0'?>
<USAddresses>
 <Address>
  <Company>John Wiley &amp; Son</Company>
  <Street>605 Third Avenue</Street>
  <City>New York</City>
  <State>NY</State>
  <ZipCode>10158-0012</ZipCode>
 </Address>
 <Address>
  <Company>Sun Microsystems Inc</Company>
  <Street>901 San Antonio Road</Street>
  <City>Palo Alto</City>
  <State>CA</State>
  <ZipCode>94303-4900</ZipCode>
 </Address>
 <Address>
  <Company>Microsoft Corporation</Company>
  <Street>1 Microsoft Way</Street>
  <City>Redmond</City>
  <State>WA</State>
  <ZipCode>98052-8300</ZipCode>
 </Address>
 <Address>
  <Company>International Business Machines Corporation</Company>
  <Street>1 New Orchard Road</Street>
  <City>Armonk</City>
  <State>NY</State>
  <ZipCode>10504-1783</ZipCode>
 </Address>
</USAddresses>
```

Listing 5.21 Addresses in the 50 U.S. states (USAddresses.xml).

```
<?xml version='1.0'?>
<xsd:schema xmlns:xsd="http://www.w3.org/2001/XMLSchema">
<xsd:element name="USAddresses">
<xsd:complexType>
<xsd:sequence>
<xsd:element name="Address" type="USAddressType" minOccurs="1"
maxOccurs="unbounded"/>
</xsd:sequence>
</xsd:complexType>
</xsd:element>

<xsd:complexType name="USAddressType">
<xsd:sequence>
<xsd:element name="Company" type="xsd:string"/>
<xsd:element name="Street" type="xsd:string"/>
<xsd:element name="City" type="xsd:string"/>
<xsd:element name="State" type="USStateType"/>
<xsd:element name="ZipCode" type="USZipCodeType"/>
</xsd:sequence>
</xsd:complexType>

<xsd:simpleType name="USStateType">
<xsd:restriction base="xsd:string">
<xsd:enumeration value="AK"/>
<xsd:enumeration value="AL"/>
<xsd:enumeration value="AR"/>
<xsd:enumeration value="AZ"/>
<xsd:enumeration value="CA"/>
<xsd:enumeration value="CO"/>
<xsd:enumeration value="CT"/>
<xsd:enumeration value="DC"/>
<xsd:enumeration value="DE"/>
<xsd:enumeration value="FL"/>
<xsd:enumeration value="GA"/>
<xsd:enumeration value="HI"/>
<xsd:enumeration value="IA"/>
<xsd:enumeration value="ID"/>
<xsd:enumeration value="IL"/>
<xsd:enumeration value="IN"/>
<xsd:enumeration value="KS"/>
<xsd:enumeration value="KY"/>
<xsd:enumeration value="LA"/>
<xsd:enumeration value="MA"/>
<xsd:enumeration value="MD"/>
<xsd:enumeration value="ME"/>
<xsd:enumeration value="MI"/>
```

Listing 5.22 Enumeration of all 50 U.S. states that also checks for conformity of zip+4 format (USAddresses.xsd).

```
<xsd:enumeration value="MN"/>
<xsd:enumeration value="MO"/>
<xsd:enumeration value="MS"/>
<xsd:enumeration value="MT"/>
<xsd:enumeration value="NC"/>
<xsd:enumeration value="ND"/>
<xsd:enumeration value="NE"/>
<xsd:enumeration value="NH"/>
<xsd:enumeration value="NJ"/>
<xsd:enumeration value="NM"/>
<xsd:enumeration value="NV"/>
<xsd:enumeration value="NY"/>
<xsd:enumeration value="OH"/>
<xsd:enumeration value="OK"/>
<xsd:enumeration value="OR"/>
<xsd:enumeration value="PA"/>
<xsd:enumeration value="RI"/>
<xsd:enumeration value="SC"/>
<xsd:enumeration value="SD"/>
<xsd:enumeration value="TN"/>
<xsd:enumeration value="TX"/>
<xsd:enumeration value="UT"/>
<xsd:enumeration value="VA"/>
<xsd:enumeration value="VT"/>
<xsd:enumeration value="WA"/>
<xsd:enumeration value="WI"/>
<xsd:enumeration value="WV"/>
<xsd:enumeration value="WY"/>
</xsd:restriction>
</xsd:simpleType>

<xsd:simpleType name="USZipCodeType">
<xsd:restriction base="xsd:string">
<xsd:pattern value="\d{5}-\d{4}"/>
</xsd:restriction>
</xsd:simpleType>

</xsd:schema>
```

Listing 5.22 Enumeration of all 50 U.S. states that also checks for conformity of zip+4 format (USAddresses.xsd). (Continued)

to the zip+4 format. Refer back to Listing 5.18 if you want to add non-extended zip codes.

The type definition for the USStateType simple type is a restriction on the permitted type xsd:string. Therefore, an <xsd:restriction> element is used to express that. The desired restriction is expressed as a long list of <xsd:enumeration> elements.

The whiteSpace Element

White space in XML jargon is indicated by space (#x20), tab (#x09), line feed (#x0A), and carriage return (#x0D) characters.

The <xsd:whiteSpace> element is the XML representation of the whiteSpace facet.

The whiteSpace facet can take one of three values:

- Preserve
- Replace
- Collapse

In order to understand the role of the whitespace facet, it is necessary to make use of the concept of *normalized value*. The XSD Schema Recommendation defines the normalized value as follows: "The *normalized value* of an element or attribute information item is an initial value whose white space, if any, has been normalized according to the value of the whitespace facet of the simple type definition used in its validation."

When the whiteSpace facet has the value of "preserve," then no normalization takes place. The normalized value is identical to the value of an attribute information item or element information item. No changes are made in whitespace.

When the whiteSpace facet has the value of "replace," then all tabs (#x09), line feed (#x0A), and carriage return (#x0D) characters are replaced by space characters (#x20).

When the whiteSpace facet has the value of "collapse," then the changes just described for "replace" are carried out, any leading or trailing space characters are removed, and any sequences of space characters within the string are converted to a single-space character.

The definition for the xsd:token type in the XSD Schema schema provides an example of the use of the collapse value for the whiteSpace facet:

```
<xsd:simpleType name='xsd:token'>
 <xsd:restriction base='xsd:normalizedString'>
  <xsd:whiteSpace value='collapse'/>
 </xsd:restriction>
</xsd:simpleType>
```

Any excess white space is collapsed as indicated by the value attribute on the <xsd:whiteSpace> element.

Summary

This chapter has examined several of the XSD Schema constraining facets. The length, maxLength, and minLength facets constrain the permitted length of content expressed in units of length that vary according to the datatype being constrained. The pattern facet enables powerful and flexible control over the content of elements or attribute by using regular expressions. The enumeration facet enables permitted values to be listed explicitly. The whiteSpace facet is used to control how white space is treated.

In Chapter 6, we will go on to examine the remainder of XSD Schema's constraining facets.

CHAPTER

6

More about Data Facets

In this chapter, we will look at the remaining constraining facets that we did not explore in Chapter 5, "Data Facets."

XSD Schema provides four facets that enable us to restrict the allowed range of values for datatypes. Two of those facets, the <xsd:maxExclusive> element and the <xsd:maxInclusive> element, enable us to constrain the maximum allowed value. The other two, the <xsd:minExclusive> and <xsd:minInclusive> elements, enable us to constrain the minimum permitted value.

Much of this chapter will relate to controlling the maximum and minimum values allowed in types that have numerical, date, or time values. Such ordered, scalar values can be constrained by using the facets just mentioned. Unfortunately, xsd:string types do not allow the use of these facets. The pattern facet can be used to achieve a similar effect on xsd:string types as maxExclusive, minExclusive, maxInclusive, or MinInclusive, however, as we will show later.

There are logical limitations to how these four facets can be used. It makes no sense, for example, to specify both a maxExclusive and maxInclusive facet in the same context. These facets can be used singly or can be used in pairs where one member of the pair defines the minimum permitted value (minExclusive or minInclusive facet) and the other member of the pair defines the maximum permitted value (maxExclusive or maxInclusive) facet.

These four facets constrain the value space so that a minimum or maximum value of the relevant data type is defined as being either included or excluded. The examples that follow will show these facets in use with a variety of datatypes.

First, let's look at the two facets that can be used to define the maximum permitted value of an element in the instance document.

The maxExclusive Element

The maxExclusive facet enables us to specify a maximum value, with the specified maximum value excluded from among the allowed values.

Suppose that we wanted to constrain the values for mean daily temperature allowed in a weather data store, as shown in Listing 6.1, in order to ensure that any data entered is within realistic limits.

```
<?xml version='1.0'?>
<TemperatureRecord>
 <Record>
  <Date>2001-10-28</Date>
  <Location>London</Location>
  <MeanTemp>58</MeanTemp>
  <Units>Fahrenheit</Units>
 </Record>
 <Record>
  <Date>2001-10-29</Date>
  <Location>London</Location>
  <MeanTemp>54</MeanTemp>
  <Units>Fahrenheit</Units>
 </Record>
 <Record>
  <Date>2001-10-30</Date>
  <Location>London</Location>
  <MeanTemp>53</MeanTemp>
  <Units>Fahrenheit</Units>
 </Record>
 <Record>
  <Date>2001-10-31</Date>
  <Location>London</Location>
  <MeanTemp>46</MeanTemp>
  <Units>Fahrenheit</Units>
  </Record>
</TemperatureRecord>
```

Listing 6.1 A database of mean daily temperature (TemperatureRecord.xml).

If we assumed that the data store was intended for storing mean temperatures from locations worldwide, a realistic maximum allowed temperature for mean daily temperature might be 109 degrees Fahrenheit. A schema to constrain, using the maxExclusive facet, the maximum value of the <MeanTemp> element is shown in Listing 6.2.

The desired maximum permitted value was 109 degrees. The maxExclusive facet shown in the definition of the MeanTempType simple type indicates that the value of 110 is disallowed but that all integer values below 110 are permitted.

We can use the maxExclusive facet on datatypes other than numeric ones. For example, if we had a data store for daily sales amounts for Quarter 1 of

```
<?xml version="1.0" encoding="UTF-8"?>
<xsd:schema xmlns:xsd="http://www.w3.org/2001/XMLSchema" >

<xsd:element name="TemperatureRecord">
 <xsd:complexType>
  <xsd:sequence>
   <xsd:element ref="Record" minOccurs="1" maxOccurs="unbounded"/>
  </xsd:sequence>
 </xsd:complexType>
</xsd:element>

<xsd:element name="Record">
 <xsd:complexType>
  <xsd:sequence>
   <xsd:element name="Date" type="xsd:date"/>
   <xsd:element name="Location" type="xsd:string"/>
   <xsd:element name="MeanTemp" type="MeanTempType"/>
   <xsd:element name="Units" type="xsd:string"/>
  </xsd:sequence>
 </xsd:complexType>
</xsd:element>

<xsd:complexType name="MeanTempType">
 <xsd:simpleContent>
   <xsd:restriction base="xsd:integer">
    <xsd:maxExclusive value="110"/>
   </xsd:restriction>
 </xsd:simpleContent>
</xsd:complexType>

</xsd:schema>
```

Listing 6.2 A schema to constrain maximum mean daily temperature (TemperatureRecord.xsd).

```
<?xml version='1.0'?>
<!-- All sales amounts expressed as $0005-->
<SalesQ12002>
<DailyReport>
 <Date>2002-03-29</Date>
 <Location>New York</Location>
 <SalesAmount>2345.00</SalesAmount>
</DailyReport>
<DailyReport>
 <Date>2002-03-30</Date>
 <Location>New York</Location>
 <SalesAmount>12345.55</SalesAmount>
</DailyReport>
<DailyReport>
 <Date>2002-03-31</Date>
 <Location>New York</Location>
 <SalesAmount>3456.12</SalesAmount>
</DailyReport>
<DailyReport>
 <Date>2002-03-31</Date>
 <Location>Tokyo</Location>
 <SalesAmount>4567.10</SalesAmount>
</DailyReport>
</SalesQ12002>
```

Listing 6.3 A record of daily sales in Q1 2002 (SalesQ12002.xml).

2002, similar to that in Listing 6.3, we can use the maxExclusive facet to constrain the allowed values for the date.

Because the desired period is Quarter 1 of 2002, then the latest allowable value for the content of the <Date> element is 2002-03-31, or March 31, 2002. A schema to enforce that constraint is shown in Listing 6.4.

The definition of the Q12002Type simple type is where we have applied the maxExclusive facet to an xsd:date type. You might recall that the format for date is CCYY-MM-DD (century, year, month, day). Thus, we want to exclude the date April 1, 2002 from the permitted values and convey that by the syntax 2002-04-01 in the value attribute of the <xsd:maxExclusive> element.

Listing 6.3 validates against the schema in Listing 6.4. If you edit Listing 6.3 to include a date of 2002-04-01 or later, an error will be reported during validation.

The maxExclusive facet can also be used with the xsd:duration or xsd:gYear types. If, for example, we had a collection of annual company reports for the 20th century (Listing 6.5), then we could use the maxExclusive facet to ensure that the year of a report was no higher than 1999 (assuming that the 21st century started in the year 2000).

```
<?xml version="1.0" encoding="UTF-8"?>
<xsd:schema xmlns:xsd="http://www.w3.org/2001/XMLSchema" >

<xsd:element name="SalesQ12002">
 <xsd:complexType>
  <xsd:sequence>
   <xsd:element name="DailyReport" type="DailyReportType"
maxOccurs="unbounded" />
  </xsd:sequence>
 </xsd:complexType>
</xsd:element>

<xsd:complexType name="DailyReportType">
 <xsd:sequence>
  <xsd:element name="Date" type="Q12002Type"/>
  <xsd:element name="Location" type="xsd:string"/>
  <xsd:element name="SalesAmount" type="xsd:decimal"/>
 </xsd:sequence>
</xsd:complexType>

<xsd:simpleType name="Q12002Type">
 <xsd:restriction base="xsd:date">
  <xsd:maxExclusive value="2002-04-01"/>
 </xsd:restriction>
</xsd:simpleType>

</xsd:schema>
```

Listing 6.4 A schema using the maxExclusive facet on a date type (SalesQ12002.xsd).

```
<?xml version='1.0'?>
<AnnualReports>
<AnnualReport>
 <Year>1999</Year>
 <Subsidiary>Wonder Fizzy Drink Company</Subsidiary>
 <Summary>A year with fizz in our sales.</Summary>
</AnnualReport>
<AnnualReport>
 <Year>1997</Year>
 <Subsidiary>Widget Manufacturing Company</Subsidiary>
 <Summary>Widget sales up 11% on year.</Summary>
</AnnualReport>
<AnnualReport>
 <Year>1994</Year>
```

Listing 6.5 A data store of annual reports from the twentieth century (AnnualReports.xml).

```
 <Subsidiary>CPU Computing Books</Subsidiary>
 <Summary>DOS and OS/2 book sales collapse.</Summary>
</AnnualReport>
</AnnualReports>
```

Listing 6.5 A data store of annual reports from the twentieth century (AnnualReports.xml).

```
<?xml version="1.0" encoding="UTF-8"?>
<xsd:schema xmlns:xsd="http://www.w3.org/2001/XMLSchema" >

<xsd:element name="AnnualReports">
 <xsd:complexType>
  <xsd:sequence>
   <xsd:element name="AnnualReport" maxOccurs="unbounded"
type="AnnualReportType"/>
  </xsd:sequence>
 </xsd:complexType>
</xsd:element>

<xsd:complexType name="AnnualReportType">
 <xsd:sequence>
  <xsd:element name="Year" type="TwentiethCenturyType"/>
  <xsd:element name="Subsidiary" type="xsd:string"/>
  <xsd:element name="Summary" type="xsd:string"/>
 </xsd:sequence>
</xsd:complexType>

<xsd:simpleType name="TwentiethCenturyType">
 <xsd:restriction base="xsd:gYear">
  <xsd:maxExclusive value="2000"/>
 </xsd:restriction>
</xsd:simpleType>

</xsd:schema>
```

Listing 6.6 A schema constraining the <Year> to the 20th century by using <xsd:maxExclusive> (AnnualReports.xsd).

A schema to constrain the maximum permitted value for content in the <Year> element is shown in Listing 6.6.

The definition of the TwentiethCenturyType simple type toward the end of the schema uses the base type xsd:gYear. We use the <xsd:exclusive> element to specify that the year 2000 is too high for inclusion as a permitted value.

NOTE **The name of an XML Schema type must correspond to XML 1.0 naming rules. Using a number as the initial character of a type name—if, for example, you attempt to create a 20thCenturyType simple type—will cause an error.**

The maxInclusive Element

The maxInclusive facet is very similar in syntax and meaning to the maxExclusive facet, with the important difference that the maxInclusive facet specifies the maximum permitted value rather than the lowest excluded value (which is what maxExclusive does).

If we wanted to create an XML-based data store of examination results for Quarter 4 of 2001, we could ensure that nobody scores above a perfect mark (100 percent) by using the maxInclusive facet. Listing 6.7 shows a simple data store of exam marks.

Listing 6.8 shows an XSD schema that constrains the maximum mark to 100 and the latest date permitted to 2001-12-31 to make sure that dates no later than December 31, 2001 are stored in this particular data store.

The definitions of the ValidDateType and ValidMarkType simple types use the maxInclusive facet to constrain the maximum permitted value. The definition of the ValidMarkType contains an implicit minimum value for a valid mark of zero because the type is xsd:nonNegativeInteger.

```
<?xml version='1.0'?>
<ExamMarks>
<Person>
 <Name>John Doe</Name>
 <Course>SVG 101</Course>
 <DateOfExam>2001-12-31</DateOfExam>
 <Mark>91</Mark>
</Person>
<Person>
 <Name>Paul Cohen</Name>
 <Course>XML Schema 101</Course>
 <DateOfExam>2001-10-08</DateOfExam>
 <Mark>84</Mark>
</Person>
</ExamMarks>
```

Listing 6.7 A data store of examination marks in Quarter 4 of 2001 in XML (ExamMarks.xml).

```
<?xml version="1.0" encoding="UTF-8"?>
<xsd:schema xmlns:xsd="http://www.w3.org/2001/XMLSchema" >

<xsd:element name="ExamMarks">
 <xsd:complexType>
  <xsd:sequence>
   <xsd:element name="Person" type="PersonType"
maxOccurs="unbounded"/>
  </xsd:sequence>
 </xsd:complexType>
</xsd:element>

<xsd:complexType name="PersonType">
 <xsd:sequence>
  <xsd:element name="Name" type="xsd:string"/>
  <xsd:element name="Course" type="ValidCourseType"/>
  <xsd:element name="DateOfExam" type="ValidDateType"/>
  <xsd:element name="Mark" type="ValidMarkType"/>
 </xsd:sequence>
</xsd:complexType>

<xsd:simpleType name="ValidCourseType">
 <xsd:restriction base="xsd:string">
  <xsd:pattern value="[A-Za-z ]{3,15}[0-9]{3}"/>
 </xsd:restriction>
</xsd:simpleType>

<xsd:simpleType name="ValidDateType">
 <xsd:restriction base="xsd:date">
  <xsd:maxInclusive value="2001-12-31"/>
 </xsd:restriction>
</xsd:simpleType>

<xsd:simpleType name="ValidMarkType">
 <xsd:restriction base="xsd:nonNegativeInteger">
  <xsd:maxInclusive value="100"/>
 </xsd:restriction>
</xsd:simpleType>

</xsd:schema>
```

Listing 6.8 A schema using the maxInclusive facet on xsd:nonNegativeInteger and xsd:date types (ExamMarks.xsd).

Notice, too, the <xsd:pattern> element where we use a regular expression to constrain the allowed names of courses that are available. The initial part of the regular expression [A-Za-z] (note the space character immediately before the closing square bracket) specifies that any alphabetic character, upper or lower case, and the space character can be used in any combination. The {3,15} indicates that a minimum of three and a maximum of 15 of those characters can be used.

Having looked at the two facets that can be used to define the maximum permitted value of an element in an XML instance document, let's now move on and look at the minExclusive and minInclusive facets. Both of these facets can be used to define the minimum permitted value of an element in the instance document.

The minExclusive Element

The <xsd:minExclusive> element enables us to define the lowest value allowed for an element in an instance document by stating the highest value that is *not* permitted.

Suppose that we had set up a new company and wanted to create an automatically incremented number for the number of invoices sent to customers. We would not want the absolute newness of the company to be evident to our first customers, and we might want to start numbering invoices at 3001.

If our instance document was similar to that in Listing 6.9, we could use an XSD schema similar to that shown in Listing 6.10 to ensure that no invoice can be numbered below 3001.

```
<?xml version='1.0'?>
<Invoice>
<InvoiceNumber>3303</InvoiceNumber>
<BillingAddress>
 <Name>K9 Services</Name>
 <FAO>Ian Barking</FAO>
 <Street1>123 Kennel Street</Street1>
 <Street2></Street2>
 <City>Dachshund City</City>
 <ZipCode>98765-4321</ZipCode>
 <State>OK</State>
</BillingAddress>
<ShippingAddress>
 <Name>K9 Services</Name>
 <FAO>Retail Dept.</FAO>
 <Street1>888 Dogbowl Street</Street1>
 <Street2></Street2>
 <City>Pet City</City>
 <ZipCode>98765-1234</ZipCode>
 <State>OK</State>
```

continues

Listing 6.9 An invoice expressed in XML (Invoice.xml).

```
</ShippingAddress>
<BilledItems>
 <Item>
  <ItemDescription>Studded Collar</ItemDescription>
  <ItemCode>K9-1234</ItemCode>
  <ItemQuantity>10</ItemQuantity>
  <ItemPrice>11.95</ItemPrice>
 </Item>
 <Item>
  <ItemDescription>K9 Pet Coat</ItemDescription>
  <ItemCode>K9-2345</ItemCode>
  <ItemQuantity>5</ItemQuantity>
  <ItemPrice>25.00</ItemPrice>
 </Item>
</BilledItems>
</Invoice>
```

Listing 6.9 An invoice expressed in XML (Invoice.xml). (Continued)

Listing 6.10 uses the minExclusive facet to ensure that the content of the <InvoiceNumber> element is at least 3001. It also includes further examples of the minExclusive facet to impact the minimum quantity to be ordered and the minimum item price. Additionally, there is a pattern facet to constrain the content of the <ItemCode> element.

```
<?xml version="1.0" encoding="UTF-8"?>
<xsd:schema xmlns:xsd="http://www.w3.org/2001/XMLSchema" >

<xsd:element name="Invoice">
 <xsd:complexType>
  <xsd:sequence>
   <xsd:element name="InvoiceNumber" type="InvoiceNumberType"/>
   <xsd:element name="BillingAddress" type="AddressType"/>
   <xsd:element name="ShippingAddress" type="AddressType"/>
   <xsd:element name="BilledItems" type="ItemsType"/>
  </xsd:sequence>
 </xsd:complexType>
</xsd:element>

<xsd:simpleType name="InvoiceNumberType">
 <xsd:restriction base="xsd:positiveInteger">
  <xsd:minExclusive value="3000"/>
 </xsd:restriction>
</xsd:simpleType>
```

Listing 6.10 A schema using the minExclusive facet to constrain the content of three elements (Invoice.xsd).

```
<xsd:complexType name="AddressType">
 <xsd:sequence>
  <xsd:element name="Name" type="xsd:string"/>
  <xsd:element name="FAO" type="xsd:string"/>
  <xsd:element name="Street1" type="xsd:string"/>
  <xsd:element name="Street2" type="xsd:string"/>
  <xsd:element name="City" type="xsd:string"/>
  <xsd:element name="ZipCode" type="USZipCodeType"/>
  <xsd:element name="State" type="xsd:string"/>
 </xsd:sequence>
</xsd:complexType>

<xsd:simpleType name="USZipCodeType">
 <xsd:restriction base="xsd:string">
  <xsd:pattern value="\d{5}|\d{5}-\d{4}"/>
 </xsd:restriction>
</xsd:simpleType>

<xsd:complexType name="ItemsType">
 <xsd:sequence>
  <xsd:element name="Item" type="ItemType" minOccurs="1"
maxOccurs="unbounded"/>
 </xsd:sequence>
</xsd:complexType>
<xsd:complexType name="ItemType">
 <xsd:sequence>
  <xsd:element name="ItemDescription" type="xsd:string"/>
  <xsd:element name="ItemCode" type="ItemCodeType"/>
  <xsd:element name="ItemQuantity" type="ItemQuantityType"/>
  <xsd:element name="ItemPrice" type="ItemPriceType"/>
 </xsd:sequence>
</xsd:complexType>

<xsd:simpleType name="ItemCodeType">
 <xsd:restriction base="xsd:string">
  <xsd:pattern value="K9-[0-9]{4}"/>
 </xsd:restriction>
</xsd:simpleType>

<xsd:simpleType name="ItemQuantityType">
 <xsd:restriction base="xsd:nonNegativeInteger">
  <xsd:minExclusive value="0" />
  <xsd:maxExclusive value="1000" />
 </xsd:restriction>
</xsd:simpleType>
```

continues

Listing 6.10 A schema using the minExclusive facet to constrain the content of three elements (Invoice.xsd).

```
<xsd:simpleType name="ItemPriceType">
 <xsd:restriction base="xsd:decimal">
  <xsd:minExclusive value="0.99" />
  <xsd:maxExclusive value="500.00" />
 </xsd:restriction>
</xsd:simpleType>

</xsd:schema>
```

Listing 6.10 A schema using the minExclusive facet to constrain the content of three elements (Invoice.xsd). (Continued)

You can see the use of the minExclusive facet in the definition of the InvoiceNumberType, ItemQuantityType, and ItemPriceType simple types. In the InvoiceNumberType, the highest value not allowed is 3000:

```
<xsd:minExclusive value="3000"/>
```

In the ItemQuantityType and ItemPriceType type definitions, the minExclusive facet is combined with use of the maxExclusive facet for the same type definition, providing an allowed range within which the value of the type is permitted. Of course, the appropriate upper and lower bounds of a value would be determined by the content in which it is being used.

We similarly could use the minExclusive and maxExclusive facets in combination to define the allowed dates for the Quarter 1 2002 sales reports that we saw earlier in Listing 6.4:

```
<xsd:simpleType name="Q12002Type">
 <xsd:restriction base="xsd:date">
  <xsd:maxExclusive value="2002-04-01"/>
  <xsd:minExclusive value="2001-12-31"/>
 </xsd:restriction>
</xsd:simpleType>
```

The minInclusive Element

The <xsd:minInclusive> element is very similar to the <xsd:minExclusive> element. The important difference is that the value specified in the value attribute of the <xsd:minInclusive> element is an allowed value, whereas the value specified in the value attribute of the <xsd:minExclusive> is the highest disallowed value.

We might use the minInclusive facet to define the earliest allowed date for a report of customer satisfaction within a particular time period. Listing 6.11 shows a possible structure for such a report.

A schema using the minInclusive facet is shown in Listing 6.12. It also includes the use of the maxInclusive facet as well as the pattern and enumeration facets.

The minInclusive and maxInclusive facets are used in the definition of the Q12003DateType simple type:

```
<xsd:simpleType name="Q12003DateType">
 <xsd:restriction base="xsd:date">
  <xsd:minInclusive value="2003-01-01"/>
  <xsd:maxInclusive value="2003-03-31"/>
 </xsd:restriction>
</xsd:simpleType>
```

```
<?xml version='1.0'?>
<CustReport Period="Q12003">
<Report>
 <Product>XML Training</Product>
 <Date>2003-01-28</Date>
 <CustID>DD-88D</CustID>
 <Summary>Trainer turned up late and seemed ill-prepared.</Summary>
 <ActionTaken>Discussed with employee</ActionTaken>
</Report>
<Report>
 <Product>SVG Consultancy</Product>
 <Date>2003-02-14</Date>
 <CustID>RD-93A</CustID>
 <Summary>Delighted with quality of solution provided to agreed time
lines.</Summary>
 <ActionTaken>Discussed with employee</ActionTaken>
</Report>
<Report>
 <Product>XML Schema Consultancy</Product>
 <Date>2003-03-08</Date>
 <CustID>IB-37M</CustID>
 <Summary>Customer needs met. High satisfaction level.</Summary>
 <ActionTaken>Employee bonus</ActionTaken>
</Report>
</CustReport>
```

Listing 6.11 A customer satisfaction report for Q1 2003 in XML (CustReportQ12003.xml).

```
<?xml version="1.0" encoding="UTF-8"?>
<xsd:schema xmlns:xsd="http://www.w3.org/2001/XMLSchema" >

<xsd:element name="CustReport">
 <xsd:complexType>
  <xsd:sequence>
   <xsd:element name="Report" type="ReportType"
maxOccurs="unbounded"/>
  </xsd:sequence>
  <xsd:attribute name="Period" type="PeriodType"/>
 </xsd:complexType>
</xsd:element>

<xsd:simpleType name="PeriodType">
 <xsd:restriction base="xsd:string">
  <xsd:pattern value="Q[1-4]{1}20[0-9]{2}"/>
 </xsd:restriction>
</xsd:simpleType>

<xsd:complexType name="ReportType">
 <xsd:sequence>
  <xsd:element name="Product" type="xsd:string"/>
  <xsd:element name="Date" type="Q12003DateType"/>
  <xsd:element name="CustID" type="CustIDType"/>
  <xsd:element name="Summary" type="xsd:string"/>
  <xsd:element name="ActionTaken" type="ActionTakenType"
maxOccurs="3"/>
 </xsd:sequence>
</xsd:complexType>

<xsd:simpleType name="Q12003DateType">
 <xsd:restriction base="xsd:date">
  <xsd:minInclusive value="2003-01-01"/>
  <xsd:maxInclusive value="2003-03-31"/>
 </xsd:restriction>
</xsd:simpleType>

<xsd:simpleType name="CustIDType">
 <xsd:restriction base="xsd:string">
  <xsd:pattern value="[A-Z]{2}-\d{2}[A-Z]{1}"/>
 </xsd:restriction>
</xsd:simpleType>

<xsd:simpleType name="ActionTakenType">
 <xsd:restriction base="xsd:string">
  <xsd:enumeration value="None"/>
```

Listing 6.12 A schema using minInclusive to constrain allowed dates (CustRportQ12003.xsd).

```
    <\<>xsd:enumeration value="Discussed with employee"/<\>>
    <\<>xsd:enumeration value="Discussed with line manager"/<\>>
    <\<>xsd:enumeration value="Employee bonus"/<\>>
  <\<>/xsd:restriction<\>>
 <\<>/xsd:simpleType<\>>

 <\<>/xsd:schema<\>>
```

Listing 6.12 A schema to constrain using minInclusive to constrain allowed dates (CustReportQ12003.xsd). (Continued)

We also define the PeriodType type using a pattern facet.

```
<xsd:pattern value="Q[1-4]{1}20[0-9]{2}"/>
```

First, we have the literal upper-case alphabetic character "Q" followed by a single digit 1 to 4 inclusive, as specified by [1-4]{1}, followed by the literal digits "20" because we are concerned with 21st century reports. Finally, we have two numeric digits from 0 to 9 inclusive, as indicated by [0-9]{2}.

The paragraphs at the beginning of the chapter indicated that the maxExclusive, maxInclusive, minExclusive, and minInclusive facets cannot be used on xsd:string types. There are situations, however, in which you might want to exercise such control of ranges over string types. For example, if you wanted to split a personnel listing into separate parts for surnames A-G, H-O, and P-Z, the <xsd:pattern> element could be used on xsd:string types to provide control of the upper or lower limits of allowed content comparable to that permitted on other datatypes by using the maxExclusive, maxInclusive, minExclusive, and minInclusive facets.

A possible instance document for surnames A-G is shown in Listing 6.13.

The <xsd:pattern> facet used in Listing 6.14 enables us to achieve the desired range of values in the xsd:string type for surnames beginning with A to G.

The type definition for the AtoGSurnameType enables us to use the pattern facet to constrain permitted values of the initial letter of the surname.

```
<xsd:simpleType name="AtoGSurnameType">
 <xsd:restriction base="xsd:string">
  <xsd:pattern value="[A-G]{1}[a-zA-Z]{1,20}"/>
 </xsd:restriction>
</xsd:simpleType>
```

The initial part of the regular expression, [A-G]{1}, permits only uppercase alphabetic characters from A to G (inclusive) to be the initial letter of a surname. The final part of the regular expression {1,20} allows from one to 20 further alphabetic characters in the allowed surnames.

```
<?xml version='1.0'?>
<Personnel>
<Person>
 <Name>
  <FirstName>George</FirstName>
  <MiddleNames>Walker</MiddleNames>
  <LastName>Bush</LastName>
 </Name>
 <Address>
  <Street>1600 Pennsylvania Avenue</Street>
  <City>Washington</City>
  <PostalCode>12345-6789</PostalCode>
  <HomeEmail>Dubya@bush.gov</HomeEmail>
  <OfficeEmail>GWB@bush.gov</OfficeEmail>
 </Address>
 <CompanyRecord>
  <DateJoined>2001-01-20</DateJoined>
  <DateLeft></DateLeft>
  <HRNumber>GWB1234 5678</HRNumber>
  <Assignment>
   <Department>President's Office</Department>
   <Location>White House</Location>
   <JobTitle>President</JobTitle>
   <DateAssigned>2001-01-20</DateAssigned>
   <DateCompleted></DateCompleted>
   <HRAssessment></HRAssessment>
  </Assignment>
 </CompanyRecord>
</Person>
<!-- Many more person records would go here. -->
</Personnel>
```

Listing 6.13 Personnel records for surnames A-G (PersonnelAtoG.xml).

```
<?xml version="1.0" encoding="UTF-8"?>
<xsd:schema xmlns:xsd="http://www.w3.org/2001/XMLSchema" >

<xsd:element name="Personnel">
 <xsd:complexType>
  <xsd:sequence>
   <xsd:element name="Person" type="PersonType" minOccurs="0"
maxOccurs="unbounded" />
  </xsd:sequence>
 </xsd:complexType>
</xsd:element>
```

Listing 6.14 Using <xsd:pattern> to set limits for xsd:string type (PersonnelAtoG.xsd).

```
<?xml version="1.0" encoding="UTF-8"?>
<xsd:schema xmlns:xsd="http://www.w3.org/2001/XMLSchema" >

<xsd:element name="Personnel">
 <xsd:complexType>
  <xsd:sequence>
   <xsd:element name="Person" type="PersonType" minOccurs="0"
maxOccurs="unbounded" />
  </xsd:sequence>
 </xsd:complexType>
</xsd:element>

<xsd:complexType name="PersonType">
 <xsd:sequence>
  <xsd:element name="Name" type="NameType"/>
  <xsd:element name="Address" type="AddressType"/>
  <xsd:element name="CompanyRecord" type="CompanyRecordType"/>
 </xsd:sequence>
</xsd:complexType>

<xsd:complexType name="NameType">
 <xsd:sequence>
  <xsd:element name="FirstName" type="xsd:string"/>
  <xsd:element name="MiddleNames" type="xsd:string"/>
  <xsd:element name="LastName" type="AtoGSurnameType"/>
 </xsd:sequence>
</xsd:complexType>

<xsd:simpleType name="AtoGSurnameType">
 <xsd:restriction base="xsd:string">
  <xsd:pattern value="[A-G]{1}[a-zA-Z]{1,20}"/>
 </xsd:restriction>
</xsd:simpleType>

<xsd:complexType name="AddressType">
 <xsd:sequence>
  <xsd:element name="Street" type="xsd:string"/>
  <xsd:element name="City" type="xsd:string"/>
  <xsd:element name="PostalCode" type="USZipCodeType"/>
  <xsd:element name="HomeEmail" type="xsd:string"/>
  <xsd:element name="OfficeEmail" type="xsd:string"/>
 </xsd:sequence>
</xsd:complexType>

<xsd:simpleType name="USZipCodeType">
 <xsd:restriction base="xsd:string">
```

continues

Listing 6.14 Using <xsd:pattern> to set limits for xsd:string type (PersonnelAtoG.xsd). (Continued)

```
    <xsd:pattern value="\d{5}|\d{5}-\d{4}"/>
  </xsd:restriction>
</xsd:simpleType>

<xsd:complexType name="CompanyRecordType">
  <xsd:sequence>
    <xsd:element name="DateJoined" type="ValidDateType" />
    <xsd:element name="DateLeft" type="LeftDateType" />
    <xsd:element name="HRNumber" type="xsd:string"/>
    <xsd:element name="Assignment" type="AssignmentType" minOccurs="1"
maxOccurs="unbounded"/>
  </xsd:sequence>
</xsd:complexType>

<xsd:complexType name="AssignmentType">
  <xsd:sequence>
    <xsd:element name="Department" type="xsd:string" />
    <xsd:element name="Location" type="ValidLocationType" />
    <xsd:element name="JobTitle" type="xsd:string"/>
    <xsd:element name="DateAssigned" type="ValidDateType"/>
    <xsd:element name="DateCompleted" type="LeftDateType"/>
    <xsd:element name="HRAssessment" type="xsd:string"/>
  </xsd:sequence>
</xsd:complexType>

<xsd:simpleType name="ValidDateType">
  <xsd:restriction base="xsd:date">
    <xsd:minExclusive value="2000-12-31"/>
    <xsd:maxExclusive value="2005-02-28"/>
  </xsd:restriction>
</xsd:simpleType>

<xsd:simpleType name="LeftDateType">
    <xsd:union>
      <xsd:simpleType>
        <xsd:restriction base="ValidDateType"/>
      </xsd:simpleType>
      <xsd:simpleType>
        <xsd:restriction base="xsd:string">
          <xsd:enumeration value=""/>
        </xsd:restriction>
      </xsd:simpleType>
    </xsd:union>
  </xsd:simpleType>
<xsd:simpleType name="ValidLocationType">
  <xsd:restriction base="xsd:string">
    <xsd:enumeration value="White House"/>
```

Listing 6.14 Using <xsd:pattern> to set limits for xsd:string type (PersonnelAtoG.xsd). (Continued)

```
    <xsd:enumeration value="Camp David"/>
   </xsd:restriction>
  </xsd:simpleType>

  </xsd:schema>
```

Listing 6.14 Using <xsd:pattern> to set limits for xsd:string type (PersonnelAtoG.xsd). (Continued)

The final two facets that we will consider, totalDigits and fractionDigits, are used to constrain the length of xsd:decimal types. They are closely connected. The value of the fractionDigits facet can never legally exceed the value of the corresponding totalDigits facet.

The totalDigits and fractionDigits Facets

The totalDigits facet, not surprisingly, constrains the total number of digits permitted in a value of type xsd:decimal.

Listing 6.15 shows a record of hourly temperature at some location. If we could measure temperature to one decimal place and we knew that the temperature would never exceed 90 degrees or go below 15 degrees, we know that there are two digits before the decimal point and one after (giving a total of three digits). We could thus use the totalDigits facet set to three and the fractionDigits facet set to one.

The schema in Listing 6.16 applies the totalDigits and fractionDigits facets to ensure the desired format for the values contained in <Temp> elements. In addition, the minInclusive and maxInclusive facets ensure that only values in the temperature range deemed realistic can be recorded.

As you can see in the type definition for the TempType type, we can combine several facets within one <xsd:restriction> element. In this case, we define a total of three digits with exactly one digit to follow the decimal point.

```
<?xml version='1.0'?>
<HourlyTemps>
<Temp>34.3</Temp>
<Temp>37.1</Temp>
<Temp>41.6</Temp>
<Temp>48.4</Temp>
</HourlyTemps>
```

Listing 6.15 A record of hourly temperature readings in XML (HourlyTemps.xml).

```
<?xml version="1.0" encoding="UTF-8"?>
<xsd:schema xmlns:xsd="http://www.w3.org/2001/XMLSchema" >

<xsd:element name="HourlyTemps">
 <xsd:complexType>
  <xsd:sequence>
   <xsd:element name="Temp" type="TempType" maxOccurs="unbounded"/>
  </xsd:sequence>
 </xsd:complexType>
</xsd:element>

<xsd:simpleType name="TempType">
 <xsd:restriction base="xsd:decimal">
  <xsd:totalDigits value="3"/>
  <xsd:fractionDigits value="1"/>
  <xsd:minInclusive value="15.0"/>
  <xsd:maxInclusive value="90.0"/>
 </xsd:restriction>
</xsd:simpleType>

</xsd:schema>
```

Listing 6.16 A schema using the totalDigits and fractionDigits facets to ensure desired numeric format (HourlyTemps.xsd).

In addition, we use the minInclusive and maxInclusive facets to define the permitted temperature range. Applying facets together allows us very useful control over permitted values.

Summary

In this chapter, we looked at the remaining constraining facets of XSD Schema. The maxInclusive and maxExclusive facets are used to define the upper allowed limit for the value of an attribute or an element's content. The minInclusive and minExclusive facets define the lower bound of allowed values. We also looked at how you can use the pattern facet on the xsd:string type to define the upper and lower bounds of allowed string content.

Finally, you saw how the totalDigits and fractionDigits facets can be used to constrain the structure of datatypes of type xsd:decimal.

Having examined the constraining facets of XSD Schema in this chapter and in Chapter 5, we will, in Chapter 7, "Grouping Elements and Attributes," go on to look at grouping elements and attributes.

CHAPTER 7

Grouping Elements and Attributes

In Chapter 1, "Elementary XML Schema," we looked briefly at a number of the options for grouping that are provided in W3C XML Schema. In this chapter, we will take a more detailed look at what grouping techniques are available and how you can use them in your XSD Schema code.

The grouping functionality for elements in XSD Schema is not limited to the <xsd:group> element. When we globally declare an element or use a named type definition, we are in a sense creating a group that we can reuse in much the same way that an <xsd:group> can be reused. We won't examine those structures again in detail in this chapter, however.

Grouping elements or attributes allows us to reuse the group, thereby reducing the number of places where XSD code has to be altered if changes are desired in the structure of instance documents. In this chapter, we will look at reusing groups within a single schema. In Chapter 10, "Bringing the Parts Together," we will look at how to reuse groups (and other definitions and declarations) across multiple schemas.

Reusing Definitions with Groups

Probably the least efficient way to code XSD Schema documents is to repeat element definitions several times in the same document. Thus, if we wanted to record both the work address and home address of a series of people, we could code XSD element declarations for each place in the instance document that we use, for example, a <Street> element. Coding in that way makes no use of code that we have already created. We have to check and debug the code at each place we use it in a schema that we have written. If we want to modify the structure of an allowed instance document—for example, to constrain a datatype more tightly—then we have to examine the code carefully to ensure that we find each (essentially duplicate) piece of information and be sure that we make each change in exactly the same way. Having a central definition or declaration that is referenced as often as it is needed is more efficient. XSD Schema provides us with several ways to group repeating parts of code.

One option that enables us to make use of the fact that address information is essentially the same in both uses is to reference globally declared elements. In Listing 7.1, you can see an address listing for a number of individuals.

```
<?xml version='1.0'?>
<PersonAddresses>
<Person>
 <Name>Patrick D. Carter</Name>
 <WorkAddress>
  <Address>
   <Street>123 Home Street</Street>
   <City>Miami</City>
   <State>FL</State>
   <ZipCode>98765-4321</ZipCode>
  </Address>
 </WorkAddress>
 <HomeAddress>
  <Address>
   <Street>987 Labor Street</Street>
   <City>Miami</City>
   <State>FL</State>
   <ZipCode>98765-1234</ZipCode>
  </Address>
 </HomeAddress>
</Person>
<Person>
 <Name>Carol J. Whittaker</Name>
 <WorkAddress>
<?xml version='1.0'?>
```

Listing 7.1 An address listing (PersonAddresses.xml).

```
<PersonAddresses>
<Person>
 <Name>Patrick D. Carter</Name>
 <WorkAddress>
  <Address>
   <Street>123 Home Street</Street>
   <City>Miami</City>
   <State>FL</State>
   <ZipCode>98765-4321</ZipCode>
  </Address>
 </WorkAddress>
 <HomeAddress>
  <Address>
   <Street>987 Labor Street</Street>
   <City>Miami</City>
   <State>FL</State>
   <ZipCode>98765-1234</ZipCode>
  </Address>
 </HomeAddress>
</Person>
<Person>
 <Name>Carol J. Whittaker</Name>
 <WorkAddress>
```

Listing 7.1 An address listing (PersonAddresses.xml). (Continued)

Notice how in the <WorkAddress> and <HomeAddress> elements we use the same elements in the same sequence within the <Address> element. Thus, without using groups, we can establish code reuse by using references to a globally declared element, the <Address> element, as you can see in Listing 7.2.

In the schema, the definitions for both the WorkAddressType type and the HomeAddressType type are identical. We exploit the identical structure needed

```
<?xml version="1.0" encoding="UTF-8"?>
<xsd:schema xmlns:xsd="http://www.w3.org/2001/XMLSchema" >

<xsd:element name="PersonAddresses">
 <xsd:complexType>
  <xsd:sequence>
   <xsd:element name="Person" type="PersonType" minOccurs="0"
maxOccurs="unbounded"/>
  </xsd:sequence>
```

continues

Listing 7.2 A schema for the address listing that references a globally declared element (PersonAddresses01.xsd).

```
  </xsd:complexType>
 </xsd:element>

 <xsd:complexType name="PersonType">
  <xsd:sequence>
   <xsd:element name="Name" type="xsd:string"/>
   <xsd:element name="WorkAddress" type="WorkAddressType"/>
   <xsd:element name="HomeAddress" type="HomeAddressType"/>
  </xsd:sequence>
 </xsd:complexType>

 <xsd:complexType name="HomeAddressType">
  <xsd:sequence>
   <xsd:element ref="Address"/>
  </xsd:sequence>
 </xsd:complexType>

 <xsd:complexType name="WorkAddressType">
  <xsd:sequence>
   <xsd:element ref="Address"/>
  </xsd:sequence>
 </xsd:complexType>

 <xsd:element name="Address">
  <xsd:complexType>
   <xsd:sequence>
    <xsd:element name="Street" type="xsd:string"/>
    <xsd:element name="City" type="xsd:string"/>
    <xsd:element name="State" type="StateType"/>
    <xsd:element name="ZipCode" type="USZipCodeType"/>
   </xsd:sequence>
  </xsd:complexType>
 </xsd:element>

 <xsd:simpleType name="StateType">
  <xsd:restriction base="xsd:string">
   <xsd:length value="2"/>
  </xsd:restriction>
 </xsd:simpleType>

 <xsd:simpleType name="USZipCodeType">
  <xsd:restriction base="xsd:string">
   <xsd:pattern value="\d{5}|\d{5}-\d{4}"/>
  </xsd:restriction>
 </xsd:simpleType>

 </xsd:schema>
```

Listing 7.2 A schema for the address listing that references a globally declared element (PersonAddresses01.xsd). (Continued)

in the instance document by referencing one globally declared element declaration for the <Address> element.

We could achieve a similar result by recoding the type definitions for the WorkAddressType and HomeAddressType types as follows so that a named complex type is used within the two named complex types HomeAddressType and WorkAddressType:

```
<xsd:complexType name="HomeAddressType">
 <xsd:sequence>
  <xsd:element name="Address" type="AddressType"/>
 </xsd:sequence>
</xsd:complexType>

<xsd:complexType name="WorkAddressType">
 <xsd:sequence>
  <xsd:element name="Address" type="AddressType"/>
 </xsd:sequence>
</xsd:complexType>
```

In parallel with those changes, we would use a named complex type definition for the AddressType type:

```
<xsd:complexType name="AddressType">
 <xsd:sequence>
  <xsd:element name="Street" type="xsd:string"/>
  <xsd:element name="City" type="xsd:string"/>
  <xsd:element name="State" type="StateType"/>
  <xsd:element name="ZipCode" type="USZipCodeType"/>
 </xsd:sequence>
</xsd:complexType>
```

The modified listing using a named complex type definition is shown in Listing 7.3.

The schemas in Listing 7.2 and 7.3 enable us to achieve code reuse without making any use of <xsd:group> elements. Groups enable us to reuse type

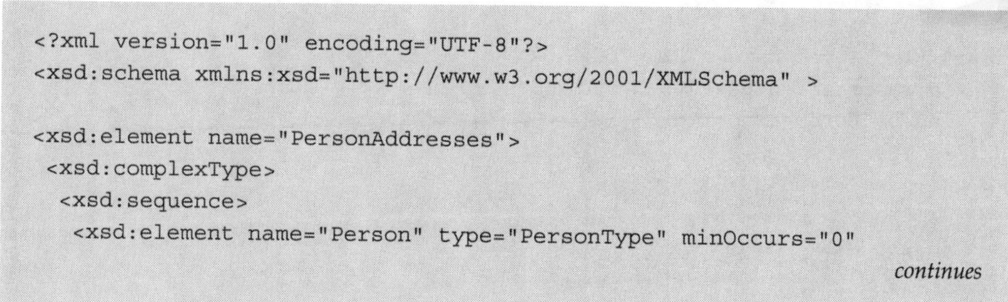

```
<?xml version="1.0" encoding="UTF-8"?>
<xsd:schema xmlns:xsd="http://www.w3.org/2001/XMLSchema" >

<xsd:element name="PersonAddresses">
 <xsd:complexType>
  <xsd:sequence>
   <xsd:element name="Person" type="PersonType" minOccurs="0"
```

continues

Listing 7.3 A modified schema using named complex types (PersonAddresses02.xsd).

```
maxOccurs="unbounded"/>
   </xsd:sequence>
  </xsd:complexType>
 </xsd:element>

 <xsd:complexType name="PersonType">
  <xsd:sequence>
   <xsd:element name="Name" type="xsd:string"/>
   <xsd:element name="WorkAddress" type="WorkAddressType"/>
   <xsd:element name="HomeAddress" type="HomeAddressType"/>
  </xsd:sequence>
 </xsd:complexType>

 <xsd:complexType name="HomeAddressType">
  <xsd:sequence>
   <xsd:element name="Address" type="AddressType"/>
  </xsd:sequence>
 </xsd:complexType>

 <xsd:complexType name="WorkAddressType">
  <xsd:sequence>
   <xsd:element name="Address" type="AddressType"/>
  </xsd:sequence>
 </xsd:complexType>

 <xsd:complexType name="AddressType">
  <xsd:sequence>
   <xsd:element name="Street" type="xsd:string"/>
   <xsd:element name="City" type="xsd:string"/>
   <xsd:element name="State" type="StateType"/>
   <xsd:element name="ZipCode" type="USZipCodeType"/>
  </xsd:sequence>
 </xsd:complexType>

 <xsd:simpleType name="StateType">
  <xsd:restriction base="xsd:string">
   <xsd:length value="2"/>
  </xsd:restriction>
 </xsd:simpleType>
 <xsd:simpleType name="USZipCodeType">
  <xsd:restriction base="xsd:string">
   <xsd:pattern value="\d{5}|\d{5}-\d{4}"/>
  </xsd:restriction>
 </xsd:simpleType>

</xsd:schema>
```

Listing 7.3 A modified schema using named complex types (PersonAddresses02.xsd). (Continued)

definitions in a way that can be a little more efficient than by using referenced global element declarations. If you look at the instance document in Listing 7.1, you might notice that the only function of the <Address> element is to act as a grouping element for the <Street>, <City>, <State>, and <ZipCode> elements. There is no attribute on the <Address> element, so if we use XSD grouping, we can dispense with the <Address> element entirely—thus reducing slightly the size of the content of each <Person> element in the instance document. In a sense, we have a choice of creating a grouping element (of whatever element type name) in the instance document or using an <xsd:group> element in the schema to achieve the same purpose.

The modified instance document, with the <Address> element removed, is shown in Listing 7.4.

Notice that the <Address> element has been removed but the information contained in the file is essentially the same. Notice, too, that the code is around 15 percent shorter than Listing 7.1, although smaller savings in code length are

```
<?xml version='1.0'?>
<PersonAddresses>
<Person>
 <Name>Patrick D. Carter</Name>
 <WorkAddress>
   <Street>123 Home Street</Street>
   <City>Miami</City>
   <State>FL</State>
   <ZipCode>98765-4321</ZipCode>
 </WorkAddress>
 <HomeAddress>
   <Street>987 Labor Street</Street>
   <City>Miami</City>
   <State>FL</State>
   <ZipCode>98765-1234</ZipCode>
 </HomeAddress>
</Person>
<Person>
 <Name>Carol J. Whittaker</Name>
 <WorkAddress>
   <Street>88 Canada Avenue</Street>
   <City>Rochester</City>
   <State>NY</State>
   <ZipCode>12345-6789</ZipCode>
 </WorkAddress>
 <HomeAddress>
   <Street>99 Cammelia Crescent</Street>
```

continues

Listing 7.4 A modified person addresses data store without the <Address> element (PersonAddresses02.xml).

```
    <City>Rochester</City>
    <State>NY</State>
    <ZipCode>12345-9876</ZipCode>
  </HomeAddress>
</Person>
<!-- More Person elements can go here. -->
</PersonAddresses>
```

Listing 7.4 A modified person addresses data store without the <Address> element (PersonAddresses02.xml). (Continued)

likely in most settings. To be able to avoid the unnecessary code in instance documents, we use the <xsd:group> element in the XSD Schema as shown in Listing 7.5.

Notice that in the complex type definition for both the WorkAddressType and the HomeAddressType types that we have replaced the <xsd:element> element with the <xsd:group> element. The content of the AddressGroup group is a sequence of elements. We reference the XSD Schema group named AddressGroup, which contains element declarations for the <Street>, <City>, <State>, and <ZipCode> elements.

```
<?xml version="1.0" encoding="UTF-8"?>
<xsd:schema xmlns:xsd="http://www.w3.org/2001/XMLSchema" >

<xsd:element name="PersonAddresses">
 <xsd:complexType>
  <xsd:sequence>
   <xsd:element name="Person" type="PersonType" minOccurs="0"
maxOccurs="unbounded"/>
  </xsd:sequence>
 </xsd:complexType>
</xsd:element>

<xsd:complexType name="PersonType">
 <xsd:sequence>
  <xsd:element name="Name" type="xsd:string"/>
  <xsd:element name="WorkAddress" type="WorkAddressType"/>
  <xsd:element name="HomeAddress" type="HomeAddressType"/>
 </xsd:sequence>
</xsd:complexType>

<xsd:complexType name="HomeAddressType">
 <xsd:sequence>
  <xsd:group ref="AddressGroup" />
```

Listing 7.5 A revised schema using the <xsd:group> element (PersonAddresses03.xsd).

```
  </xsd:sequence>
 </xsd:complexType>

 <xsd:complexType name="WorkAddressType">
  <xsd:sequence>
   <xsd:group ref="AddressGroup"/>
  </xsd:sequence>
 </xsd:complexType>

 <xsd:group name="AddressGroup">
   <xsd:sequence>
    <xsd:element name="Street" type="xsd:string"/>
    <xsd:element name="City" type="xsd:string"/>
    <xsd:element name="State" type="StateType"/>
    <xsd:element name="ZipCode" type="USZipCodeType"/>
   </xsd:sequence>
 </xsd:group>

 <xsd:simpleType name="StateType">
  <xsd:restriction base="xsd:string">
   <xsd:length value="2"/>
  </xsd:restriction>
 </xsd:simpleType>
 <xsd:simpleType name="USZipCodeType">
  <xsd:restriction base="xsd:string">
   <xsd:pattern value="\d{5}|\d{5}-\d{4}"/>
  </xsd:restriction>
 </xsd:simpleType>

 </xsd:schema>
```

Listing 7.5 A revised schema using the <xsd:group> element (PersonAddresses03.xsd). (Continued)

Nesting Sequence Groups

We can nest one XSD group within another to create fairly complex structures. As an example, let's suppose that we wished for some reason to group the declarations for the <State> and <ZipCode> elements so that we could create a StateZipCodeGroup group, which is referenced from within the definition of the AddressGroup group. The code is shown in Listing 7.6.

In our simple example, this action provides no direct productivity gain, but by creating groups that we use as reusable components of a schema, we can—with more extensive schemas—build up a library of code contained in <xsd:group> elements that has already been tested. With those advantages of reuse in mind, it is important, in a production setting, to document the purpose and characteristics of each group by adding <xsd:annotation> and

<xsd:documentation> elements to each group of which you plan to make repeated use. In the more extensive example to be developed in Chapter 10, "Bringing the Parts Together," we will see how a schema and an associated type library can be documented to aid understanding.

```
<?xml version="1.0" encoding="UTF-8"?>
<xsd:schema xmlns:xsd="http://www.w3.org/2001/XMLSchema" >

<xsd:element name="PersonAddresses">
 <xsd:complexType>
  <xsd:sequence>
   <xsd:element name="Person" type="PersonType" minOccurs="0"
maxOccurs="unbounded"/>
  </xsd:sequence>
 </xsd:complexType>
</xsd:element>

<xsd:complexType name="PersonType">
 <xsd:sequence>
  <xsd:element name="Name" type="xsd:string"/>
  <xsd:element name="WorkAddress" type="WorkAddressType"/>
  <xsd:element name="HomeAddress" type="HomeAddressType"/>
 </xsd:sequence>
</xsd:complexType>

<xsd:complexType name="HomeAddressType">
 <xsd:sequence>
  <xsd:group ref="AddressGroup" />
 </xsd:sequence>
</xsd:complexType>

<xsd:complexType name="WorkAddressType">
 <xsd:sequence>
  <xsd:group ref="AddressGroup"/>
 </xsd:sequence>
</xsd:complexType>

<xsd:group name="AddressGroup">
  <xsd:sequence>
   <xsd:element name="Street" type="xsd:string"/>
   <xsd:element name="City" type="xsd:string"/>
   <xsd:group ref="StateZipCodeGroup"/>
  </xsd:sequence>
</xsd:group>

<xsd:group name="StateZipCodeGroup">
 <xsd:sequence>
  <xsd:element name="State" type="StateType"/>
```

Listing 7.6 Nesting element group definitions in a schema (PersonAddresses04.xsd).

```
   <xsd:element name="ZipCode" type="USZipCodeType"/>
  </xsd:sequence>
 </xsd:group>
 <xsd:simpleType name="StateType">
  <xsd:restriction base="xsd:string">
   <xsd:length value="2"/>
  </xsd:restriction>
 </xsd:simpleType>

 <xsd:simpleType name="USZipCodeType">
  <xsd:restriction base="xsd:string">
   <xsd:pattern value="\d{5}|\d{5}-\d{4}"/>
  </xsd:restriction>
 </xsd:simpleType>

 </xsd:schema>
```

Listing 7.6 Nesting element group definitions in a schema (PersonAddresses04.xsd). (Continued)

Nesting Choice Groups

XSD Schema enables us to use the <xsd:group> element to contain a sequence of elements, as we have just seen, or a choice of either elements or further groups. Any groups that are referenced must be declared globally.

Just as we can nest sequence groups, we can also nest choice groups. Suppose that we had an online health questionnaire for a life insurance company. Part of that questionnaire to assess future disease risk might differ depending on gender. Not many men, for example, are likely to have been pregnant. A possible instance document is shown in Listing 7.7. Because several nested choices are to be made within the schema which follows, the instance document is fairly long in order to allow testing against the schema.

```
<?xml version='1.0'?>
<Questionnaire>
 <Person gender="Female">
  <Name>Jane Doe</Name>
  <SmokingHistory>
   <NeverSmoked>Yes</NeverSmoked>
  </SmokingHistory>
  <FemaleGenderRelated>
   <NumberofPregnancies>0</NumberofPregnancies>
   <LastCervicalSmear>1999-12-14</LastCervicalSmear>
```

continues

Listing 7.7 A health questionnaire expressed in XML (Questionnaire.xml).

```
    <BreastSelfExamination>Yes</BreastSelfExamination>
    <GynCaFamilyHistory>No</GynCaFamilyHistory>
   </FemaleGenderRelated>
  </Person>
  <Person gender="Male">
   <Name>John Doe</Name>
   <SmokingHistory>
    <EverSmoked>Yes</EverSmoked>
    <AgeFirstSmoked>12</AgeFirstSmoked>
    <MaxCigsPerDay>50</MaxCigsPerDay>
    <CurrentSmoker>No</CurrentSmoker>
   </SmokingHistory>
   <MaleGenderRelated>
    <TesticularSelfExamination>No</TesticularSelfExamination>
   </MaleGenderRelated>
  </Person>
  <Person gender="Female">
   <Name>Jane Smith</Name>
    <SmokingHistory>
     <EverSmoked>Yes</EverSmoked>
     <AgeFirstSmoked>14</AgeFirstSmoked>
     <MaxCigsPerDay>25</MaxCigsPerDay>
     <CurrentSmoker>Yes</CurrentSmoker>
    </SmokingHistory>
   <FemaleGenderRelated>
    <NumberofPregnancies>3</NumberofPregnancies>
    <LastCervicalSmear>2000-01-01</LastCervicalSmear>
    <BreastSelfExamination>No</BreastSelfExamination>
    <GynCaFamilyHistory>Yes</GynCaFamilyHistory>
   </FemaleGenderRelated>
 </Person>
 </Questionnaire>
```

Listing 7.7 A health questionnaire expressed in XML (Questionnaire.xml). (Continued)

Each person has a <Name> element recording his or her name. A smoking history is taken, and if the person is a never-smoker, a <NeverSmoked> element is used. If the person has ever smoked, however, a series of pieces of information is collected. The choice between the <NeverSmoked> element and the supplementary questions for a past or current smoker is guided by a choice group. Following the smoking-related information, some additional information is collected that is appropriate to the person's gender. Again, a choice group is used to allow data appropriate to the gender of the person to be collected and stored.

Clearly, there are many choices to be made about what questions might sensibly be asked in the questionnaire. It is pointless asking questions about the age when a person first smoked and maximum cigarettes per day to someone who has never smoked. Similarly, if we know that the person's gender is female, there are aspects of personal or medical history that apply only to females and need not be asked of males (and vice-versa). Notice how in Listing 7.8 we use nested choice groups to reflect the logical flow of which data it is relevant to seek, and therefore to store.

```
<?xml version="1.0" encoding="UTF-8"?>
<xsd:schema xmlns:xsd="http://www.w3.org/2001/XMLSchema" >

<xsd:element name="Questionnaire">
 <xsd:complexType>
  <xsd:sequence>
   <xsd:element name="Person" type="PersonType" maxOccurs="unbounded"/>
  </xsd:sequence>
 </xsd:complexType>
</xsd:element>

<xsd:complexType name="PersonType">
 <xsd:sequence>
  <xsd:group ref="BasicDataGroup" />
  <xsd:element name="SmokingHistory">
   <xsd:complexType>
    <xsd:group ref="SmokingHistoryGroup"/>
   </xsd:complexType>
  </xsd:element>
  <xsd:group ref="GenderRelatedGroup"/>
 </xsd:sequence>
 <xsd:attribute name="gender" type="xsd:string"/>
</xsd:complexType>

<xsd:group name="BasicDataGroup">
 <xsd:choice>
  <xsd:element name="Name" type="xsd:string"/>
  <xsd:element name="Anonymous" type="xsd:string"/>
 </xsd:choice>
</xsd:group>

<xsd:group name="SmokingHistoryGroup">
 <xsd:choice>
  <xsd:element name="NeverSmoked" type="xsd:string"/>
  <xsd:group ref="EverSmokedGroup"/>
 </xsd:choice>
</xsd:group>

<xsd:group name="EverSmokedGroup">
 <xsd:sequence>
  <xsd:element name="EverSmoked" type="xsd:string"/>
  <xsd:element name="AgeFirstSmoked" type="xsd:positiveInteger"/>
```

continues

Listing 7.8 A schema for the health questionnaire (Questionnaire.xsd).

```
   <xsd:element name="MaxCigsPerDay" type="xsd:positiveInteger"/>
   <xsd:group ref="CurrentSmokerGroup"/>
  </xsd:sequence>
 </xsd:group>

 <xsd:group name="CurrentSmokerGroup">
 <xsd:annotation>
  <xsd:documentation>
  Extend this group to another level of nested choice group if you want
 to add questions for current smokers only.
  </xsd:documentation>
 </xsd:annotation>
  <xsd:sequence>
   <xsd:element name="CurrentSmoker" type="xsd:string"/>
  </xsd:sequence>
 </xsd:group>

 <xsd:group name="GenderRelatedGroup">
  <xsd:choice>
   <xsd:group ref="FemaleGenderGroup"/>
   <xsd:group ref="MaleGenderGroup"/>
  </xsd:choice>
 </xsd:group>

 <xsd:group name="FemaleGenderGroup">
  <xsd:sequence>
   <xsd:element name="FemaleGenderRelated">
    <xsd:complexType>
     <xsd:sequence>
      <xsd:element name="NumberofPregnancies"
 type="xsd:nonNegativeInteger"/>
      <xsd:element name="LastCervicalSmear" type="xsd:date"/>
      <xsd:element name="BreastSelfExamination" type="xsd:string"/>
      <xsd:element name="GynCaFamilyHistory" type="xsd:string"/>
     </xsd:sequence>
    </xsd:complexType>
    </xsd:element>
  </xsd:sequence>
 </xsd:group>

 <xsd:group name="MaleGenderGroup">
  <xsd:sequence>
   <xsd:element name="MaleGenderRelated">
    <xsd:complexType>
     <xsd:sequence>
      <xsd:element name="TesticularSelfExamination" type="xsd:string"/>
     </xsd:sequence>
    </xsd:complexType>
```

Listing 7.8 A schema for the health questionnaire (Questionnaire.xsd). (Continued)

```
    </xsd:element>
  </xsd:sequence>
</xsd:group>

</xsd:schema>
```

Listing 7.8 A schema for the health questionnaire (Questionnaire.xsd). (Continued)

The structure of the schema follows the design of the instance questionnaire described a little earlier. Hopefully you will be able, having started at the element declaration for the <Questionnaire> element, to follow the logical flow of allowed and appropriate choices for the data that is to be collected. The definition of the SmokingHistoryGroup enables us to choose either a <Never-Smoked> element or a further choice group named EverSmokedGroup. The final member of the sequence within the EverSmokedGroup group is a Current-SmokerGroup group. In the schema as written, that group contains only a single element. The group could be extended further to explore questions about current smoking habits, however—perhaps incorporating a choice of CurrentHeavy-SmokerGroup, CurrentModerateSmokerGroup, or CurrentLightSmokerGroup groups.

The GenderRelatedGroup group enables us to include content appropriate to each gender. Just as with the smoking history questions, we could nest further choice or sequence groups. For example, if there was a family history of gynecological cancer as indicated by the content of the <GynCaFamilyHistory> element, then further questions could be added in another more deeply nested group.

You should be able to see that <xsd:group> elements can be used to create complex nested structures that can, when sensibly used, reflect the logic of the information that it is appropriate to record (depending on the circumstances that apply).

XSD Schema provides a further mechanism to enable us to choose which type of element to display in a particular setting. In this case, we are constrained to the inclusion of elements of the same datatype. Let's go on and examine substitution groups.

Substitution Groups

It can be useful to allow substitution of one element for another in instance documents without having to create a new schema. In XSD Schema, the notion of substitution groups provides functionality that achieves this goal. The elements that can be substituted one for another must be of the same named datatype, however. Additionally, the element for which a substitution can be made has to be declared globally.

Let's suppose that we want to create an instance document that consists of a data store about modes of transport. It might look a little like Listing 7.9.

A schema for Listing 7.9 is shown in Listing 7.10.

It might be useful, however, to allow a variety of more specific elements within the instance document so that it looks like the instance document shown in Listing 7.11. In the example, we would be allowed to use <Car> and

```
<?xml version='1.0'?>
<ModesOfTransport>
 <Vehicle>
  <Type>Car</Type>
  <Wheels>4</Wheels>
  <Wings>0</Wings>
 </Vehicle>
 <Vehicle>
  <Type>Aeroplane</Type>
  <Wheels>5</Wheels>
  <Wings>2</Wings>
  </Vehicle>
</ModesOfTransport>
```

Listing 7.9 Modes of transport expressed in XML (Transport01.xml).

```
<?xml version="1.0" encoding="UTF-8"?>
<xsd:schema xmlns:xsd="http://www.w3.org/2001/XMLSchema" >

<xsd:element name="ModesOfTransport">
 <xsd:complexType>
  <xsd:sequence>
   <xsd:element name="Vehicle" type="VehicleType"
maxOccurs="unbounded"/>
  </xsd:sequence>
 </xsd:complexType>
</xsd:element>

<xsd:complexType name="VehicleType">
 <xsd:sequence>
  <xsd:element name="Type" type="xsd:string"/>
  <xsd:element name="Wheels" type="xsd:nonNegativeInteger"/>
  <xsd:element name="Wings" type="xsd:nonNegativeInteger"/>
 </xsd:sequence>
</xsd:complexType>

</xsd:schema>
```

Listing 7.10 A schema (without substitution group) for the modes of transport instance document (Transport01.xsd).

```
<?xml version='1.0'?>
<ModesOfTransport>
 <Aeroplane>
  <Type>Boeing 777</Type>
  <Wheels>5</Wheels>
  <Wings>2</Wings>
 </Aeroplane>
 <Car>
  <Type>Rolls Royce</Type>
  <Wheels>4</Wheels>
  <Wings>0</Wings>
 </Car>
 <Aeroplane>
  <Type>Boeing 767</Type>
  <Wheels>5</Wheels>
  <Wings>2</Wings>
 </Aeroplane>
 <Car>
  <Type>Ferrari</Type>
  <Wheels>4</Wheels>
  <Wings>0</Wings>
 </Car>
</ModesOfTransport>
```

Listing 7.11 A modified instance document allowing element substitution (Transport02.xml).

<Aeroplane> elements in the same place in the content model as <Vehicle> elements are permitted. Notice that the content model for the <Car> and <Aeroplane> elements is the same as the content model for the <Vehicle> element shown earlier in Listing 7.9.

XSD Schema enables us to specify a collection of elements that are allowed as substitutes for the <Vehicle> element. In the following schema, the collection of substitution elements will contain two elements. In this context, the <Vehicle> element is termed the *head element*. Listing 7.12 shows a schema that describes Listing 7.11.

Notice that the schema has been modified. The <Vehicle> element has been declared as a global element declaration (it has to be, if substitution is to work correctly). It also now has an abstract attribute with the value of "true." You will notice, too, the two new global element declarations for the <Car> and <Aeroplane> elements. The type attribute of each of those <xsd:element> elements specifies the datatype to be the same as that of the <Vehicle> element. The substitutionGroup attribute denotes that each of the two elements can be substituted in an instance document in the same position in the content model as the <Vehicle> element is allowed.

```
<?xml version="1.0" encoding="UTF-8"?>
<xsd:schema xmlns:xsd="http://www.w3.org/2001/XMLSchema" >

<xsd:element name="ModesOfTransport">
 <xsd:complexType>
  <xsd:sequence>
   <xsd:element ref="Vehicle" maxOccurs="unbounded"/>
  </xsd:sequence>
 </xsd:complexType>
</xsd:element>

<xsd:element name="Vehicle" type="VehicleType" abstract="true"/>

<xsd:element name="Car" type="VehicleType"
substitutionGroup="Vehicle"/>
<xsd:element name="Aeroplane" type="VehicleType"
substitutionGroup="Vehicle"/>

<xsd:complexType name="VehicleType">
 <xsd:sequence>
  <xsd:element name="Type" type="xsd:string"/>
  <xsd:element name="Wheels" type="xsd:nonNegativeInteger"/>
  <xsd:element name="Wings" type="xsd:nonNegativeInteger"/>
 </xsd:sequence>
</xsd:complexType>

</xsd:schema>
```

Listing 7.12 A schema using a substitution group (Transport02.xsd).

The presence of an abstract attribute with value true on the element declaration for the <Vehicle> element means that we cannot include a <Vehicle> element in the instance document. Thus, we can use only <Aeroplane> and <Car> elements but not the <Vehicle> element itself. Removing the abstract attribute allows us to mix freely <Vehicle>, <Aeroplane>, and <Car> elements in the instance document.

NOTE **Turbo XML 2.2.1 will enable you, incorrectly, to include <Vehicle> elements when abstract is set to "true."**

Substitution groups used as they are in the previous paragraphs can save us from having to repeat type definitions for each element. But the alternate technique of having a choice group with three element declarations each with type attribute relating to a named VehicleType complex definition would have achieved the same result.

Having looked at several grouping techniques that are relevant to elements, let's go on to look at attribute groups.

Attribute Groups

Attribute groups enable us to reuse code in a way similar to the benefits of using element-related groups. It enables us to declare a group of attributes that we might want to reuse in several places in the same schema or that we want to use in a type library so that the group can be referenced from other XSD schemas. The elements to enable reuse of information contained in external schemas are described in Chapter 10, "Bringing the Parts Together."

A simple invoice document might look like that shown in Listing 7.13.

The <InvoiceNumber> element has two attributes: checkedBy and Department. We could add the attribute declarations separately in the schema. Alternatively, we could group the attributes using an <xsd:attributeGroup> element so that we could reuse them, as a group, in some other setting.

A schema using a simple attribute grouping is shown in Listing 7.14. Note that the <xsd:attributeGroup> element must be global in order to be referenced correctly.

```
<?xml version='1.0'?>
<SimpleInvoice>
<InvoiceNumber
  checkedBy="Mary"
  Department="Despatch"
  >
  01234
  </InvoiceNumber>
<Customer>WonderWidgets</Customer>
<Items>
 <Item>A thing</Item>
 <Item>Some other thing</Item>
 <Item>A third thing</Item>
</Items>
</SimpleInvoice>
```

Listing 7.13 A simple invoice using attributes (SimpleInvoice.xml).

```
<?xml version="1.0" encoding="UTF-8"?>
<xsd:schema xmlns:xsd="http://www.w3.org/2001/XMLSchema" >

<xsd:element name="SimpleInvoice">
 <xsd:complexType>
  <xsd:sequence>
   <xsd:element name="InvoiceNumber" type="xsd:positiveInteger"/>
```

continues

Listing 7.14 A schema using an attribute group (SimpleInvoice.xsd).

```
    <xsd:element name="Customer" type="xsd:string"/>
    <xsd:element name="Items" type="ItemsType"/>
   </xsd:sequence>
   <xsd:attributeGroup ref="CheckedAndDeptAttributesGroup"/>
  </xsd:complexType>
 </xsd:element>

 <xsd:complexType name="ItemsType">
  <xsd:sequence>
   <xsd:element name="Item" type="xsd:string"/>
  </xsd:sequence>
 </xsd:complexType>

 <xsd:attributeGroup name="CheckedAndDeptAttributesGroup">
  <xsd:attribute name="checkedBy" type="xsd:string"/>
  <xsd:attribute name="Department" type="xsd:string"/>
 </xsd:attributeGroup>

 </xsd:schema>
```

Listing 7.14 A schema using an attribute group (SimpleInvoice.xsd). (Continued)

The attribute group we created could be reused in other settings where documents or actions must be documented as checked by a particular individual from a particular department.

Summary

In this chapter, we have looked at the improvement in efficiency that grouping of definitions or declarations within an XSD schema can produce. We have examined the use of <xsd:group> elements with either sequence or choice content. We then went on to look at how nesting choice groups can enable us to represent a hierarchy of choices in an instance document. Finally, we have looked briefly at the use of attribute groups.

In Chapter 8, we go on to examine how we can create new datatypes customized for our particular need from those datatypes that XSD Schema provides for us.

CHAPTER

8

Deriving Types

One of the most powerful innovations in XSD Schema is the ability to create new user-defined datatypes that are derived from datatypes provided by the XSD Schema Recommendation itself or from derived datatypes created earlier by you or by other schema authors. The existence of built-in datatypes in XSD Schema takes it substantially beyond the capabilities of DTDs, but the ability to derive new datatypes specifically crafted for a particular use (from either primitive or derived datatypes) is a major advance.

In earlier chapters, we have seen (in passing) many examples of deriving new data types. In this chapter, we will focus specifically on how we can use XSD Schema to derive new datatypes in a number of settings.

The facility within XSD Schema to derive new datatypes enables the reuse of existing types in a way that is similar to that in which object inheritance is used in object-oriented programming. In creating a derived datatype, we can simply make use of an existing datatype and modify some part of it for our specific intended use. There is no need to code or create new datatypes from scratch—we can, as we gain experience in XSD Schema, make use of a growing resource of existing XSD Schema code. This functionality has great advantages in allowing the reuse of code, rather than repetitive creation of new code that then has to go through a full debugging process. As you will see in Chapter 10, "Bringing the Parts Together," XSD Schema also enables code to be reused outside the schema in which it was created.

As well as those advantages in reducing repetitive XSD Schema code, the flexibility and specificity of XSD Schema-derived datatypes enables a significant decrease in application-specific coding for type checking. There is no need for much of the custom-written code that would have been necessary using documents that were validated by using DTDs.

XSD Schema provides four methods of deriving new datatypes:

- By extension (complex types only)
- By restriction (simple and complex types)
- By list (simple types only)
- By union (simple types only)

In conjunction with the elements <xsd:extension>, <xsd:restriction>, <xsd:list>, and <xsd:union>, we can apply the facets that were discussed in Chapters 5, "Data Facets," and 6, "More about Data Facets." Many of these facets will be shown in the examples in this chapter. The type from which a new type is derived is termed the *base type*, which is typically expressed as a base attribute in one of the elements just mentioned. In the case of the list type, the type from which the new type is derived is termed the item type. It is expressed as an itemType attribute of the <xsd:list> element.

When we apply constraining facets in order to create a new datatype, we can restrict the allowed values in either the *lexical space* or the *value space* of a datatype. A floating point number can have a single expression of 50 in the value space of the datatype but can be expressed in several ways, such as 50 or 50.0 or 5.0e1 in the lexical space. Restriction of the value space can be done directly or indirectly. For example, the value attribute of the <xsd:pattern> element, which we discussed in Chapter 5, constrains the lexical space of a type and thereby indirectly controls the value space of the type.

In the final section of the chapter, we will briefly look at the xsi:type attribute. First, let's look at deriving new types by extension.

Deriving Types by Extension

The <xsd:extension> element provides us with several techniques implemented by XSD Schema facets by which we can extend an existing datatype in order to create a new datatype. We can extend a type by code reuse without actually using the <xsd:extension> element, however. First, we will examine a simple example of code reuse and then go on to use the <xsd:extension> element.

Let's take a simple example of a short schema for information about a person. An instance document might look like that in Listing 8.1.

An XSD schema that would define the content of the <Person> element in Listing 8.1 is shown in Listing 8.2.

```
<?xml version='1.0'?>
<PersonList>
 <Person>
  <Name>
   <FirstName>John</FirstName>
   <MiddleInitial>X</MiddleInitial>
   <LastName>Smith</LastName>
  </Name>
 </Person>
 <Person>
  <Name>
   <FirstName>Janet</FirstName>
   <MiddleInitial>X</MiddleInitial>
   <LastName>Chang</LastName>
  </Name>
 </Person>
</PersonList>
```

Listing 8.1 A simple instance document describing a person (PersonList.xml).

```
<?xml version='1.0'?>
<xsd:schema xmlns:xsd="http://www.w3.org/2001/XMLSchema">
 <xsd:annotation>
  <xsd:documentation>
  This schema provides only the most basic person related data and will
  need to be extended to be used other than for very local purposes.
  </xsd:documentation>
 </xsd:annotation>

<xsd:element name="PersonList">
 <xsd:annotation>
  <xsd:documentation>
  The &lt;PersonList&gt; element is simply a sequence of
&lt;Person&gt; elements.
  The &lt;Person&gt; element can be replaced by the definition of an
extended derived datatype if desired.
  </xsd:documentation>
 </xsd:annotation>
 <xsd:complexType>
```

continues

Listing 8.2 An XSD schema for Listing 8.1 (PersonList.xsd).

```
    <xsd:sequence>
     <xsd:element name="Person" type="BasicPersonType" minOccurs="0"
     maxOccurs="unbounded"/>
    </xsd:sequence>
   </xsd:complexType>
  </xsd:element>

  <xsd:complexType name="BasicPersonType">
   <xsd:sequence>
    <xsd:element name="Name" type="BasicNameType" minOccurs="1"
  maxOccurs="1"/>
   </xsd:sequence>
  </xsd:complexType>

  <xsd:complexType name="BasicNameType">
   <xsd:sequence>
    <xsd:element name="FirstName" type="xsd:string" />
    <xsd:element name="MiddleInitial" type="xsd:string" minOccurs="0"
    maxOccurs="10"/>
    <xsd:element name="LastName" type="xsd:string"/>
   </xsd:sequence>
  </xsd:complexType>

  </xsd:schema>
```

Listing 8.2 An XSD schema for Listing 8.1 (PersonList.xsd). (Continued)

Information that is as limited as this about a person would likely be adequate only in the most localized of settings—in any corporate setting, the possibility of duplication of names arises as the number of persons increases beyond a few. As a basic addition to the information about the person, we could add standard address information. Listing 8.3 shows the modified instance document.

We have inserted address information into each <Person> element following the <Name> element.

An amended schema is shown in Listing 8.4.

The PersonWithAddressType type can be viewed as being the BasicNameType from Listing 8.2 with the added property of the BasicAddressType type. Thus, we have extended the BasicNameType type without using the <xsd: extension> element directly.

Let's go on to extend both the content model for the <Person> and <Address> elements and add a new <CreditHistory> element so that the personal information is adapted and extended for use in credit rating purposes. Listing 8.5 shows an instance document.

```
<?xml version='1.0'?>
<PersonList>
 <Person>
  <Name>
   <FirstName>John</FirstName>
   <MiddleInitial>X</MiddleInitial>
   <LastName>Smith</LastName>
  </Name>
  <Address>
   <Street1>45678 2nd Street</Street1>
   <Street2></Street2>
   <City>Tampa</City>
   <State>FL</State>
   <ZipCode>34567</ZipCode>
   <Country>USA</Country>
  </Address>
 </Person>
 <Person>
  <Name>
   <FirstName>Janet</FirstName>
   <MiddleInitial>X</MiddleInitial>
   <LastName>Chang</LastName>
  </Name>
  <Address>
   <Street1>34567 Ronald Reagan Avenue</Street1>
   <Street2></Street2>
   <City>Sacramento</City>
   <State>CA</State>
   <ZipCode>98765</ZipCode>
   <Country></Country>
  </Address>
 </Person>
</PersonList>
```

Listing 8.3 A person list with added address information (PersonList02.xml).

```
<?xml version='1.0'?>
<xsd:schema xmlns:xsd="http://www.w3.org/2001/XMLSchema">

<xsd:annotation>
 <xsd:documentation>
  This schema provides only basic person related data with added
address data and will need to be extended to be used other than for
  local purposes.
 </xsd:documentation>
</xsd:annotation>
```

continues

Listing 8.4 A schema for persons with added address data (PersonList02.xsd).

```
<xsd:element name="PersonList">
 <xsd:annotation>
  <xsd:documentation>
  The &lt;PersonList&gt; element remains a sequence of &lt;Person&gt;
elements.
  The &lt; Person&gt; element can be replaced by the definition of an
extended derived datatype if desired.
  </xsd:documentation>
 </xsd:annotation>
 <xsd:complexType>
  <xsd:sequence>
   <xsd:element name="Person" type="PersonWithAddressType"
minOccurs="0"
   maxOccurs="unbounded"/>
  </xsd:sequence>
 </xsd:complexType>
</xsd:element>

<xsd:complexType name="PersonWithAddressType">
 <xsd:sequence>
  <xsd:element name="Name" type="BasicNameType" minOccurs="1"
maxOccurs="1"/>
  <xsd:element name="Address" type="BasicAddressType" minOccurs="1"
  maxOccurs="1"/>
 </xsd:sequence>
</xsd:complexType>

<xsd:complexType name="BasicNameType">
 <xsd:sequence>
  <xsd:element name="FirstName" type="xsd:string" />
  <xsd:element name="MiddleInitial" type="xsd:string" minOccurs="0"
  maxOccurs="10"/>
  <xsd:element name="LastName" type="xsd:string"/>
 </xsd:sequence>
</xsd:complexType>
<xsd:complexType name="BasicAddressType">
 <xsd:sequence>
  <xsd:element name="Street1" type="xsd:string"/>
  <xsd:element name="Street2" type="xsd:string" minOccurs="0"
maxOccurs="1" />
  <xsd:element name="City" type="xsd:string" />
  <xsd:element name="State" type="xsd:string"/>
  <xsd:element name="ZipCode" type="xsd:integer" />
  <xsd:element name="Country" type="xsd:string" minOccurs="0"
```

Listing 8.4 A schema for persons with added address data (PersonList02.xsd). (Continued)

```
maxOccurs="1" />
 </xsd:sequence>
</xsd:complexType>

</xsd:schema>
```

Listing 8.4 A schema for persons with added address data (PersonList02.xsd). (Continued)

```
<?xml version='1.0'?>
<PersonList>
 <Person>
  <Name>
   <FirstName>John</FirstName>
   <MiddleInitial>X</MiddleInitial>
   <LastName>Smith</LastName>
   <EmailAddress></EmailAddress>
  </Name>
  <Address>
   <Street1>45678 2nd Street</Street1>
   <Street2></Street2>
   <City>Tampa</City>
   <State>FL</State>
   <ZipCode>34567</ZipCode>
   <Country>USA</Country>
   <TimeAtAddress>3 months</TimeAtAddress>
  </Address>
  <CreditInformation>
   <CreditCards>
    <CreditCard number="0987654321098765" type="Mastercard"
status="OK"
    time="4 years"/>
    <CreditCard number="9876543210987654" type="Visa" status="OK"
    time="3 years 9 months"/>
    <CreditCard number="5678901234567890" type="Diner&apos;s"
status="OK"
    time="6 months"/>
   </CreditCards>
   <CreditHistory status="" NumberEvents="1">
    <CreditEvent>Overdue payment on Visa card, September
2002</CreditEvent>
   </CreditHistory>
  </CreditInformation>
```

continues

Listing 8.5 An instance document with added credit history information (PersonList03.xml).

```
  </Person>
  <Person>
   <Name>
    <FirstName>Janet</FirstName>
    <MiddleInitial>X</MiddleInitial>
    <LastName>Chang</LastName>
    <EmailAddress></EmailAddress>
   </Name>
   <Address>
    <Street1>34567 Ronald Reagan Avenue</Street1>
    <Street2></Street2>
    <City>Sacramento</City>
    <State>CA</State>
    <ZipCode>98765</ZipCode>
    <Country></Country>
    <TimeAtAddress>2 years</TimeAtAddress>
   </Address>
   <CreditInformation>
    <CreditCards>
     <CreditCard number="1234567890123456" type="Visa" status="OK"
time="2 years"/>
     <CreditCard number="2345678901234567" type="Mastercard"
status="OK"
     time="3 years"/>
    </CreditCards>
    <CreditHistory status="Clear" NumberEvents="0">
     <CreditEvent></CreditEvent>
    </CreditHistory>
   </CreditInformation>
  </Person>
 </PersonList>
```

Listing 8.5 An instance document with added credit history information (PersonList03.xml). (Continued)

Notice in the instance document that we have extended the <Name> element by adding an <EmailAddress> subelement, extended the <Address> element by adding a <TimeAtAddress> subelement, and added a new subelement <CreditInformation> to the <Person> element. The <CreditInformation> element has <CreditCards>, <CreditHistory>, and <CreditEvent> subelements, some of which in turn have subelements.

A schema reflecting the new elements that we have added is shown in Listing 8.6.

```
<?xml version='1.0'?>
<xsd:schema xmlns:xsd="http://www.w3.org/2001/XMLSchema">

<xsd:annotation>
 <xsd:documentation>
  This schema provides basic person related data plus information
directly relevant for credit rating purposes.
 </xsd:documentation>
</xsd:annotation>

<xsd:element name="PersonList">
 <xsd:annotation>
  <xsd:documentation>
  The &lt;PersonList&gt; element remains a sequence of &lt;Person&gt;
elements.
  The &lt;Person&gt; element can be replaced by the definition of an
extended derived datatype if desired.
 </xsd:documentation>
 </xsd:annotation>
 <xsd:complexType>
  <xsd:sequence>
   <xsd:element name="Person" type="PersonWithCreditInfoType"
minOccurs="0"
   maxOccurs="unbounded"/>
  </xsd:sequence>
 </xsd:complexType>
</xsd:element>

<xsd:complexType name="PersonWithCreditInfoType">
 <xsd:sequence>
  <xsd:element name="Name" type="NameWithEmailType" minOccurs="1"
maxOccurs="1"/>
  <xsd:element name="Address" type="AddressWithTimeType" minOccurs="1"
  maxOccurs="1"/>
  <xsd:element name="CreditInformation" type="CreditInformationType"
  minOccurs="1" maxOccurs="1"/>
 </xsd:sequence>
</xsd:complexType>

<xsd:complexType name="NameWithEmailType">
 <xsd:complexContent>
  <xsd:extension base="BasicName">
   <xsd:sequence>
    <xsd:element name="EmailAddress" type="xsd:string" minOccurs="0"
maxOccurs="4"/>
```

continues

Listing 8.6 A schema with added credit information (PersonList03.xsd).

```
    </xsd:sequence>
   </xsd:extension>
  </xsd:complexContent>
 </xsd:complexType>

 <xsd:complexType name="BasicNameType">
  <xsd:sequence>
   <xsd:element name="FirstName" type="xsd:string" />
   <xsd:element name="MiddleInitial" type="xsd:string" minOccurs="0"
   maxOccurs="10"/>
   <xsd:element name="LastName" type="xsd:string"/>
  </xsd:sequence>
 </xsd:complexType>

 <xsd:complexType name="AddressWithTimeType">
  <xsd:complexContent>
   <xsd:extension base="BasicAddressType">
    <xsd:sequence>
     <xsd:element name="TimeAtAddress" type="xsd:string" minOccurs="1"
     maxOccurs="1"/>
    </xsd:sequence>
   </xsd:extension>
  </xsd:complexContent>
 </xsd:complexType>

 <xsd:complexType name="BasicAddressType">
  <xsd:sequence>
   <xsd:element name="Street1" type="xsd:string"/>
   <xsd:element name="Street2" type="xsd:string" minOccurs="0"
 maxOccurs="1" />
   <xsd:element name="City" type="xsd:string" />
   <xsd:element name="State" type="xsd:string"/>
   <xsd:element name="ZipCode" type="xsd:integer" />
   <xsd:element name="Country" type="xsd:string" minOccurs="0"
 maxOccurs="1" />
  </xsd:sequence>
 </xsd:complexType>

 <xsd:complexType name="CreditInformationType">
  <xsd:sequence>
   <xsd:element name="CreditCards" type="CreditCardsType" minOccurs="1"
   maxOccurs="1"/>
   <xsd:element name="CreditHistory" type="CreditHistoryType"
 minOccurs="1"
   maxOccurs="1"/>
  </xsd:sequence>
 </xsd:complexType>
```

Listing 8.6 A schema with added credit information (PersonList03.xsd). (Continued)

```
<xsd:complexType name="CreditCardsType">
 <xsd:sequence>
  <xsd:element ref="CreditCard" minOccurs="0" maxOccurs="20"/>
 </xsd:sequence>
</xsd:complexType>

<xsd:element name="CreditCard">
 <xsd:complexType>
  <xsd:simpleContent>
   <xsd:extension base="xsd:string">
    <xsd:attribute name="number" type="xsd:long"/>
    <xsd:attribute name="type" type="xsd:string"/>
    <xsd:attribute name="status" type="xsd:string"/>
    <xsd:attribute name="time" type="xsd:string"/>
   </xsd:extension>
  </xsd:simpleContent>
 </xsd:complexType>
</xsd:element>

<xsd:complexType name="CreditHistoryType">
 <xsd:sequence>
  <xsd:element name="CreditEvent" type="xsd:string" minOccurs="0"
  maxOccurs="unbounded"/>
 </xsd:sequence>
 <xsd:attribute name="status" type="xsd:string"/>
 <xsd:attribute name="NumberEvents" type="xsd:integer"/>
</xsd:complexType>

</xsd:schema>
```

Listing 8.6 A schema with added credit information (PersonList03.xsd). (Continued)

In Listing 8.6, we have used the <xsd:extension> element in three places: in the definition of the NameWithEmailType type, in the AddressWithTimeType type (where we add an element to a complex type definition), and in the definition of the <CreditCard> element (where we add attributes to an element that has simple content).

First, let's look at the NameWithEmailType type:

```
<xsd:complexType name="NameWithEmailType">
 <xsd:complexContent>
  <xsd:extension base="BasicNameType">
   <xsd:sequence>
    <xsd:element name="EmailAddress" type="xsd:string" minOccurs="0"
maxOccurs="4"/>
   </xsd:sequence>
```

```
    </xsd:extension>
  </xsd:complexContent>
</xsd:complexType>
```

The base type for the derived NameWithEmailType type is the BasicNameType type, which we saw earlier. The <xsd:extension> element adds a further declaration for an <EmailAddress> element by means of the <xsd:sequence> and <xsd:element> elements, which is of type xsd:string and has a cardinality of 0 to 4. The resulting type defines a complex type that has a declaration for a sequence of <FirstName>, <MiddleInitial>, <LastName>, and <EmailAddress> elements.

The second type which uses the <xsd:extension> element is the AddressWithTimeType type:

```
<xsd:complexType name="AddressWithTimeType">
 <xsd:complexContent>
  <xsd:extension base="BasicAddressType">
   <xsd:sequence>
    <xsd:element name="TimeAtAddress" type="xsd:string" minOccurs="1"
    maxOccurs="1"/>
   </xsd:sequence>
  </xsd:extension>
 </xsd:complexContent>
</xsd:complexType>
```

Here, we have used the <xsd:extension> element in a similar way. The base type is the BasicAddressType type. We add a declaration for a <TimeAtAddress> element to the definition of the base type.

Finally, let's look at how we add attributes to the <CreditCard> element:

```
<xsd:element name="CreditCard">
 <xsd:complexType>
  <xsd:simpleContent>
   <xsd:extension base="xsd:string">
    <xsd:attribute name="number" type="xsd:long"/>
    <xsd:attribute name="type" type="xsd:string"/>
    <xsd:attribute name="status" type="xsd:string"/>
    <xsd:attribute name="time" type="xsd:string"/>
   </xsd:extension>
  </xsd:simpleContent>
 </xsd:complexType>
</xsd:element>
```

Remember that any element with either (or both) element content or one or more attributes is deemed in XSD Schema to be of complex type. Thus, the declaration for the <CreditCard> element uses an <xsd:complexType> element. We specify that the element will have content of simple type, that it will have no elements as content, by using the <xsd:simpleContent> element. We then use the <xsd:extension> element to extend the base type xsd:string by adding four attributes to the <CreditCard> element.

Deriving Types by Restriction

Deriving new types by restriction is a powerful tool in the use of XSD schemas. If we can precisely define the allowed values of the content of an element or the value of an attribute, we can avoid or minimize writing custom code. XSD Schema provides us with many tools that we can apply singly or together in order to restrict the permitted values of attributes or content of elements. In Chapters 5 and 6, you saw examples of how we can use XSD Schema constraining facets to constrain the permitted values of derived types.

One of the most straightforward types of restriction to achieve is the restriction of allowed values—for example, of purchases or credit. Let's look first at a simple credit database that restricts the maximum credit allowed to any individual to $25,000. Within that global credit ceiling, individuals might have their personal credit limit, but the schema checks that nobody has a credit limit in excess of $25,000. The following examples make use of the length and maxInclusive facets in conjunction with the <xsd:restriction> element.

An instance document might look like CreditRatings.xml in Listing 8.7.

```
<?xml version='1.0'?>
<CreditRatings>
 <Person>
  <Name>
   <FirstName>John</FirstName>
   <MiddleInitial>F</MiddleInitial>
   <LastName>Kennedy</LastName>
  </Name>
  <Address>
   <Street1>88 East Street</Street1>
   <Street2></Street2>
   <City>Any Town</City>
   <State>OH</State>
   <Zip>87654</Zip>
  </Address>
  <CreditRating>
   <RiskRating>Good</RiskRating>
   <CreditMaximum>12500</CreditMaximum>
  </CreditRating>
```

continues

Listing 8.7 Credit ratings expressed in XML (CreditRatings.xml).

```
  </Person>
  <Person>
   <Name>
    <FirstName>Mary</FirstName>
    <MiddleInitial>J</MiddleInitial>
    <LastName>Drachmanik</LastName>
   </Name>
   <Address>
    <Street1>99 Bridge Street</Street1>
    <Street2>Eastington</Street2>
    <City>New Town</City>
    <State>MN</State>
    <Zip>33388</Zip>
   </Address>
   <CreditRating>
    <RiskRating>Medium</RiskRating>
    <CreditMaximum>3000</CreditMaximum>
   </CreditRating>
  </Person>
 <!-- Many other Person records could go here. -->
 </CreditRatings>
```

Listing 8.7 Credit ratings expressed in XML (CreditRatings.xml). (Continued)

One specific purpose in creating the schema in Listing 8.8 is to define the maximum ceiling for credit as $25,000. So, we need to restrict the content allowed in the <CreditMaximum> element. Listing 8.8 shows a schema that restricts the value of the <CreditMaximum> element as well as defining or declaring the other parts of the instance document.

The schema in Listing 8.8 contains several <xsd:restriction> elements. The first is contained within the <xsd:simpleType> element named InitialType:

```
<xsd:simpleType name="InitialType">
 <xsd:restriction base="xsd:string">
  <xsd:length value="1"/>
 </xsd:restriction>
</xsd:simpleType>
```

We use the <xsd:restriction> element with the value of the base attribute equal to xsd:string. Nested within the <xsd:restriction> element is an <xsd:length> element by means of which we constrain the middle initial to a length of 1. Note that the <xsd:simpleType> element has no indication of the frequency with which a middle initial can occur. That is defined by using the minOccurs and maxOccurs attributes on the declaration of the <xsd:element> element with name attribute of "MiddleInitial."

```
<?xml version='1.0'?>
<xsd:schema xmlns:xsd="http://www.w3.org/2001/XMLSchema">

<xsd:element name="CreditRatings">
 <xsd:complexType>
  <xsd:sequence>
   <xsd:element name="Person" type="PersonType" minOccurs="0"
   maxOccurs="unbounded"/>
  </xsd:sequence>
 </xsd:complexType>
</xsd:element>

<xsd:complexType name="PersonType">
 <xsd:sequence>
  <xsd:element name="Name" type="NameType"/>
  <xsd:element name="Address" type="AddressType"/>
  <xsd:element name="CreditRating" type="CreditRatingType"/>
 </xsd:sequence>
</xsd:complexType>

<xsd:complexType name="NameType">
 <xsd:sequence>
  <xsd:element name="FirstName" type="xsd:string"/>
  <xsd:element name="MiddleInitial" type="InitialType" minOccurs="0"
  maxOccurs="5"/>
  <xsd:element name="LastName" type="xsd:string"/>
 </xsd:sequence>
</xsd:complexType>

<xsd:simpleType name="InitialType">
 <xsd:restriction base="xsd:string">
  <xsd:length value="1"/>
 </xsd:restriction>
</xsd:simpleType>

<xsd:complexType name="AddressType">
 <xsd:sequence>
  <xsd:element name="Street1" type="xsd:string"/>
  <xsd:element name="Street2" type="xsd:string"/>
  <xsd:element name="City" type="xsd:string"/>
  <xsd:element name="State" type="StateType"/>
  <xsd:element name="Zip" type="ZipCodeType"/>
 </xsd:sequence>
</xsd:complexType>

<xsd:simpleType name="StateType">
 <xsd:restriction base="xsd:string">
```

continues

Listing 8.8 An XSD Schema for Listing 8.7 (CreditRatings.xsd).

```
    <xsd:length value="2"/>
  </xsd:restriction>
 </xsd:simpleType>

 <xsd:simpleType name="ZipCodeType">
  <xsd:restriction base="xsd:positiveInteger">
   <xsd:length value="5"/>
  </xsd:restriction>
 </xsd:simpleType>

 <xsd:complexType name="CreditRatingType">
  <xsd:sequence>
   <xsd:element name="RiskRating" type="xsd:string"/>
   <xsd:element name="CreditMaximum" type="CreditMaximumType"/>
  </xsd:sequence>
 </xsd:complexType>

 <xsd:simpleType name="CreditMaximumType">
  <xsd:restriction base="xsd:decimal">
   <xsd:maxInclusive value="25000.00"/>
  </xsd:restriction>
 </xsd:simpleType>

 </xsd:schema>
```

Listing 8.8 An XSD Schema for Listing 8.7 (CreditRatings.xsd). (Continued)

The second <xsd:restriction> element is used to constrain the length of the <State> element to strings of two characters in length:

```
<xsd:simpleType name="StateType">
 <xsd:restriction base="xsd:string">
  <xsd:length value="2"/>
 </xsd:restriction>
</xsd:simpleType>
```

The restriction that we have used is a very simple one. The <xsd:length> element nested within the <xsd:restriction> element simply constrains the length to two characters. For many, it will be obvious that in the context of an address, the <State> element is intended to use the USPS state codes, which were shown in full in an example in Chapter 5. In this example, however, there is nothing in this schema that constrains the content to the USPS codes. We could have, if we wanted a value in a <State> element of "XX" or "OO." Because of the use of the length facet, however, we cannot have "Ohio" or "Montana" as the content of the <State> element because those words are too long to be permitted by the schema. In practice, we would likely include the

USStateType type used in Listing 5.22. It is not used in Listing 8.8 for reasons of space.

The third restriction is used to constrain the length of the zip code:

```
<xsd:simpleType name="ZipCodeType">
 <xsd:restriction base="xsd:positiveInteger">
  <xsd:length value="5"/>
 </xsd:restriction>
</xsd:simpleType>
```

The base type of the restriction is xsd:positiveInteger. Nested within the <xsd:restriction> element is an <xsd:length> element whose value attribute has a value of "5." Taken together, these constrain the values permitted within the <Zip> element to positive integers whose length is no more and no less than five digits.

The final restriction is on the maximum value of credit permitted for any person in the database:

```
<xsd:simpleType name="CreditMaximumType">
 <xsd:restriction base="xsd:decimal">
  <xsd:maxInclusive value="25000.00"/>
 </xsd:restriction>
</xsd:simpleType>
```

The <xsd:restriction> element has a base attribute with value of xsd:decimal. Nested within the <xsd:restriction> element, the <xsd:maxInclusive> element defines the maximum permitted value of the content of the <CreditMaximum> element as being exactly $25,000.00 Notice, of course, that because the content is an xsd:decimal, the $ sign and the comma are not included within the content of the <CreditMaximum> element.

In the following example in this section, we will look at the use of the <xsd:pattern> element in types that are used as extensions of a schema author created-derived type.

Let's look at the situation of an international database of customers—in the United States, Canada, and the United Kingdom. For the customers, we will use a base complex type for addresses that we will extend to produce derived address types for each of the three chosen countries.

Listing 8.9 shows an example of three customers, one for each of the three address types derived by extension.

A schema for Listing 8.9 is shown in Listing 8.10.

The address for a customer in each of the three countries is based on a derived complex type called BasicAddressType. For each of the countries, a country-specific address type is derived by extension from the BasicAddressType type. See the type definitions for the USAddressType, UKAddressType, and Canada-AddressType types in the schema. The element that is added to the base type while added by means of an <xsd:extension> element is itself a derived type

```
<?xml version='1.0'?>
<Customers>
 <Customer>
  <Name>
   <FirstName>William</FirstName>
   <MiddleNames>Jefferson</MiddleNames>
   <LastName>Clinton</LastName>
  </Name>
  <USAddress>
   <Street>123 Any Street</Street>
   <City>Phoenix</City>
   <Locality>Arizona</Locality>
   <Country>USA</Country>
   <USZipCode>12345-6789</USZipCode>
  </USAddress>
  <!-- Further customer related information could go here. -->
 </Customer>
 <Customer>
  <Name>
   <FirstName>David</FirstName>
   <MiddleNames></MiddleNames>
   <LastName>Steel</LastName>
  </Name>
  <UKAddress>
   <Street>987 High Street</Street>
   <City>Edinburgh</City>
   <Locality>Midlothian</Locality>
   <Country>UK</Country>
   <UKPostalCode>EH1 1XX</UKPostalCode>
  </UKAddress>
  <!-- Further customer related information could go here. -->
 </Customer>
 <Customer>
  <Name>
   <FirstName>Jacques</FirstName>
   <MiddleNames>Michel</MiddleNames>
   <LastName>Chirac</LastName>
  </Name>
  <CanadaAddress>
   <Street>678 Pierre Street</Street>
   <City>Montreal</City>
   <Locality>Quebec</Locality>
   <Country>Canada</Country>
   <CanadaPostalCode>A1A 9Z9</CanadaPostalCode>
  </CanadaAddress>
  <!-- Further customer related information could go here. -->
 </Customer>
</Customers>
```

Listing 8.9 An international customer database (Customers.xml).

```
<?xml version="1.0" encoding="UTF-8"?>
<xsd:schema xmlns:xsd="http://www.w3.org/2001/XMLSchema" >

<xsd:element name="Customers">
 <xsd:complexType>
  <xsd:sequence>
   <xsd:element name="Customer" type="CustomerType"
maxOccurs="unbounded"/>
  </xsd:sequence>
 </xsd:complexType>
</xsd:element>

<xsd:complexType name="CustomerType">
 <xsd:sequence>
  <xsd:element name="Name" type="NameType"/>
  <xsd:group ref="AddressChoiceGroup"/>
 </xsd:sequence>
</xsd:complexType>

<xsd:complexType name="NameType">
 <xsd:sequence>
  <xsd:element name="FirstName" type="xsd:string"/>
  <xsd:element name="MiddleNames" type="xsd:string"/>
  <xsd:element name="LastName" type="xsd:string"/>
 </xsd:sequence>
</xsd:complexType>

<xsd:group name="AddressChoiceGroup">
 <xsd:choice>
  <xsd:element name="USAddress" type="USAddressType"/>
  <xsd:element name="UKAddress" type="UKAddressType"/>
  <xsd:element name="CanadaAddress" type="CanadaAddressType"/>
 </xsd:choice>
</xsd:group>

<xsd:complexType name="BasicAddressType">
 <xsd:sequence>
  <xsd:element name="Street" type="xsd:string"/>
  <xsd:element name="City" type="xsd:string"/>
  <xsd:element name="Locality" type="xsd:string"/>
  <xsd:element name="Country" type="xsd:string"/>
 </xsd:sequence>
</xsd:complexType>

<xsd:complexType name="USAddressType">
 <xsd:complexContent>
  <xsd:extension base="BasicAddressType">
```

continues

Listing 8.10 A schema using restrictions together with extension derived types and choice groups (Customers.xsd).

```
    <xsd:sequence>
     <xsd:element name="USZipCode" type="USZipCodeType"/>
    </xsd:sequence>
   </xsd:extension>
  </xsd:complexContent>
 </xsd:complexType>

 <xsd:simpleType name="USZipCodeType">
  <xsd:restriction base="xsd:string">
   <xsd:pattern value="[0-9]{5}|[0-9]{5}-[0-9]{4}"/>
  </xsd:restriction>
 </xsd:simpleType>

 <xsd:complexType name="UKAddressType">
  <xsd:complexContent>
   <xsd:extension base="BasicAddressType">
    <xsd:sequence>
     <xsd:element name="UKPostalCode" type="UKPostalCodeType"/>
    </xsd:sequence>
   </xsd:extension>
  </xsd:complexContent>
 </xsd:complexType>

 <xsd:simpleType name="UKPostalCodeType">
  <xsd:restriction base="xsd:string">
   <xsd:pattern value="[A-Z]{1,2}[0-9]{1,2} [0-9]{1}[A-Z]{2}"/>
  </xsd:restriction>
 </xsd:simpleType>

 <xsd:complexType name="CanadaAddressType">
  <xsd:complexContent>
   <xsd:extension base="BasicAddressType">
    <xsd:sequence>
     <xsd:element name="CanadaPostalCode" type="CanadaPostalCodeType"/>
    </xsd:sequence>
   </xsd:extension>
  </xsd:complexContent>
 </xsd:complexType>

 <xsd:simpleType name="CanadaPostalCodeType">
  <xsd:restriction base="xsd:string">
   <xsd:pattern value="[A-Z]{1}[0-9]{1}[A-Z]{1} [0-9]{1}[A-Z]{1}[0-
9]{1}"/>
  </xsd:restriction>
 </xsd:simpleType>

 </xsd:schema>
```

Listing 8.10 A schema using restrictions together with extension derived types and choice groups (Customers.xsd). (Continued)

that is derived by restriction. Those types derived by restriction are, respectively for the three countries, the USZipCodeType, UKPostalCodeType, and CanadaPostalCodeType types.

Let's look at the type definition of the CanadaAddressType type. As you can see, it is a complex type. The <xsd:complexContent> element is used to nest the <xsd:extension> element. The only other permitted child of an <xsd:complexContent> element is an <xsd:restriction> element. The <xsd:extension> element uses the base type BasicAddressType to which we add a sequence, in this case a sequence of one, where the declaration for the <CanadaPostalCode> element is present:

```
<xsd:complexType name="CanadaAddressType">
 <xsd:complexContent>
  <xsd:extension base="BasicAddressType">
   <xsd:sequence>
    <xsd:element name="CanadaPostalCode" type="CanadaPostalCodeType"/>
   </xsd:sequence>
  </xsd:extension>
 </xsd:complexContent>
</xsd:complexType>
```

Let's take a closer look at the CanadaPostalCodeType type definition. As you have just seen, it is the type of the <CanadaPostalCode> element that extends the BasicAddressType type. Its type, however, is derived by restriction:

```
<xsd:simpleType name="CanadaPostalCodeType">
 <xsd:restriction base="xsd:string">
  <xsd:pattern value="[A-Z]{1}[0-9]{1}[A-Z]{1} [0-9]{1}[A-Z]{1}[0-9]{1}"/>
 </xsd:restriction>
</xsd:simpleType>
```

The pattern facet reflects the structure of a Canadian postal code: one upper-case alphabetic character, followed by a single numeric digit, followed by one upper-case alphabetic character. Then follows a literal space character, a further single numeric digit, a single upper-case alphabetic character, and finally comes a single numeric digit.

Notice, too, that the content of the CustomerType complex type involves an <xsd:group> element that references the AddressChoiceGroup choice group.

The enumeration Element

Enumeration is a special case of restriction. Rather than restricting, say, the content of an element to a certain length, the enumeration facility in XSD Schema enables specific values to be specified as the only permitted values allowed to occur at certain points in an instance document.

The XML 1.0 DTD enables the values of attributes to be enumerated. XSD Schema extends the facility to constrain values in that way to element content.

Listing 8.11 shows a simple example of how the <xsd:enumeration> element can be used in a clothes catalog scenario.

The XSD schema shown in Listing 8.12 makes use of two <xsd:enumeration> elements in order to define the allowed sizes for garments.

Let's take a look at each of the enumerations used in the schema. The first type definition is as follows:

```
<xsd:simpleType name="SizeType">
<xsd:restriction base="xsd:string">
 <xsd:enumeration value="S"/>
 <xsd:enumeration value="M"/>
 <xsd:enumeration value="L"/>
 <xsd:enumeration value="XL"/>
</xsd:restriction>
</xsd:simpleType>
```

This type definition limits the possible content of the <Size> element to four strings representing available sizes: S, M, L, and XL. Notice that the <Size> element being of SizeType is a simple type—it only contains text content—and that the xsd:string type is restricted by applying an <xsd:restriction> element

```
<?xml version='1.0'?>
<ClothesCatalog>
<Garment>
 <Type>Shirt</Type>
 <Size>S</Size>
 <Color>Light Blue</Color>
 <Price currency="USD">49.99</Price>
</Garment>
<Garment>
 <Type>Shirt</Type>
 <Size>L</Size>
 <Color>Navy Blue</Color>
 <Price currency="USD">55.49</Price>
</Garment>
<Garment>
 <Type>Shirt</Type>
 <Size>XL</Size>
 <Color>Cerise</Color>
 <Price currency="USD">99.99</Price>
</Garment>
</ClothesCatalog>
```

Listing 8.11 A clothes catalog expressed in XML (ClothesCatalog.xml).

```
<?xml version='1.0'?>
<xsd:schema xmlns:xsd="http://www.w3.org/2001/XMLSchema">
<xsd:element name="ClothesCatalog">
 <xsd:complexType>
  <xsd:sequence>
   <xsd:element name="Garment" type="GarmentType"
maxOccurs="unbounded"/>
  </xsd:sequence>
 </xsd:complexType>
</xsd:element>

<xsd:complexType name="GarmentType">
 <xsd:sequence>
  <xsd:element name="Type" type="xsd:string"/>
  <xsd:element name="Size" type="SizeType"/>
  <xsd:element name="Color" type="xsd:string"/>
  <xsd:element ref="Price" />
 </xsd:sequence>
</xsd:complexType>

<xsd:simpleType name="SizeType">
 <xsd:restriction base="xsd:string">
  <xsd:enumeration value="S"/>
  <xsd:enumeration value="M"/>
  <xsd:enumeration value="L"/>
  <xsd:enumeration value="XL"/>
 </xsd:restriction>
</xsd:simpleType>

<xsd:element name="Price">
 <xsd:complexType>
  <xsd:simpleContent>
   <xsd:extension base="xsd:string">
    <xsd:attribute name="currency">
     <xsd:simpleType>
      <xsd:restriction base="xsd:string">
       <xsd:enumeration value="USD"/>
       <xsd:enumeration value="GBP"/>
       <xsd:enumeration value="JPY"/>
      </xsd:restriction>
     </xsd:simpleType>
    </xsd:attribute>
   </xsd:extension>
  </xsd:simpleContent>
 </xsd:complexType>
</xsd:element>

</xsd:schema>
```

Listing 8.12 An XSD schema demonstrating enumerations (ClothesCatalog.xsd).

with nested <xsd:enumeration> elements with permitted content as just mentioned.

The second use of an enumeration is in the declaration for the <Price> element, as follows:

```
<xsd:element name="Price">
 <xsd:complexType>
  <xsd:simpleContent>
   <xsd:extension base="xsd:string">
    <xsd:attribute name="currency">
     <xsd:simpleType>
      <xsd:restriction base="xsd:string">
       <xsd:enumeration value="USD"/>
       <xsd:enumeration value="GBP"/>
       <xsd:enumeration value="JPY"/>
      </xsd:restriction>
     </xsd:simpleType>
    </xsd:attribute>
   </xsd:extension>
  </xsd:simpleContent>
 </xsd:complexType>
</xsd:element>
```

The element declaration includes an anonymous complex type definition and constrains the permitted currencies to be used in the currency attribute of the <Price> element to be U.S. dollars, British Pounds, and Japanese Yen, abbreviated to the three character strings: USD, GBP and JPY.

The pattern Element

We have already looked at the <xsd:pattern> element in Chapter 5. When the <xsd:pattern> element is being used, then a new datatype is being derived by restriction of the base type (which is the value of the base attribute located in the containing <xsd:restriction> element).

Let's look at a further example of how we can use the <xsd:pattern> element to create new datatypes.

Listing 8.13 shows sales figures for XMML.com expressed in a simple instance document.

A schema for those sales figures that uses the <xsd:pattern> element to ensure that the value of the Year attribute is between 2001 and 2005, inclusive, is shown in Listing 8.14.

```
<?xml version='1.0'?>
<SalesFigures Company="XMML.com">
 <Sales Year="2001">1234.56</Sales>
 <Sales Year="2002">2345.67</Sales>
 <Sales Year="2003">3456.78</Sales>
 <Sales Year="2004">4567.89</Sales>
 <Sales Year="2005">5678.90</Sales>
</SalesFigures>
```

Listing 8.13 Sales figures expressed in XML (SalesFigures.xml).

```
<?xml version="1.0" encoding="UTF-8"?>
<xsd:schema xmlns:xsd="http://www.w3.org/2001/XMLSchema" >

<xsd:element name="SalesFigures">
 <xsd:complexType>
  <xsd:sequence>
   <xsd:element name="Sales" type="SalesType" maxOccurs="10"/>
  </xsd:sequence>
  <xsd:attribute name="Company" type="xsd:string"/>
 </xsd:complexType>
</xsd:element>

<xsd:complexType name="SalesType">
 <xsd:simpleContent>
  <xsd:extension base="xsd:string">
   <xsd:attribute name="Year" type="FiveYearType"/>
  </xsd:extension>
 </xsd:simpleContent>
</xsd:complexType>

<xsd:simpleType name="FiveYearType">
 <xsd:restriction base="xsd:string">
  <xsd:pattern value="200[1-5]{1}"/>
 </xsd:restriction>
</xsd:simpleType>

</xsd:schema>
```

Listing 8.14 A schema to constrain figures to years 2001 to 2005 (SalesFigures.xsd).

The value attribute of the <xsd:pattern> element begins with the literal character "200," which is followed by one literal character from 1 to 5 (inclusive). In other words, the value of the Year attribute needs to be from 2001 to 2005 (inclusive).

The xsi:type Attribute

The definition of an XSD Schema simple type or complex type is typically contained within the XSD schema, which is associated with a particular instance document. The W3C XML Schema Recommendation, however, enables information about the type of an element to be declared in an instance document.

If we had an instance document like that in Listing 8.15, you can see that the type of the <Sales> element is declared to be of type SalesType. The value of the xsi:type attribute must be a QName that is either a built-in XSD Schema datatype or a schema author-derived datatype.

Notice that within the start tag of the <SalesFigures> element, there is a namespace declaration:

```
xmlns:xsi="http://www.w3.org/2001/XMLSchema-instance"
```

This declaration associates the URI http://www.w3.org/2001/XMLSchema-instance with the namespace prefix "xsi." The XML Schema instance namespace is what enables us to declare types within the instance document. The W3C XML Schema specification defines the semantics of the type attribute within the XML Schema instance namespace. Thus, when an XML Schema processor meets an xsi:type attribute, it knows how to interpret that because it is in the XML Schema instance namespace as an indication of the type to be applied to the <Sales> elements within the instance document.

```
<?xml version='1.0'?>
<SalesFigures Company="XMML.com"
 xmlns:xsi="http://www.w3.org/2001/XMLSchema-instance">
 <Sales Year="2001" xsi:type="SalesType">1234.56</Sales>
 <Sales Year="2002">2345.67</Sales>
 <Sales Year="2003">3456.78</Sales>
 <Sales Year="2004">4567.89</Sales>
 <Sales Year="2005">5678.90</Sales>
</SalesFigures>
```

Listing 8.15 Using the xsi:type attribute (SalesFigures02.xml).

Summary

In this chapter, we have explored the derivation of new datatypes by using some of the data facets that we examined in Chapters 5 and 6. We have seen, for example, how we can combine extension and restriction to produce types that both reuse and build on existing code and yet have precisely focused constraints on the extended type. In the final part of the chapter, we have looked at declaring types within an instance document by using the xsi:type attribute, which is present in the XML Schema Instance namespace.

In Chapter 9, "Uniqueness and Keys in XSD Schema," we go on to consider some further XSD Schema issues and techniques—in particular, identity-constraint definitions.

Next Steps

CHAPTER

9

Uniqueness and Keys in XSD Schema

In this chapter, we will briefly examine some aspects of XSD Schema that are relevant when you wish to store data in XML but want to maintain some characteristics of the data such that it resembles data stored in a *relational database management system* (RDBMS). In particular, we will examine identity-constraint definitions in W3C XML Schema and how these provide functionality and flexibility, which improves significantly on that provided in XML 1.0 DTDs.

Identity-Constraint Definitions

In Chapter 4, "Applying Datatypes," you were introduced to the xsd:ID, xsd:IDREF, and xsd:IDREFS simple types. Those closely mirror the equivalent functionality provided in XML 1.0 DTDs. When documents were typically standalone, then it was pretty much appropriate for an identity constraint to extend document-wide. As documents are increasingly being created by combining components from different sources, however, the potential need of multiple identity constraints within a single document becomes real.

If, for example, we had an XML-based data store of purchase order and invoice information, there would be a real potential for conflict, because a customer is likely to choose, say, purchase order numbers without attaching great importance to how our invoices were numbered. In a sizeable database, you could possibly have a purchase order number from one (or more) customers with a value of "12345" while your company might also have an invoice numbered as "12345." If these numbers were stored as attributes, which were designated in an accompanying DTD or DTDs as ID attributes, then in XML 1.0 an error might well occur.

There is no intrinsic reason why an ID attribute should be document-wide in the scope of its uniqueness, however, just as in a relational database there is no reason why a particular value couldn't occur in more than one primary key database. If it were possible to limit the scope of an ID attribute "12345" to the purchase order, then another ID attribute with a value of "12345" could legitimately occur in the invoice section of the same data store without causing conflict.

XSD Schema provides three categories of identity-constraint definitions: xsd:key, xsd:keyref, and xsd:unique.

First we will look at the <xsd:unique> element.

The <xsd:unique> Element

The <xsd:unique> element enables us to designate a particular part of an instance document as having to contain a value, whether in the content of an element or an attribute, that is unique. The <xsd:unique> element has some similarities to an XML ID attribute value but provides functionality over the approach of using the XML 1.0 ID type. The XML 1.0 ID type is limited in scope to attribute values only; it has to be unique across a whole document, and such values are not permitted to start with a number or contain space characters.

XSD Schema offers several advantages over the ID type. An XSD Schema identity constraint can be applied to both element content and attribute values and so is not limited to attribute values as the ID type was. A unique value in XSD Schema can start with a number and can be of any datatype. The value can be unique within some specified part of the document and need not be unique document-wide. It is possible in XSD Schema to create unique values that are made up of a composite of values. For example, we might have numbered paragraphs within numbered chapters, in which case we could use the combined information from the chapter number and paragraph number as an indicator of uniqueness.

Let's look at the scenario where a business has business customers and personal customers and wants to allocate an ID that is unique across the whole data store of customers but applies to business customers only.

An instance document in Listing 9.1 shows how, in an abbreviated customer data store, information for a business customer and personal customer are stored.

```
<?xml version='1.0'?>
<Customers>
 <BusinessCustomer uniqueCustomerID="12345">
  <BusinessName>ACME Web Design</BusinessName>
  <BusinessContact>Jim Smith</BusinessContact>
  <BusinessContactEmail>Jim@ACMEWeb.com</BusinessContactEmail>
  <BusinessContactTelephone>(999) 123 4567</BusinessContactTelephone>
  <BusinessContactFax>(999) 234 5678</BusinessContactFax>
  <ShippingAddress>
   <Street1>234 Any Street</Street1>
   <City>Fiction Town</City>
   <State>CA</State>
   <ZipCode>99999</ZipCode>
  </ShippingAddress>
  <Discount Allowed="Yes">
   <DiscountTo10k>10</DiscountTo10k>
   <DiscountTo50k>12</DiscountTo50k>
   <DiscountTo100k>15</DiscountTo100k>
   <DiscountOver100k>20</DiscountOver100k>
  </Discount>
 </BusinessCustomer>
 <PersonalCustomer CustomerID="23456">
  <PersonName>Anna Jessop</PersonName>
  <Address>
   <Street1>345678 Long Street</Street1>
   <City>Fiction Town</City>
   <State>CA</State>
   <ZipCode>99999</ZipCode>
  </Address>
 </PersonalCustomer>
 <BusinessCustomer uniqueCustomerID="12346">
  <BusinessName>SVGenius.com</BusinessName>
  <BusinessContact>Patrick Head</BusinessContact>
<BusinessContactEmail>PatrickHead@SVGenius.com</BusinessContactEmail>
  <BusinessContactTelephone>(777) 123 4567</BusinessContactTelephone>
  <BusinessContactFax>(777) 234 5678</BusinessContactFax>
  <ShippingAddress>
   <Street1>897 Any Street</Street1>
   <City>None Town</City>
   <State>WA</State>
   <ZipCode>77777</ZipCode>
  </ShippingAddress>
  <Discount Allowed="Yes">
   <DiscountTo10k>8</DiscountTo10k>
   <DiscountTo50k>10</DiscountTo50k>
   <DiscountTo100k>12</DiscountTo100k>
```

continues

Listing 9.1 A data store of customer information in XML (Customers.xml).

```
    <DiscountOver100k>17.5</DiscountOver100k>
   </Discount>
  </BusinessCustomer>
 </Customers>
```

Listing 9.1 A data store of customer information in XML (Customers.xml). (continued)

As you can see from this code, we collect additional contact information for business customers: the contact with whom we interact at a business customer as well as allowing business customers a sliding-scale discount, based on size of spending.

The schema for the instance document shown in Listing 9.1 is shown in Listing 9.2.

```
<?xml version='1.0'?>
<xsd:schema xmlns:xsd="http://www.w3.org/2001/XMLSchema">

<xsd:element name="Customers">
 <xsd:complexType>
  <xsd:sequence>
   <xsd:choice minOccurs="1" maxOccurs="unbounded">
    <xsd:element name="BusinessCustomer" type="BusinessCustomerType"/>
    <xsd:element name="PersonalCustomer" type="PersonalCustomerType"/>
   </xsd:choice>
  </xsd:sequence>
 </xsd:complexType>
 <xsd:unique name="uniqueCustomerIDType">
  <xsd:selector xpath="BusinessCustomer"/>
  <xsd:field xpath="@uniqueCustomerID" />
 </xsd:unique>
</xsd:element>

<xsd:complexType name="BusinessCustomerType">
 <xsd:sequence>
  <xsd:element name="BusinessName" type="xsd:string"/>
  <xsd:element name="BusinessContact" type="xsd:string"/>
  <xsd:element name="BusinessContactEmail" type="xsd:string"/>
  <xsd:element name="BusinessContactTelephone" type="xsd:string"/>
  <xsd:element name="BusinessContactFax" type="xsd:string"/>
  <xsd:element name="ShippingAddress" type="ShippingAddressType"/>
  <xsd:element name="Discount" type="DiscountType"/>
 </xsd:sequence>
 <xsd:attribute name="uniqueCustomerID" type="CustomerIDType"/>
</xsd:complexType>
```

Listing 9.2 A schema using the <xsd:unique> element (Customers.xsd).

```
<xsd:complexType name="ShippingAddressType">
 <xsd:sequence>
  <xsd:element name="Street1" type="xsd:string"/>
  <xsd:element name="City" type="xsd:string"/>
  <xsd:element name="State" type="xsd:string"/>
  <xsd:element name="ZipCode" type="xsd:string"/>
 </xsd:sequence>
</xsd:complexType>

<xsd:complexType name="DiscountType">
 <xsd:sequence>
  <xsd:element name="DiscountTo10k" type="DiscountPercentageType"/>
  <xsd:element name="DiscountTo50k" type="DiscountPercentageType"/>
  <xsd:element name="DiscountTo100k" type="DiscountPercentageType"/>
  <xsd:element name="DiscountOver100k" type="DiscountPercentageType"/>
 </xsd:sequence>
 <xsd:attribute name="Allowed" type="DiscountAllowedType"/>
</xsd:complexType>

<xsd:simpleType name="CustomerIDType">
 <xsd:restriction base="xsd:integer">
  <xsd:length value="5"/>
 </xsd:restriction>
</xsd:simpleType>

<xsd:simpleType name="DiscountPercentageType">
 <xsd:restriction base="xsd:decimal">
  <xsd:minInclusive value="5.0"/>
  <xsd:maxInclusive value="50.0"/>
 </xsd:restriction>
</xsd:simpleType>

<xsd:simpleType name="DiscountAllowedType">
 <xsd:restriction base="xsd:string">
  <xsd:enumeration value="Yes"/>
  <xsd:enumeration value="No"/>
 </xsd:restriction>
</xsd:simpleType>

<xsd:complexType name="PersonalCustomerType">
 <xsd:sequence>
  <xsd:element name="PersonName" type="xsd:string"/>
  <xsd:element name="Address" type="ShippingAddressType"/>
 </xsd:sequence>
 <xsd:attribute name="CustomerID" type="CustomerIDType"/>
</xsd:complexType>

</xsd:schema>
```

Listing 9.2 A schema using the <xsd:unique> element (Customers.xsd).

The important part of the schema as far as identity constraints are concerned is contained in the element declaration for the <Customers> element as follows:

```
<xsd:element name="Customers">
 <xsd:complexType>
  <xsd:sequence>
   <xsd:choice minOccurs="1" maxOccurs="unbounded">
    <xsd:element name="BusinessCustomer" type="BusinessCustomerType"/>
    <xsd:element name="PersonalCustomer" type="PersonalCustomerType"/>
   </xsd:choice>
  </xsd:sequence>
 </xsd:complexType>
 <xsd:unique name="uniqueCustomerIDType">
  <xsd:selector xpath="BusinessCustomer"/>
  <xsd:field xpath="@uniqueCustomerID" />
 </xsd:unique>
</xsd:element>
```

The declaration for the <Customers> element contains a complex type definition. The content of the <Customers> element is essentially an unbounded succession of either <BusinessCustomer> or <PersonalCustomer> elements.

How do we tell which part of that succession of elements and attributes is to be unique? The scope of application of the <xsd:unique> element is defined by the subelements <xsd:selector> and <xsd:field>. Each of those subelements possesses an xpath attribute. Not surprisingly, the value of the xpath attribute contains an XPath (XML Path Language) location path. The value of the xpath attribute in the <xsd:selector> element indicates that it is the <BusinessCustomer> element to which the <xsd:unique> element applies. The value of the xpath attribute of the <xsd:field> element makes it known that it is the uniqueCustomerID attribute of the <BusinessCustomer> element that is specifically the focus of the <xsd:unique> element. In other words, throughout the instance document an error would be reported if a value were present in more than one uniqueCustomerID attribute belonging to a <BusinessCustomer> element.

In XPath, there is always a context node relative to which a location path is determined. In this XSD schema, the context node corresponds to the <Customers> element (more strictly, it is the element node that represents in memory the <Customers> element). The xpath attribute of the <xsd:selector> element has the value of BusinessCustomer. The default axis in XPath is the child axis. Thus, we know that the <xsd:selector> is indicating a BusinessCustomer element node that is a child of the context node, an element node representing the <Customers> element. The <xsd:field> element then has the value of @uniqueCustomerID. The "@" character is abbreviated XPath syntax for an attribute. The remainder of the value, uniqueCustomerID, tells us which attribute of the <BusinessCustomer> element to which we are referring.

If we create an instance document such as CustomersB.xml (available for download), which has identical values in two different uniqueCustomerID attributes belonging to <BusinessCustomer> elements, then an error is present. It is correctly reported by XML Spy but was not reported by Turbo XML in the version used at this writing. This situation illustrates the types of difference between XSD Schema tools, such as XML Spy and Turbo XML, which was mentioned in Chapter 1, "Elementary XML Schema."

Sometimes uniqueness is appropriately expressed by using a combination of values rather than a single value. One possible scenario where this situation might occur is in a collection of data about houses in a city. Inevitably, most streets will have houses that have a number 1, 2, 3, and so on. So, we could not base a unique value on house number alone but would need to bring in at least one other value such as street name (or, in a large city, perhaps a district or other locality name, too) to provide a meaningful, unique value.

Similar issues arise when we consider the identification of unique paragraph numbering in an extensive document. Listing 9.3 is a simplified version of such a document.

Listing 9.4 contains a schema that describes the content of the instance document in Listing 9.3.

```
<?xml version='1.0'?>
<Book>
<Introduction>
 <Paragraph ParaID="001">This is the first para of the
introduction.</Paragraph>
 <Paragraph ParaID="002">This is the second para of the
introduction.</Paragraph>
 <Paragraph ParaID="003">This is the third para of the
introduction.</Paragraph>
</Introduction>
<Chapter ChapterID="01">
 <Paragraph ParaID="001">This is the first para of the Chapter
1.</Paragraph>
 <Paragraph ParaID="001">This is the second para of the Chapter
1.</Paragraph>
 <Paragraph ParaID="001">This is the third para of the Chapter
1.</Paragraph>
```

continues

Listing 9.3 A simulated lengthy document in XML (Book.xml).

```
 <Paragraph ParaID="001">This is the fourth para of the Chapter
1.</Paragraph>
</Chapter>
<Chapter ChapterID="02">
 <Paragraph ParaID="001">This is the first para of the Chapter
2.</Paragraph>
 <Paragraph ParaID="002">This is the second para of the Chapter
2.</Paragraph>
 <Paragraph ParaID="003">This is the third para of the Chapter
2.</Paragraph>
 <Paragraph ParaID="004">This is the fourth para of the Chapter
2.</Paragraph>
</Chapter>
<!-- Many more chapters with realistically long paragraphs could go
here. -->
</Book>
```

Listing 9.3 A simulated lengthy document in XML (Book.xml). (Continued)

```
<?xml version="1.0" encoding="UTF-8"?>
<xsd:schema xmlns:xsd="http://www.w3.org/2001/XMLSchema" >

<xsd:element name="Book">
 <xsd:complexType>
  <xsd:sequence>
   <xsd:element name="Introduction" type="IntroductionType"/>
   <xsd:element ref="Chapter" maxOccurs="unbounded"/>
  </xsd:sequence>
 </xsd:complexType>
</xsd:element>

<xsd:complexType name="IntroductionType">
 <xsd:sequence>
  <xsd:element name="Paragraph" type="ParagraphType"
maxOccurs="unbounded"/>
 </xsd:sequence>
</xsd:complexType>

<xsd:element name="Chapter">
<xsd:complexType>
 <xsd:sequence>
  <xsd:element name="Paragraph" maxOccurs="unbounded">
   <xsd:complexType>
    <xsd:simpleContent>
     <xsd:extension base="xsd:string">
```

Listing 9.4 A schema using <xsd:unique> on a combination of values (Book.xsd).

```
        <xsd:attribute name="ParaID">
         <xsd:simpleType>
          <xsd:restriction>
           <xsd:pattern value="[0-9]{3}"/>
          </xsd:restriction>
         </xsd:simpleType>
        </xsd:attribute>
       </xsd:extension>
      </xsd:simpleContent>
     </xsd:complexType>
    </xsd:element>
   </xsd:sequence>
   <xsd:attribute name="ChapterID">
    <xsd:simpleType>
     <xsd:restriction>
      <xsd:pattern value="[0-9]{2}"/>
     </xsd:restriction>
    </xsd:simpleType>
   </xsd:attribute>
  </xsd:complexType>
    <xsd:unique>
     <xsd:selector xpath="/Book/Chapter" />
     <xsd:field xpath="@ChapterID"/>
     <xsd:field xpath="Paragraph/@ParaID"/>
    </xsd:unique>
  </xsd:element>

  <xsd:complexType name="ParagraphType">
   <xsd:simpleContent>
    <xsd:extension base="xsd:string">
     <xsd:attribute name="ParaID">
      <xsd:simpleType>
       <xsd:restriction>
        <xsd:pattern value="[0-9]{3}"/>
       </xsd:restriction>
      </xsd:simpleType>
     </xsd:attribute>
    </xsd:extension>
   </xsd:simpleContent>
  </xsd:complexType>

  </xsd:schema>
```

Listing 9.4 A schema using <xsd:unique> on a combination of values (Book.xsd). (Continued)

Notice how the <xsd:unique> element is used:

```
<xsd:unique>
 <xsd:selector xpath="/Book/Chapter" />
 <xsd:field xpath="@ChapterID"/>
```

```
  <xsd:field xpath="Paragraph/@ParaID"/>
</xsd:unique>
```

The <xsd:selector> element uses an absolute location path, /Book/Chapter, which indicates that starting from the root node, we select a Chapter element node that has a Book element node parent that is a child node of the root node. The presence of two <xsd:field> elements indicates that we must take into account the value of both xpath attributes before arriving at a knowledge of what combination of values is to be unique. In other words, we are aiming to create a unique value that incorporates both the value of the ChapterID attribute of the <Chapter> element and the ParaID attribute of the <Paragraph> element. Thus, we might have more than one ParaID attribute with value of 002, but only when they are in different chapters.

Having looked at some examples of specifying uniqueness, let's move on to take a look at the <xsd:key> and <xsd:keyref> elements.

The <xsd:key> and <xsd:keyref> Elements

The ID and IDREF datatypes of XML 1.0 are limited in the extent to which they can represent relational database structures. The W3C XML Schema Working Group had as one of its objectives the creation of a schema language that would better support relational database structures. The <xsd:key> and <xsd:keyref> elements provide improvements in this context.

An ID/IDREF relationship relates to an entire document. Computationally, it can be demanding to process the references in large documents. As you will see, the <xsd:key>/<xsd:keyref> relationships use XPath location paths, thereby defining the scope of the relationship and allowing a processor to focus on accessing only relevant parts of a document.

In XML 1.0, an ID type is a datatype. In XSD Schema, it is possible to specify the identity constraint and the datatype separately.

XSD Schema extends the facility to define identity constraints to element content. In XML 1.0, the use of the ID attribute was limited to use in attribute values only.

One of the principles of database usage is that information should be entered in one place only. Doing so reduces the likelihood of entering incorrect data in one location, of what could be many locations, where the same data is held. It also facilitates changes, corrections, or updates being made to data because the data needs to be changed or updated once only.

As an example of the use of the <xsd:key> and <xsd:keyref> elements, let's look at the scenario in which employees in a multinational company have their location specified as part of the data recorded about them.

An instance document for employees of XMML.com is shown in Listing 9.5.

Because it is possible that the company might at some future date relocate its offices in a particular locality (in the example, it is Langley), it would be

```
<?xml version='1.0'?>
<XMMLPersonnel>
<Staff>
<!-- For brevity only Name and CompanyRecord data will be shown. -->
<Person locationID="3" employeeID="71">
 <Name>
  <FirstName>Cinder</FirstName>
  <MiddleNames>Ella</MiddleNames>
  <LastName>Goodfairy</LastName>
 </Name>
 <CompanyRecord>
  <DateJoined>2001-01-20</DateJoined>
  <DateLeft></DateLeft>
  <HRNumber>CEG1234 1234</HRNumber>
  <Assignment>
   <Department>Sister support</Department>
   <JobTitle>Assistant</JobTitle>
   <DateAssigned>2001-01-20</DateAssigned>
   <DateCompleted></DateCompleted>
   <HRAssessment></HRAssessment>
  </Assignment>
 </CompanyRecord>
</Person>
<!-- Other Person elements go here. -->
</Staff>


<Locations>
<!-- Content of Location elements abbreviated to Street and City
only -->
<Location LocationID="1">
 <Street>123 First Street</Street>
 <City>New York</City>
</Location>
<Location LocationID="2">
 <Street>23435 Regent Street</Street>
 <City>London</City>
</Location>
<Location LocationID="3">
 <Street>99 Spook Street</Street>
 <City>Langley</City>
</Location>
</Locations>

</XMMLPersonnel>
```

Listing 9.5 A listing of XMML.com staff (XMMLPersonnel.xml).

inefficient to store information about the street, city, postal code, and so on within each <Person> element. Thus, it makes sense, and corresponds closely to how tables in an RDBMS might be set up, for us to store information about locations separately. If, in the terms of the example, location 3 is relocated, we need only update street and city information (and other information in a real-life setting) in one location in the instance document: the <Location> element for LocationID 3.

A schema corresponding to the instance document in Listing 9.5 that uses the <xsd:key> and <xsd:keyref> elements is shown in Listing 9.6. As you read the definition for the <XMMLPersonnel> element, take a close look at the <xsd:key> and <xsd:keyref> elements.

```
<?xml version="1.0" encoding="UTF-8"?>
<xsd:schema xmlns:xsd="http://www.w3.org/2001/XMLSchema" >

<xsd:element name="XMMLPersonnel">
 <xsd:complexType>
  <xsd:sequence>
   <xsd:element name="Staff" type="StaffType"/>
   <xsd:element name="Locations" type="LocationsType"/>
  </xsd:sequence>
 </xsd:complexType>
 <xsd:keyref name="PersonToLocationRef"
            refer="PersonToLocationKey" >
  <xsd:selector xpath="Staff/Person" />
  <xsd:field xpath="@LocationID"/>
  </xsd:keyref>
  <xsd:key name="PersonToLocationKey">
   <xsd:selector xpath="Locations/Location"/>
   <xsd:field xpath="@LocationID"/>
  </xsd:key>
</xsd:element>

<xsd:complexType name="StaffType">
 <xsd:sequence>
  <xsd:element ref="Person" maxOccurs="unbounded"/>
 </xsd:sequence>
</xsd:complexType>

<xsd:element name="Person">
<xsd:complexType >
 <xsd:sequence>
  <xsd:element name="Name" type="BasicNameType"/>
  <xsd:element name="CompanyRecord" type="CompanyRecordType"/>
```

Listing 9.6 A schema using the <xsd:key> and <xsd:keyref> elements (XMMLPersonnel.xsd).

```
  </xsd:sequence>
  <xsd:attribute name="locationID" type="xsd:positiveInteger"/>
  <xsd:attribute name="employeeID" type="xsd:positiveInteger"/>
</xsd:complexType>
</xsd:element>

<xsd:complexType name="BasicNameType">
 <xsd:sequence>
  <xsd:element name="FirstName" type="xsd:string"/>
  <xsd:element name="MiddleNames" type="xsd:string"/>
  <xsd:element name="LastName" type="xsd:string"/>
 </xsd:sequence>
</xsd:complexType>

<xsd:complexType name="CompanyRecordType">
 <xsd:sequence>
  <xsd:element name="DateJoined" type="ValidDateType" />
  <xsd:element name="DateLeft" type="LeftDateType" />
  <xsd:element name="HRNumber" type="xsd:string"/>
  <xsd:element name="Assignment" type="AssignmentType" minOccurs="1"
maxOccurs="unbounded"/>
 </xsd:sequence>
</xsd:complexType>

<xsd:complexType name="AssignmentType">
 <xsd:sequence>
  <xsd:element name="Department" type="xsd:string" />
  <xsd:element name="JobTitle" type="xsd:string"/>
  <xsd:element name="DateAssigned" type="ValidDateType"/>
  <xsd:element name="DateCompleted" type="LeftDateType"/>
  <xsd:element name="HRAssessment" type="xsd:string"/>
 </xsd:sequence>
</xsd:complexType>

<xsd:simpleType name="ValidDateType">
 <xsd:restriction base="xsd:date">
  <xsd:minExclusive value="2000-12-31"/>
  <xsd:maxExclusive value="2005-02-28"/>
 </xsd:restriction>
</xsd:simpleType>

<xsd:simpleType name="LeftDateType">
  <xsd:union>
   <xsd:simpleType>
    <xsd:restriction base="ValidDateType"/>
```

continues

Listing 9.6 A schema using the <xsd:key> and <xsd:keyref> elements (XMMLPersonnel.xsd). (Continued)

```
    </xsd:simpleType>
    <xsd:simpleType>
     <xsd:restriction base="xsd:string">
       <xsd:enumeration value=""/>
     </xsd:restriction>
    </xsd:simpleType>
   </xsd:union>
  </xsd:simpleType>

 <xsd:complexType name="LocationsType">
  <xsd:sequence>
   <xsd:element name="Location" type="LocationType"
 maxOccurs="unbounded"/>
  </xsd:sequence>
 </xsd:complexType>

 <xsd:complexType name="LocationType">
  <xsd:sequence>
   <xsd:element name="Street" type="xsd:string"/>
   <xsd:element name="City" type="xsd:string"/>
  </xsd:sequence>
  <xsd:attribute name="LocationID" type="xsd:positiveInteger"/>
 </xsd:complexType>

 </xsd:schema>
```

Listing 9.6 A schema using the <xsd:key> and <xsd:keyref> elements (XMMLPersonnel .xsd). (Continued)

Let's look more closely at the use of the key and the key reference.

```
<xsd:keyref name="PersonToLocationRef"
            refer="PersonToLocationKey" >
 <xsd:selector xpath="Staff/Person" />
 <xsd:field xpath="@LocationID"/>
</xsd:keyref>
<xsd:key name="PersonToLocationKey">
 <xsd:selector xpath="Locations/Location"/>
 <xsd:field xpath="@LocationID"/>
</xsd:key>
```

The <xsd:keyref> element contains an <xsd:selector> element and an <xsd:field> element. The xpath attributes of those elements indicates by means of two XPath location paths that the key information (sorry for the pun!) is located in the LocationID attribute of the <Person> element, which is a child of the <Staff> element. The <xsd:keyref> element indicates where a reference is being made to a key. Its refer attribute contains the name of the key that is being referenced.

The value in the refer attribute of the <xsd:keyref> element must match the value of a name attribute of an <xsd:key> element. That is the mechanism by which, in more complex documents, we can be sure that we are associating the appropriate pair of key and key reference. Within the <xsd:key> element, we find an <xsd:selector> element and an <xsd:field> element. The values of the xpath attributes of those elements define the location of the key in the instance document. The XPath location paths show that the key is contained in the LocationID attribute of the <Location> element that is a child of a <Locations> element.

Summary

In this chapter, we have looked briefly at the improved flexibility in specifying uniqueness constraints in XSD Schema compared to the fairly primitive constraints present in the XML 1.0 DTD. In addition, we have examined how we can use the <xsd:key> and <xsd:keyref> elements to represent data structures similar to those that you can expect to find in the tables of a relational database.

In Chapter 10, "Bringing the Parts Together," we will explore the use of type definitions and element declarations across multiple schema documents and also bring many of the ideas and techniques that you have seen together in a more substantial example than we have created so far.

CHAPTER

10

Bringing the Parts Together

In this chapter, we will bring the parts together in two senses. First, we will examine how we can modularize XSD schemas and reassemble the parts to enable code reuse and thereby achieve improvements in maintenance of schemas. Second, we will create a significantly longer example than we have seen in earlier chapters, because the document uses many of the techniques already discussed in this book.

Modularizing Schemas

You might have already noticed that schemas, even in examples in earlier chapters, can become fairly complex. Particularly with longer schemas, it can be a considerable task to orient yourself within the schema. Increasingly, as you apply schemas to real-world situations, it makes good sense, on grounds of convenience alone, to modularize schemas and then reference those modularized schemas.

The modular approach also has advantages in efficiency of maintenance of the information in schemas. If the schema structure for a particular type of information, let's say addresses, is held in a separate schema file, it is easy to locate the schema and update the necessary structure of address information in one file. Any other schemas that reference the definitions or declarations within the modified file will reflect those updates. A nonmodular approach would require updating address information in, perhaps, several places with additional time spent on the task and the attendant risks of creating inconsistencies in structure by unintentionally making slightly different changes in each schema document.

We might want others to be able to access and use type definitions that we have created. Alternatively, we might want to access type definitions in XSD Schema documents created by others. While we might want to use an industry-standard schema as it stands, we might alternatively want to adapt the standard schema to reflect our company's data needs. In any of these scenarios, the ability to access more than one schema document is a typical requirement.

The notion of modular schemas is one of growing importance throughout the XML world. You might be aware that XHTML has been modularized in version 1.1 (see www.w3.org/TR/xhtml11). Profiles for different types of user agents will make use of a range of the XHTML 1.1 modules appropriate to the user agent capabilities. To do that, the user agent must be able to make use of schema information from several schema modules. Similar modularization changes are proposed for other XML-based languages, such as the Scalable Vector Graphics specification in version 1.1 (see www.w3.org/TR/SVG11). So, you can see that an understanding of how to combine schema modules will be a highly relevant skill in the future of XML application languages.

In some settings, we might well be satisfied with simply using definitions from a referenced schema exactly as they are defined in the schema that we have referenced. Sometimes, however, it might be advantageous to adapt definitions from the referenced schema to the specific needs of information storage in a particular setting. You have seen how useful it can be to derive new datatypes from types within the same schema as the derived type. We will look at the syntax that we need to use to exploit referenced schema definitions to create new datatypes or elements within the referencing schema.

Let's move on to look at the syntax we need in order to be able to make use of schema information contained in referenced schema modules.

How to Use Schema Modules

In order to make use of schema components in a referenced schema, we need the schema components to be named. There is no way to reference an anonymous type in another module. In addition, we can reference only globally declared or defined schema components. Thus, the schema components that we can use include element and attribute declarations (which, of course, are named), named complex type definitions, named simple type definitions, named model groups, and named attribute groups.

First, let's look at the mechanism that enables us to make use of external XSD Schema documents but that limits us to using the referenced elements, types, or groups exactly as they are specified in the referenced schema.

The <xsd:include> Mechanism

For example, let's look at a simple scenario in which we have a staff and a customer database—a situation similar to the example that we will be developing later in the chapter.

An instance document for staff would, in a highly simplified form, be similar to Listing 10.1.

A simplified instance document for customer data is shown in Listing 10.2.

I hope you can see that both Listing 10.1 and Listing 10.2 contain name information with identical structures. We could, of course, simply create XSD schema components in each of two schemas for these instance documents, or we could, perhaps unwisely, attempt to create one large schema that would allow the structures of both instance documents in one schema document. We want to look at how to reuse schema components, however, so we will create a simple schema that we will reference from the schema that we will use for our instance documents. In other words, we will have two instance documents and two schemas, and each of those two schemas will reference a type library (which itself is an XSD Schema schema). The common definitions or declarations go in the type library.

The schema to be referenced, which is sometimes called a type library, is shown in Listing 10.3.

Notice that a type library must have, as document element, an <xsd:schema> element with an appropriate namespace declaration for the xsd namespace prefix. It is important to include some documentation in a type library in order to ensure that the overall purpose of the type library is clear and that each type

```
<?xml version='1.0'?>
<SimpleStaff>
<Person>
 <Name>
  <FirstName>John</FirstName>
  <MiddleNames>Rivaldo</MiddleNames>
  <LastName>Doe</LastName>
 </Name>
 <EmployeeInformation>
  <EmployeeID>98765</EmployeeID>
  <DateJoined>2003-01-08</DateJoined>
  <!-- Other information would go here -->
 </EmployeeInformation>
</Person>
</SimpleStaff>
```

Listing 10.1 A simplified staff instance document (SimpleStaff.xml).

```
<?xml version='1.0'?>
<SimpleCustomer>
<Customer>
 <Name>
  <FirstName>John</FirstName>
  <MiddleNames>Pyotr</MiddleNames>
  <LastName>Mikhailovich</LastName>
 </Name>
 <CustomerAddress>
  <Street>444 Fore Street</Street>
  <City>Fore Town</City>
  <State>MN</State>
  <ZipCode>54321</ZipCode>
 </CustomerAddress>
<!-- More customer information would go here. -->
</Customer>
<!-- More customers would go here. -->
</SimpleCustomer>
```

Listing 10.2 A simplified customer instance document (SimpleCustomer.xml).

```
<?xml version="1.0" encoding="UTF-8"?>
<xsd:schema xmlns:xsd="http://www.w3.org/2001/XMLSchema" >

<xsd:annotation>
 <xsd:documentation>
  This is a simplified type library for use in Chapter 10 of XML
Schema Essentials.
  It has been designed to be referenced by SimpleStaff.xsd and
SimpleCustomer.xsd [and in real life probably others]
 </xsd:documentation>
</xsd:annotation>

<xsd:complexType name="Name">
<xsd:annotation>
 <xsd:documentation>
  This is a complex type containing basic name information.
 </xsd:documentation>
</xsd:annotation>
 <xsd:sequence>
  <xsd:element name="FirstName" type="xsd:string"/>
  <xsd:element name="MiddleNames" type="xsd:string"/>
  <xsd:element name="LastName" type="xsd:string"/>
 </xsd:sequence>
</xsd:complexType>

</xsd:schema>
```

Listing 10.3 A simple type library (SimpleTypeLib.xsd).

definition, element declaration, and so on is clearly described. I suggest that in practice you document each type definition, too. If you take that approach and make the text in the documentation clear and comprehensive, you can apply the XSLT stylesheet demonstrated in Chapter 1, "Elementary XML Schema," to the type library to produce basic documentation for it in HTML—thereby enabling you or colleagues to quickly get an overview of the purpose and content of the type library.

Now that we have created our type library, let's move on to look at how we can reference it from the schemas to be created for SimpleStaff.xml and SimpleCustomer.xml. Listing 10.4 shows the schema for SimpleStaff.xml.

```
<?xml version="1.0" encoding="UTF-8"?>
<xsd:schema xmlns:xsd="http://www.w3.org/2001/XMLSchema" >
<xsd:include schemaLocation="SimpleTypeLib.xsd"/>

<xsd:annotation>
 <xsd:documentation>
  This schema references SimpleTypeLib.xsd to reference the structure
for the Name element.
  Ensure that the SimpleTypeLib.xsd schema is in the same directory as
this schema if the reference is to work correctly.
 </xsd:documentation>
</xsd:annotation>

<xsd:element name="SimpleStaff">
 <xsd:complexType>
  <xsd:sequence>
   <xsd:element name="Person" type="PersonType"
maxOccurs="unbounded"/>
  </xsd:sequence>
 </xsd:complexType>
</xsd:element>

<xsd:complexType name="PersonType">
  <xsd:annotation>
   <xsd:documentation>
    The Name element declaration in this complex type definition uses
a complex type definition from the SimpleTypeLib.xsd schema and we use
the type attribute as normal.
   </xsd:documentation>
  </xsd:annotation>
 <xsd:sequence>
  <xsd:element name="Name" type="NameType"/>
```

continues

Listing 10.4 A schema for SimpleStaff.xml using <xsd:include> (SimpleStaff.xsd).

```
    <xsd:element name="EmployeeInformation"
  type="EmployeeInformationType"/>
   </xsd:sequence>
  </xsd:complexType>

  <xsd:complexType name="EmployeeInformationType">
   <xsd:sequence>
    <xsd:element name="EmployeeID" type="xsd:string"/>
    <xsd:element name="DateJoined" type="xsd:date"/>
   </xsd:sequence>
  </xsd:complexType>

  </xsd:schema>
```

Listing 10.4 A schema for SimpleStaff.xml using <xsd:include> (SimpleStaff.xsd). (Continued)

The third line of the schema,

```
<xsd:include schemaLocation="SimpleTypeLib.xsd"/>
```

is the mechanism by which we can reference the type definition in SimpleTypeLib.xsd. In effect, it is equivalent to copying code from the type library and pasting into the referencing schema all the type definitions (and so on) that such a referenced schema might contain. Notice the schemaLocation attribute of the <xsd:include> element, which is essential for the XML Schema processor to locate the desired type library. The value of the schemaLocation attribute can be any URI. In the present example, the file SimpleTypeLib.xsd must be in the same directory as SimpleStaff.xsd because it is from that file that the reference is being made. If you want to share a type library among several groups of colleagues, you will likely want to choose a full URL on an intranet or position the type library publicly on the Internet depending on the scope of access to the type library that you desire.

In this instance, the referenced type library contains only one complex type definition—for the NameType complex type. Because conceptually, the <xsd: include> element effectively copies the complex type definition into the SimpleStaff.xsd schema, we can reference the NameType type by using the element declaration in the normal way:

```
<xsd:element name="Name" type="NameType"/>
```

The type definition is for a NameType type contained in SimpleTypeLib.xsd. Because it has been "included" in the SimpleStaff.xsd schema, however, we use syntax identical to that we would use if it were physically included (written) in SimpleStaff.xsd.

Similarly, Listing 10.5 shows a schema, SimpleCustomer.xsd, that also uses an <xsd:include> element for SimpleCustomer.xml.

```
<?xml version="1.0" encoding="UTF-8"?>
<xsd:schema xmlns:xsd="http://www.w3.org/2001/XMLSchema" >
<xsd:include schemaLocation="SimpleTypeLib.xsd"/>

<xsd:annotation>
 <xsd:documentation>
  This schema references SimpleTypeLib.xsd to reference the structure
for the Name element.
  Ensure that the SimpleTypeLib.xsd schema is in the same directory as
this schema if the reference is to work correctly.
 </xsd:documentation>
</xsd:annotation>

<xsd:element name="SimpleCustomer">
 <xsd:complexType>
  <xsd:sequence>
   <xsd:element name="Customer" type="CustomerType"
maxOccurs="unbounded"/>
  </xsd:sequence>
 </xsd:complexType>
</xsd:element>

<xsd:complexType name="CustomerType">
  <xsd:annotation>
   <xsd:documentation>
    The Name element declaration in this complex type definition uses
a complex type definition from the SimpleTypeLib.xsd schema and we use
    the type attribute as normal.
   </xsd:documentation>
  </xsd:annotation>
 <xsd:sequence>
  <xsd:element name="Name" type="NameType"/>
  <xsd:element name="CustomerAddress" type="CustomerAddressType"/>
 </xsd:sequence>
</xsd:complexType>
<xsd:complexType name="CustomerAddressType">
 <xsd:sequence>
```

continues

Listing 10.5 A schema using <xsd:include> for SimpleCustomer.xml (SimpleCustomer.xsd).

```
    <xsd:element name="Street" type="xsd:string"/>
    <xsd:element name="City" type="xsd:string"/>
    <xsd:element name="State" type="xsd:string"/>
    <xsd:element name="ZipCode" type="xsd:string"/>
  </xsd:sequence>
 </xsd:complexType>

</xsd:schema>
```

Listing 10.5 A schema using <xsd:include> for SimpleCustomer.xml (SimpleCustomer.xsd). (Continued)

We can post type libraries at URIs that are publicly accessible. If, for example, we wanted the file SimpleTypeLib.xsd to be accessible on the XMML.com Web site, we could amend the schemaLocation attribute to have the value of "http://www.XMML.com/TypeLibraries/SimpleTypeLib.xsd".

If we consider Listings 10.1 to 10.5, we have two separate instance documents—each of which has its own XSD schema document. Each of those XSD Schema documents is incomplete on its own, however, and references—by using the <xsd:include> element—a type definition contained in a type library.

This type of interrelationship enables us to reuse code only when the code in the type library is exactly in the form that we want to use. In many situations, we might want to extend or restrict the types or elements contained in the type library. Suppose that we wanted to add <Title> and <FormOfAddress> elements to the Name element. The following section shows how to do that. If we want to extend or otherwise adapt the code in the type library, we need to make use of the <xsd:redefine> element.

The <xsd:redefine> Mechanism

As mentioned in the previous section on the <xsd:include> element, we can consider a referenced type definition, named group, named element, or attribute as being copied and pasted into the referencing schema. If we had simply written a type definition in the referencing schema, we would expect to be able to derive new datatypes from it by the methods we looked at in Chapter 8, "Deriving Types." If we want to be able to derive new types from a type definition in a referenced type library, we need to use the <xsd:redefine> element rather than the <xsd:include> element to reference the type library. When we use the <xsd:include> element, we use the referenced definition or declaration unchanged. If we want to change it, we use the <xsd:redefine> element and nest the syntax to derive the new datatype within the <xsd:redefine> element.

If we add <Title>, <FormOfAddress>, and <Comment> elements to our instance document for customer data, we have an instance document, SimpleCustomer02.xml, shown in Listing 10.6.

We could, of course, remove the reference to NameType in SimpleTypeLib.xsd and create a CustomerNameType type from scratch, but we don't need to perform this task. We can derive a new CustomerNameType from the existing NameType by extension, as you were shown in Chapter 8.

Listing 10.7 shows a schema using <xsd:redefine> to extend the NameType type definition so that we can use the modified structure of the customer information that you saw in Listing 10.6. The schema has internal documentation to help you understand how the parts fit together.

```
<?xml version='1.0'?>
<SimpleCustomer>
<Customer>
 <Name>
  <FirstName>John</FirstName>
  <MiddleNames>Pyotr</MiddleNames>
  <LastName>Mikhailovich</LastName>
  <Title>Mr</Title>
  <FormOfAddress>Mr. Mikhailovich</FormOfAddress>
  <Comment>He hates being called John.</Comment>
 </Name>
 <CustomerAddress>
  <Street>444 Fore Street</Street>
  <City>Fore Town</City>
  <State>MN</State>
  <ZipCode>54321</ZipCode>
 </CustomerAddress>
<!-- More customer information would go here. -->
</Customer>
<!-- More customers would go here. -->
</SimpleCustomer>
```

Listing 10.6 Adding elements to the instance document (SimpleCustomer02.xml).

```
<?xml version="1.0" encoding="UTF-8"?>
<xsd:schema xmlns:xsd="http://www.w3.org/2001/XMLSchema" >

<xsd:redefine schemaLocation="SimpleTypeLib.xsd">
```

continues

Listing 10.7 A schema using <xsd:redefine> to extend the NameType type definition (SimpleCustomer02.xsd).

```
 <xsd:complexType name="NameType">
  <xsd:annotation>
   <xsd:documentation>
    This complex type definition redefines the NameType type.
    Note that the base complex type definition NameType is contained
in SimpleTypeLib.xsd not in this schema.
   </xsd:documentation>
  </xsd:annotation>
  <xsd:complexContent>
   <xsd:extension base="NameType">
    <xsd:sequence>
     <xsd:element name="Title" type="xsd:string"/>
     <xsd:element name="FormOfAddress" type="xsd:string"/>
     <xsd:element name="Comment" type="xsd:string"/>
    </xsd:sequence>
   </xsd:extension>
  </xsd:complexContent>
 </xsd:complexType>
</xsd:redefine>

<xsd:annotation>
 <xsd:documentation>
  This schema references SimpleTypeLib.xsd to reference the complex
type for the Name type.
  Ensure that the SimpleTypeLib.xsd schema is in the same directory as
this schema if the reference is to work correctly.
 </xsd:documentation>
</xsd:annotation>

<xsd:element name="SimpleCustomer">
 <xsd:complexType>
  <xsd:sequence>
   <xsd:element name="Customer" type="CustomerType"
maxOccurs="unbounded"/>
  </xsd:sequence>
 </xsd:complexType>
</xsd:element>

<xsd:complexType name="CustomerType">
  <xsd:annotation>
   <xsd:documentation>
    The Name element declaration in this complex type definition uses
a complex type definition from the SimpleTypeLib.xsd schema and we use
the type attribute as normal.
```

Listing 10.7 A schema using <xsd:redefine> to extend the NameType type definition (SimpleCustomer02.xsd). (Continued)

```
    The type definition CustomerNameType extends the Name type
referenced from SimpleTypeLib.xsd.
   </xsd:documentation>
  </xsd:annotation>
 <xsd:sequence>
  <xsd:element name="Name" type="NameType"/>
  <xsd:element name="CustomerAddress" type="CustomerAddressType"/>
 </xsd:sequence>
</xsd:complexType>

<xsd:complexType name="CustomerAddressType">
 <xsd:sequence>
  <xsd:element name="Street" type="xsd:string"/>
  <xsd:element name="City" type="xsd:string"/>
  <xsd:element name="State" type="xsd:string"/>
  <xsd:element name="ZipCode" type="xsd:string"/>
 </xsd:sequence>
</xsd:complexType>

</xsd:schema>
```

Listing 10.7 A schema using <xsd:redefine> to extend the NameType type definition (SimpleCustomer02.xsd). (Continued)

Notice that the <xsd:redefine> element comes immediately after the <xsd: schema> element. There are four elements in XSD Schema that must occur (if they are present at all) before type definitions and element declarations: <xsd:include>, <xsd:import>, <xsd:redefine>, and <xsd:annotation>. We will look at the <xsd:import> element soon. Within that prioritized group, the four named elements can occur in any order. Of course, <xsd:annotation> can also be used as a child element of other XSD Schema elements within a schema document, not only as a child of the <xsd:schema> element.

In the element redefinition that follows, you can see the syntax to extend the type definition for the NameType type:

```
<xsd:redefine schemaLocation="SimpleTypeLib.xsd">
 <xsd:complexType name="NameType">
  <xsd:annotation>
   <xsd:documentation>
    This complex type definition redefines the NameType type.
    Note that the base complex type definition NameType is contained in
SimpleTypeLib.xsd not in this schema.
   </xsd:documentation>
```

```
    </xsd:annotation>
    <xsd:complexContent>
     <xsd:extension base="NameType">
      <xsd:sequence>
       <xsd:element name="Title" type="xsd:string"/>
       <xsd:element name="FormOfAddress" type="xsd:string"/>
       <xsd:element name="Comment" type="xsd:string"/>
      </xsd:sequence>
     </xsd:extension>
    </xsd:complexContent>
   </xsd:complexType>
  </xsd:redefine>
```

Like the <xsd:include> element, there is a schemaLocation attribute on the <xsd:redefine> element. It, too, can take any URI value. In this case, the type library is in the same directory as the referencing schema.

To achieve the derivation of a new datatype, we nest a <xsd:complexContent> element within the <xsd:complexType> element. Within the <xsd:complexContent> element is nested an <xsd:extension> element. We specify the NameType type (located in the type library) as the base type from which the new datatype is derived. We add a sequence of element declarations to the end of the existing type definition, which we express by a sequence of <xsd:element> elements nested within an <xsd:sequence> element.

Use of the <xsd:redefine> element enables us to modify the structure of types or elements referenced from the type library.

Let's move on to examine how we can use the <xsd:import> element to make use of namespace-qualified documents.

The <xsd:import> Mechanism

The third of the mechanisms that XSD Schema provides to reference schema components in external schema documents is the <xsd:import> element.

Use of the <xsd:import> element can involve the use of namespaces, which is a topic we haven't yet looked at in detail in this book.

Namespace and W3C XML Schema

Up to this point in the book, we have simply used XSD schemas without considering namespace issues in any detail. In order to use the <xsd:import> element, we must have some understanding of how namespaces are treated in XSD Schema. The good news is that XSD Schema, unlike DTDs in XML 1.0, has namespace support built in. The not-so-good news is that expressing namespaces and the relevant syntax correctly can become a little complex.

Review of XML Namespaces

In this section, we will briefly review key points of XML namespaces. The Namespaces in XML Recommendation is the background for the use of namespaces in XSD Schema and is located at www.w3.org/TR/REC-xml-names/ if you wish to review the official documentation.

The Namespaces in XML Recommendation addresses the difficulties that would likely arise when we mix elements or attributes from different XML application languages together in one document. Listings 10.8 and 10.9 show two simple XML documents that use a <Title> element. If we create a composite document that combines information about Wiley books and Wiley authors, the potential ambiguity as to which <Title> element is being referred to and what its content should be is probably obvious to you. We would have two <Title> elements with identical element type names but different context and meaning.

Listing 10.8 shows a simple data store that contains brief descriptions of a couple of Wiley titles on XML.

Listing 10.9 shows a simple data store expressed as XML that lists a couple of Wiley authors.

So, how do we handle the situation in which we might want to combine in one document the <Title> element that gives us some information about an author with the <Title> element that gives us some information about a book? The Namespaces in XML Recommendation provides a solution to mixing elements from different vocabularies by means of the namespace URI, the association of a namespace URI with a namespace prefix by means of a namespace declaration, and the use of the namespace prefix in element type names in XML documents. The following is an example start tag that contains a namespace declaration:

```
<myPrefix:AnElement xmlns:myPrefix="http://www.XMML.com/Namespace">
```

```
<?xml version='1.0'?>
<BookList>
 <Book>
  <Title>XPath Essentials</Title>
  <Series>XML Essentials</Series>
 </Book>
 <Book>
  <Title>XML Schema Essentials</Title>
  <Series>XML Essentials</Series>
 </Book>
</BookList>
```

Listing 10.8 A simple book list in XML (BookList.xml).

```
<?xml version='1.0'?>
<Authors>
 <Author>
  <Title>Mr.</Title>
  <FirstAndMiddleNames>R. Allen</FirstAndMiddleNames>
  <LastName>Wyke</LastName>
 </Author>
 <Author>
  <Title>Mr.</Title>
  <FirstAndMiddleNames>Andrew</FirstAndMiddleNames>
  <LastName>Watt</LastName>
 </Author>
</Authors>
```

Listing 10.9 A list of authors in XML (Authors.xml).

To use a namespace prefix, it must have been declared as just shown. Typically, the namespace declaration occurs either in the outermost element in an XML document or in the outermost element where the namespace prefix is actually used. The namespace declaration is the string xmlns followed by a single colon character followed by the namespace prefix that we will use in the relevant part of the XML document. The string in quotes following the xmlns:myPrefix is the namespace URI (sometimes also called the namespace name).

To use a declared namespace but to avoid needing to use namespace prefixes, we can use a default namespace declaration that uses xmlns (with no following colon and no namespace prefix):

```
<AnElement xmlns="http://www.XMML.com/Namespace">
```

This element has no namespace prefix but is declared as being associated with the namespace URI http://www.XMML.com/Namespace.

In a namespace prefix, only certain XML names are permitted. It is not permitted to use a colon character, which is a legal XML names character. An XML name in which a colon character is not used is called an NCName: a non-colon name. The reason for that, hopefully, will be obvious. If the colon character were permitted in a namespace prefix, a namespace-aware XML processor would have difficulty in interpreting an element called

```
my:Element:Name
```

Is the namespace prefix my and the element type name Element:Name? Or is the namespace prefix my:Element and the element type name Name? Excluding the use of the colon character in NCNames avoids such ambiguity.

Returning to our example, if we add a namespace declaration to our two XML documents that contain <Title> elements and consistently use the relevant namespace prefix, the source of potential confusion to a document author and to an XML processor is removed. The <bk:Title> element is distinguishable from the <au:Title> element to both human readers and to an XML processor.

Listings 10.10 and 10.11, respectively, show the book list and the list of authors with a namespace declaration and namespace prefix.

Listing 10.11 shows the authors list rewritten by using a namespace URI and namespace prefix.

```
<?xml version='1.0'?>
<bk:BookList
  xmlns:bk="http://www.WileyBooks.com/Namespace">
 <bk:Book>
  <bk:Title>XPath Essentials</bk:Title>
  <bk:Series>XML Essentials</bk:Series>
 </bk:Book>
 <bk:Book>
  <bk:Title>XML Schema Essentials</bk:Title>
  <bk:Series>XML Essentials</bk:Series>
 </bk:Book>
</bk:BookList>
```

Listing 10.10 The book list with namespace prefix (BookList02.xml).

```
<?xml version='1.0'?>
<au:Authors
  xmlns:au="http://www.WileyAuthors.com/Namespace">
 <au:Author>
  <au:Title>Mr.</au:Title>
  <au:FirstAndMiddleNames>R. Allen</au:FirstAndMiddleNames>
  <au:LastName>Wyke</au:LastName>
 </au:Author>
 <au:Author>
  <au:Title>Mr.</au:Title>
  <au:FirstAndMiddleNames>Andrew</au:FirstAndMiddleNames>
  <au:LastName>Watt</au:LastName>
 </au:Author>
</au:Authors>
```

Listing 10.11 The authors list with namespace prefix (Authors02.xml).

Thus, we could use the <bk:Title> element and <au:Title> element in a single document without fear of ambiguity, because for the human reader the two are distinguishable by the different namespace prefixes—and for XML processors, they are distinguishable because they refer to different namespace URIs. Of course, at appropriate places in the document we would need to include namespace declarations for each of the two namespace URIs that we intend to use.

Let's move on to look at a simple schema that uses namespaces and namespace prefixes.

Schemas for Instance Documents That Use Namespaces

Let's look, for example, at how to express a schema that we could use as the schema for the namespace-qualified authors list shown earlier in Listing 10.11. The schema is shown in Listing 10.12.

Notice that on the <xsd:schema> element, the targetNamespace attribute and the default namespace declaration (xmlns="http://www.WileyAuthors

```
<?xml version="1.0" encoding="UTF-8"?>
<xsd:schema xmlns:xsd="http://www.w3.org/2001/XMLSchema"
 targetNamespace="http://www.WileyAuthors.com/Namespace"
 xmlns="http://www.WileyAuthors.com/Namespace"
 elementFormDefault="qualified"
 attributeFormDefault="unqualified">

<xsd:element name="Authors">
 <xsd:complexType>
  <xsd:sequence>
   <xsd:element name="Author" type="AuthorType"
maxOccurs="unbounded"/>
  </xsd:sequence>
 </xsd:complexType>
</xsd:element>

<xsd:complexType name="AuthorType">
 <xsd:sequence>
  <xsd:element name="Title" type="xsd:string"/>
  <xsd:element name="FirstAndMiddleNames" type="xsd:string"/>
  <xsd:element name="LastName" type="xsd:string"/>
 </xsd:sequence>
</xsd:complexType>

</xsd:schema>
```

Listing 10.12 A schema for the authors list including namespaces (Authors02.xsd).

.com/Namespace") both refer to the same namespace URI. The elementForm-Default attribute has a value of "qualified," meaning that when the elements defined in the schema are used in an instance document, a namespace prefix is, by default, to be used.

Notice, too, that when we declare an element in the namespace in the schema

```
<xsd:element name="Authors">
```

we don't include the namespace prefix. As indicated by the elementForm-Default attribute, however, we do use the element type name in "qualified" form in an instance document. A qualified name, or QName, includes the namespace prefix and the colon character. So, although we see "Authors" in the element declaration in the XSD schema, in the instance we see <au:Authors> or the use of some other specified namespace prefix.

Let's move on and look at how we can use the <xsd:import> element.

Using the <xsd:import> Element

To illustrate the use of <xsd:import>, we need an instance document that includes namespaces, an XSD Schema document, and a type library that is referenced by the XSD Schema document.

The instance document that includes elements from two namespace is shown in Listing 10.13. Notice that there are two namespace prefixes in use. The namespace prefix XMML is associated with the namespace URI http://www.XMML.com/CoreSchema (which, as we will see in a moment, relates to the type library), and the namespace prefix cust is associated with the namespace URI http://www.XMML.com/Customers.

```
<?xml version='1.0'?>
<cust:SimpleCustomer
  xmlns:xsi="http://www.w3.org/2001/XMLSchema-instance"
  xsi:schemaLocation="http://www.XMML.com/Customers
SimpleCustomer03.xsd"
  xmlns:cust="http://www.XMML.com/Customers"
  xmlns:XMML="http://www.XMML.com/CoreSchema"
  >
<cust:Customer>
 <XMML:Name xmlns:XMML="http://www.XMML.com/CoreSchema">
  <XMML:FirstName>John</XMML:FirstName>
```

continues

Listing 10.13 An XML document using two namespaces (SimpleCustomer03.xml).

```
    <XMML:MiddleNames>Pyotr</XMML:MiddleNames>
    <XMML:LastName>Mikhailovich</XMML:LastName>
   </XMML:Name>
   <cust:CustomerAddress >
    <cust:Street>444 Fore Street</cust:Street>
    <cust:City>Fore Town</cust:City>
    <cust:State>MN</cust:State>
    <cust:ZipCode>54321</cust:ZipCode>
   </cust:CustomerAddress>
  <!-- More customer information would go here. -->
  </cust:Customer>
  <!-- More customers would go here. -->
  </cust:SimpleCustomer>
```

Listing 10.13 An XML document using two namespaces (SimpleCustomer03.xml). (Continued)

Notice the attributes on the document element for Listing 10.13. We use the xsi:schemaLocation attribute to associate the namespace URI, http://www .XMML.com/Customers, with an actual file location. So that the XSD Schema processor will understand what the namespace prefix xsi refers to, we must also include a namespace declaration association: the namespace prefix xsi with the URI http:www.w3.org/2001/XMLSchema-instance, the W3C XML Schema Instance namespace URI.

```
<cust:SimpleCustomer
  xmlns:xsi="http://www.w3.org/2001/XMLSchema-instance"
  xsi:schemaLocation="http://www.XMML.com/Customers
SimpleCustomer03.xsd"
  xmlns:cust="http://www.XMML.com/Customers"
  xmlns:XMML="http://www.XMML.com/CoreSchema"
  >
```

In addition, we associate the cust and XMML namespace prefixes with their respective URIs.

The XSD Schema associated with the instance document is shown in Listing 10.14. Notice the namespace declarations on the <xsd:schema> element that declare the namespace URIs http://www.XMML.com/Customers and http://www.XMML.com/CoreSchema. Notice, too, the namespace and schemaLocation attributes of the <xsd:import> element. In the schema, the namespace URI http://www.XMML.com/Customers is now the default namespace. Notice, too, that the <xsd:import> element comes earlier in the schema than element declarations or type definitions.

And finally, Listing 10.15 shows the type library using namespaces. Notice that the namespace URI in the type library is also declared in the SimpleCustomer03.xsd schema and in the instance document SimpleCustomer03.xml.

```
<?xml version="1.0" encoding="UTF-8"?>
<xsd:schema xmlns:xsd="http://www.w3.org/2001/XMLSchema"
 xmlns="http://www.XMML.com/Customers"
 xmlns:XMML="http://www.XMML.com/CoreSchema"
 targetNamespace="http://www.XMML.com/Customers"
 elementFormDefault="qualified">

<xsd:import namespace="http://www.XMML.com/CoreSchema"
   schemaLocation="SimpleTypeLib02.xsd"/>

<xsd:annotation>
 <xsd:documentation>
  This schema references SimpleTypeLib02.xsd to reference the Name
element.
  Ensure that the SimpleTypeLib02.xsd schema is in the same directory
as this schema if the reference is to work correctly.
 </xsd:documentation>
</xsd:annotation>

<xsd:element name="SimpleCustomer">
 <xsd:complexType>
  <xsd:sequence>
   <xsd:element name="Customer" type="CustomerType"
maxOccurs="unbounded"/>
  </xsd:sequence>
 </xsd:complexType>
</xsd:element>

<xsd:complexType name="CustomerType">
  <xsd:annotation>
   <xsd:documentation>
    The XMML:Name element declaration in this complex type definition
references an element declaration from the SimpleTypeLib02.xsd schema.
    </xsd:documentation>
  </xsd:annotation>
 <xsd:sequence>
  <xsd:element ref="XMML:Name" />
  <xsd:element name="CustomerAddress" type="CustomerAddressType"/>
 </xsd:sequence>
</xsd:complexType>

<xsd:complexType name="CustomerAddressType">
 <xsd:sequence>
  <xsd:element name="Street" type="xsd:string"/>
  <xsd:element name="City" type="xsd:string"/>
  <xsd:element name="State" type="xsd:string"/>
```

continues

Listing 10.14 An XSD schema that uses the <xsd:import> element (SimpleCustomer03.xsd).

```
  <xsd:element name="ZipCode" type="xsd:string"/>
 </xsd:sequence>
</xsd:complexType>

</xsd:schema>
```

Listing 10.14 An XSD schema that uses the <xsd:import> element (SimpleCustomer03.xsd). (Continued)

```
<?xml version="1.0" encoding="UTF-8"?>
<xsd:schema xmlns:xsd="http://www.w3.org/2001/XMLSchema"
 targetNamespace="http://www.XMML.com/CoreSchema"
 xmlns="http://www.XMML.com/CoreSchema"
 elementFormDefault="unqualified"
 >

<xsd:annotation>
 <xsd:documentation>
  This is a simplified type library for use in Chapter 10 of XML
Schema Essentials.
  It has been designed to be referenced by SimpleStaff.xml and
SimpleCustomer.xml
 </xsd:documentation>
</xsd:annotation>

<xsd:element name="Name">
<xsd:complexType >
<xsd:annotation>
 <xsd:documentation>
  This is a complex type containing basic name information.
 </xsd:documentation>
</xsd:annotation>
 <xsd:sequence>
  <xsd:element name="FirstName" type="xsd:string"/>
  <xsd:element name="MiddleNames" type="xsd:string"/>
  <xsd:element name="LastName" type="xsd:string"/>
 </xsd:sequence>
</xsd:complexType>
</xsd:element>

</xsd:schema>
```

Listing 10.15 The type library using a namespace. (SimpleTypeLib02.xsd).

Notice that within the <xsd:schema> element, we set both the targetNamespace attribute and the default namespace declaration to point to the same URI.

In the available space, it isn't possible to give an exhaustive description of the use of <xsd:include>, <xsd:redefine>, and <xsd:import>. The examples given for the use of these elements provide working code to illustrate one way to use them.

Having looked at putting things together, in the sense of combining XSD Schema modules, using <xsd:include>, <xsd:redefine>, and <xsd:import>, let's move on to create an example that makes use of many, but not all, of the techniques of XSD Schema that you have been introduced to earlier in the book.

Creating the Example

The earlier chapters in this book have introduced you to many of the most useful techniques available in XSD Schema, but inevitably, because we were introducing topics individually, the examples used were short and relatively simple in order to help you understand how each part of XSD Schema is used. In this chapter, we will create a more substantial schema that will incorporate many techniques that you have already seen but will apply them in combination rather than individually as self-contained techniques. We will also use the example to reinforce your understanding of techniques for accessing type definitions that are spread across more than one XSD Schema document.

The example that we will create will relate to the data store of XMML.com, a consultancy in XML and related technologies. Later, we will consider what information a company of that type might need to store and discuss options as to how we might create a schema to ensure that instance documents are appropriately and consistently structured.

Planning the Example

In order to plan the schemas we want to create, we must define what the existing data stores might be and the information needs of the company. To simplify the situation, we will assume that there are no existing relevant data stores.

Defining the Information Needs

In this section, we will consider what information a consultancy might need to store as XML. Of course, although this example will be more complex than others you have seen, it will still, because of space constraints, be significantly more limited than is likely to adequately meet the information needs of all but the least ambitious companies. We will assume that you are familiar with the process of information needs gathering from a client and the importance of listening to what the client needs to do and needs to know.

The business needs of a consultancy are many. We will focus only on the information needs about people which are relevant to XMML.com and so create two XML instance documents: one a data store of information about staff of the company, and the second a data store about customers. Because both XML data stores will contain information about people, there will be a commonality of data structures that will enable us to explore the reuse of XSD Schema code as well as several other techniques that you have seen applied in shorter schemas.

We will assume that XMML.com operates in three countries: the United States, Canada, and the United Kingdom. Staff will be relocated from one country to the other as workload requires, so we will need to be able to handle address and telephone information from three countries.

In the staff data store, we will need to have information about names of staff members. In addition, we will store address information and information about an individual's history of employment at XMML.com. The latter information is specific to the staff data store.

In the customer data store, we will need to store information about customers' names. Contact information and form of address will be directly relevant in that context.

Because we will store information about names in both the staff and customer data stores, we will create a type library with basic name information and address information.

Documenting the Schema

As soon as we make the transition from creating example schemas, such as those you have seen earlier in this book, to the preparation of production (or similar) schemas, the issue of documentation becomes immensely important. Good documentation allows easier revision of the schema by the schema author or someone else at a future date. If we want our schema to be accessed and used by schema authors, it is much easier to spread the use of a schema we have authored if it is well documented and if other parties find it easy to understand and apply.

As we work through the creation of the individual parts of the schemas developed in this chapter, we will ensure that we consider what we should document and provide sufficient information in the <xsd:documentation> elements so that anyone reading the schemas at a future date will be able to interpret the structure and also understand the business process or practice reasons for the design choices that we make.

Basic Schema Templates

If you are planning to do any hand coding in XSD Schema, you should create a file of templates to save you a lot of typing. A good setup of files is to keep copies, for example, of the basic template for an XSD schema as well as common structures for complex type and simple type definitions in one file. Note that Listing 10.16, which you might want to adapt for your own template needs, is not a well-formed XSD Schema. It simply has code snippets that are suitable for cutting and pasting.

Of course, if you and your colleagues are going to adopt an approach like this one, it makes sense to ensure that you are all using the same namespace prefix in such templates. If you don't, then you will, unless you take appropriate precautions, run into problems on any schema where you are working jointly or where you mix schemas from different authors. We discussed importing existing schemas earlier in this chapter.

```
<?xml version='1.0'?>
<XSDTemplates>

<!-- A bare XSD Schema document template. -->
<?xml version="1.0" encoding="UTF-8"?>
<xsd:schema xmlns:xsd="http://www.w3.org/2001/XMLSchema" >
</xsd:schema>

<!-- An XSD Schema document template with xsd:annotation. -->
<?xml version="1.0" encoding="UTF-8"?>
<xsd:schema xmlns:xsd="http://www.w3.org/2001/XMLSchema" >
<xsd:annotation>
 <xsd:documentation>

 </xsd:documentation>
</xsd:annotation>
</xsd:schema>

<!-- A simple type definition template for restriction with pattern. -->
<xsd:simpleType name="">
 <xsd:restriction base="">
  <xsd:pattern value=""/>
 </xsd:restriction>
</xsd:simpleType>
<!-- A simple type definition template for restriction with
enumeration. -->
```

continues

Listing 10.16 A set of XSD Schema text templates in an XML file (XSDTemplates.xml).

```
<xsd:simpleType name="">
 <xsd:restriction base="">
  <xsd:enumeration value=""/>
 </xsd:restriction>
</xsd:simpleType>

<!-- A simple type definition template for union type. May not use
xsd:pattern and xsd:enumeration -->
<xsd:simpleType>
  <xsd:union>
   <xsd:simpleType>
    <xsd:restriction base="">
     <xsd:pattern value=""/>
    </xsd:restriction>
   </xsd:simpleType>
   <xsd:simpleType>
    <xsd:restriction base="">
      <xsd:enumeration value=""/>
    </xsd:restriction>
   </xsd:simpleType>
  </xsd:union>
 </xsd:simpleType>

<!-- Complex type definition -->
<xsd:complexType name="">
 <xsd:sequence>
   <xsd:element name="" type=""/>
   <xsd:element ref=""/>
 </xsd:sequence>
</xsd:complexType>

</XSDTemplates>
```

Listing 10.16 A set of XSD Schema text templates in an XML file (XSDTemplates.xml). (Continued)

Modularizing the Schemas

The data in the staff and customer information requirements suggests that it would be appropriate to create a type library to hold information about names and addresses.

So, we will plan to create three schema documents. XMMLHRFile.xsd will be the schema document for the staff file, and XMMLCustomers.xsd will be the schema document for the customers file. XMMLCore.xsd will be the type library, which will be referenced by both of the other schemas.

For ease of presentation, the creation of the various schemas will be described as separate processes. In practice, you would plan out top-level design for each of the schemas and the type library and analyze those initial decisions for any inappropriate interactions between the proposed schemas.

Creating the Staff Schema

Having looked at some of the issues that we need to bear in mind when creating a production schema, let's proceed to construct the schema step by step.

An instance document that is to be described by the schema we want to develop is shown in Listing 10.17. Notice that the instance document is much longer than those used previously. In part, this reflects the fact that we want to collect a more real-life set of data. Also, variants of the possible data structures within the instance document have been constructed so as to test many of the cardinality and other constraints in the XSD Schema that we will construct later. If you make your instance documents too simple or too short during the development process, you won't be testing the possible constraints adequately with possible errors arising later when the untested situations arise in the use of real data. For the schema author, that is an embarrassing situation.

```
<?xml version='1.0'?>
<XMMLHRFile>
<Person>
 <Name>
  <FirstName>Nelson</FirstName>
  <MiddleNames>Zebulun</MiddleNames>
  <LastName>Mandela</LastName>
 </Name>
 <Demographics>
  <DateOfBirth>1975-12-03</DateOfBirth>
  <Gender>Male</Gender>
 </Demographics>
 <Residence>
  <CurrentAddress>
   <Street1>888 Uptown Avenue</Street1>
   <Street2></Street2>
   <City>Any Town</City>
```

continues

Listing 10.17 An instance document for the staff list (XMMLHRFile.xml).

```
    <State>FL</State>
    <ZipCode>12345-6789</ZipCode>
    <Country>USA</Country>
   </CurrentAddress>
   <PastAddresses>
    <PastAddress>
     <Street1>85 Regent Street</Street1>
     <Street2></Street2>
     <City>London</City>
     <County></County>
     <UKPostalCode>WC8 9XX</UKPostalCode>
     <Country>UK</Country>
    </PastAddress>
   </PastAddresses>
  </Residence>
  <CompanyExperience>
   <DateJoined>1999-10-08</DateJoined>
   <DateLeft></DateLeft>
   <HRNumber>NZM1234</HRNumber>
   <CurrentAssignment>
    <Department>Sales</Department>
    <Location>USA</Location>
    <JobTitle>VP Sales</JobTitle>
    <DateAssigned>2001-01-20</DateAssigned>
    <DateCompleted></DateCompleted>
    <HRAssessment></HRAssessment>
   </CurrentAssignment>
   <PreviousAssignments>
    <PreviousAssignment>
     <Department>Sales</Department>
     <Location>Canada</Location>
     <JobTitle>Sales Manager</JobTitle>
     <DateAssigned>1999-10-08</DateAssigned>
     <DateCompleted>2001-01-19</DateCompleted>
     <HRAssessment>Excellent progress. Promoted to VP Sales. Relocated
to US office.</HRAssessment>
     </PreviousAssignment>
   </PreviousAssignments>
  </CompanyExperience>
</Person>
<Person>
  <Name>
   <FirstName>Jacqui</FirstName>
   <MiddleNames>Mary</MiddleNames>
   <LastName>Kennedy</LastName>
  </Name>
  <Demographics>
   <DateOfBirth>1958-10-07</DateOfBirth>
```

Listing 10.17 An instance document for the staff list (XMMLHRFile.xml). (Continued)

```
    <Gender>Female</Gender>
   </Demographics>
   <Residence>
    <CurrentAddress>
     <Street1>999 Sylvia Street</Street1>
     <Street2></Street2>
     <City>Vancouver</City>
     <Province>British Columbia</Province>
     <CanadaPostalCode>A1A 8A8</CanadaPostalCode>
     <Country>Canada</Country>
    </CurrentAddress>
    <PastAddresses>
     <PastAddress>
      <Street1>97 Peter Street</Street1>
      <Street2></Street2>
      <City>London</City>
      <County></County>
      <UKPostalCode>W1 8DB</UKPostalCode>
      <Country>UK</Country>
     </PastAddress>
     <PastAddress>
      <Street1>888 Camellia Avenue</Street1>
      <Street2></Street2>
      <City>Miami</City>
      <State>FL</State>
      <ZipCode>23456-7890</ZipCode>
      <Country>USA</Country>
     </PastAddress>
    </PastAddresses>
   </Residence>
   <CompanyExperience>
    <DateJoined>2000-09-18</DateJoined>
    <DateLeft></DateLeft>
    <HRNumber>JMK7890</HRNumber>
    <CurrentAssignment>
     <Department>Customer Support</Department>
     <Location>Canada</Location>
     <JobTitle>Customer Support Representative</JobTitle>
     <DateAssigned>2001-09-18</DateAssigned>
     <DateCompleted></DateCompleted>
     <HRAssessment>Good initial progress.</HRAssessment>
    </CurrentAssignment>
    <PreviousAssignments>
    </PreviousAssignments>
   </CompanyExperience>
  </Person>
  <!-- A third person and subsequent persons would go here. -->
  </XMMLHRFile>
```

Listing 10.17 An instance document for the staff list (XMMLHRFile.xml). (continued)

```
<?xml version="1.0" encoding="UTF-8"?>
<xsd:schema xmlns:xsd="http://www.w3.org/2001/XMLSchema" >
<xsd:annotation>
 <xsd:documentation>
  A hypothetical schema for the human resources information needs for
XMML.com.
  This version is dated 2001-11-10. Version 0.01.
  The schema accesses and uses type definitions from the XMMLCore.xsd
file.
 </xsd:documentation>
</xsd:annotation>

</xsd:schema>
```

Listing 10.18 A first version of the Human Resources schema (XMMLHRSchema001.xsd).

The instance document contains an unbounded number of <Person> elements. Within each <Person> element, you will see <Name>, <Demographics>, <Residence>, and <CompanyExperience> elements. The structures within those elements vary depending on the personal situation of the individuals being described. In addition, there are differing constraints for the permitted content of some elements and attributes.

Let's move on and begin to create the schema. In practice, you might be using a tool, such as XML Spy or Turbo XML, which will assist you in creating a schema. As we create the example, we will hand code each step in the process of building up the final schema.

Starting the Schema

Each XSD schema has a standard template that includes the <xsd:schema> element and a namespace declaration for the W3C XML Schema namespace. To that, we add some documentation about the nature and the overall purpose of the schema, as shown in Listing 10.18.

Notice that a version number is used in the filename for the schema. The version number and date is also expressed in the <xsd:documentation> element. If those are out of synchronization, it is a marker that something is not quite right.

The next step is to add an element declaration for the element root of the human resources instance document. This is shown in Listing 10.19.

The declaration for the <XMMLHRFile> element indicates that it contains a sequence of <Person> elements, each of PersonType type. The next step, shown in Listing 10.20, is to add the complex type definition for the PersonType type.

```
<?xml version="1.0" encoding="UTF-8"?>
<xsd:schema xmlns:xsd="http://www.w3.org/2001/XMLSchema" >
<xsd:annotation>
 <xsd:documentation>
  A hypothetical schema for the human resources information needs for
XMML.com.
  This version is dated 2001-11-10. Version 0.02.
  The schema accesses and uses type definitions from the XMMLCore.xsd
file.
 </xsd:documentation>
</xsd:annotation>

<xsd:element name="XMMLHRFile">
<xsd:annotation>
 <xsd:documentation>
  The XMMLHRFile element is the document element for the XMMLHR
schema. It has a sequence of Person child elements, which are
unbounded in number.
 </xsd:documentation>
</xsd:annotation>
 <xsd:complexType>
  <xsd:element name="Person" type="PersonType" maxOccurs="unbounded"/>
 </xsd:complexType>
</xsd:element>

</xsd:schema>
```

Listing 10.19 A second version of the human resources schema (XMMLHRSchema002.xsd).

```
<?xml version="1.0" encoding="UTF-8"?>
<xsd:schema xmlns:xsd="http://www.w3.org/2001/XMLSchema" >
<xsd:annotation>
 <xsd:documentation>
  A hypothetical schema for the human resources information needs for
XMML.com.
  This version is dated 2001-11-10. Version 0.03.
  The schema accesses and uses type definitions from the XMMLCore.xsd
file.
 </xsd:documentation>
</xsd:annotation>

<xsd:element name="XMMLHRFile">
```

continues

Listing 10.20 The staff schema after the type definition for PersonType has been added (XMMLHRFile003.xsd).

```
<xsd:annotation>
 <xsd:documentation>
  The XMMLHRFile element is the document element for the XMMLHR
schema. It has a sequence of Person child elements, which are
unbounded in number.
 </xsd:documentation>
</xsd:annotation>
 <xsd:complexType>
  <xsd:element name="Person" type="PersonType" maxOccurs="unbounded"/>
 </xsd:complexType>
</xsd:element>

<xsd:complexType name="PersonType">
<xsd:annotation>
 <xsd:documentation>
  The PersonType complex type consists of a sequence of four elements.
  The Name element is referenced from the XMMLCore.xsd type library.
  The Demographics element is of a complex type derived in this
schema.
  The Residence element is of a complex type derived in this schema.
  The CompanyExperience element is of type derived in this schema.
 </xsd:documentation>
</xsd:annotation>
 <xsd:sequence>
  <xsd:element ref="Name" />
  <xsd:element name="Demographics" type="DemographicsType"/>
  <xsd:element name="Residence" type="ResidenceType"/>
  <xsd:element name="CompanyExperience" type="CompanyExperienceType"/>
 </xsd:sequence>
</xsd:complexType>

</xsd:schema>
```

Listing 10.20 The staff schema after the type definition for PersonType has been added (XMMLHRFile003.xsd). (Continued)

Notice that we have updated the version information in the documentation. In addition, within the documentation of the PersonType complex type definition, design decisions (which might have to be changed at a later time if there is some flaw in the design logic) are documented so it is explicit what the design intentions are.

In practice, you will build up the schema by analyzing element by element or type by type the content of an element or type and creating further element declarations or type definitions. At each step, you will be considering—in the light of the overall information requirements—whether there is any information in the schema that you are creating that is common with some other schema that you will need to create. In our example, there are only two XSD Schema documents (as well as the type library). As we progress through consideration of the design, however, it will become clear that there is a common structure to address information within the staff and customer schemas. Therefore, address information will be stored in the type library, XMML-Core.xsd.

This process of design and review continues until the final schema and the referenced documents are completed. The final schema, XMMLHRFileFinal.xsd, is shown in Listing 10.21. The schema is copiously documented with <xsd:documentation> elements, partly so that it provides an example of a documented schema of reasonable length and partly to help you understand what is happening as you read through the code. If you take time to read through the schema, you should find sufficient information to enable you to understand what the schema is about and how it relates to XMMLCustomers.xsd and XMMLCore.xsd.

```
<?xml version="1.0" encoding="UTF-8"?>
<xsd:schema xmlns:xsd="http://www.w3.org/2001/XMLSchema" >
<xsd:annotation>
 <xsd:documentation>
  A hypothetical schema for the human resources information needs for
XMML.com.
  This version is dated 2001-11-10. Version 1.0.
  The schema accesses and uses type definitions and/or element
declarations from the XMMLCore.xsd file.
 </xsd:documentation>
</xsd:annotation>

<xsd:include schemaLocation="XMMLCore.xsd"/>

<xsd:element name="XMMLHRFile">
<xsd:annotation>
 <xsd:documentation>
  The XMMLHRFile element is the document element for the XMMLHR
schema. It has a sequence of Person child elements, which are
unbounded in number.
 </xsd:documentation>
</xsd:annotation>
 <xsd:complexType>
  <xsd:sequence>
```

continues

Listing 10.21 The final Human Resources schema (XMMLHRFileFinal.xsd).

```
    <xsd:element name="Person" type="PersonType" minOccurs="0"
maxOccurs="unbounded"/>
   </xsd:sequence>
  </xsd:complexType>
</xsd:element>

<xsd:complexType name="PersonType">
<xsd:annotation>
 <xsd:documentation>
  The PersonType complex type consists of a sequence of four elements.
  The Name element is referenced from the XMMLCore.xsd type library.
  The Demographics element is of a complex type derived in this
schema.
  The Residence element is of a complex type derived in this schema.
  The CompanyExperience element is of type derived in this schema.
 </xsd:documentation>
</xsd:annotation>
 <xsd:sequence>
  <xsd:element ref="Name" />
  <xsd:element name="Demographics" type="DemographicsType"/>
  <xsd:element name="Residence" type="ResidenceType"/>
  <xsd:element name="CompanyExperience" type="CompanyExperienceType"/>
 </xsd:sequence>
</xsd:complexType>

<xsd:complexType name="DemographicsType">
<xsd:annotation>
 <xsd:documentation>
  The DemographicsType complex type consists of two elements, the
DateOfBirth element and the Gender element.
 </xsd:documentation>
</xsd:annotation>
 <xsd:sequence>
  <xsd:element name="DateOfBirth" type="DOBType"/>
  <xsd:element name="Gender" type="GenderType"/>
 </xsd:sequence>
</xsd:complexType>

<xsd:simpleType name="DOBType">
<xsd:annotation>
 <xsd:documentation>
  The DOBType is a simple type for defining a date of birth. We
restrict the xsd:date type. We apply minInclusive and maxInclusive
facets to represent what we see as realistic limits of age and youth
for recruits to XMML.com.
 </xsd:documentation>
</xsd:annotation>
```

Listing 10.21 The final Human Resources schema (XMMLHRFileFinal.xsd). (Continued)

```
  <xsd:restriction base="xsd:date">
   <xsd:minInclusive value="1935-01-01"/>
   <xsd:maxInclusive value="1984-01-01"/>
  </xsd:restriction>
 </xsd:simpleType>

 <xsd:simpleType name="GenderType">
 <xsd:annotation>
  <xsd:documentation>
   For obvious biological reasons the GenderType simple type is an
 enumeration of two possible values.
  </xsd:documentation>
 </xsd:annotation>
  <xsd:restriction base="xsd:string">
   <xsd:enumeration value="Female"/>
   <xsd:enumeration value="Male"/>
  </xsd:restriction>
 </xsd:simpleType>

 <xsd:complexType name="ResidenceType">
 <xsd:annotation>
  <xsd:documentation>
   The ResidenceType complex type has two compulsory elements declared
 within it.
   The CurrentAddress type is defined later but references
 XMMLCore.xsd.
   The PastAddresses element is of PastAddressesType type described
 later in this schema.
  </xsd:documentation>
 </xsd:annotation>
  <xsd:sequence>
    <xsd:element name="CurrentAddress" type="CurrentAddressType"/>
    <xsd:element name="PastAddresses" type="PastAddressesType"/>
  </xsd:sequence>
 </xsd:complexType>

 <xsd:complexType name="CurrentAddressType">
 <xsd:annotation>
  <xsd:documentation>
   This type definition references a group definition in the
 XMMLCore.xsd type library.
   It could have been omitted by creating an additional Address element
 in the instance document and a corresponding Address element
 declaration in XMMLCore.xsd.
  </xsd:documentation>
 </xsd:annotation>
```

continues

Listing 10.21 The final Human Resources schema (XMMLHRFileFinal.xsd). (Continued)

```
 <xsd:sequence>
  <xsd:group ref="AddressGroup"/>
 </xsd:sequence>
</xsd:complexType>

<xsd:complexType name="PastAddressesType">
<xsd:annotation>
 <xsd:documentation>
  The PastAddressesType type simply consists of a sequence of zero or
more past addresses.
 </xsd:documentation>
</xsd:annotation>
 <xsd:sequence>
  <xsd:element name="PastAddress" type="PastAddressType" minOccurs="0"
maxOccurs="unbounded"/>
 </xsd:sequence>
</xsd:complexType>

<xsd:complexType name="PastAddressType">
<xsd:annotation>
 <xsd:documentation>
  This type definition references a group definition in the
XMMLCore.xsd type library.
  It could have been omitted by creating an additional Address element
in the instance document and a corresponding Address element
declaration in XMMLCore.xsd.
 </xsd:documentation>
</xsd:annotation>
 <xsd:sequence>
  <xsd:group ref="AddressGroup"/>
 </xsd:sequence>
</xsd:complexType>

<xsd:complexType name="CompanyExperienceType">
<xsd:annotation>
 <xsd:documentation>
  The CompanyExperienceType type contains information specific to the
XMMLHRFile.xml instance document.
  Therefore there is no reference out to any other type library from
it.
 </xsd:documentation>
</xsd:annotation>
 <xsd:sequence>
  <xsd:element name="DateJoined" type="DateJoinedType"/>
  <xsd:element name="DateLeft" type="DateLeftType"/>
  <xsd:element name="HRNumber" type="HRNumberType"/>
  <xsd:element name="CurrentAssignment" type="CurrentAssignmentType"/>
```

Listing 10.21 The final Human Resources schema (XMMLHRFileFinal.xsd). (Continued)

```
  <xsd:element name="PreviousAssignments"
type="PreviousAssignmentsType"/>
 </xsd:sequence>
</xsd:complexType>

<xsd:simpleType name="DateJoinedType">
<xsd:annotation>
 <xsd:documentation>
  The DateJoinedType is a simple type for defining the date an
individual joined XMML.com.
  We restrict the xsd:date type. We apply a minInclusive facet to
represent the date XMML.com was founded.
 </xsd:documentation>
</xsd:annotation>
 <xsd:restriction base="xsd:date">
  <xsd:minInclusive value="1995-01-01"/>
 </xsd:restriction>
</xsd:simpleType>


<xsd:simpleType name="DateLeftType">
<xsd:annotation>
 <xsd:documentation>
  The DateLeftType is a simple type for defining the date an
individual left XMML.com.
  We restrict the xsd:date type. We apply a minInclusive facet to
represent the date XMML.com was founded since a staff member can't
have left the company before it was founded.
  A union type is created to allow for the empty string, which would
occur during the period a member of staff was employed by XMML.com
 </xsd:documentation>
</xsd:annotation>
<xsd:union>
 <xsd:simpleType>
  <xsd:restriction base="xsd:date">
   <xsd:minInclusive value="1995-01-01"/>
  </xsd:restriction>
 </xsd:simpleType>
 <xsd:simpleType>
  <xsd:restriction base='xsd:string'>
    <xsd:enumeration value=''/>
  </xsd:restriction>
 </xsd:simpleType>
</xsd:union>
</xsd:simpleType>
```

continues

Listing 10.21 The final Human Resources schema (XMMLHRFileFinal.xsd). (Continued)

```
<xsd:simpleType name="HRNumberType">
<xsd:annotation>
 <xsd:documentation>
  The HRNumberType type is a simple type which uses the pattern facet.
  The regular expression indicates three upper case characters
followed by four digits in the range from zero to nine inclusive.
  The three uppercase characters represent the initials of the staff
member (first initial, first middleinitial if any plus initial of last
name)
  If no middle initial then X is substituted.
 </xsd:documentation>
</xsd:annotation>
 <xsd:restriction base="xsd:string">
  <xsd:pattern value="[A-Z]{3}[0-9]{4}"/>
 </xsd:restriction>
</xsd:simpleType>

<xsd:complexType name="CurrentAssignmentType">
<xsd:annotation>
 <xsd:documentation>
  The CurrentAssignmentType type references an xsd:group named
AssignmentGroup.
 </xsd:documentation>
</xsd:annotation>
 <xsd:sequence>
  <xsd:group ref="AssignmentGroup"/>
 </xsd:sequence>
</xsd:complexType>

<xsd:complexType name="PreviousAssignmentsType">
 <xsd:sequence>
  <xsd:element name="PreviousAssignment" type="PreviousAssignmentType"
minOccurs="0"/>
 </xsd:sequence>
</xsd:complexType>

<xsd:complexType name="PreviousAssignmentType">
 <xsd:sequence>
  <xsd:group ref="AssignmentGroup" minOccurs="0" maxOccurs="5"/>
 </xsd:sequence>
</xsd:complexType>

<xsd:group name="AssignmentGroup">
<xsd:annotation>
 <xsd:documentation>
  The DateAssigned element uses the DateJoinedType since similar
constraints apply.
```

Listing 10.21 The final Human Resources schema (XMMLHRFileFinal.xsd). (Continued)

```
  </xsd:documentation>
 </xsd:annotation>
  <xsd:sequence>
   <xsd:element name="Department" type="xsd:string"/>
   <xsd:element name="Location" type="LocationType"/>
   <xsd:element name="JobTitle" type="xsd:string"/>
   <xsd:element name="DateAssigned" type="DateJoinedType"/>
   <xsd:element name="DateCompleted" type="DateLeftType"/>
   <xsd:element name="HRAssessment" type="xsd:string"/>
  </xsd:sequence>
 </xsd:group>

 <xsd:simpleType name="LocationType">
 <xsd:annotation>
  <xsd:documentation>
   The LocationType type may take one of three enumerated values
 corresponding to the three countries in which XMML.com is assumed to
 operate.
  </xsd:documentation>
 </xsd:annotation>
  <xsd:restriction>
   <xsd:enumeration value="UK"/>
   <xsd:enumeration value="USA"/>
   <xsd:enumeration value="Canada"/>
  </xsd:restriction>
 </xsd:simpleType>

 <xsd:simpleType name="DateCompletedType">
 <xsd:annotation>
  <xsd:documentation>
   The DateCompletedType is a simple type for defining the date an
 individual completed a past assignment for XMML.com.
   We restrict the xsd:date type. We apply a minInclusive facet to
 represent the date XMML.com was founded since a staff member can't
 have left the company before it was founded.
   A union type is not created to allow for the empty string, since
 unlike the DateLeftType the DateCompletedType is only used for past
 (completed) assignments.
  </xsd:documentation>
 </xsd:annotation>
  <xsd:restriction base="xsd:date">
   <xsd:minInclusive value="1995-01-01"/>
  </xsd:restriction>
 </xsd:simpleType>

 </xsd:schema>
```

Listing 10.21 The final Human Resources schema (XMMLHRFileFinal.xsd). (Continued)

As you read through Listing 10.21, you should have recognized uses of techniques to which you have been introduced in earlier chapters and with which you have begun to have some familiarity and comfort.

Let's move on to consider how to create the schema for the customer data store.

Creating the Customer Schema

To create the XMMLCustomers.xsd schema, we would follow a similar process: Define the company's information needs, create an instance document that will reflect the allowed variability in customer information that is likely to be held when the data store goes live, then proceed in an iterative way to build up an appropriately structured XSD schema to reflect the chosen structure of needed customer information. Then, we create the type library.

Creating the Type Library

The type library, XMMLCore.xsd, will contain element declarations and type definitions that will be referenced by each of the two other XSD Schema documents: XMMLHRSchemaFinal.xsd and (the hypothetical) XMMLCustomers.xsd.

In Listing 10.22, you see the type library that is referenced by XMMLHR-SchemaFinal.xsd. The name-related structures you should find straightforward. When looking at the structures that relate to addresses, remember that the United States, United Kingdom, and Canada use different names for localities (state, county, and province) and have different structure for zip or postal codes.

```
<?xml version="1.0" encoding="UTF-8"?>
<xsd:schema xmlns:xsd="http://www.w3.org/2001/XMLSchema" >
<xsd:annotation>
 <xsd:documentation>
  This schema contains type definitions which are accessed by XSD
schemas which define the Human Resources and Customer data stores.
The referencing schemas are held in XMMLHRSchema.xsd and
XMMLCustomers.xsd.
 </xsd:documentation>
</xsd:annotation>
```

Listing 10.22 The type library referenced by the two schemas (XMMLCore.xsd).

```
<xsd:element name="Name">
<xsd:annotation>
 <xsd:documentation>
 This element declaration is reference by XMMLHRFinal.xsd and
XMMLCustomers.xsd.
 It has three subelements each of which is of type xsd:string.
 </xsd:documentation>
</xsd:annotation>
 <xsd:complexType>
  <xsd:sequence>
   <xsd:element name="FirstName" type="xsd:string"/>
   <xsd:element name="MiddleNames" type="xsd:string"/>
   <xsd:element name="LastName" type="xsd:string"/>
  </xsd:sequence>
 </xsd:complexType>
</xsd:element>

<xsd:group name="AddressGroup">
<xsd:annotation>
 <xsd:documentation>

 </xsd:documentation>
</xsd:annotation>
 <xsd:sequence>
  <xsd:element name="Street1" type="xsd:string"/>
  <xsd:element name="Street2" type="xsd:string"/>
  <xsd:element name="City" type="xsd:string"/>
  <xsd:group ref="CountryChoiceGroup"/>
 </xsd:sequence>
</xsd:group>

<xsd:group name="CountryChoiceGroup">
 <xsd:choice>
  <xsd:group ref="USAddressGroup"/>
  <xsd:group ref="UKAddressGroup"/>
  <xsd:group ref="CanadaAddressGroup"/>
 </xsd:choice>
</xsd:group>

<xsd:group name="USAddressGroup">
<xsd:annotation>
 <xsd:documentation>

 </xsd:documentation>
</xsd:annotation>
 <xsd:sequence>
```

continues

Listing 10.22 The type library referenced by the two schemas (XMMLCore.xsd). (Continued)

```
  <xsd:element name="State" type="USStateType"/>
  <xsd:element name="ZipCode" type="USZipCodeType"/>
  <xsd:element name="Country" type="USCountryType"/>
 </xsd:sequence>
</xsd:group>

<xsd:simpleType name="USStateType">
<xsd:restriction base="xsd:string">
<xsd:enumeration value="AK"/>
<xsd:enumeration value="AL"/>
<xsd:enumeration value="AR"/>
<xsd:enumeration value="AZ"/>
<xsd:enumeration value="CA"/>
<xsd:enumeration value="CO"/>
<xsd:enumeration value="CT"/>
<xsd:enumeration value="DC"/>
<xsd:enumeration value="DE"/>
<xsd:enumeration value="FL"/>
<xsd:enumeration value="GA"/>
<xsd:enumeration value="HI"/>
<xsd:enumeration value="IA"/>
<xsd:enumeration value="ID"/>
<xsd:enumeration value="IL"/>
<xsd:enumeration value="IN"/>
<xsd:enumeration value="KS"/>
<xsd:enumeration value="KY"/>
<xsd:enumeration value="LA"/>
<xsd:enumeration value="MA"/>
<xsd:enumeration value="MD"/>
<xsd:enumeration value="ME"/>
<xsd:enumeration value="MI"/>
<xsd:enumeration value="MN"/>
<xsd:enumeration value="MO"/>
<xsd:enumeration value="MS"/>
<xsd:enumeration value="MT"/>
<xsd:enumeration value="NC"/>
<xsd:enumeration value="ND"/>
<xsd:enumeration value="NE"/>
<xsd:enumeration value="NH"/>
<xsd:enumeration value="NJ"/>
<xsd:enumeration value="NM"/>
<xsd:enumeration value="NV"/>
<xsd:enumeration value="NY"/>
<xsd:enumeration value="OH"/>
<xsd:enumeration value="OK"/>
<xsd:enumeration value="OR"/>
<xsd:enumeration value="PA"/>
```

Listing 10.22 The type library referenced by the two schemas (XMMLCore.xsd). (Continued)

```
<xsd:enumeration value="RI"/>
<xsd:enumeration value="SC"/>
<xsd:enumeration value="SD"/>
<xsd:enumeration value="TN"/>
<xsd:enumeration value="TX"/>
<xsd:enumeration value="UT"/>
<xsd:enumeration value="VA"/>
<xsd:enumeration value="VT"/>
<xsd:enumeration value="WA"/>
<xsd:enumeration value="WI"/>
<xsd:enumeration value="WV"/>
<xsd:enumeration value="WY"/>
</xsd:restriction>
</xsd:simpleType>

<xsd:simpleType name="USZipCodeType">
 <xsd:restriction base="xsd:string">
  <xsd:pattern value="\d{5}|\d{5}-\d{4}"/>
 </xsd:restriction>
</xsd:simpleType>

<xsd:simpleType name="USCountryType">
 <xsd:restriction base="xsd:string">
  <xsd:pattern value="USA"/>
 </xsd:restriction>
</xsd:simpleType>

<xsd:group name="UKAddressGroup">
<xsd:annotation>
 <xsd:documentation>
  The three elements which make up a UK address.
 </xsd:documentation>
</xsd:annotation>
 <xsd:sequence>
  <xsd:element name="County" type="xsd:string"/>
  <xsd:element name="UKPostalCode" type="UKPostalCodeType"/>
  <xsd:element name="Country" type="UKCountryType"/>
 </xsd:sequence>
</xsd:group>

<xsd:simpleType name="UKPostalCodeType">
 <xsd:restriction base="xsd:string">
  <xsd:pattern value="[A-Z]{1,2}\d{1,2} \d{1}[A-Z]{2}"/>
 </xsd:restriction>
</xsd:simpleType>
```

continues

Listing 10.22 The type library referenced by the two schemas (XMMLCore.xsd). (Continued)

```
<xsd:simpleType name="UKCountryType">
 <xsd:restriction base="xsd:string">
  <xsd:pattern value="UK"/>
 </xsd:restriction>
</xsd:simpleType>

 <xsd:group name="CanadaAddressGroup">
<xsd:annotation>
 <xsd:documentation>

 </xsd:documentation>
</xsd:annotation>
 <xsd:sequence>
  <xsd:element name="Province" type="xsd:string"/>
  <xsd:element name="CanadaPostalCode" type="CanadaPostalCodeType"/>
  <xsd:element name="Country" type="CanadaCountryType"/>
 </xsd:sequence>
</xsd:group>

<xsd:simpleType name="CanadaPostalCodeType">
 <xsd:restriction base="xsd:string">
  <xsd:pattern value="[A-Z]{1}[0-9]{1}[A-Z]{1} [0-9]{1}[A-Z]{1}[0-
9]{1}"/>
 </xsd:restriction>
</xsd:simpleType>

<xsd:simpleType name="CanadaCountryType">
 <xsd:restriction base="xsd:string">
  <xsd:pattern value="Canada"/>
 </xsd:restriction>
</xsd:simpleType>

</xsd:schema>
```

Listing 10.22 The type library referenced by the two schemas (XMMLCore.xsd). (Continued)

This creation of a more substantial example should help to reinforce or illuminate the techniques that you read about earlier in the book. In a book of this length, only the essentials of XSD Schema can be discussed—but the W3C XML Schema Recommendation is of great complexity and flexibility. Understanding it fully is a demanding task. Hopefully, you are glad that you have started on that journey.

Appendixes

APPENDIX

A

Datatypes

Datatypes are very important when defining schemas. While XSD enables you to easily describe the structure of a set of data, knowing and understanding the types of data, such as a date or a decimal, enables applications to properly interpret and process the data. Having this information will make it easier to create database tables that might be ultimately storing the data or even displaying in user interfaces (you don't want a date showing up as a numerical value).

Within this appendix, two types of datatypes are examined: *primitive* datatypes, which represent the core datatypes present in XML Schema, and *derived* datatypes, which are derived from the core datatypes and other derived datatypes.

Primitive Datatypes

These are datatypes that are not derived from other datatypes. In other words, they are not built on top of, nor do they represent a collection of other datatypes. Within this section of the appendix, we are going to examine each of the primitive datatypes present in the XML Schema Part 2: Datatype Recommendation. We also are going to include what datatypes have been derived from these primitive types, and in Appendix B, what facets are associated with them.

anyURI

The anyURI datatype represents an absolute or relative URI. While many seemingly valid characters can be used to represent a URI, you are encouraged to use the proper encoding for special characters (for example, space is represented by %20).

The following list contains the facets available in the anyURI datatype:

- enumeration
- length
- maxLength
- minLength
- pattern
- whiteSpace

base64Binary

The base64Binary datatype represents Base64-encoded arbitrary binary data. In other words, the data is encoded by using the Base64 Content-Transfer-Encoding defined in Section 6.8 of RFC 2045.

NOTE **For more information about RFC 2045, see www.ietf.org/rfc/rfc2045.txt.**

The following list contains the facets available in the base64Binary datatype:

- enumeration
- length
- maxLength
- minLength
- pattern
- whiteSpace

boolean

The boolean datatype represents the ability of an item to be valued as true or false, as in mathematical binary-valued logic. With this type, possible values are true, false, 1, and 0, where 1 is analogous to true and 0 is analogous to false.

The following list contains the facets available in the boolean datatype:

- pattern
- whiteSpace

date

The date datatype represents a given day in a given month in a given year, regardless of time, in the Gregorian calendar as defined by ISO 8601 (www.iso.ch/markete/8601.pdf). For instance, you could write 2002-10-23 (October 23, 2002). The following list contains the facets available in the date datatype:

- enumeration
- maxExclusive
- maxInclusive
- minExclusive
- minInclusive
- pattern
- whiteSpace

dateTime

The dateTime datatype represents a given day in a given month in a given year at a given time (hour, minute, seconds) in the Gregorian calendar as defined by ISO 8601 (www.iso.ch/markete/8601.pdf). For instance, 2002-10-23T00:10:00 (October 23, 2002 12:10 A.M.). Optionally, if you wish to specify a time zone, you can accomplish this task by passing the offset from *Coordinated Universal Time* (UTC). Using our previous example, 2002-10-23T00:10:00-05:00 signifies *Eastern Standard Time* (EST), which is five hours behind UTC.

The following list contains the facets available in the date datatype:

- enumeration
- maxExclusive
- maxInclusive
- minExclusive
- minInclusive
- pattern
- whiteSpace

decimal

The decimal datatype represents arbitrary precision decimal numbers that can be either positive or negative. Negative decimals must have a preceding – sign, while the lack thereof assumes positive. As defined in XSD, a minimal supporting processor must support at least 18 decimal digits. Additionally, the built-in integer datatype is derived from decimal.

The following list contains the facets available in the decimal datatype:

- enumeration
- fractionDigits
- maxExclusive
- maxInclusive
- minExclusive
- minInclusive
- pattern
- totalDigits
- whiteSpace

double

The double datatype, which corresponds to IEEE double-precision 64-bit floating point type, consists of the values m x 2^e, where m is an integer whose absolute value is less than 2^53 and e is an integer between –1,075 and 970, inclusively. A double consists of the decimal part of a logarithm (in other words, digits after decimal) followed by an optional e or E to represent an integer exponent. Additionally, double has defined special values for positive and negative zero, positive and negative infinity, and not-a-number. These are 0, –0, INF, –INF, and NaN, respectively.

NOTE A float datatype is different from a double in that it is a 32-bit floating point number. It is essentially half the size of the double.

The following list contains the facets available in the double datatype:

- enumeration
- maxExclusive
- maxInclusive

- minExclusive
- minInclusive
- pattern
- whiteSpace

duration

The duration datatype represents a duration of time made up of a year, month, day, hour, minute, and second within a Gregorian calendar. These components are defined by ISO 8601 (www.iso.ch/markete/8601.pdf). For instance, P28Y10M23DT10H30M45S represents a duration of 28 years, 10 months, 23 days, 10 hours, 30 minutes, and 45 seconds. Note that not all items are required (such as P28Y10 would represent 28 years and 10 months). Additionally, a negative value can be passed, such as –P28H, to represent a duration of minus 28 hours. The following list contains the facets available in the duration datatype:

- enumeration
- maxExclusive
- maxInclusive
- minExclusive
- minInclusive
- pattern
- whiteSpace

float

The float datatype, which corresponds to the IEEE single-precision 32-bit floating point type, consists of the values m x 2^e, where m is an integer whose absolute value is less than 2^24 and e is an integer between –149 and 104, inclusively. A float consists of the decimal part of a logarithm (in other words, digits after decimal) followed by an optional e^ or ^E to represent an integer exponent. Additionally, float has defined special values for positive and negative zero, positive and negative infinity, and not-a-number. These are 0, –0, INF, –INF, and NaN, respectively.

NOTE A double datatype is different from a float in that it is a 64-bit floating point number. It is essentially double the size of the float.

The following list contains the facets available in the float datatype:

- enumeration
- maxExclusive
- maxInclusive
- minExclusive
- minInclusive
- pattern
- whiteSpace

gDay

The gDay datatype represents a reoccurring day in a given month in the Gregorian calendar as defined by ISO 8601 (www.iso.ch/markete/8601.pdf); for instance, the 23rd of each month. The following list contains the facets available in the gDay datatype:

- enumeration
- maxExclusive
- maxInclusive
- minExclusive
- minInclusive
- pattern
- whiteSpace

gMonth

The gMonth datatype represents a reoccurring month every year in the Gregorian calendar as defined by ISO 8601 (www.iso.ch/markete/8601.pdf)—for instance, October. The following list contains the facets available in the gMonth datatype:

- enumeration
- maxExclusive
- maxInclusive
- minExclusive
- minInclusive
- pattern
- whiteSpace

gMonthDay

The gMonthDay datatype represents a reoccurring day every year in the Gregorian calendar as defined by ISO 8601 (www.iso.ch/markete/8601.pdf)—for instance, the 23rd of October. The following list contains the facets available in the gMonthDay datatype:

- enumeration
- maxExclusive
- maxInclusive
- minExclusive
- minInclusive
- pattern
- whiteSpace

gYear

The gYear datatype represents a given year in the Gregorian calendar as defined by ISO 8601 (www.iso.ch/markete/8601.pdf)—for instance, 2002. The following list contains the facets available in the gYear datatype:

- enumeration
- maxExclusive
- maxInclusive
- minExclusive
- minInclusive
- pattern
- whiteSpace

gYearMonth

The gYearMonth datatype represents a specific month in a specific year in the Gregorian calendar as defined by ISO 8601 (www.iso.ch/markete/8601.pdf)—for instance, October 2002. The following list contains the facets available in the gYearMonth datatype:

- enumeration
- maxExclusive
- maxInclusive

- minExclusive
- minInclusive
- pattern
- whiteSpace

hexBinary

The hexBinary datatype represents binary data that has been hex-encoded. The following list contains the facets available in the hexBinary datatype:

- enumeration
- length
- maxLength
- minLength
- pattern
- whiteSpace

NOTATION

The NOTATION datatype represents a NOTATION attribute type as defined in XML 1.0. It is illegal for NOTATION to be used directly in a schema, and therefore only datatypes that derive from NOTATION can be used. You perform this task by specifying a value for enumeration.

The following list contains the facets available in the NOTATION datatype:

- enumeration
- length
- maxLength
- minLength
- pattern
- whiteSpace

QName

The QName datatype represents XML qualified names. These names are broken into a Prefix, which represents the appropriate namespace, and a Local-

Part, which defines the local part, or name, of the qualified name. The following list contains the facets available in the QName datatype:

- enumeration
- length
- maxLength
- minLength
- pattern
- whiteSpace

string

The string datatype represents a finite-length sequence of character as defined in XML 1.0. The string datatype is simple type and therefore cannot contain child elements. In these cases, you should consider the use of a complex type that allows for mixed content, of which one could be a string. The built-in normalizeString datatype is derived from string.

The following list contains the facets available in the string datatype:

- enumeration
- length
- maxLength
- minLength
- pattern
- whiteSpace

time

The time datatype represents an instance in time in a given day, with values ranging from 00:00:00 (midnight) to 23:59:59. Optionally, if you wish to specify a time zone, this task can be accomplished by passing the offset from UTC. Using our previous example, 00:00:00-05:00 signifies midnight EST, which is five hours behind UTC.

The following list contains the facets available in the time datatype:

- enumeration
- maxExclusive
- maxInclusive

- minExclusive
- minInclusive
- pattern
- whiteSpace

Derived Datatypes

Derived datatypes, which are also defined in the XML Schema Part 2: Datatype Recommendation, refer to datatypes that are in fact derived from the core primitive datatypes. This section of the appendix includes a comprehensive reference for the derived datatypes that are defined in the recommendation so that it will be easy for you to learn and better understand how to use them. Also included are what facets are associated with these datatypes (see Appendix B for more on facets), as well as any additional datatypes that might be further derived.

byte

The byte datatype, which is derived from short, represents a value between –128 and 127. The following list contains the facets available in the byte datatype:

- enumeration
- fractionDigits
- maxExclusive
- maxInclusive
- minExclusive
- minInclusive
- pattern
- totalDigits
- whiteSpace

ENTITIES

The ENTITIES datatype, which is derived from ENTITY, represents the ENTITIES attribute as defined in XML 1.0. It is a finite, non-zero-length sequence of ENTITY datatype instances that have been declared as unparsed entities in a DTD. The following list contains the facets available in the ENTITIES datatype:

- enumeration
- length
- maxLength
- minLength
- whiteSpace

ENTITY

The ENTITY datatype, which is derived from NCName, represents the ENTITY attribute as defined in XML 1.0. It is the set of all strings that match the NCName production in Namespaces in XML and that have been declared as unparsed entities in a DTD. The ENTITIES datatype is derived from the ENTITY datatype.

The following list contains the facets available in the ENTITY datatype:

- enumeration
- length
- maxLength
- minLength
- pattern
- whiteSpace

ID

The ID datatype, which is derived from NCName, represents the ID attribute as defined in XML 1.0. It is the set of all strings that match the NCName production in Namespaces in XML. The following list contains the facets available in the ID datatype:

- enumeration
- length
- maxLength
- minLength
- pattern
- whiteSpace

IDREF

The IDREF datatype represents the IDREF attribute as defined in XML 1.0. It is the set of all strings that match the NCName production in Namespaces in XML. The IDREFS datatype is derived from the IDREF datatype.

The following list contains the facets available in the IDREF datatype:

- enumeration
- length
- maxLength
- minLength
- pattern
- whiteSpace

IDREFS

The IDREFS datatype, which is derived from IDREF, represents the IDREFS attribute as defined in XML 1.0. It is the set of finite, non-zero-length sequences of IDREFs. The following list contains the facets available in the IDREFS datatype:

- enumeration
- length
- maxLength
- minLength
- whiteSpace

int

The int datatype, which is derived from long, represents a value between −2147483648 and 2147483647. The short datatype is derived from the int datatype. The following list contains the facets available in the int datatype:

- enumeration
- fractionDigits
- maxExclusive
- maxInclusive
- minExclusive
- minInclusive

- pattern
- totalDigits
- whiteSpace

integer

The integer datatype, which is derived from the decimal primitive datatype, represents a whole number with no decimal places (in other words, equivalent to all values after the decimal equal to 0). The following list contains a list of datatypes that are additionally derived from integer:

- long
- nonNegativeInteger
- nonPositiveInteger

The following list contains the facets available in the integer datatype:

- enumeration
- fractionDigits
- maxExclusive
- maxInclusive
- minExclusive
- minInclusive
- pattern
- totalDigits
- whiteSpace

language

The language datatype, which is derived from token, represents natural language identifiers as defined in RFC 1766 (www.ietf.org/rfc/rfc1766.txt). The following list contains the facets available in the language datatype:

- enumeration
- length
- maxLength
- minLength
- pattern
- whiteSpace

long

The long datatype, which is derived from integer, represents a value between –223372036854775808 and 9223372036854775807. The int datatype is derived from the long datatype. The following list contains the facets available in the long datatype:

- enumeration
- fractionDigits
- maxExclusive
- maxInclusive
- minExclusive
- minInclusive
- pattern
- totalDigits
- whiteSpace

Name

The Name datatype, which is derived from token, represents Names as defined in XML 1.0. The NCName datatype is derived from the Name datatype. The following list contains the facets available in the Name datatype:

- enumeration
- length
- maxLength
- minLength
- pattern
- whiteSpace

NCName

The NCName datatype, which is derived from Name, represents "noncolonized" Names as defined in XML 1.0. The following list contains a list of datatypes that are additionally derived from NCName:

- ENTITY
- ID
- IDREF

The following list contains the facets available in the NCName datatype:

- enumeration
- length
- maxLength
- minLength
- pattern
- whiteSpace

negativeInteger

The negativeInteger datatype, which is derived from nonPositiveInteger, represents any negative integer. Remember that an integer is defined as a whole number with no decimal values (for example, equivalent to all values after the decimal equal to 0). The following list contains the facets available in the negativeInteger datatype:

- enumeration
- fractionDigits
- maxExclusive
- maxInclusive
- minExclusive
- minInclusive
- pattern
- totalDigits
- whiteSpace

NMTOKEN

The NMTOKEN datatype, which is derived from token, represents the NMTOKEN attribute as defined in XML 1.0. This datatype is a set of tokens that match the Nmtoken production. The NMTOKENS datatype is derived from the NMTOKEN dataype. The following list contains the facets available in the NMTOKEN datatype:

- enumeration
- length
- maxLength
- minLength
- pattern
- whiteSpace

NMTOKENS

The NMTOKENS datatype, which is derived from NMTOKEN, represents the NMTOKENS attribute as defined in XML 1.0. This datatype is a set of finite, non-zero-length sequences of NMTOKENs. The following list contains the facets available in the NMTOKENS datatype:

- enumeration
- length
- maxLength
- minLength
- whiteSpace

nonNegativeInteger

The nonNegativeInteger datatype, which is derived from integer, represents any positive integer. Remember that an integer is defined as a whole number with no decimal values (in other words, equivalent to all values after the decimal equal to 0). The following list contains a list of datatypes that are additionally derived from nonNegativeInteger:

- positiveInteger
- unsignedLong

The following list contains the facets available in the nonNegativeInteger datatype:

- enumeration
- fractionDigits
- maxExclusive
- maxInclusive
- minExclusive
- minInclusive
- pattern
- totalDigits
- whiteSpace

nonPositiveInteger

The nonPositiveInteger datatype, which is derived from integer, represents any negative integer. Remember that an integer is defined as a whole number with no decimal values (in other words, equivalent to all values after the decimal equal to 0). The negativeInteger datatype is derived from the nonPositiveInteger datatype.

The following list contains the facets available in the nonPositiveInteger datatype:

- enumeration
- fractionDigits
- maxExclusive
- maxInclusive
- minExclusive
- minInclusive
- pattern
- totalDigits
- whiteSpace

normalizedString

The normalizedString datatype, which is derived from the string primitive datatype, represents whiteSpace normalized strings that do not carry a carriage return, line feed, or tab character. The token datatype is derived from the normalizedString datatype.

The following list contains the facets available in the normalizedString datatype:

- enumeration
- length
- maxLength
- minLength
- pattern
- whiteSpace

positiveInteger

The positiveInteger datatype, which is derived from nonNegativeInteger, represents any positive integer. Remember that an integer is defined as a whole number with no decimal values (for example, equivalent to all values after the decimal equal to 0). The following list contains the facets available in the positiveInteger datatype:

- enumeration
- fractionDigits
- maxExclusive
- maxInclusive
- minExclusive
- minInclusive
- pattern
- totalDigits
- whiteSpace

short

The short datatype, which is derived from int, represents a value between −32768 and 32767. The byte datatype is derived from the short datatype. The following list contains the facets available in the short datatype:

- enumeration
- fractionDigits
- maxExclusive
- maxInclusive
- minExclusive
- minInclusive
- pattern
- totalDigits
- whiteSpace

token

The token datatype, which is derived from normalizedString, represents tokenized strings. This datatype refers to a set of strings that do not contain a line feed or tab character and that have no leading or trailing spaces. They also cannot have internal sequences of two or more spaces. The following list contains a list of datatypes that are additionally derived from token:

- language
- Name
- NMTOKEN

The following list contains the facets available in the token datatype:

- enumeration
- length
- maxLength
- minLength
- pattern
- whiteSpace

unsignedByte

The unsignedByte datatype, which is derived from unsignedShort, represents a number with an upper bound of 255. The following list contains the facets available in the unsignedByte datatype:

- enumeration
- fractionDigits
- maxExclusive
- maxInclusive
- minExclusive
- minInclusive
- pattern
- totalDigits
- whiteSpace

unsignedInt

The unsignedInt datatype, which is derived from unsignedLong, represents a number with an upper bound of 4294967295. The unsignedShort datatype is derived from the unsignedInt datatype. The following list contains the facets available in the unsignedInt datatype:

- enumeration
- fractionDigits
- maxExclusive
- maxInclusive
- minExclusive

- minInclusive
- pattern
- totalDigits
- whiteSpace

unsignedLong

The unsignedLong datatype, which is derived from nonNegativeInteger, represents a number with an upper bound of 18446744073709551615. The unsignedInt datatype is derived from the unsignedLong datatype.

The following list contains the facets available in the unsignedLong datatype:

- enumeration
- fractionDigits
- maxExclusive
- maxInclusive
- minExclusive
- minInclusive
- pattern
- totalDigits
- whiteSpace

unsignedShort

The unsignedShort datatype, which is derived from unsignedInt, represents a number with an upper bound of 65535. The unsignedByte datatype is derived from the unsignedShort datatype.

The following list contains the facets available in the unsignedShort datatype:

- enumeration
- fractionDigits
- maxExclusive
- maxInclusive
- minExclusive

- minInclusive
- pattern
- totalDigits
- whiteSpace

Summary

In this appendix we provided a reference for the two types of datatypes defined with XML Schema. As we discussed throughout the book, primitive datatypes represent the core datatypes present in XML Schema, while derived datatypes are derived from these core primitive datatypes. Datatypes are extremely important, so we hope you found this reference beneficial.

APPENDIX

B

Data Facets

This appendix will summarize the characteristics of the data facets provided by XSD Schema. A brief summary of the fundamental facets will be followed by information about the constraining facets that XSD Schema provides. Examples of usage of the constraining facets are to be found in Chapters 5 and 6.

Facets are defined fully in Chapter 4.2 of Part 2 of the W3C XML Schema Recommendation, located at www.w3.org/TR/2001/REC-xmlschema-2-20010502/.

NOTE **The names of datatypes and elements in this appendix will be expressed as QNames, such as xsd:string, indicating that the type (or element) is in the namespace of W3C XML Schema. An appropriate namespace declaration will be assumed to apply.**

A facet is a single defining aspect of a *value space*. Most facets work in separate axes; that is, the way in which you set one facet generally leaves you free to define others as you choose within the set of facets available in a particular context of a datatype.

Fundamental Facets

XSD Schema lists five fundamental facets:

- equal
- ordered
- bounded
- cardinality
- numeric

The fundamental facets of a datatype determine which operations, including comparisons, can be performed on values of that type.

The equal Facet

The equal facet applies in all value spaces. In other words, it applies to all XSD Schema datatypes.

The equal facet enables comparisons to be made between values and equality (for example, X=Y) to be determined or not (X!=Y). Comparisons of string values for equality are case sensitive, thus ABC != abc.

There is no *schema component* corresponding to the equal facet.

The ordered Facet

The ordered facet applies in all value spaces.

Number, date, and some other datatypes have values that are ordered. This feature permits comparisons of the type *greater than* (X>Y) or *less than* (X<Y).

There is an *ordered* schema component for the ordered facet. It can take the values of false, partial, or total.

The bounded Facet

The bounded facet applies in all value spaces.

For ordered datatypes, by setting a maximum permitted value and a minimum permitted value, bounds of permissible values can be defined. Thus, for a value of X, we can expect a minimum value to be less than or equal to X (which, in turn, is less than or equal to a maximum value).

There is a *bounded* schema component that can take the boolean values of true or false.

The cardinality Facet

The cardinality facet applies in all value spaces.

The cardinality facet defines the permitted number of values in a value space. The cardinality can be zero, one, unbounded, or some specified positive integer number.

There is a *cardinality* schema component that can take the values *finite* or *countably infinite*.

The numeric Facet

The numeric facet applies in all value spaces.

The numeric facet distinguishes values that are a number from those that are not.

There is a *numeric* schema component that can take the boolean values of true or false.

Constraining Facets

XSD Schema describes 12 constraining facets:

- enumeration
- fractionDigits
- length
- maxExclusive
- maxInclusive
- maxLength
- minExclusive
- minInclusive
- minLength
- pattern
- totalDigits
- whiteSpace

Examples of how to use each of these constraining facets are to be found in Chapters 5, Data Facets," and 6, "More about Data Facets."

The enumeration Facet

The enumeration facet applies in all value spaces except for xsd:boolean.

The enumeration facet constrains the permitted values in a value space to a specified set of values.

The schema component for the enumeration facet is the <xsd:enumeration> element. The enumeration schema component has a value property and an optional annotation property. The value property is expressed as the value attribute of the <xsd:enumeration> element. The annotation property is expressed by using an <xsd:annotation> element.

The fractionDigits Facet

The fractionDigits facet applies in the xsd:decimal value space, and the value spaces of types derived from xsd:decimal.

The fractionDigits facet specifies the number of digits that can occur after the decimal point in a value of type xsd:decimal.

The schema component for the fractionDigits facet is the <xsd:fractionDigits> element. The fractionDigits facet has value, fixed, and annotation properties. The value property is expressed as the value of the value attribute of the <xsd:fractionDigits> element. The fixed property of the fractionDigits facet is expressed as the value of the fixed attribute of the <xsd:fractionDigits> element. The annotation property is expressed as an <xsd:annotation> element.

The length Facet

The length facet applies in the value spaces xsd:string (and types derived from xsd:string, such as xsd:normalizedString and xsd:token) and binary encoding types (xsd:hexBinary and xsd:base64Binary).

The length facet constrains the length of a type, as specified in *units of length*. The units of length vary by the type being constrained. For xsd:string types (and derived types from xsd:string), the unit of length is the character. For binary encoding types, the unit of length is an octet of bits. For list simple types, the unit of length is a list item.

The schema component for the length facet is the <xsd:length> element. It has value, fixed, and annotation properties. The value and fixed properties are expressed as attributes of the <xsd:length> element. An annotation is optional and is expressed by using an <xsd:annotation> element.

The maxExclusive Facet

The maxExclusive facet applies in the value spaces for numeric and date/time datatypes.

The maxExclusive facet defines the lowest value that exceeds the permitted values of the type.

The schema component for the maxExclusive facet is the <xsd:maxExclusive> element. The maxExclusive facet has value, fixed, and annotation properties. The value property is expressed as the value of the value attribute of the <xsd:maxExclusive> element. The fixed property is expressed as the fixed attribute of the <xsd:maxExclusive> element and takes a boolean value. The optional annotation property is expressed in an <xsd:annotation> element.

The maxInclusive Facet

The maxInclusive facet applies in the value spaces for numeric and date/time datatypes.

The maxInclusive facet defines the maximum permitted value of the type.

The schema component for the maxInclusive facet is the <xsd:maxInclusive> element. The maxInclusive facet has value, fixed, and annotation properties. The value property is expressed as the value of the value attribute of the <xsd:maxInclusive> element. The fixed property is expressed as the fixed attribute of the <xsd:maxInclusive> element and takes a boolean value. The optional annotation property is expressed in an <xsd:annotation> element.

The maxLength Facet

The maxLength facet applies in the value spaces xsd:string (and types derived from xsd:string, such as xsd:normalizedString and xsd:token) and binary encoding types (xsd:hexBinary and xsd:base64Binary).

The maxLength facet is defined as units of length that vary by datatype, as described for the length facet.

The schema component for the maxLength facet is the <xsd:maxLength> element.

It has value, fixed, and annotation properties. The value and fixed properties are expressed as attributes of the <xsd:maxLength> element. An annotation is optional and is expressed by using an <xsd:annotation> element.

The minExclusive Facet

The minExclusive facet applies in the value spaces for numeric and date/time datatypes.

The minExclusive facet defines the maximum value that is less than the permitted values of the type.

The schema component for the minExclusive facet is the <xsd:minExclusive> element. The minExclusive facet has value, fixed, and annotation properties. The value property is expressed as the value of the value attribute of the

<xsd:minExclusive> element. The fixed property is expressed as the fixed attribute of the <xsd:minExclusive> element and takes a boolean value. The optional annotation property is expressed in an <xsd:annotation> element.

The minInclusive Facet

The minInclusive facet applies in the value spaces for numeric and date/time datatypes.

The minInclusive facet defines the minimum permitted value of the type.

The schema component for the minInclusive facet is the <xsd:minInclusive> element. The minInclusive facet has value, fixed, and annotation properties. The value property is expressed as the value of the value attribute of the <xsd:minInclusive> element. The fixed property is expressed as the fixed attribute of the <xsd:minInclusive> element and takes a boolean value. The optional annotation property is expressed in an <xsd:annotation> element.

The minLength Facet

The minLength facet applies in the value spaces xsd:string (and types derived from xsd:string, such as xsd:normalizedString and xsd:token) and binary encoding types (xsd:hexBinary and xsd:base64Binary).

The minLength facet declares the minimum length of a datatype and is defined as units of length that vary by datatype, as described for the length facet.

The schema component for the minLength facet is the <xsd:minLength> element.

It has value, fixed, and annotation properties. The value and fixed properties are expressed as attributes of the <xsd:minLength> element. An annotation is optional and is expressed by using an <xsd:annotation> element.

The pattern Facet

The pattern facet applies in all value spaces except those for xsd:IDREFS and xsd:ENTITIES.

The pattern facet indirectly constrains the value space type by limiting the values permitted in the lexical space to those that match a specified pattern. The value of the pattern must be a regular expression.

The schema component for the pattern facet is the <xsd:pattern> element. The pattern schema component has a value property and an optional annotation property. The value property is expressed, by means of a regular expression, as the value of the value attribute of an <xsd:pattern> element.

The totalDigits Facet

The totalDigits facet applies in the xsd:decimal value space and the value spaces of types derived from xsd:decimal.

The totalDigits facet specifies the number of digits that can occur before and after the decimal point in a value of type xsd:decimal.

The schema component for the totalDigits facet is the <xsd:totalDigits> element. The totalDigits facet has value, fixed, and annotation properties. The value property is expressed as the value of the value attribute of the <xsd:totalDigits> element. The fixed property of the totalDigits facet is expressed as the value of the fixed attribute of the <xsd:totalDigits> element. The annotation property is expressed as an <xsd:annotation> element.

The whiteSpace Facet

The whiteSpace facet applies in the xsd:string value space and the value spaces of types derived from xsd:string.

The whiteSpace facet specifies how white space is to be handled in terms of XML normalization as described in the XML 1.0 Recommendation. Three values are permitted: preserve, replace, or collapse. When the value is preserve, then the value is not changed. When the value is replace, then any #x9 (tab), #xA (line feed), or #xD (carriage return) characters are replaced by space characters (#x20). When the value is collapse, then the normalization described for replace is carried out. In addition, any sequences of space characters are collapsed to a single space character.

The schema component for the whiteSpace facet is the <xsd:whiteSpace> element. The whiteSpace facet has value, fixed, and annotation properties. The value property may take the values of preserve, replace, or collapse and is expressed as the value of the value attribute of the <xsd:whiteSpace> element. The fixed property may take the boolean values, true or false. The optional annotation property is expressed in an <xsd:annotation> element.

Index

E

Y–Z